The Deity of Christ in Modern Translations

A Response to the Claims of Jason BeDuhn
and
A Defense of the Biblical Testimony that Jesus is God

By

Thomas A. Howe, Ph.D.

©2015 by Thomas A. Howe. All rights reserved. No part of this book may be reproduced in any form without the written permission of Thomas A. Howe

Thomas A. Howe, Ph.D.
drthowe@att.net

The Linguist Software LaserHebrew II and LaserSyriac fonts used to print this work are available from Linguist's Software, Inc., PO Box 580, Edmonds, WA 98020-0580 USA tel (425) 775-1130 www.linguistsoftware.com.

TABLE OF CONTENTS

LIST OF ILLUSTRATIONS.. iv
LIST OF TABLES... v
ABBREVIATIONS.. viii
INTRODUCTION... 1
CHAPTER 1: TRANSLATING THE BIBLE............................. 13
CHAPTER 2: WORSHIPING CHRIST................................... 24
CHAPTER 3: IN THE FORM OF GOD.................................. 54
CHAPTER 4: BY HIM ALL THINGS WERE CREATED........... 65
CHAPTER 5: OUR GOD AND SAVIOR JESUS CHRIST......... 83
CHAPTER 6: THY THRONE O GOD..................................... 100
CHAPTER 7: BEFORE ABRAHAM WAS............................... 109
CHAPTER 8: THE WORD IS GOD....................................... 114
CHAPTER 9: THE SPIRIT AND THE TRINITY..................... 174
CHAPTER 10: THE FINAL WORD.. 219
CHAPTER 11: "YHWH" NOT "JEHOVAH"............................ 230
BIBLIOGRAPHY.. 240

LIST OF ILLUSTRATIONS

Figure 1: Titus 2:13 and 1:4. 84
Figure 2: Titus 2:13 and 1:4 Disparity. 85
Figure 3: Titus 2:13 and 2 Thess. 1:12 Disparity. 87
Figure 4: Titus 2:13 and 2 Thess. 1:12. 87
Figure 5: Titus 2:13 and 2 Pet. 1:2. 89
Figure 6: Titus 2:13 and 2 Pet. 1:1. 89
Figure 7: 2 Pet. 1:1 and 2 Pet. 1:2.. 90
Figure 8: 2 Pet. 1:1 & 1:11. 91
Figure 9: Titus 2:13 Diagraming.. 99
Figure 10: Textual Variants of Mk. 12:27. 130
Figure 11: Definite Predicate Nominative After the Verb. 145
Figure 12: Definite Predicate Nominative Before the Verb. 145
Figure 13: Jn. 6:0 and 1:1c Diagraming. 161
Figure 14: Adonai to Yehovah. 231
Figure 15: 1 Pet. 2:3–4 Antecedent of 'Him'. 235

LIST OF TABLES

Table #1: Acts 13:4–12. ... 28
Table #2: Acts 13:6. ... 29
Table #3: Acts 13:8. ... 30
Table #4: GSEPT Occurrences of μάγος. ... 31
Table #5: Προσκυνέω in Matthew's Gospel. ... 35
Table #6: 2 Chron. 29:30. ... 39
Table #7: Job 1:20. ... 40
Table #8: Dan. 3:5. ... 41
Table #9: Dan. 3:6. ... 41
Table #10: Dan. 3:10. ... 41
Table #11: Dan. 3:11. ... 41
Table #12: Dan. 3:15. ... 42
Table #13: Matt. 14:33. ... 48
Table #14: Matt. 28:16–17. ... 50
Table #15: Phil. 2:5–6. ... 54
Table #16: "Image" and "Form" in the New Testament. ... 57
Table #17: Judg. 8:18. ... 59
Table #18: Phil. 2:7–8. ... 61
Table #19: Gen. 5:1–3. ... 63
Table #20: Col. 1:15–20. ... 65
Table #21: Col. 1:16–17. ... 72
Table #22: Paul's Use of "The All". ... 73
Table #23: Eph. 3:9. ... 77
Table #24: Col. 2:9. ... 79
Table #25: Titus 2:13. ... 83
Table #26: 2 Thess. 1:2. ... 86
Table #27: 2 Pet. 1:1–2. ... 88
Table #28: 2 Pet. 1:1 and 1:2. ... 89
Table #29: Parallels to Titus 2:13. ... 96
Table #30: Parallels with Titus 2:13. ... 97
Table #31: Heb. 1:8. ... 100
Table #32: Ps. 45:7. ... 102
Table #33: Ps. 44:7 and Heb. 1:8. ... 102
Table #34: Gen. 41:38. ... 103
Table #35: GSEPT and BHS of Ps. 45:7. ... 104
Table #36: ὁ θεός as Vocative. ... 105
Table #37: Ps. 40:9. ... 107
Table #38: Ps. 39:9 (GSEPT). ... 107
Table #39: Ps. 39:9 (GSEPT), Ps. 40:9 (BHS), Heb. 10:7. ... 108
Table #40: Jn. 8:58. ... 109
Table #41: Jn. 1:1. ... 114

Table #42: Jn. 1:6. 115
Table #43: Anarthrous Instances of θεός. 117
Table #44: Anarthrous, Definite Uses of θεός. 119
Table #45: Anarthrous *theos* as Definite Predicate Nominatives. 123
Table #46: Comparative List of Anarthrous Uses of θεός. 124
Table #47: Definite Predicate Nominatives of θεός. 125
Table #48: θεὸς in John With and Without the Definite Article. 125
Table #49: Mk. 12:27 and Lk. 20:38. 131
Table #50: Phil. 2:13. 135
Table #51: 2 Thess. 2:4. 137
Table #52: Jn. 10:34. 140
Table #53: Ps. 81:6 GSEPT. 140
Table #54: Ps. 82:6 BHS. 141
Table #55: Ex. 7:1. 142
Table #56: Ex. 7:16. 143
Table #57: Jer. 16:20. 143
Table #58: Ex. 22:8–9. 144
Table #59: Jn. 4:19. 149
Table #60: Supposed Parallels with Jn. 1:1. 149
Table #61: Jn. 1:1c and Jn. 18:35. 155
Table #62: Jn. 1:1 and Jn. 18:37. 156
Table #63: Jn. 18:33 and Jn. 18:39. 156
Table #64: Jn. 19:21. 157
Table #65: Jn. 1:49. 158
Table #66: Jn. 6:60 and Jn. 1:1c. 160
Table #67: Jn. 1:1 and 4:24. 163
Table #68: Jn. 7:39 and Jn. 20:22. 163
Table #69: Acts 8:39. 164
Table #70: Rom. 8:11. 164
Table #71: Heb. 7:5. 175
Table #72: Matt. 4:7c. 176
Table #73: Deut. 6:16 (BHS). 176
Table #74: Deut. 6:16 (GSEPT). 177
Table #75: Acts 8:15. 177
Table #76: ἐπιπίπτω in Acts. 178
Table #77: Acts 8:17–19. 180
Table #78: Acts 2:38c. 181
Table #79: Acts 10:38. 181
Table #80: Acts 1:8. 182
Table #81: Acts 19:2. 182
Table #82: Acts 19:2b. 183
Table #83: "Receiving the Holy Spirit" in Luke-Acts. 183
Table #84: Λαμβάνω in Luke-Acts. 184

Table #85: Lk. 2:25	188
Table #86: Lk. 2:26a	188
Table #87: Lk. 11:13	189
Table #88: τοῦ ἁγίου πνεύματος in Luke Acts	190
Table #89: Jn. 20:22	191
Table #90: "Spirit Holy" in John	191
Table #91: Jn. 7:39 & 14:17	192
Table #92: Gen. 2:7	193
Table #93: Ezek. 37:9	194
Table #94: Matt. 12:43–45	196
Table #95: Neuter Nouns Referring to Persons	196
Table #96: Παράκλητος	199
Table #97: Acts 5:32	200
Table #98: Eph. 4:30	200
Table #99: "Grieve" in the New Testament	201
Table #100: 1 Cor. 6:19	204
Table #101: Jn. 14:26	205
Table #102: Jn. 6:63	207
Table #103: The Spirit Gives Life	208
Table #104: John's Use of τὸ πνεῦμα	209
Table #105: Jn. 4:23–24	211
Table #106: Jesus Life-Giving Spirit	213
Table #107: "The Spirit of Truth"	213
Table #108: 2 Thess. 1:9	232
Table #109: Isa. 2:10, 19, 21	233
Table #110: 1 Pet. 2:3	234
Table #111: Ps. 34:8 (H9; GSEPT9)	234
Table #112: 1 Pet. 3:15	235
Table #113: Isa. 8:13	235

ABBREVIATIONS

BDAG	-	Arndt, William, Frederick W. Danker, and Walter Bauer. *A Greek-English Lexicon of the New Testament and Other Early Christian Literature.* Chicago: University of Chicago Press, 2000.
BHS	-	*Biblia Hebraica Stuttgartensia.* German Bible Society, 2003.
CSD	-	Smith, R. Payne, *A Compendious Syriac Dictionary.* Oxford: Oxford University Press, 1902.
GSEPT	-	*Vetus Testamentum Graecum. Auctoritate Academiae Scientiarum Gottingensis Editum.* Göttingen: Vandenhoeck & Ruprecht, 1931–2006.
GGBTB	-	Wallace, Daniel B. *Greek Grammar Beyond the Basics: Exegetical Syntax of the New Testament.* Zondervan Publishing House and Galaxie Software, 1999.
KBH	-	Koehler, Ludwig, Walter Baumgartner, M. E. J. Richardson, and Johann Jakob Stamm. *The Hebrew and Aramaic Lexicon of the Old Testament.* Leiden; New York: E.J. Brill, 1999.
LPeshitta	-	*Leiden Peshitta.* Leiden: Peshitta Institute Leiden, 2008.
LSL	-	Liddell, Henry George, Robert Scott, Henry Stuart Jones, and Roderick McKenzie. *A Greek-English Lexicon.* Oxford: Clarendon Press, 1996.
NA28	-	Aland, Barbara, et al. *Novum Testamentum Graece*, 28th Edition. Deutsche Bibelgesellschaft, 2012.
NASBU	-	*New American Standard Bible: 1995 Update.* LaHabra, CA: The Lockman Foundation, 1995.
NIDNTTE	-	Silva, Moisés, ed. *New International Dictionary of New Testament Theology and Exegesis.* Grand Rapids: Zondervan, 2014.
NIDOTTE	-	VanGemeren, Willem, ed. *New International Dictionary of Old Testament Theology & Exegesis.* Grand Rapids: Zondervan Publishing House, 1997.
SSL	-	Sokoloff, Michael. *A Syriac Lexicon.* Winona Lake, Indiana: Eisenbrauns, 2009.
TWOT	-	Harris, R. Laird, Gleason L. Archer Jr., and Bruce K. Waltke, eds. *Theological Wordbook of the Old Testament.* Chicago: Moody Press, 1999.
UBS4	-	Aland, Kurt, et al. *The Greek New Testament, Fourth Revised Edition.* Deutsche Bibelgesellschaft, 1993; 2006.

INTRODUCTION

This book is a defense of the accuracy of contemporary translations of the New Testament in depicting Jesus Christ as God in the flesh. Recently, Dr. Jason BeDuhn has published a book titled *Truth in Translation*,[1] that has become a primary weapon in the arsenal of the Jehovah's Witnesses in their efforts to deny that Jesus is God. Arguing from the Greek of the New Testament, BeDuhn attempts to demonstrate that the New World Translation (identified by the initials NW in BeDuhn's book) is the most accurate of modern translations. For anyone who is familiar with the claims of the Jehovah's Witnesses, this means that according to NW and Jason BeDuhn, the New Testament does not teach that Jesus is God or that there is a Trinity of Persons. In fact, according to the Jehovah's Witnesses and BeDuhn's arguments from such passages as Col. 1:15–20, Jesus is a created being.

Such claims must be addressed directly. Those who are witnessing to the Jehovah's Witnesses are usually not Greek scholars, so the technical discussions presented by BeDuhn are often beyond the scope of training of most evangelical apologists. Consequently, Christians on the front lines are being challenged with BeDuhn's claims, and most of them are unable to make a response. This book addresses each one of BeDuhn's arguments in order to provide understandable explanations that can be used to respond to the attacks of Jehovah's Witnesses. In order to respond to BeDuhn's arguments it will be necessary to deal with the technical aspects of his presentation. I have endeavored to make this as transparent as the subject matter will allow.

At publication, Jason BeDuhn was associate professor of religious studies at Northern Arizona University in Flagstaff. He received a Ph.D. in Comparative Study of Religions at Indiana University. In his introduction he presents himself as a qualified Greek scholar who believes he is able, where all others have failed, to give an objective, unbiased account of the accuracy, or rather the inaccuracy, and bias in modern translations. He says, "Most people interested enough to undertake the arduous work of making a Bible translation have an investment in a particular understanding of

---

[1] Jason David BeDuhn, *Truth in Translation: Accuracy and Bias in English Translations of the New Testament* (Lanham, Maryland: University Press of America, 2003).

Christianity, and this investment can affect their objectivity."[2] BeDuhn supposes himself immune to any influence that might compromise his objectivity. Having set forth his own qualifications to make judgments of others' accomplishments, BeDuhn declares, "But just as importantly [as the academic qualifications], I have an attitude that puts me at a distinct advantage to write a book such as this. I am a committed historian dedicated to discovering what Christians said and did two thousand years ago. I have no stake in proving that *those* Christians are most like a particular modern denomination of Christianity, or that they adhered to a particular doctrines that match those of modern Christians."[3]

But BeDuhn tips his hand early in the book. He says, "Accuracy in Bible translation has nothing to do with majority votes; it has to do with letting the biblical authors speak, regardless of where their words might lead. It has to do with strictly excluding bias towards later developments of Christian thought."[4] For those familiar with the claims of Jehovah's Witnesses and with Church history, the implications of BeDuhn's remark cannot be missed. He is, of course, poisoning the well for the reader, alerting the reader that any translations that may seem to indicate a belief that Jesus is God are automatically considered biased and inaccurate as a "later development." BeDuhn does not explain why later developments in Christian thought ought not to be considered in understanding what a text is saying. This kind of tactic would eliminate the entire notion of typology and prophecy—it assumes that what God put in His word cannot be more than what first century Christians could understand.

BeDuhn claims that accuracy "has to do with letting the biblical authors speak, regardless of where their words might lead. . . . Avoiding bias involves obeying probable meaning rather than wished-for meaning. The first choice when faced with options of how best to translate the original Greek usually should be the most obvious, straightforward, unspecialized understanding of the word or phrase."[5] However, anyone who has studied translation theory knows that all translation involves interpretation. As Mark Strauss points out, "Every translation is an interpretation. When confronted with an original text, the translator must interpret the meaning of the original text before he or she can translate the meaning of it into another language."[6] Who decides what is the "most obvious, straightforward, unspecialized understanding" of a word or phrase? Of the possible meanings of words or phrases in the source language, there are a number of possible words or phrases that can be selected from the target language. Each one of these choices involves interpretation—for BeDuhn no less than for any other translator. For BeDuhn to present the work of translation as a simple matter of selecting

---

[2] Ibid., xv.
[3] Ibid., xix.
[4] Ibid.
[5] Ibid., xvi.
[6] Mark L. Strauss, *Distorting Scripture? The Challenge of Bible Translation and Gender Accuracy* (Downers Grove, Illinois: InterVarsity Press, 1998), 85.

Introduction

the "most obvious, straightforward, unspecialized" meaning in each instance is disingenuous at best and deliberately misleading at worst.

BeDuhn claims that in order to analyze translations "you have to know how to read Greek, and the particular kind of Greek in which the New Testament was originally written (something known as *Koinē*, or 'common' Greek)."[7] But BeDuhn says nothing about other qualifications that are equally necessary. What about linguistics and philosophy of language in order to analyze translations? What about a background in translation studies? None of these areas of academic background are mentioned by BeDuhn. BeDuhn also makes no mention of textual criticism, hermeneutics, and theology. Can one effectively evaluate a translation without competency in each of these areas?

BeDuhn decries the tendency of translators to employ their theological bias in translation, but when did such a practice become illegitimate? Why is it wrong to appeal to one's theology to help understand what a passage means? Granted, this can become an illegitimate practice, but it is a perfectly acceptable practice when properly controlled. In fact, it is ultimately an unavoidable practice with reference to many passages. As we interact with BeDuhn's analyses we will see that he is by far not immune to practicing the imposition of his own theological bias on his analysis of others' translations and of the text itself.

But our efforts will not be wholly directed at a critique of BeDuhn's claims. We will also want to analyze each passage in order to demonstrate how these passages support and teach that Jesus Christ is God in the flesh. We will work to provide apologists and witnesses with the ammunition not only to respond to the claims of Jehovah's Witnesses who are appealing to the conclusions of BeDuhn, but to present a positive case from these very Scriptures that Jesus is God, the Second Person of the Trinity, uncreated, the only Son of God, eternally begotten of the Father, true God from true God, begotten, not made, of one Being with the Father, through Whom all things were made. But before we begin the task of analyzing particular arguments, let us consider what BeDuhn says he is trying to do.

BeDuhn's Argument

The Basic Task

BeDuhn begins his book by recognizing the significant impact that the King James Version of the Bible has had on Western, English-speaking culture. All to often, as BeDuhn observes, loyalty to the KJV has produced a myopic perspective and an intolerance toward changes and new translations even among those who would not otherwise be classified among the KJV-only crowd. BeDuhn argues that not all

---

[7] BeDuhn, *Translation*, xvii.

translations accurately present the meaning of the underlying Greek text. According to BeDuhn, "The important thing in judgments of accuracy is that the translators have found English words and phrases that correspond to the known meaning of the Greek, and put them together into English sentences that dutifully follow what the Greek syntax communicates."[8] Consequently, the Greek text provides the standard by which translations ought to be judged: "If a translator chooses rare or otherwise unattested meanings for Greek words, and constructs English sentences which do not straightforwardly communicate the most likely sense of the original, then he or she is producing an inaccurate translation."[9]

BeDuhn also addresses what he sees as a bias in some translations: "Bias comes into the picture when we try to identify why a translation shows inaccuracy in its handling of the original Greek text."[10] BeDuhn is not interested in automatically charging translators with bias, so he first examines a translation's faithfulness to the Greek text, and if the translation appears to be more than simply a mistake, he addresses the possibility of bias. BeDuhn realizes that translations can legitimately differ simply because "there are several ways to convey the meaning of the original."[11] So, in such circumstances he is not quick to attribute inaccuracy to theological or philosophical prejudices.

How then does one know whether a difference in translation is more than a legitimate difference or a mistake? BeDuhn says, "Bias is involved when differences in translation cannot be explained by reasons based in the likely meaning of the original Greek."[12] Translations are the product of persons who have a particular theological perspective, and sometimes, according to BeDuhn, this perspective can "affect their objectivity" as translators.[13] BeDuhn's analysis is presented as if from someone who has no theological axe to grind. He observes that bias can come from any denominational and confessional commitment: "The New American Bible was prepared by Catholics . . . The New World Translation was produced by Jehovah's Witnesses. The New International Version . . . 'evangelical' . . ."[14] But bias does not come only from a particular confessional commitment, as BeDuhn points out: "But even translations made by broad inter-denominational committees can be subject to the collective, 'mainstream Christian' bias of the translators."[15]

BeDuhn seeks to analyze translations in terms of whether they let the biblical authors speak for themselves, "regardless of where their words lead."[16] Translations

---

[8] Ibid., xiv.
[9] Ibid.
[10] Ibid.
[11] Ibid., xv.
[12] Ibid.
[13] Ibid.
[14] Ibid.
[15] Ibid.
[16] Ibid.

Introduction

should not, according to BeDuhn, reflect theological positions that may have developed later than the actual New Testament documents. BeDuhn believes that translators should not read back into the New Testament documents theological positions or doctrines that developed only after years of debate and discussion. Rather, according to BeDuhn, accuracy in translation involves the "most obvious, straightforward, unspecialized understanding of the word or phrase."[17] However, BeDuhn does not want automatically to rule out translations that may at first seem to be inaccurate or less obvious: "Any other choice needs to be justified by strong evidence from the literary context or historical and cultural environment."[18] The evidence must be there, however, and a translation that seems to deviate from the straightforward meaning of the text must be justified from "the known rules of the Greek language."[19]

Even though translators may seek to be as faithful to the text as possible, BeDuhn realizes that sometimes rival meanings cannot be easily resolved. In such cases, translators my legitimately choose the meaning that best fits their beliefs, but BeDuhn warns, "they owe it to their readers to make a note of the uncertainty."[20] Nor is BeDuhn quick to reject a translation or accuse translators of bias under these circumstances. "If the translation given is at least within the realm of possibility for the meaning of the Greek text, we must grant that fact and not be too hard on the translators for preferring one possible meaning over another."[21]

So, from what we have seen thus far, BeDuhn has set himself the task of discovering the accuracy and bias of modern translations of the New Testament. By implication, BeDuhn approaches this task as a non-partisan observer, not affiliated with or committed to a particular confessional tradition. The standard of accuracy and unbiased translation will be the Greek text and the grammatical and syntactical aspects of the Greek language as this is found in the Greek New Testament. The Greek of the New Testament that will form this standard will not necessarily be the Greek of the later church Fathers or of later theological development, but will be the language as it was employed by the New Testament authors in their own time. In other words, BeDuhn will work from a synchronic rather than a diachronic understanding of the Greek of the New Testament.

Specific Tasks

BeDuhn spells out what he believes constitutes an accurate and unbiased translation: "Accurate, unbiased translations are based on (1) linguistic content, (2)

---

[17] Ibid., xvi.
[18] Ibid.
[19] Ibid.
[20] Ibid.
[21] Ibid.

literary context, and (3) historical and cultural environment."²² These three principles are not different from the principles that govern good exegesis and hermeneutics. BeDuhn also spells out why he makes these points the basis of his test for accuracy:

> We use these three bases for making and assessing New Testament translations because we presume certain things about how the New Testament was written by its authors. Our reliance on linguistic content presupposes that an author used Greek correctly, in line with the linguistic conventions of his or her time. If he or she didn't, we really have no way to know what might be meant. Our use of literary context assumes that an author was relatively consistent and non-contradictory in what he or she said. If the author has not assembled a coherent piece of writing, we would be unable to judge our ability to understand it. Our attention to the historical and cultural environment presumes that an author worked with images and ideas available in his or her world (even if working to redefine or transform them), and that a contemporaneous audience was the intended readership. If the books of the New Testament were written in a way that was incomprehensible to the earliest Christians, they never would have been valued, preserved, and collected into scripture.²³

Not only does BeDuhn enumerate the basic principles by which he will assess the accuracy of a translation, he also describes the qualifications of an individual who will perform the analysis. For BeDuhn, such an individual must have a working knowledge of the Greek language of the authors. Although this qualification seems obvious, as BeDuhn points out, many who condemn other translations do so without this capacity. As BeDuhn observes, "In practice, people who do not read Greek compare a new translation with an existing one of which they approve."²⁴ But, non-Greek readers are not equipped to assess the accuracy or bias of a given translation.

The next qualification is the capacity to recognize the various kinds of literature one finds in the New Testament and to employ the appropriate hermeneutical principles. But, as BeDuhn points out, the capacity to recognize and interpret specific kinds of writing in the New Testament "is only the beginning. The books of the New Testament belong to a larger literary context that includes early Jewish and Christian traditions of writing."²⁵ In order effectively to interpret a passage of the New Testament, the interpreter must have a grasp of the larger literary context, the practices and styles that were commonly used in the period. As BeDuhn explains, "Other Jewish and Christian writings produced at the same time as the New Testament, such as the Dead Sea Scrolls or the Christian apostolic fathers, help us grasp the literary conventions followed in the New Testament as well as the characteristics that set the New Testament apart."²⁶ This involves much more than simply reading a commentary that elucidates the immediate

---

²² Ibid., xvi.
²³ Ibid.
²⁴ Ibid., xvii.
²⁵ Ibid., xviii.
²⁶ Ibid.

historical background of a book or passage. A working knowledge of these factors prepares one to fulfill the second principle of evaluation, the literary context.

The third qualification is a grasp of the grammar and syntax of the Greek language of the authors' day. Being able to look up words in a lexicon is inadequate to make the kinds of assessments that BeDuhn wants to make. A translator, or one who seeks to assess the adequacy of a translation, must understand the nature of language, how words change their meanings, how words are impacted by their cultural surroundings, how the meanings of words are found in "references and allusions of our imagery, metaphors, and figures of speech."[27] As BeDuhn points out, "a great deal of what Jesus had to say refers to and builds upon the ideas and images of 1st century Judaism."[28] This requires a broad knowledge of the linguistic context as well as the literary context.

Finally, BeDuhn briefly discusses the fact that one who seeks to assess the accuracy of a translation must have a knowledge of the historical background against which the New Testament was composed: "The exact nuance of a phrase or argument in the New Testament may depend on this background knowledge. So it is important to have some credentials in this area."[29] BeDuhn is not saying that in order to understand what the New Testament is teaching, that one much be a scholar with all these credentials. What he is saying is that one who wishes to assess the adequacy, accuracy, and possible bias of a translation of the New Testament must indeed have these qualifications, and those who do not are not equipped to make such judgments.

BeDuhn has set for himself the specific task of assessing, on the basis of the three basic principles, the accuracy of modern translations and of discovering whether or not some translations betray a theological or philosophical bias in the way the translators present the meaning of the Greek New Testament text. As we have mentioned, BeDuhn believes that he is uniquely qualified for this task because, as he puts it, "I am a committed historian dedicated to discovering what Christians said and did two thousand years ago. I have no stake in proving that *those* Christians are most like a particular modern denomination of Christianity, or that they adhered to particular doctrines that match those of modern Christians."[30] BeDuhn commits himself to follow the evidence wherever it leads. If a translation accurately presents the meaning of the Greek text, then for him it does not matter who those translators were or to which confession or set of doctrines they are committed, he is committed simply to report this facts as he finds them. And likewise, if a translation proves to be inaccurate or driven by confessional or doctrinal bias, BeDuhn commits himself simply to report that as well.

---

[27] Ibid.
[28] Ibid.
[29] Ibid.
[30] Ibid., xix.

The Challenge

BeDuhn invites the reader to scrutinize his arguments and test his claims. He promises to present evidence—linguistic, literary, and historical—to persuade the reader of his conclusions. And this is what I propose to do in the following pages. BeDuhn has thrown down the gauntlet. Like BeDuhn, I have many years of teaching on a graduate level biblical languages, biblical literature, and biblical backgrounds. Additionally, I have training in theology and philosophy that equips me to be able to uncover and assess presuppositions and assumptions upon which an author operates often without his even realizing it. As Richard Rorty once said, "Uncovering the presuppositions of those who think they have none is one of the principal means by which philosophers find new issues to debate."[31] In the pages that follow, I will take up BeDuhn's gauntlet. I will scrutinize his arguments. I will check his claims. I will attempt to uncover his own bias. In the closing comments of his introduction, BeDuhn said that by the end of the book, "I hope you will be motivated to continue your exploration and to develop your ability to use these tools to pursue further questions on your own."[32] By the end of my book, I hope you will see that BeDuhn has a dog in this fight, just like everyone else. BeDuhn promises to uncover bias and inaccuracy in modern translations. I hope to uncover BeDuhn's own bias and inaccuracy in his assessment of modern translations.

The Roadmap

Let set out for you where we are going and how we are going to get there. Jason BeDuhn claims that New Testament translations are frequently inaccurate. They often betray a theological or philosophical bias that has led the translators to provide an English translation that supports this bias even though the underlying Greek text does not. To accomplish this task, BeDuhn has selected certain passages to analyze. In each one of these passages, the inaccuracy and bias has to do with the Deity of Jesus Christ. Our book will basically follow the chapter divisions of BeDuhn's book so that we can address each of his arguments in the context of his presentations.

BeDuhn's book is composed of thirteen chapters with an introduction and an appendix. The first three chapters are dedicated to some important background information about modern translations; how we got or English Bibles, what is the nature of translation, and a synopsis of the major English translations. We discuss some important issues and respond to BeDuhn's discussion about translation in Chapter One, "TRANSLATING THE BIBLE." However, it is not until chapter four that BeDuhn

---

[31] Richard M. Rorty, "Introduction: Metaphilosophical Difficulties of Linguistic Philosophy," in *The Linguistic Turn*, ed. Richard M. Rorty (Chicago: The University of Chicago Press, 1992), 2.

[32] BeDuhn, *Truth in Translation*, xix.

Introduction

begins his analysis of specific instances of inaccuracy and bias. The chapters that deal specifically with this issue are given below with a brief synopsis of each:

Chapter Two —WORSHIPING CHRIST: In his chapter titled "Bowing to Bias,"[33] chapter four in his book, BeDuhn attempts to demonstrate that "the accuracy of the translation is hampered by a bias towards restricted, theological importance invested in a term."[34] BeDuhn focuses on the Greek word *proskuneō* (προσκυνέω). Whereas in several instances, many modern translations translate this word as "worship," especially when the action is directed to Jesus, BeDuhn seeks to show that this is in fact not the meaning of this term. BeDuhn argues that in these contexts, the word simply indicates the custom of bowing or prostration designed to show respect, but not indicating that the one bowing is worshiping someone. So, in those passages where someone is bowing before Christ, the bias of modern translators has led them to translate this as "worship" when in fact all that is being said is that the bowing was a customary gesture of respect.

Chapter Three — IN THE FORM OF GOD: In chapter five of his book, titled "Grasping At Accuracy,"[35] BeDuhn focuses on Phil. 2:5–11. The critical statement for BeDuhn is found in verse 6: "who, although He existed in the form of God, did not regard equality with God a thing to be grasped" (NASB). Initially BeDuhn focuses on the translation of the word *morphē* (μορφή), translated "form." He argues that this does not necessarily indicate that Jesus is God, and that modern translators have prevented their audiences from see the word as having any other possible meaning. Although BeDuhn acknowledges that there is a certain amount of interpretation in any translation, he claims that modern translations have actually gone too far in imposing their interpretations upon these verses. Next he turns his attention to the word *harpagmos* (ἁρπαγμός) that is translated "a thing to be grasped." BeDuhn claims, "The NW translators, on the other hand, have understood *harpagmos* accurately as grasping at something one does not have, that is, a 'seizure.'"[36] In other words, this verse is not teaching that Jesus, being God, did not hold onto his position as God, but was rather grasping after equality with God.

In chapter six of his book, "When Is A Man Not A Man?"[37] BeDuhn discusses the use of gender in New Testament Greek and how this impacts or is evident in modern translations. This is a fairly straightforward discussion that does not present any seriously objectionable claims, so we will not dedicate a chapter to BeDuhn's discussion. Only one observation is in order and can be dealt with here. BeDuhn starts off the chapter by claiming that both the language and culture of the New Testament were male-dominated. He then says, "Both have grammatical rules that are male-based."[38] Strictly speaking, grammatical rules are not male-based. Rather, it is the

---

[33] Ibid., 41–49.
[34] Ibid., 41.
[35] Ibid., 51–62.
[36] Ibid., 61.
[37] Ibid., 63–74.
[38] Ibid., 63.

lexical structure of a language that can be considered male-based. In fact, throughout BeDuhn's discussion, it is always the meanings of words, not the grammatical rules, that are the focus of discussion. Such a misuse of terminology occurs frequently in his book and serves to confuse the reader, and it raises the question of whether BeDuhn was not exaggerating his competence to deal with the issues of translation.

Chapter Four — BY HIM ALL THINGS WERE CREATED: BeDuhn begins his chapter seven, "Probing the Implicit Meaning,"[39] by acknowledging that some times translators must add words in order for the text to make sense in English. He discusses the notion that there are implicit meanings that translators sometimes make explicit in their translations and sometimes do not. He focuses in on Col. 1:15–20 concerning which he says, "It is a tricky passage where every translation does and must 'add words.'"[40] Along these lines, BeDuhn considers how the New World translation has added the word 'other' to their translation of Col. 1:16. The NW translation renders this verse as, "because by means of him all [other] things were created." BeDuhn justifies this addition with a discussion of the Greek Genitive case. In this chapter he also discusses the word 'firstborn,' and then he questions the validity of adding the word 'his' in verse 19, which the NIV renders, "For *God* was pleased to have all *his* fullness dwell in him."

Chapter Five — OUR GOD AND SAVIOR JESUS CHRIST: In chapter eight of his book, "Words Together and Apart"[41] BeDuhn focuses on the specific statement in Titus 2:13. BeDuhn renders the statement as "the great God and our savior Christ Jesus."[42] This is a fairly literal translation, and BeDuhn argues that this phrase is a reference to God and Christ Jesus as two distinct individuals. Most modern translations treat this phrase as if it were a reference only to Christ Jesus. For example, the NASB renders it, "our great God and Savior, Christ Jesus." In this chapter, BeDuhn appeals to various passages that claims have identical grammatical structures[43] and demonstrate that the Titus 2:13 must be translated in such a way as to make explicit that the phrase is in fact referring to two distinct individuals, God and Jesus.

Chapter Six — THY THRONE O GOD: In Heb. 1:8 the verb 'is' does not appear. Consequently, it is up to the translators to decide whether to add the verb in the English, and if so, where to put it. The placement of this relatively small verb makes a great deal of difference in communicating to the reader what the translators believe this verse means. In chapter nine of his book, "An Uncertain Throne,"[44] BeDuhn argues that modern translations have actually misrepresented this verse by adding the verb 'is' after the word 'God' instead of before it. The New World translation renders this verse as follows: "But with reference to the Son: 'God is your throne forever and ever, and [the]

---

[39] Ibid., 75–88.
[40] Ibid., 77.
[41] Ibid., 89–95.
[42] Ibid., 89.
[43] Ibid., 92.
[44] Ibid., 97–101.

Introduction

scepter of your kingdom is the scepter of uprightness,'" and BeDuhn argues that this placement is correct because the word 'God' is not a direct address.

Chapter Seven — BEFORE ABRAHAM WAS: In chapter ten of his book, "Tampering With Tenses"[45] BeDuhn discusses the unusual expression in Jn. 8:58, "Before Abraham was, I am." BeDuhn argues that this is a Greek idiom and that the English translation should not try to reproduce the disparity between the verb tenses because this would not be proper English. Also, BeDuhn criticizes modern translations for departing from proper English word order.

Chapter Eight — THE WORD IS GOD: BeDuhn titles his eleventh chapter, "And the Word was . . . What?" This is arguably the longest chapter in his book. This may be because it deals with one of the most important verses, or at least one of the most popular verses, expressing the fact that Jesus is God—Jn. 1:1, especially the last sentence, "And the Word was God." There has been much debate between orthodox Christians and Jehovah's Witnesses over the precise meaning of the word 'God.' Is this short sentence really asserting that Jesus is God, or is it simply saying Jesus is a god. BeDuhn argues for the latter interpretation. Because of the importance of this small sentence, and because of the nature of the arguments put forward by BeDuhn, this is certainly be the longest and perhaps the most technical chapter in our book.

Chapter Nine — THE SPIRIT AND THE TRINITY: According to the Jehovah's Witnesses, the Holy Spirit is not the third Person of the Trinity. In fact, the Holy Spirit, according to the JWs, is not a Person at all. Rather, they believe that the Holy Spirit is "the invisible active force of the Almighty God."[46] They argue, "There is no basis for concluding that the Holy Spirit is a Person."[47] In lockstep with the Jehovah's Witnesses, BeDuhn attempts to show that the Holy Spirit is an "it." He calls chapter twelve on this topic, "The Spirit Writ Large."[48] Appealing to an account of the history of Christian doctrine, BeDuhn asserts, "Later Christian theology also applied technical status of a 'person' on the Holy Spirit, which has led modern translators and readers to think of the Holy Spirit in human terms as a 'who,' even a 'he,' rather than an 'it' that transcends human measures of personhood."[49] BeDuhn tries to argue that the doctrine of the Trinity and the belief that the Holy Spirit is a Person and the third Person of the Trinity was a later development in Christian thought and was not a part of the New Testament.

Chapter Ten — THE FINAL WORD: Although BeDuhn titles his thirteenth chapter "A Final Word,"[50] he follows this chapter with more words. His thirteenth chapter is a

---

[45] Ibid., 103–12.
[46] Watch Tower Bible and Tract Society, *Let God Be True* (n.p.: Watch Tower Bible and Tract Society, 1952), 108; quoted in Walter Martin, *The Kingdom of the Cults* (Minneapolis: Bethany Fellowship, 1977), 47.
[47] Watch Tower Bible and Tract Society, "Watch Tower" (January 1, 1952): 24; quoted in Martin, *Kingdom of Cults*, 47.
[48] BeDuhn, *Translation*, 135–60.
[49] Ibid., 136.
[50] Ibid., 161–68.

summary of his arguments throughout the book. Although this is a short chapter, in it BeDuhn presents a summary of what he believes he has accomplished in each of his chapters. Our goal is to consider each of BeDuhn's summaries and then to summarize our critique of his arguments and claims in the respective chapters.

Chapter Eleven — "YHWH" NOT "JEHOVAH": This material deals with BeDuhn's arguments in his Appendix titled, "The Use of 'Jehovah' in the NW."[51] After a brief discussion of how the word 'Jehovah' came to be, BeDuhn argues that the NW editors have legitimately used the word 'Jehovah' in many places in the NT. BeDuhn claims that the practice of the editors of the NW in their use of the name "Jehovah" in the NT is for "Carefully distinguishing God from Jesus by using the name of Jehovah for the former." He claims they have sought to resolve the "ambiguity in a way that keeps these two personages distinct and aids in the formulation of theology and christology by showing which entity is responsible for which activities in the thinking of the biblical authors."[52]

Chapter Ten in our book actually serves as the conclusion for the whole book as well as an analysis of BeDuhn's chapter thirteen. Our material in Chapter Eleven is actually a response to BeDuhn's Appendix. Much of the material in this book is technical, and we have attempted to explain these technical aspects so that those who have no training in the biblical languages can still follow the arguments. Consequently, when you who have this training run across this explanatory material, please be patient and keep in mind that this is for the benefit of others. It is hoped that this material will help to train and support those who are on the front lines of apologetics and evangelism in defending the historic Christian doctrine of the deity of Jesus Christ and the Divine Trinity.

---

[51] Ibid., 169–81.
[52] Ibid., 176.

CHAPTER 1

TRANSLATING THE BIBLE

Introduction

This chapter will focus primarily upon BeDuhn's presentation in the chapter titled "The Work of Translation,"[1] which is actually chapter two in BeDuhn's book. Although we will refer to some comments made by BeDuhn in chapter one of his book and in his introduction, the focus of these sections of BeDuhn's book are very general in character and do not present material that necessarily supports his claim that the New World translation is the best modern translation. In chapter two however, BeDuhn attempts to limit the resources for the study in a way that stacks the deck against anyone attempting to critique his thesis. BeDuhn argues for the superiority of reference works that he thinks are supportive of his arguments, and he attempts to disparage other reference materials that he believes would present information that would tend to undermine his thesis.

In chapter two of his book, BeDuhn purports to give the reader an overview of the nature of the task of translation. He begins by briefly discussing what he takes to be the first step in the practice of translation, identifying each Greek word and discovering its meaning in context.

Translation and Lexicons

Of course, one of the tools of a translator is going to be a standard lexicon of the language of the document(s) studied. For the study of the Greek New Testament, BeDuhn advocates the Liddell & Scott Greek lexicon—Henry George Liddell and Robert Scott, *A Greek-English Lexicon* (Oxford: Clarendon Press, 1996). No doubt this is a standard Greek lexicon, but it is primarily a standard of classical Greek, not

---

[1] BeDuhn, *Translation*, 11–26.

particularly of Koine Greek, as Cyril Barber points out. Barber calls it "the most important resource tool to the classical period of Greek literature . . ."[2]

BeDuhn marginalizes the standard New Testament lexicon—Walter Bauer, Frederick William Danker, W. F. Arndt, and F. W. Gingrich, *A Greek-English Lexicon of the New Testament and Other Early Christian Literature*, 3d ed. (Chicago: The University of Chicago Press, 2000). He says, "A more specialized lexicon is the one originally edited by Walter Bauer (which has also been revised by many later editors), published by the University of Chicago Press and focused more on the later Greek of the Christian period."[3] However, contrary to BeDuhn's claim, the lexicon itself claims to focus on the New Testament period: "It is the purpose of this lexicon to facilitate the understanding of the texts that were composed in the late Greek described above."[4] According to Bauer, the "late Geek" period is the period begun approximately 300 BC and known as the Hellenistic period of Koine Greek.

Of this and other such specialized lexicons, BeDuhn asserts, "in the work of Bible translation, these should be used only secondarily, if at all."[5] BeDuhn believes that these lexicons have many weaknesses, one of which is that they "tend to be based on existing English translations, rather than offering resources for fresh translation."[6] Unfortunately BeDuhn offers no explanation why being based on existing English translations is a weakness, nor does he explain why being based on existing translations makes it impossible for such a lexicon to offer resources for fresh translations. Additionally, BeDuhn seems to assume that fresh translations are better than existing translations, and he likewise offers no explanation why anyone should think this is the case.

BeDuhn also believes that these specialized lexicons are "deeply flawed by containing information only from the Bible itself, instead of including information from Greek literature in general."[7] But it seems to be BeDuhn's belief that is deeply flawed. A lexicon is designed to be a presentation of how the lexical units of a language are or were used. A lexicon can be specialized in that it presents lexical units only of a specialized field—legal field—or a specialized period of history—New Testament and other early Christian literature—or of a specialized range of function—contemporary idioms. No one would consider a legal lexicon to be flawed because it did not include information from biology or engineering, nor should a lexicon on the use of Greek in the New Testament be considered flawed simply because it does not include information about how words were used in the Classical period.

---

[2] Cyril J. Barber, *Introduction to Theological Research* (Chicago: Moody Press, 1982), 93. Barber is not only an accomplished theologian but also holds an advanced degree in library science.

[3] BeDuhn, *Translation*, 12.

[4] Walter Bauer, "An Introduction to the Lexicon of the Greek New Testament," in BDAG, xxii.

[5] BeDuhn, *Translation*, 12.

[6] Ibid.

[7] Ibid.

Chapter 1: Translating the Bible

BeDuhn should have spent a few minutes reading the Preface to the Liddell & Scott Lexicon. He would have discovered that this lexicon is primarily a lexicon of Attic Greek. Even though through the years plans and efforts were made to expand the scope of the lexicon to exhaustively include Greek material through the centuries, the vast amount of extant Greek material accumulated through the centuries made such a task financially and practically impossible. In fact, H. Stuart Jones points out in the Preface to the 1925 edition, the last major update of the lexicon, that he relied upon "Moulton and Milligan's *Vocabulary of the Greek Testament*, which (within its natural limits) may almost be regarded as a Lexicon of the κοινή as a whole."[8] In other words, the last updater of the Liddell&Scott lexicon recognized the superior value of specialized New Testament lexicons.

Since the Liddell&Scott Lexicon is primarily a lexicon of Attic Greek, the need for a New Testament lexicon is evident from the differences between Koine and Attic Greek. As Chrys C. Caragounis points out,

> while the Attic dialect was becoming a world language, it also embarked upon a course that would inevitably lead it to its 'collapse.' The agents to whom it owed its world domination were not the architects who had curved it with feeling and taste, but soldiers, engineers, technicians, physicians and second rate literati from every corner of the Greek world. When the barbarians, too, were in time invited to feast on its sumptuous table, the havoc was complete. All those features that had made it what it had been began to fall away. The precision, the delicateness, the expressiveness, the aesthetic beauty began to wane, to leave behind them the bare structure, imposing though it still was. Stripped of its finest, most intricate and delicate elements, it received the less sensitive equivalents from the other dialects, as well as new patterns that gave it a new appearance. Attic now became Koine.[9]

In other words, Attic Greek gave way to Koine with many drastic changes imposed upon the language by non-native Greek speakers. Although Liddell&Scott incorporate many of these differences into its articles, it was deemed by the revisors to be impossible to include all those features that became common to the Koine form of the language. Consequently, contrary to BeDuhn's chronological snobbery, the New Testament Lexicon by Bauer, Danker, Arndt, and Gingrich is a necessary and in many ways superior lexical source simply because it focuses on the Koine Greek of the New Testament; a form of Greek that has incorporated into it some of the distinctive features of writers whose native language was Semitic.

A lexicon of the New Testament is designed to present to the user of the lexicon information on how the lexical units of the New Testament were used in New Testament and early Christian users of Koine Greek. It is not designed to tell the user how lexical units were used outside the circumscribed period covered by the lexicon. Although the

---

[8] H. Stuart Jones, "Preface," in *A Greek-English Lexicon* (Oxford: At The Clarendon Press, 1969), ix.

[9] Chrys C. Caragounis, *The Development of Greek and the New Testament: Morphology, Syntax, Phonology, and Textual Transmission* (Grand Rapids: Baker Academic, 2006), 102–3.

lexicon may indeed include such information, it is not designed necessarily to include this. BeDuhn's error is to assume that just because the lexicon includes information only about the New Testament that its meanings are not informed by earlier usage. The lexicographers no doubt consulted earlier as well as later uses as well as the New Testament in compiling the lexicon. BeDuhn says that these kinds of lexicons are "inherently biased towards harmonization of meaning for a particular word among its many uses in the Bible."[10] But BeDuhn nowhere demonstrates that this is the case either in the New Testament lexicon or in any other lexicon. This kind of unsupported declaration, as we will see, is characteristic of BeDuhn's argument style.

One can make the same charge against the Liddell&Scott lexicon—it is inherently biased toward harmonization of meaning for a particular word among its many uses in the history of the Greek language particularly focusing on the Attic dialect. The flaw in BeDuhn's reasoning is that a New Testament Greek lexicon is different from the Liddell&Scott lexicon only in the range of use considered. But when does one cross the line in range of use to become "inherently biased toward harmonization of meaning"? Does a lexicon become inherently biased when it considers only one period in the history of the Greek language? But this is true of the Liddell&Scott lexicon since it does not consider the use of modern Greek. BeDuhn's own bias against orthodox Christian doctrine leads him to attempt to poison the well against any reference material that would tend to undermine or not to support his point of view. But, as we will repeatedly see, BeDuhn's own speculations about meaning and use of Greek words is often not supported by his favorite lexicon either.

Translation and Etymology

BeDuhn criticizes biblical lexicons because, according to him, they are "handicapped by a mistaken etymological approach to word meanings."[11] What at first may seem like a minor point may also be indicative of a larger problem of a lack of familiarity with the principles of linguistics in general and of translation in particular. BeDuhn says, "Older and less sophisticated applications of formal equivalence often lapse into the etymological fallacy. That is, translators make the mistake of thinking a word has a core meaning based upon the lexical meaning of its constituent parts that are *always* the same and *always* intended when the word is used, regardless of context."[12] A problem with BeDuhn's statement is that this is in fact not the "etymological fallacy." John Lyons, Master of Trinity Hall in the University of Cambridge, fellow of the British Academy, and Honorary Member of the Linguistics Society of America, defines the etymological fallacy as "the common belief that the meaning of words can be determined by investigating their origins. The etymology of a lexeme is, in principle,

---

[10] Ibid.
[11] Ibid.
[12] Ibid., 14.

Chapter 1: Translating the Bible

synchronically irrelevant. The fact that the word 'curious,' for example, can be traced back to the Latin 'curiosus' meaning 'careful' or 'fastidious' (and that it also had this meaning in earlier stages of English) does not imply that this, rather than 'inquisitive,' is its true or correct meaning in present-day standard English."[13] The *International Encyclopedia of Linguistics* says, "Taken most strictly as a relationship, an etymology is the history and prehistory of a locution."[14]

BeDuhn's misunderstanding of what is the etymological fallacy stems from his basic misunderstanding of what etymology is. David Alan Black gives an accurate sense of what etymology is: "The ancient Greek debated whether the meaning of a word is to be found in its nature (φύσις) or whether meaning is a matter of convention and usage (νόμος). The Stoics opted for the former position, and through their influence the idea of ἔτυμον ('real meaning') became firmly implanted in linguistic investigation."[15] Of course, the astute observer may think that we have committed the etymological fallacy by quoting Black's explanation of the term according to its historical roots. However, that is not the case since the term 'etymology' is a technical term that is purposely built upon its historic meaning, and Black does not recount the history of the word for the purposes of determining contemporary meaning, but to compare the error of the Stoics with the tendency of modern commentators to attempt to find "the 'real meaning' of a word merely by looking up its etymology, without paying attention to the context in which the word occurs."[16]

In fact, not only does BeDuhn seem to have the wrong meaning of 'etymology,' he actually seems to advocate what experts in the field identify as the etymological fallacy. BeDuhn says, "Most biblical lexicons are handicapped by a mistaken etymological approach to word meanings. This is the idea that words only mean what their constituent parts mean. The actual history of use is much more reliable in determining a word's meaning."[17] Of course, etymology is not the effort to discover the meaning of a word based on the meaning of the constituent parts at a given point in the history of the word. Etymology certainly includes the effort to discover the meaning of the constituent parts of a word, but this aspect of etymology involves the distinction between diachronic and synchronic elements in semantics.[18] That is, the difference between the history of a word's meaning, diachronic meaning, and the use of a word in a particular historical period, synchronic meaning. In fact, Black goes on to point out that the proper use of etymology, the history of a word's meaning, is not for discovering meaning: "The

---

[13] John Lyons, *Semantics* (Cambridge: Cambridge University Press, 1977), 244. The term 'lexeme' indicates a lexical unit, or more loosely, a vocabulary entry.

[14] Eric P. Hamp, "Etymology," in *International Encyclopedia of Linguistics*, 2d ed. ed. William J. Frawley (Oxford: Oxford University Press, 2003), 2.7.

[15] David Alan Black, *Linguistics for Students of New Testament Greek* (Grand Rapids: Baker Book House, 1988), 121.

[16] Ibid.

[17] BeDuhn, *Translation*, 12.

[18] See Lyons, *Semantics*, 244.

proper way to use etymology and other historical information is for the sake of comparison and background, not for determining later meanings."[19]

Now we can give BeDuhn the benefit of the doubt (as we will see, something he is unwilling to do for the motives of modern translators). BeDuhn may be using his definition of 'etymology' and 'etymological fallacy' to refer to the historical construction of words from roots, assuming of course that this is the way words were formed. In fact Black uses this very kind of example as a case of the etymological fallacy. He says, "The Greek word ἐκκλησία is a notorious victim of etymologizing. Its etymology suggests the meaning, 'a called-out group' (ἐκκλησία is formed from a combination of the preposition ἐκ ['out of'] and the root καλ ['to call'])."[20] The difference is that the word ἐκκλησία is actually the combination of two historically distinct lexemes, but not all words are composed of such combinations. Nevertheless, all words do have a history of meaning. But even with this benefit of the doubt, BeDuhn has nevertheless misused the standard linguistic terminology, and BeDuhn's apparent lack of familiarity with standard terminology in linguistics may be indicative of a larger lack of familiarity with linguistics in general and how principles of language relate to the process of translation in particular.

Of course, some will say this is an example of an *ad hominem* attack and is therefore a logical fallacy. But, this kind of response reveals a lack of familiarity with the basic principles of logic. Not all *ad hominem* arguments are fallacious. As Howard Kahane points out, "But *ad hominem* arguments are not always fallacious. For instance, a lawyer who attacks the testimony of a witness by questioning his moral character argues *ad hominem*, but does not commit a fallacy."[21] We will discuss this in more detail later, but the point is, if a person professes to be an expert in a field, then an analysis of his abilities is warranted, and questions about his knowledge or ability in the supposed field of his expertise is not an *ad hominem* fallacy. BeDuhn claims to be able to instruct his reader on the basic principles of translation, and yet he seems unfamiliar with the basic terminology of linguistics and translation. Kahane goes on to point out that this kind of analysis, *ad hominem* that is not a fallacy, does not prove that what the supposed expert is saying is false, but it does justify the disregarding of what the expert is saying. BeDuhn purports to be an expert, but his discussion of translation seems to indicate otherwise.

Translation and Proper English

BeDuhn criticizes the KJV (King James Version) and other translations that he claims follow a formal equivalence method of translation. As an example, he presents

---

[19] Black, *Linguistics*, 122.
[20] Ibid., 121.
[21] Howard Kahane, *Logic and Philosophy*, 2d ed. (Belmont, California: Wadsworth Publishing Company, 1973), 240.

Chapter 1: Translating the Bible

translations of 1 Thess. 4:3–6 from the KJV, NW (New World Translation), and the NASB (New American Standard Bible).[22] BeDuhn accuses the KJV of using phrases that are "not recognizable as proper English (for example: 'even as the Gentiles which know not God'), while the NW sounds stilted and wooden."[23] BeDuhn does not tell the reader why he considers this to be unrecognizable as proper English other than perhaps the use of the term "Gentiles." BeDuhn says, "The KJV and NASB retain the archaic English word 'Gentiles,' while the NW translates more accurately as 'nations.'"[24] But BeDuhn has ignored his own principle of understanding the meaning of a word in its historical and literary context. The word translated "Gentiles" (ἔθνη, *ethnē*) is frequently used of those outside the covenant relation of the nation of Israel, that is to say, the covenant that God established with Israel, and in many instances the term 'Gentiles' is used to refer to non-Jews specifically. By relying too heavily on the LSL BeDuhn has missed the peculiar NT usage. And yet even LSL gives this information about the use of the word in the NT:

b. later, τὰ ἔ *foreign, barbarous nations*, opp. Ἕλληνες, Arist.Pol.1324b10; ἔ. νομάδων, of Bedawin, LW2203 (Syria.); at Athens, athletic *clubs of non-Athenians*, IG2.444, al.; in Lxx, *non-Jews*, Ps.2.1, al., cf. Act.Ap.7.45; *Gentiles*, τῶν ἐθνέων τε καὶ Ἰουδαίων ib.14.5, etc.; used of *Gentile Christians*, Ep.Rom.15.27.[25]

BDAG gives the following as a possible meaning: "those who do not belong to groups professing faith in the God of Israel, **the nations, gentiles, unbelievers**."[26] In 2 Thess. 4:5, Paul is not merely saying that this is done by "the nations," but specifically by unbelievers, and the use of the word "nations" in this context gives the English reader the wrong idea that Paul is simply referring to nationalities and not to a distinction based on belief or unbelief in the God of Israel. Consequently, the translation as the more generic "nations" gives the reader of the NW the wrong meaning. Now whether this convinces anyone is not the point. The point is, there are other ways of understanding this reference, and BeDuhn's practice of unilaterally condemning the KJV, *et al.*, translations as "inaccurate" is neither warranted nor helpful. BeDuhn's judgment in this instance is entirely his personal preference and has nothing to do with "proper English." But, as we will see, this is characteristic of BeDuhn's treatment of modern translations. He makes unilateral condemnations that

---

[22] "For this is the will of God, your sanctification; *that is*, that you abstain from sexual immorality; that each of you know how to possess his own vessel in sanctification and honor, not in lustful passion, like the Gentiles [τὰ ἔθνη, *ta ethnē*] who do not know God; *and* that no man transgress and defraud his brother in the matter because the Lord is the avenger in all these things, just as we also told you before and solemnly warned *you*" (1The 4:3–6 NASB).

[23] BeDuhn, *Translation*, 16.

[24] Ibid.

[25] LSL, s.v. "ἔθνος." The initials LXX in the quote refer to the Greek Old Testament generally referred to as the Septuagint.

[26] BDAG, s.v. "ἔθνος."

ultimately are based only on his own private bias. Unfortunately, he has a habit of trying to make his biases appear to be required by Greek grammar and syntax or "proper" English usage.

A good example of this practice is his comment about certain translations of the 1 Thessalonians passage and Paul's use of the expression τὸ ἑαυτοῦ σκεῦος κτᾶσθαι, which is translated by the NASBU as "to posses his own vessel." BeDuhn comments, "The NASB quite properly suggests some possible understandings of the expression in a footnote ('I.e., body; or possibly, wife'). The meaning of this expression is not clear to the modern reader as it stands, but these translations are careful not to promote a possible interpretation to the status of scripture. Interpretation built upon the literal rendering of Paul's words is left to the reader."[27] The problem with this observation is that BeDuhn seems oblivious to the fact that translation always involves some level of interpretation, and to refer to a distinction between interpretation and "literal rendering" as if these function in clearly defined spheres is arbitrary and predicated upon BeDuhn's own judgment about what constitutes each.

BeDuhn chides the KJV for interpretively adding the word 'any' in its translation of the phrase "defraud his brother in *any* matter." BeDuhn says, "That's a nice sentiment, but it is not what the Greek says."[28] On what basis does BeDuhn make the judgment that adding 'any' is not what the Greek says? Does he say this simply because the English word 'any' does not have a specifically individual lexeme to which it might correspond in the Greek text? This cannot be the case since BeDuhn himself advocates adding words: "Some words should be dropped because they are not necessary in English (such as the article 'the' before 'fornication'), and other words need to be added to complete the sense (for example a verb such as 'do' in the clause 'according to which the nations also *do*')."[29] Now, since BeDuhn advocates adding words "to complete the sense," why does he chide the KJV translators for adding 'any'? It's not simply because the word is added, but because BeDuhn thinks it's not necessary to complete the sense. But, that is a personal judgment that is not demanded by the Greek text as BeDuhn wants his reader to think. In fact, the translators of the KJV seem to think that it is *in fact* what the Greek says, which is why they added it. But apparently BeDuhn thinks he is the only one qualified to make such a determination. And let us repeat. It is not on the basis of the Greek text that BeDuhn makes this statement since BeDuhn himself advocates adding words when this completes the sense. It is because, in BeDuhn's own judgment, he thinks it is not necessary to complete the sense, and yet he portrays his own judgment about what should "complete the sense" as if this is dictated by what the Greek says. This tendency to present his own personal preferences and his own personal judgment as if this is what the Greek says is his constant practice. As is repeatedly the case throughout his book, BeDuhn condemns modern translators as being theologically biased and producing inaccurate translations, and yet ultimately BeDuhn condemns

---

[27] BeDuhn, *Translation*, 16–17.
[28] Ibid., 17.
[29] Ibid., 13.

these translators because they do not agree with his own personal judgment about what should be included and excluded in a translation. He leads the reader to think that his judgments are actually the requirements of Greek grammar and syntax, a pretense that is disingenuous at best and misleading at worst.

Translation and Equivalence

BeDuhn enters into a discussion of the translation theories known as Formal Equivalence and Dynamic or Functional Equivalence. In this discussion he attempts to consider the strengths and weaknesses of each approach. After his evaluations, BeDuhn advocates an approach that does not serve either a Formal Equivalence or a Dynamic/Functional Equivalence, but one that combines "the best features of each while avoiding the chief pitfalls."[30] He says, "But whichever [approach] one prefers, the key word in both is 'equivalence.' Both [Formal Equivalence and Dynamic Equivalence] are committed to this. . . . But the test of a translation of either kind is *equivalence* — that is, does the translation actually convey a meaning equivalent to the one readers in the original linguistic, literary, and cultural setting received?"[31] Although this statement sounds good at first, it betrays a lack of awareness of the problems with the whole notion of equivalence.

In contemporary Translation Studies, the concept of "equivalence" is recognized as an ambiguous and problematic concept. Dorothy Kenny provides a typical definition of 'equivalence': "equivalence [is] the relationship between source text (ST) and a target text (TT) that allows the TT to be considered as a translation of the ST in the first place."[32] Kenny goes on to point out the problem with even trying to define equivalence: "The above definition of equivalence is not unproblematic, however. Pym, for one, has pointed to its circularity: equivalence is supposed to define translation, and translation, in turn, defines equivalence."[33] Jeremy Munday observes that translation studies and theory have marginalized the notion of equivalence: "equivalence is an issue that will remain central to the practice of translation, even if translation studies and translation theory has, for the time being at least, marginalized it."[34] Translation studies has marginalized the debate over the meaning of equivalence precisely because it is so problematic. In order to go on with translation studies, the debate over equivalence has to be set aside so as not to forestall the progress of the entire discipline. This fact indicates BeDuhn's complete lack of awareness of this problem by the fact that he so easily tosses the term about as if its definition were obvious.

---

[30] Ibid., 26.
[31] Ibid. (emphasis in original).
[32] Dorothy Kenny, "Equivalence," in *Routledge Encyclopedia of Translation Studies*, ed. Mona Baker (London: Routledge, 2000), 77.
[33] Ibid.
[34] Jeremy Munday, *Introducing Translation Studies: Theories and Applications* (London: Routledge, 2001), 50.

W. V. O. Quine is one who has disrupted the dogmatic slumbers of translators by his analysis of translation. In one instance Quine declared, "manuals for translating one language into another can be set up in divergent ways, all compatible with the totality of speech dispositions, yet incompatible with one another. In countless places they will diverge in giving, as their respective translations of a sentence of the one language, sentences of the other language which stand to each other in no plausible sort of equivalence however loose."[35] Translation studies is still reeling from this and other blows to the notion of equivalence even though, as Munday says, the question of equivalence has been shoved under the carpet for now.

Although the notion of equivalence is a central part of theories of translation, as Kenny notes,

> it is also a controversial one. Approaches to the question of equivalence can differ radically: some theorists define translation in terms of equivalence relations (Catford 1965; Nida and Taber 1969; Toury 1980a; Pym 1992a, 1995; Koller 1995) while other reject the theoretical notion of equivalence, claiming it is either irrelevant (Snell-Hornby 1988) or damaging (Gentzler 1993) to translation studies. Yet other theorists steer a middle course: Baker uses the notion of equivalence 'for the sake of convenience – because most translators are used to it rather than because it has any theoretical status' (1992: 5–6). Thus equivalence is variously regarded as a necessary condition for translation, an obstacle to progress in translation studies, or a useful category for describing translations.[36]

In spite of the difficulties with the notion of equivalence, BeDuhn continues to talk as if equivalence is unproblematic and a virtually self-evident concept. And yet as if demonstrating the problem with the concept, he defined "equivalence" by whether or not the translation is equivalent. He says, "does a translation actually convey a meaning equivalent to . . ."[37] For BeDuhn, the test of equivalence is whether the meanings are equivalent. But using in one's definition the term being defined does not actually define the term. Consequently, BeDuhn offers no definition of what constitutes equivalence, and yet he makes this a major standard of analysis in his test of whether there is theological bias in various translations. Since equivalence is so difficult to define, and since BeDuhn cannot define it and yet makes it the standard of analysis, his entire project is undermined.

BeDuhn may respond that a book for the general public is not the place to enter into a debate about equivalence, but this response is meaningless. BeDuhn professes to be a scholar in the field—he says, "We — that is scholars, translators, and religious leaders . . ." Yet he does not give evidence of being aware of the central debate in translation theory. And if a book on translation, and a chapter on the work of translation, is not the place at least to acknowledge the substance of the debate, then what place is there to

---

[35] W. V. O. Quine, *Word and Object* (Cambridge, Massachusetts: The Technology Press of The Massachusetts Institute of Technology, 1960), 27.

[36] Kenny, "Equivalence," 75.

[37] BeDuhn, *Truth in Translation*, 26.

alert the general public to an issue that strikes at the very heart of BeDuhn's claims? BeDuhn could at least acknowledge, perhaps in a footnote as he so often rebukes translators for not doing, that these debates, and the very question of the nature of equivalence, present issues that tend to make his claims tentative.

Conclusion

Granted, BeDuhn is attempting to reach the general reader, but reaching the general reader ought not to include distorting the facts. BeDuhn does not give evidence of being familiar with the basic issues either of translation or linguistics, much less philosophy of language or philosophy, all of which play a critical role in the task of Bible translation. This lack of familiarity allows BeDuhn to make statements that sound definitive but are grounded on principles that are debated by scholars and experts in the field of translation theory, or are simply false. Nevertheless, even the most obscure debates can be explained on the level of the general reader. The abundance of books for the general reader introducing the philosophy of science in general and physics in particular is evidence of this.[38] And to think that these issues are not relevant to the task of informing the general reader betrays a philosophical bias in one's approach to the task of translation. The general reader ought to be told up front that BeDuhn's claims and conclusions are debatable and based on principles that themselves are not as certainly established as BeDuhn would like to make us think. If the basic principles of his project are debatable and debated by actual scholars, then the conclusions he reaches are only as certain as the principles upon which they are grounded. BeDuhn's whole project is not what he makes it out to be. Translation is not simply a matter of "equivalence," whatever that may mean. It is not simply a matter of selecting English words and arranging them in proper, "contemporary" English order. Translation involves the world view of the translator, it is grounded in the translators theological and philosophical commitments, just as much for BeDuhn as for anyone else. As a task, translation is much more complex than BeDuhn makes it out to be, and because of his simplistic understanding, the value of his assessment of the success of others is questionable at best.

---

[38] For example, Jim Baggott, *Beyond Measure: Modern Physics, Philosophy and the Meaning of Quantum Theory* (Oxford: Oxford University Press, 2004); Stephen M. Barr, *Modern Physics and Ancient Faith* (Notre Dame: University of Notre Dame Press, 2003); Enrico Cantore, *Atomic Order: An Introduction to the Philosophy of Microphysics* (Cambridge, Massachusetts: The MIT Press, 1969): George Couvalis, *The Philosophy of Science: Science and Objectivity* (London: SAGE Publications, 1997); John Gribbin, *In Search of Schrödinger's Cat: Quantum Physics and Reality* (Toronto, Canada: Bantam Books, 1988); Robert Klee, *Introduction to the Philosophy of Science: Cutting Nature at its Seams* (New York: Oxford University Press, 1997).

CHAPTER 2

WORSHIPING CHRIST

Introduction

Modern translations indicate that, in Matt. 2:11, the Magi bowed down and worshiped the child. For example, the New American Standard Bible, Updated, translates the middle part of verse 11, "and they fell to the ground and worshiped Him." The English Standard Version gives a similar translation: "and they fell down and worshiped him." The New King James Version, like the NASB, has, "and they fell down to the ground and worshiped Him." There are several other passages in Matthew's Gospel where modern translations use the word "worship" to translate the Greek word προσκυνέω (*proskuneō*) indicating that Jesus is worthy of being worshiped as God.

It is this concept that constitutes BeDuhn's first study of bias in translation. His analysis focuses on the Greek word προσκυνέω (*proskuneō*). The passages on which BeDuhn concentrates most of his criticism of modern translations include the relevant verses in Matthew chapter 2 and the story of the visit of the Magi (μάγοι, *magoi*). Concerning the cultural background of the use of the word, BeDuhn says,

> Ancient Mediterranean societies tended to be very hierarchical. It was a world where everyone knew their place in relation to countless superiors and inferiors. Those who neglected to forget this stratification of rank would be readily reminded by those around. In the highest place stood God or the gods. Below that in the Roman empire, ranked the Emperor, followed by senators, governors, and a very complex system of local officials, priests, and landowners. The very bottom was occupied by slaves, who might be owned by the lowest of peasant.
> Social convention dictated gestures of deference and respect from inferior to superior at every point along this hierarchy. In the presence of some one of high rank, low bows or prostrations were expected. The Greek verb that expresses making such prostration was

proskuneō. In the modern world, the best example of a prostration can be seen in the prayers of Moslems. Dropping to your knees, you been to forward and lower your head to the ground.[1]

Immediately the reader confronts a problem with BeDuhn's argument. BeDuhn provides no references by which a reader can discover from where he obtained his information, or whether his information is accurate or has been accurately interpreted. Whether BeDuhn is writing to a lay audience or not, it is common practice to provide the reader with an indication of the resources that have been used by the author. People often make claims about customs and practices in the ancient world, and unless the author supplies references, a reader is unable to tell whether the author has any actual historical documentation for his claims. However, we will pass over this problem for now.

Magi in Matthew

After making several observations about the translation of Greek words in several passages and comparing different versions and making observations, BeDuhn comes to treat Matt. 2:1–2, 8, 11. He gives a lengthy translation of this material from the NAB:

When Jesus was born in Bethlehem of Judea, in the days of teen Herod, behold, Magi from the East arrived in Jerusalem, saying, 'Where is the newborn keening of the Jews? We saw his star at its rising and have come to do him homage.' . . . He sent them to Bethlehem and said, 'Go and search diligently for the child. When you have found him, bring me word, that I too may go and do him homage." . . . and on entering the house they saw the child with Mary his mother. They prostrated themselves and did him homage.[2]

BeDuhn provides quotes of a portion of verse 11 from several other translations:

NW:	. . . falling down, they did obeisance to it.
NASB:	. . . fell down and worshiped Him.
NIV:	. . . bowed down and worshiped him.
NRSV:	. . . knelt down and paid him homage.
TEV:	. . . they knelt down and worshiped him.
AB:	. . . fell down and worshiped Him.
LB:	. . . they threw themselves down before him, worshiping.
KJV:	. . . fell down, and worshipped him.[3]

---

[1] BeDuhn, *Translation*, 41–42.
[2] Ibid., 44.
[3] NW = New World translation; NASB = New American Standard Bible; NIV = New International Version; NRSV = New Revised Standard Version; TEV = Today's English Version; AB = Amplified Bible; LB = Living Bible; KJV = King James Version.

At this point, BeDun makes the following comments: "The magi drop to their knees and prostrate themselves to the baby Jesus. They do so because he is the 'king' their astrological observations had led them to. The majority of translations (NASB, NIV, TEV, AB, LB) lapse into language of 'worship' that simply does not apply to this context. Rendering homage to a king is not the same as worshiping a god."[4] On what basis does BeDuhn conclude that the magi are not worshiping Jesus? As he explains, "the Magi were priests of the Zoroastrian faith, which like Judaism is monotheistic. In this story, their astrological talents have revealed to them the birth of a new king. Herod and his advisors correctly discern that this new king — not one of Herod's sons — must be the Messiah. So Herod feigns willingness to go himself to render homage to the new king. In the Jewish tradition, the Messiah is merely a chosen human being; there is no suggestion that he is a divine being. The whole episode works with royal images and privileges, and language of 'worship' has no place here."[5] BeDuhn has already told us in his introduction that, "Accurate, unbiased translations are based on (1) linguistic content, (2) literary context, and (3) historical and cultural environment."[6] So, following these three points, we will look at BeDuhn's assertions about this passage.

Linguistic Content

The Linguist Content of Matthew

We will start our examination by looking at the linguistic content of the passage. First, there is no statement in the text of Matthew that would necessarily indicate that these magi were of the Zoroastrian faith. The word in the text that is translated "magi" is the Greek word μάγος (*magos*). Employing the lexicon that BeDuhn says is the best, we find the following possible meanings of the word 'μάγος':

> Μάγος [ᾰ], ου, ὁ, Magian, one of a Median tribe, Hdt.1.101, Str.15.3.1: hence, as belonging to this tribe, 2. *one of the priests and wise men in Persia* who interpreted dreams, Hdt.7.37, al., Arist.*Fr*.36, Phoen.1.5, *Ev. Matt*.2.1. b. perh. a priest in Mithraic worship, Mitchell N. Galatia 404. 3. *enchanter, wizard*, esp. in bad sense, *impostor, charlatan*, Heraclit.14, S.*OT* 387, E.*Or*.1498 (lyr.), Pl.*R*.572e, *Act.Ap*.13.6, Vett.Val.74.17: also fem., Luc.*Asin*.4, AP5.15 (Marc. Arg.). II. μάγος, ον, as Adj., magical, μάγῳ τέχνῃ πράττειν τι Philostr. *VA* 1.2; κεστοῦ φωνεῦσα μαγώτερα *AP* 5.120 (Phld.). (Opers. *maguš* 'Μαγιαν'.)[7]

---

[4] BeDuhn, *Translation*, 45.
[5] Ibid.
[6] Ibid., xvi.
[7] LSL, s.v. "Μάγος." Hereinafter referred to as LSL.

There is no reference in the "best" Greek lexicon, as BeDuhn characterizes it,[8] to the μάγος necessarily being priests of the Zoroastrian faith. In fact, there is no reference to Zoroastrianism at all. Let us look, then, at the BDAG:

μάγος, ου, ὁ (s. μαγεία, μαγεύω)—❶ *a Magus*, a (Persian [Snyberg, D. Rel. d. alten Iran '38], then also Babylonian) wise man and priest, who was expert in astrology, interpretation of dreams and various other occult arts . . . ❷ *magician* (trag. et al.; Aeschin. 3, 137 [μάγος = πονηρός] . . .[9]

The article on μάγος in BDAG is quite long, but, as with LSL, BDAG does not say anything about the Zoroastrian faith. So, right away we can see that BeDuhn does not have linguistic justification for making reference to the Zoroastrian faith. In other words, just because the word 'μάγος' is used to identify these persons, the word itself does not necessarily link them with Zoroastrianism. To round out the references to lexicons, the *Greek-English Lexicon of the New Testament Based on Semantic Domains* has two separate entries for the word μάγος, but in neither one is there any mention of the Zoroastrian faith in connection with the word. Since there are no references to Zoroastrianism in the standard lexicons, let us expand our search to theological dictionaries.

The index of *The New International Dictionary of New Testament Theology* indicates five references to "Zoroastrianism," but not one of these has anything to do with the Greek term μάγος, and in the article on this term, they make no mention of the Zoroastrian faith. The *Theological Dictionary of the New Testament* says the following:

There is no means of determining whether the μάγοι ἀπ' ἀνατολῶν of Mt. 2:1 (7, 16) are specifically Babylonian astrologers or astrologers in general. The former is more likely, since it is only in Babylon, by contrast with the exiles, that the μάγοι would acquire an interest in the Jewish king (Messiah). μάγος here means "possessor of a special (secret) wisdom," especially concerning the meaning of the course of the stars and its interconnection with world events.[10]

Throughout the rest of the article, TDNT makes no mention of the Zoroastrian faith. In the immediate context of Matthew's Gospel, there is no mention of Zoroastrian faith. In fact, Matthew does not specify who these magi are, and he says only that the came from the East. So, in addition to the fact that Matthew makes no connection with the Zoroastrian faith, it seems that the word itself as it is used in the NT has no connection with the Zoroastrian faith. Also, simply on the basis of the reference to the east (ἀνατολή, *anatolē*) in this passage, one cannot assume that the magi were of the Zoroastrian faith. The connection must be proven, not assumed. The term 'east' is

---

[8] BeDuhn, *Translation*, 12.
[9] BDAG, s.v. "μάγος."
[10] *Theological Dictionary of the New Testament* (1978), s.v. "μάγος." Hereinafter referred to as TDNT.

indicative of a direction, not a religious commitment. From a study of the standard reference works there seems to be no necessary connection, if any connection at all, between the word μάγος and the Zoroastrian faith.

The Linguistic Content of Other Passages

New Testament Occurrences:

Although there is no mention of the Zoroastrian faith in the text of Matthew, let us look at other passages in the Bible to see if these passages make some connection. The term is used in two other passages of the NT, specifically Acts 13:6 and 8. We will look at these passages in turn. The text is printed below in the NASB translation and the Greek text.

Table #1: Acts 13:4–12

4	So, being sent out by the Holy Spirit, they went down to Seleucia and from there they sailed to Cyprus.
	Αὐτοὶ μὲν οὖν ἐκπεμφθέντες ὑπὸ τοῦ ἁγίου πνεύματος κατῆλθον εἰς Σελεύκειαν, ἐκεῖθέν τε ἀπέπλευσαν εἰς Κύπρον
5	When they reached Salamis, they *began* to proclaim the word of God in the synagogues of the Jews; and they also had John as their helper
	καὶ γενόμενοι ἐν Σαλαμῖνι κατήγγελλον τὸν λόγον τοῦ θεοῦ ἐν ταῖς συναγωγαῖς τῶν Ἰουδαίων. εἶχον δὲ καὶ Ἰωάννην ὑπηρέτην.
6	When they had gone through the whole island as far as Paphos, they found a magician, a Jewish false prophet whose name was Bar-Jesus,
	Διελθόντες δὲ ὅλην τὴν νῆσον ἄχρι Πάφου εὗρον ἄνδρα τινὰ μάγον ψευδοπροφήτην Ἰουδαῖον ᾧ ὄνομα Βαριησοῦ
7	who was with the proconsul, Sergius Paulus, a man of intelligence. This man summoned Barnabas and Saul and sought to hear the word of God.
	ὃς ἦν σὺν τῷ ἀνθυπάτῳ Σεργίῳ Παύλῳ, ἀνδρὶ συνετῷ. οὗτος προσκαλεσάμενος Βαρναβᾶν καὶ Σαῦλον ἐπεζήτησεν ἀκοῦσαι τὸν λόγον τοῦ θεοῦ.
8	But Elymas the magician (for so his name is translated) was opposing them, seeking to turn the proconsul away from the faith.
	ἀνθίστατο δὲ αὐτοῖς Ἐλύμας ὁ μάγος, οὕτως γὰρ μεθερμηνεύεται τὸ ὄνομα αὐτοῦ, ζητῶν διαστρέψαι τὸν ἀνθύπατον ἀπὸ τῆς πίστεως.

Chapter 2: Worshiping Christ

9	But Saul, who was also *known as* Paul, filled with the Holy Spirit, fixed his gaze on him,
	Σαῦλος δέ, ὁ καὶ Παῦλος, πλησθεὶς πνεύματος ἁγίου ἀτενίσας εἰς αὐτὸν
10	and said, "You who are full of all deceit and fraud, you son of the devil, you enemy of all righteousness, will you not cease to make crooked the straight ways of the Lord?
	εἶπεν· ὦ πλήρης παντὸς δόλου καὶ πάσης ῥᾳδιουργίας, υἱὲ διαβόλου, ἐχθρὲ πάσης δικαιοσύνης, οὐ παύσῃ διαστρέφων τὰς ὁδοὺς (τοῦ) κυρίου τὰς εὐθείας
11	"Now, behold, the hand of the Lord is upon you, and you will be blind and not see the sun for a time." And immediately a mist and a darkness fell upon him, and he went about seeking those who would lead him by the hand.
	καὶ νῦν ἰδοὺ χεὶρ κυρίου ἐπὶ σὲ καὶ ἔσῃ τυφλὸς μὴ βλέπων τὸν ἥλιον ἄχρι καιροῦ. παραχρῆμά τε ἔπεσεν ἐπ' αὐτὸν ἀχλὺς καὶ σκότος καὶ περιάγων ἐζήτει χειραγωγούς.
12	Then the proconsul believed when he saw what had happened, being amazed at the teaching of the Lord.
	τότε ἰδὼν ὁ ἀνθύπατος τὸ γεγονὸς ἐπίστευσεν ἐκπλησσόμενος ἐπὶ τῇ διδαχῇ τοῦ κυρίου.

The first occurrence of the term is in verse 6 is set out below with an interlinear word-for-word translation.

Table #2: Acts 13:6

Διελθόντες	δὲ	ὅλην	τὴν
After having gone through	but	whole	the
νῆσον	ἄχρι	Πάφου	εὗρον
island	as far as	Paphos	they found
ἄνδρα	τινὰ	μάγον	ψευδοπροφήτην
man	certain	magician/ magon	pseudo-prophet
Ἰουδαῖον	ᾧ	ὄνομα	Βαριησοῦ
Jew	to whom	name	Bar-Jesus

The author of this passage specifically identifies this μάγος as a Jew and a pseudo-prophet. The NASB translates the word μάγον as "magician." There is no mention of the Zoroastrian faith, and it seems very unlikely that a Jew pseudo-prophet would be a Zoroastrian.

Verse 8 is set out below in the same fashion.

Table #3: Acts 13:8

ἀνθίστατο	δὲ	αὐτοῖς	Ἐλύμας
was opposing	but	to them	Elymas
ὁ	μάγος,	οὕτως	γὰρ
the	magician/magos	thus	for
μεθερμηνεύεται	τὸ	ὄνομα	αὐτοῦ,
being translated	the	name	of him,
ζητῶν	διαστρέψαι	τὸν	ἀνθύπατον
seeking	to mislead	the	proconsul
ἀπὸ	τῆς	πίστεως.	
from	the	faith.	

Verse 8 recounts the further encounter with the same *magos* who is introduced in verse 6. So, there is no reason to take this to be anyone other than the Jew pseudo-prophet. And, once again, there is no mention of the Zoroastrian faith. It would seem that the simple occurrence of the word in the NT does not necessarily indicate that the person or persons are priests of the Zoroastrian faith. Since we were unsuccessful in finding in the NT any necessary relationship between the word μάγος and the Zoroastrian faith, it may be helpful to consider the use of the term in the Septuagint.

Septuagint Occurrences:

The word occurs eight times in the Greek OT, and all of them occur in the book of Daniel.[11]

---

[11] There are actually two Greek versions of the book of Daniel—OG, which indicates the Old Greek version, and θ, which indicates Theodotian's Greek translation of Daniel. The Greek texts presented throughout this book are taken from θ, in Joseph Ziegler, ed. *Susanna, Daniel, Bel et*

Chapter 2: Worshiping Christ

Table #4: GSEPT Occurrences of μάγος

Dan. 1:20	καὶ ἐν παντὶ ῥήματι σοφίας καὶ ἐπιστήμης ὧν ἐζήτησεν παρ' αὐτῶν ὁ βασιλεὺς εὗρεν αὐτοὺς δεκαπλασίονας παρὰ πάντας τοὺς ἐπαοιδοὺς καὶ τοὺς μάγους [הָאַשָּׁפִים] τοὺς ὄντας ἐν πάσῃ τῇ βασιλείᾳ αὐτοῦ וְכֹל דְּבַר חָכְמַת בִּינָה אֲשֶׁר־בִּקֵּשׁ מֵהֶם הַמֶּלֶךְ וַיִּמְצָאֵם עֶשֶׂר יָדוֹת עַל כָּל־הַחַרְטֻמִּים הָאַשָּׁפִים [μάγους] אֲשֶׁר בְּכָל־מַלְכוּתוֹ׃ As for every matter of wisdom and understanding about which the king consulted them, he found them ten times better than all the magicians *and* conjurers [μάγους, הָאַשָּׁפִים] who *were* in all his realm.
Dan. 2:2	καὶ εἶπεν ὁ βασιλεὺς καλέσαι τοὺς ἐπαοιδοὺς καὶ τοὺς μάγους [וְלָאַשָּׁפִים] καὶ τοὺς φαρμακοὺς καὶ τοὺς Χαλδαίους τοῦ ἀναγγεῖλαι τῷ βασιλεῖ τὰ ἐνύπνια αὐτοῦ καὶ ἦλθαν καὶ ἔστησαν ἐνώπιον τοῦ βασιλέω וַיֹּאמֶר הַמֶּלֶךְ לִקְרֹא לַחַרְטֻמִּים וְלָאַשָּׁפִים [μάγους] וְלַמְכַשְּׁפִים וְלַכַּשְׂדִּים לְהַגִּיד לַמֶּלֶךְ חֲלֹמֹתָיו וַיָּבֹאוּ וַיַּעַמְדוּ לִפְנֵי הַמֶּלֶךְ׃ Then the king gave orders to call in the magicians, the conjurers [μάγους, וְלָאַשָּׁפִים], the sorcerers and the Chaldeans to tell the king his dreams. So they came in and stood before the king.
Dan. 2:10	ἀπεκρίθησαν οἱ Χαλδαῖοι ἐνώπιον τοῦ βασιλέως καὶ λέγουσιν οὐκ ἔστιν ἄνθρωπος ἐπὶ τῆς ξηρᾶς ὅστις τὸ ῥῆμα τοῦ βασιλέως δυνήσεται γνωρίσαι καθότι πᾶς βασιλεὺς μέγας καὶ ἄρχων ῥῆμα τοιοῦτο οὐκ ἐπερωτᾷ ἐπαοιδὸν μάγον [וְאָשַׁף] καὶ Χαλδαῖον עֲנוֹ כַשְׂדָּיֵא קֳדָם־מַלְכָּא וְאָמְרִין לָא־אִיתַי אֱנָשׁ עַל־יַבֶּשְׁתָּא דִּי מִלַּת מַלְכָּא יוּכַל לְהַחֲוָיָה כָּל־קֳבֵל דִּי כָּל־מֶלֶךְ רַב וְשַׁלִּיט מִלָּה כִדְנָה לָא שְׁאֵל לְכָל־חַרְטֹם וְאָשַׁף [μάγον] וְכַשְׂדָּי׃ The Chaldeans answered the king and said, "There is not a man on earth who could declare the matter for the king, inasmuch as no great king or ruler has [ever] asked anything like this of any magician, conjurer [μάγον, וְאָשַׁף] or Chaldean."

Draco, vol. 165/2, *Septuaginta Vetus Testamentum Graecum* (Göttingen: Vandenhoeck & Ruprecht, 1999). For a discussion about these issues in the book of Daniel, see Karen H. Jobes and Moisés Silva, *Invitation to the Septuagint* (Grand Rapids: Baker Academic, 2000).

	καὶ ἀπεκρίθη Δανιηλ ἐνώπιον τοῦ βασιλέως καὶ λέγει τὸ μυστήριον ὃ ὁ βασιλεὺς ἐπερωτᾷ οὐκ ἔστιν σοφῶν μάγων [אָֽשְׁפִין] ἐπαοιδῶν γαζαρηνῶν ἀναγγεῖλαι τῷ βασιλεῖ
Dan. 2:27	עָנֵה דָנִיֵּאל קֳדָם מַלְכָּא וְאָמַר רָזָה דִּי־מַלְכָּא שָׁאֵל לָא חַכִּימִין אָשְׁפִין [μάγων] חַרְטֻמִּין גָּזְרִין יָכְלִין לְהַחֲוָיָה לְמַלְכָּא׃
	Daniel answered before the king and said, "As for the mystery about which the king has inquired, neither wise men, conjurers [μάγων, אָֽשְׁפִין], magicians *nor* diviners are able to declare *it* to the king."

	καὶ εἰσεπορεύοντο οἱ ἐπαοιδοὶ μάγοι [אָֽשְׁפַיָּא] γαζαρηνοὶ Χαλδαῖοι καὶ τὸ ἐνύπνιον εἶπα ἐγὼ ἐνώπιον αὐτῶν καὶ τὴν σύγκρισιν αὐτοῦ οὐκ ἐγνώρισάν μοι
Dan. 4:7 (A4)	בֵּאדַיִן עָלְלִין חַרְטֻמַּיָּא אָֽשְׁפַיָּא [μάγοι] כַּשְׂדָּיֵא וְגָזְרַיָּא וְחֶלְמָא אָמַר אֲנָה קֳדָמֵיהוֹן וּפִשְׁרֵהּ לָא־מְהוֹדְעִין לִי׃
	Then the magicians, the conjurers [μάγοι, אָֽשְׁפַיָּא], the Chaldeans and the diviners came in and I related the dream to them, but they could not make its interpretation known to me.

	καὶ ἐβόησεν ὁ βασιλεὺς ἐν ἰσχύι τοῦ εἰσαγαγεῖν μάγους [לְאָֽשְׁפַיָּא] Χαλδαίους γαζαρηνοὺς καὶ εἶπεν τοῖς σοφοῖς Βαβυλῶνος ὃς ἂν ἀναγνῷ τὴν γραφὴν ταύτην καὶ τὴν σύγκρισιν γνωρίσῃ μοι πορφύραν ἐνδύσεται καὶ ὁ μανιάκης ὁ χρυσοῦς ἐπὶ τὸν τράχηλον αὐτοῦ καὶ τρίτος ἐν τῇ βασιλείᾳ μου ἄρξει
Dan. 5:7	קָרֵא מַלְכָּא בְּחַיִל לְהֶעָלָה לְאָֽשְׁפַיָּא [μάγους] כַּשְׂדָּיֵא וְגָזְרַיָּא עָנֵה מַלְכָּא וְאָמַר לְחַכִּימֵי בָבֶל דִּי כָל־אֱנָשׁ דִּי־יִקְרֵה כְּתָבָה דְנָה וּפִשְׁרֵהּ יְחַוִּנַּנִי אַרְגְּוָנָא יִלְבַּשׁ וְהַמּוֹנְכָא דִי־דַהֲבָא עַל־צַוְּארֵהּ וְתַלְתִּי בְמַלְכוּתָא יִשְׁלַט׃
	The king called aloud to bring in the conjurers [μάγους, לְאָֽשְׁפַיָּא], the Chaldeans and the diviners. The king spoke and said to the wise men of Babylon, "Any man who can read this inscription and explain its interpretation to me shall be clothed with purple and *have* a necklace of gold around his neck, and have authority as third *ruler* in the kingdom."

Chapter 2: Worshiping Christ

	ἔστιν ἀνὴρ ἐν τῇ βασιλείᾳ σου ἐν ᾧ πνεῦμα θεοῦ καὶ ἐν ταῖς ἡμέραις τοῦ πατρός σου γρηγόρησις καὶ σύνεσις εὑρέθη ἐν αὐτῷ καὶ ὁ βασιλεὺς Ναβουχοδονοσορ ὁ πατήρ σου ἄρχοντα ἐπαοιδῶν μάγων [אָשְׁפִין] Χαλδαίων γαζαρηνῶν κατέστησεν αὐτόν
Dan. 5:11	אִיתַי גְּבַר בְּמַלְכוּתָךְ דִּי רוּחַ אֱלָהִין קַדִּישִׁין בֵּהּ וּבְיוֹמֵי אֲבוּךְ נַהִירוּ וְשָׂכְלְתָנוּ וְחָכְמָה כְּחָכְמַת־אֱלָהִין הִשְׁתְּכַחַת בֵּהּ וּמַלְכָּא נְבֻכַדְנֶצַּר אֲבוּךְ רַב חַרְטֻמִּין אָשְׁפִין [μάγων] כַּשְׂדָּאִין גָּזְרִין הֲקִימֵהּ אֲבוּךְ מַלְכָּא׃

"There is a man in your kingdom in whom is a spirit of the holy gods; and in the days of your father, illumination, insight and wisdom like the wisdom of the gods were found in him. And King Nebuchadnezzar, your father, your father the king, appointed him chief of the magicians, conjurers [μάγων, אָשְׁפִין], Chaldeans *and* diviners."

	καὶ νῦν εἰσῆλθον ἐνώπιόν μου οἱ σοφοὶ μάγοι [אָשְׁפַיָּא] γαζαρηνοί ἵνα τὴν γραφὴν ταύτην ἀναγνῶσιν καὶ τὴν σύγκρισιν αὐτῆς γνωρίσωσίν μοι καὶ οὐκ ἠδυνήθησαν ἀναγγεῖλαί μοι
Dan. 5:15	וּכְעַן הֻעַלּוּ קָדָמַי חַכִּימַיָּא אָשְׁפַיָּא [μάγοι] דִּי־כְתָבָה דְנָה יִקְרוֹן וּפִשְׁרֵהּ לְהוֹדָעֻתַנִי וְלָא־כָהֲלִין פְּשַׁר־מִלְּתָא לְהַחֲוָיָה׃

"Just now the wise men *and* the conjurers [μάγοι, אָשְׁפַיָּא] were brought in before me that they might read this inscription and make its interpretation known to me, but they could not declare the interpretation of the message."

The word occurs only in the book of Daniel and mostly in the Aramaic sections of the book. However, the one Hebrew occurrence is Dan. 1:20. The word is the same in Hebrew and Aramaic, אַשָּׁף. According to the standard Hebrew/Aramaic Lexicon, the Hebrew word means "conjurer,"[12] and the Aramaic means "enchanter, sorcerer."[13] KBH makes no specific reference to the Zoroastrian faith in connection with either the Hebrew or the Aramaic word.

The TWOT says the following about the word:

The meaning of this word must be determined solely by context, since no etymology is apparent. Perhaps it is a loan word from Babylonia and related to the Assyrian *shiptu* ("conjuration"). Since the word is found only in Daniel, this is all the more likely. The Hebrew

---

[12] KBH, s.v. "אַשָּׁף."
[13] KBH, s.v. "אַשָּׁף."

word 'ašpâ is made from the same letters and means "quiver" (Job 39:23; Ps 127:5; Isa 22:6, 49:2; Jer 5:16; Lam 3:13), but any connection of meaning would be a guess although arrows were sometimes used in divination (Ezk 21:21 [H 27]).[14]

The NIDOTTE gives the same meanings for the Hebrew and Aramaic terms—"conjurer" and "exorcist."[15] Like the other reference works at which we have looked, TWOT makes no mention of the Zoroastrian faith connected with the term 'magi.'

For good measure we will consider the meaning of the Syriac cognate. Syriac and Aramaic are related languages, and both the OT and the NT were translated into Syriac. Many of the Eastern Church fathers wrote in Syriac. Also, Syriac is a Semitic language, like Hebrew, and along with the Greek version of the OT, Syriac is an important language in the textual criticism of the OT. According to the Syriac dictionary, the Syriac term ܐܫܘܦ ` means "snake-charmer, user of charms."[16] Once again there is no mention of the Zoroastrian faith connected with this term. There does not seem to be any linguistic reason for necessarily connecting the magi of Matthew with the Zoroastrian faith. Since even a Jew could be identified as a magos, association with the Zoroastrian faith is not a necessary conclusion simply on the basis of the word alone. So, BeDuhn's unsupported claim that the magi were of the Zoroastrian faith is not supported by the linguistic evidence. Perhaps this information will be found in the second of BeDuhn's criteria for accuracy and unbiased translation, literary context.

Literary Context

It seems that the first of BeDuhn's points upon which to base an accurate and unbiased translation has failed, so let us move on to the second point, "(2) literary context."[17] BeDuhn's notion of literary context "assumes that an author was relatively consistent and non-contradictory in what he or she said. If the author has not assembled a coherent piece of writing, we would be unable to judge our ability to understand it."[18] Unfortunately, there is not much in the way of literary context that can assist us in discovering whether the μάγοι are priests of the Zoroastrian faith. So, although this does not hurt BeDuhn's case, it does not help it either.

---

[14] TWOT, s.v. "אַשָּׁף."
[15] NIDOTTE (1997), s.v. "אַשָּׁף."
[16] CSD, s.v. "ܐܫܘܦ." SSL, s.v. "ܐܫܦ."
[17] BeDuhn, *Translation*, xvi.
[18] Ibid.

Chapter 2: Worshiping Christ

'Worship' in Matthew

Let us consider Matthew's use of the word προσκυνέω (*proskuneō*) to see if there are any instances in which the literary context of these uses might lead to a connection with Zoroastrianism. Matthew uses the term προσκυνέω 13 times through his Gospel.

Table #5: Προσκυνέω in Matthew's Gospel

Matt. 2:2	λέγοντες· ποῦ ἐστιν ὁ τεχθεὶς βασιλεὺς τῶν Ἰουδαίων εἴδομεν γὰρ αὐτοῦ τὸν ἀστέρα ἐν τῇ ἀνατολῇ καὶ ἤλθομεν προσκυνῆσαι αὐτῷ.
	"Where is He who has been born King of the Jews? For we saw His star in the east and have come to worship [προσκυνῆσαι] Him."
Matt. 2:8	καὶ πέμψας αὐτοὺς εἰς Βηθλέεμ εἶπεν· πορευθέντες ἐξετάσατε ἀκριβῶς περὶ τοῦ παιδίου· ἐπὰν δὲ εὕρητε, ἀπαγγείλατέ μοι, ὅπως κἀγὼ ἐλθὼν προσκυνήσω αὐτῷ.
	And he sent them to Bethlehem and said, "Go and search carefully for the Child; and when you have found *Him*, report to me, so that I too may come and worship [προσκυνήσω] Him."
Matt. 2:11	καὶ ἐλθόντες εἰς τὴν οἰκίαν εἶδον τὸ παιδίον μετὰ Μαρίας τῆς μητρὸς αὐτοῦ, καὶ πεσόντες προσεκύνησαν αὐτῷ καὶ ἀνοίξαντες τοὺς θησαυροὺς αὐτῶν προσήνεγκαν αὐτῷ δῶρα, χρυσὸν καὶ λίβανον καὶ σμύρναν.
	After coming into the house they saw the Child with Mary His mother; and they fell to the ground and worshiped [προσεκύνησαν] Him. Then, opening their treasures, they presented to Him gifts of gold, frankincense, and myrrh.
Matt. 4:9	καὶ εἶπεν αὐτῷ· ταῦτά σοι πάντα δώσω, ἐὰν πεσὼν προσκυνήσῃς μοι.
	and he said to Him, "All these things I will give You, if You fall down and worship [προσκυνήσῃς] me."
Matt. 4:10	τότε λέγει αὐτῷ ὁ Ἰησοῦς· ὕπαγε, σατανᾶ· γέγραπται γάρ· κύριον τὸν θεόν σου προσκυνήσεις καὶ αὐτῷ μόνῳ λατρεύσεις.
	Then Jesus said to him, "Go, Satan! For it is written, 'You shall worship [προσκυνήσεις] the Lord your God, and serve Him only.'"
Matt. 8:2	καὶ ἰδοὺ λεπρὸς προσελθὼν προσεκύνει αὐτῷ λέγων· κύριε, ἐὰν θέλῃς δύνασαί με καθαρίσαι.
	And a leper came to Him and bowed down [προσεκύνει] before Him, and said, "Lord, if You are willing, You can make me clean."

Matt. 9:18	Ταῦτα αὐτοῦ λαλοῦντος αὐτοῖς, ἰδοὺ ἄρχων εἷς ἐλθὼν προσεκύνει αὐτῷ λέγων ὅτι ἡ θυγάτηρ μου ἄρτι ἐτελεύτησεν· ἀλλὰ ἐλθὼν ἐπίθες τὴν χεῖρά σου ἐπ' αὐτήν, καὶ ζήσεται. While He was saying these things to them, a *synagogue* official came and bowed down [προσεκύνει] before Him, and said, "My daughter has just died; but come and lay Your hand on her, and she will live."
Matt. 14:33	οἱ δὲ ἐν τῷ πλοίῳ προσεκύνησαν αὐτῷ λέγοντες· ἀληθῶς θεοῦ υἱὸς εἶ. And those who were in the boat worshiped [προσεκύνησαν] Him, saying, "You are certainly God's Son!"
Matt. 15:25	ἡ δὲ ἐλθοῦσα προσεκύνει αὐτῷ λέγουσα· κύριε, βοήθει μοι. But she came and *began* to bow down [προσεκύνει] before Him, saying, "Lord, help me!"
Matt. 18:26	πεσὼν οὖν ὁ δοῦλος προσεκύνει αὐτῷ λέγων· μακροθύμησον ἐπ' ἐμοί, καὶ πάντα ἀποδώσω σοι. "So the slave fell *to the ground* and prostrated [προσεκύνει] himself before him, saying, 'Have patience with me and I will repay you everything.'"
Matt. 20:20	Τότε προσῆλθεν αὐτῷ ἡ μήτηρ τῶν υἱῶν Ζεβεδαίου μετὰ τῶν υἱῶν αὐτῆς προσκυνοῦσα καὶ αἰτοῦσά τι ἀπ' αὐτοῦ. Then the mother of the sons of Zebedee came to Jesus with her sons, bowing down [προσκυνοῦσα] and making a request of Him.
Matt. 28:9	καὶ ἰδοὺ Ἰησοῦς ὑπήντησεν αὐταῖς λέγων· χαίρετε. αἱ δὲ προσελθοῦσαι ἐκράτησαν αὐτοῦ τοὺς πόδας καὶ προσεκύνησαν αὐτῷ. And behold, Jesus met them and greeted them. And they came up and took hold of His feet and worshiped [προσεκύνησαν] Him.
Matt. 28:17	καὶ ἰδόντες αὐτὸν προσεκύνησαν, οἱ δὲ ἐδίστασαν. When they saw Him, they worshiped [προσεκύνησαν] *Him*; but some were doubtful.

Of the 13 times this word is used in Matthew's Gospel, only 3 are not used of prostrating before Jesus. The first instance is Matt. 4:9 in which Satan is testing Jesus: "and said to Him, 'All these *things* I will give to you, if you will bow down and worship me" (my translation).[19] The NASBU translates this verse this way: "and he said to Him, 'All these things I will give You, if You fall down and worship [προσκυνήσῃς,

---

[19] καὶ εἶπεν αὐτῷ· ταῦτά σοι πάντα δώσω, ἐὰν πεσὼν προσκυνήσῃς μοι. (Matt. 4:9).

proskunēsēs] me.'" This is clearly more than simply an instance in which Satan wants Jesus only to bow down to him. Satan obviously wants Jesus to worship him. Notice the word πεσὼν (*pesōn*) before the word προσκυνήσῃς. This word is translated "bow down" in the NASBU. The lexical form of this word is πίπτω (*piptō*). LSL gives a long article for this word. Its initial entry is: "**A**. Radical sense, *fall down*, and (when intentional) *cast oneself down . . . fall* in the dust, i.e., to rise no more . . .".[20] If, as BeDuhn claims, the word *proskuneō* means to prostrate oneself, it would be rather redundant for Satan to say, "fall down and prostrate yourself," since "to prostrate oneself" would necessarily involve falling down or casting oneself down. We will look at the combination of these two words after we have examined *proskuneō* in Matthew.

That Satan wants Jesus to worship him is clear from Jesus' response in verse 10.[21] The NASBU gives the following translation: "Then Jesus said to him, 'Go, Satan! For it is written, "You shall worship [προσκυνήσεις] the Lord your God, and serve Him only."'" Not only is it clear from Jesus' response that Satan is soliciting Jesus' worship, Jesus' statement is particularly problematic for BeDuhn's claims. According to BeDuhn's own principle of literary context, the translator must assume that the author is non-contradictory in what he says. Jesus says that one should perform the action indicated by the word προσκυνέω only to God: "You shall worship [προσκυνήσεις, *proskunēseis*] the Lord your God, and serve Him only [αὐτῷ μόνῳ, *autō monō*]" (Matt. 4:10). Regardless of how one wishes to translate the word—worship, prostrate, bow down, render homage, etc.—Jesus said that this action should be performed only with reference to God. Interestingly, BeDuhn neglects to make any comment about this statement. It would seem that Matthew would become inconsistent and contradictory if he should use this word with reference to Jesus and yet not mean by its use an action that should be performed only to God. At the very least this statement requires BeDuhn's consideration in order to support his claim that it cannot mean worship in our verse.

The second instance in which the word is used of this action performed with reference to someone other than Jesus is in fact Jesus' response to Satan's test. Jesus says that we should perform this action only toward God, Matt. 4:10.

The third instance is Matt. 18:26. The NASBU gives the following translation of this verse: "So the slave fell *to the ground* and prostrated [προσεκύνει] himself before him, saying, 'Have patience with me, and I will repay you everything.'"[22] This verse occurs in the text of the parable of the unforgiving servant. With reference to this parable, Craig Blomberg makes the following comments:

---

[20] LSL, s.v. "πίπτω."
[21] τότε λέγει αὐτῷ ὁ Ἰησοῦς· ὕπαγε, σατανᾶ· γέγραπται γάρ· κύριον τὸν θεόν σου προσκυνήσεις καὶ αὐτῷ μόνῳ λατρεύσεις. (Matt. 4:10).
[22] πεσὼν οὖν ὁ δοῦλος προσεκύνει αὐτῷ λέγων· μακροθύμησον ἐπ' ἐμοί, καὶ πάντα ἀποδώσω σοι. (Matt. 18:26).

One lesson also emerges from each subdivision. *(1) The first section magnificently illustrates the boundless grace of God in forgiving sins, as the king forgave his servant. (2) In the middle section, the second servant underlines the absurdity of grace spurned; one who has been forgiven so much and yet so mistreats his fellow debtor does not deserve to live. (3) The final section depicts the frightful fate awaiting the unforgiving, as the wicked servant discovered to his ruin.*[23]

Blomberg's understanding of the significance of the parable is by no means unique. Almost all commentators understand this parable to be depicting the grace of God and the kind of attitude of forgiveness we ought all to have in the face of the great debt of sin that God has forgiven us. In the parable, then, the master to whom the servant bows is representative of God. So, the bowing down of the servant in the parable does not violate the principle that Jesus had asserted in His response to Satan's testing—the action indicated by the verb προσκυνέω ought to be performed only to God. Here the parable is designed to illustrate the fact that we should worship God because of who He is and also because of the boundless grace that He has extended to all who believe. Employing BeDuhn's principle of literary context, then, we ought to understand Matthew's use of the term in our passage as referring to the kind of action that one would perform to God, that is, worship. It appears as if BeDuhn's translation has failed his second criterion for accuracy and unbiased translation. But before we draw this conclusion, let us go back to the two words we found in 4:9.

'Fall Down' and 'Worship' in the NT

There are only three other instances in the NT besides Matt. 4:9 in which these two verbs πίπτω (*piptō*), "to fall down," and προσκυνέω (*proskuneō*) "to prostrate" are used together. These are Matt. 2:11, Rev. 5:14, and 22:8:

> Matt. 2:11 "After coming into the house they saw the Child with Mary His mother; and they fell to the ground [πεσόντες] and worshiped [προσεκύνησαν] Him. Then, opening their treasures, they presented to Him gifts of gold, frankincense, and myrrh" (NASBU).

> Rev. 5:14: "And the four living creatures kept saying, 'Amen.' And the elders fell down [ἔπεσαν] and worshiped [προσεκύνησαν]" (NASBU).

> Rev. 22:8: "I, John, am the one who heard and saw these things. And when I heard and saw, I fell down [ἔπεσα] to worship [προσκυνῆσαι] at the feet of the angel who showed me these things" (NASBU).

Of course Matt. 2:11 is one of the verses that is contested, so we won't use it to establish our point. However, consider the two passages in Revelation. In 5:14 the one

---

[23] Craig L. Blomberg, *Interpreting the Parables* (Downers Grove, Illinois: InterVarsity Press, 1990), 242–43 (emphasis in original).

Chapter 2: Worshiping Christ

before whom the elders (πρεσβύτεροι, *presbuteroi*) fall down is "Lamb that was slain" (5:13). Notice what the angels/messengers, the living creatures, and the elders are saying in verse 12: "Worthy is the Lamb that was slain to receive power and riches and wisdom and might and honor and glory and blessing." Verse 13 states, "And every created thing which is in heaven and on the earth and under the earth and on the sea, and all things in them, I heard saying, 'To Him who sits on the throne, and to the Lamb, *be* blessing and honor and glory and dominion forever and ever.'" This certainly sounds like worship. In Rev. 5:14, rather than using πίπτω and προσκυνέω in a redundant sense, the one indicates falling down before the Lamb that was slain while the other indicates worship. The Lamb, of course, is Jesus.

The context of Rev. 22:8 is the vision of the tree of life. John falls down to worship the angel: "... I fell down [ἔπεσα, *epesa*] to worship [προσκυνῆσαι, *proskunēsai*] at the feet of the angel..." But the angel objects to John's action: "But he said to me, 'Do not do that. I am a fellow servant of yours and of your brethren the prophets and of those who heed the words of this book. Worship God'" (Rev. 22:9). Notice particularly the last statement of verse 9: "Worship God!" Here the Greek word is the imperative form of *proskuneō* — τῷ θεῷ προσκύνησον (*tō theō proskuneson*). Coupled with the fact that in Matt. 4:9 Jesus contradicts Satan's statement and declares that worshiping ought to be performed with reference to God, there can be little doubt that the word '*proskuneō*' in the contexts of Matthew's Gospel means "worship" and not simply "prostrate oneself," especially in those verses in which the two words 'fall down' and 'worship' occur together. And, these two words do in fact occur together in Matt. 2:11, one of the verses concerning which BeDuhn says it cannot possibly mean "worship."

'Fall Down' and 'Worship' in the GSEPT

Before we move on to the historical and cultural principle, let us look at how these two words are used together in the GSEPT. The combination of these two verbs is used seven times in the GSEPT, and five of these occur in Daniel chapter 3: (2 Chron. 29:30; Job 1:20: Dan. 3:5, 6, 10, 11, 15).

Table #6: 2 Chron. 29:30

"Moreover, King Hezekiah and the officials ordered the Levites to sing praises to the Lord with the words of David and Asaph the seer. So they sang praises with joy, and bowed down [ἔπεσον, וַיִּקְּדוּ] and worshiped [προσεκύνησαν, וַיִּשְׁתַּחֲוּוּ]" (NASBU)
καὶ εἶπεν Εζεκιας ὁ βασιλεὺς καὶ οἱ ἄρχοντες τοῖς Λευίταις ὑμνεῖν τὸν κύριον ἐν λόγοις Δαυιδ καὶ Ασαφ τοῦ προφήτου καὶ ὕμνουν ἐν εὐφροσύνῃ καὶ ἔπεσον καὶ προσεκύνησαν. (GSEPT)
וַיֹּאמֶר יְחִזְקִיָּהוּ הַמֶּלֶךְ וְהַשָּׂרִים לַלְוִיִּם לְהַלֵּל לַיהוָה בְּדִבְרֵי דָוִיד וְאָסָף הַחֹזֶה וַיְהַלְלוּ עַד־לְשִׂמְחָה וַיִּקְּדוּ וַיִּשְׁתַּחֲוּוּ: (BHS)

The context of 2 Chron. 29:30 is the re-establishing of the Temple and the worship of the Lord God of Israel. Clearly this is an instance of worship. When they sang, Hezekiah and the officials bowed down and worshiped God. Here the two Greek words, πίπτω and προσκυνέω are used, and clearly the meaning of *proskuneō* is "worship." Concerning the words in the GSEPT, the TWOT states, "The Greek word *proskuneō*, which is used to translate *hištaḥăwâ* 148 times in the GSEPT, had a semantic development similar to the Hebrew word. Like it *proskuneō* can mean either 'prostration' or 'worship.'"[24]

Table #7: Job 1:20

"Then Job arose and tore his robe and shaved his head, and he fell [πεσών, וַיִּפֹּל] to the ground and worshiped [προσεκύνησεν, וַיִּשְׁתָּחוּ]" (NASBU).
οὕτως ἀναστὰς Ιωβ διέρρηξεν τὰ ἱμάτια αὐτοῦ καὶ ἐκείρατο τὴν κόμην τῆς κεφαλῆς αὐτοῦ καὶ πεσὼν χαμαὶ προσεκύνησεν καὶ εἶπεν (GSEPT)
וַיָּקָם אִיּוֹב וַיִּקְרַע אֶת־מְעִלוֹ וַיָּגָז אֶת־רֹאשׁוֹ וַיִּפֹּל אַרְצָה וַיִּשְׁתָּחוּ:

The context of Job 1:20 is immediately following the disasters that have befallen Job. Job expresses his worship in a poem:

Naked I came from my mother's womb,	עָרֹם יָצָתִי מִבֶּטֶן אִמִּי
And naked I shall return there.	וְעָרֹם אָשׁוּב שָׁמָּה
The Lord gave and the Lord has taken away.	יְהוָה נָתַן וַיהוָה לָקָח
Blessed be the name of the Lord	יְהִי שֵׁם יְהוָה מְבֹרָךְ:
(Job 1:21 NASBU).	

Once again these two words express the physical action and the spiritual action, falling down followed by worship. Again the Hebrew word for worship is translated by the Greek word *proskuneō*.

Since the rest of the texts occur in Daniel chapter 3, and they all concern Nebuchadnezzar's command that everyone fall down and worship the image, we will treat these together.

---

[24] TWOT, s.v. "חָוָה."

Chapter 2: Worshiping Christ

Table #8: Dan. 3:5

"that at the moment you hear the sound of the horn, flute, lyre, trigon, psaltery, bagpipe and all kinds of music, you are to fall down [πίπτοντες, וְתִפְּלוּן] and worship [προσκυνεῖτε, וְתִסְגְּדוּן] the golden image that Nebuchadnezzar the king has set up." (NASBU).

ᾗ ἂν ὥρᾳ ἀκούσητε τῆς φωνῆς τῆς σάλπιγγος σύριγγός τε καὶ κιθάρας σαμβύκης καὶ ψαλτηρίου καὶ συμφωνίας καὶ παντὸς γένους μουσικῶν πίπτοντες προσκυνεῖτε τῇ εἰκόνι τῇ χρυσῇ ᾗ ἔστησεν Ναβουχοδονοσορ ὁ βασιλεύ. (GSEPT)

בְּעִדָּנָא דִּי־תִשְׁמְעוּן קָל קַרְנָא מַשְׁרוֹקִיתָא קַתְרוֹס סַבְּכָא פְּסַנְתֵּרִין סוּמְפֹּנְיָה וְכֹל זְנֵי זְמָרָא תִּפְּלוּן וְתִסְגְּדוּן לְצֶלֶם דַּהֲבָא דִּי הֲקֵים נְבוּכַדְנֶצַּר מַלְכָּא: (BHS)

Table #9: Dan. 3:6

"But whoever does not fall down and worship shall immediately be cast into the midst of a furnace of blazing fire" (NASBU).

καὶ ὃς ἂν μὴ πεσὼν προσκυνήσῃ αὐτῇ τῇ ὥρᾳ ἐμβληθήσεται εἰς τὴν κάμινον τοῦ πυρὸς τὴν καιομένη (GSEPT)

וּמַן־דִּי־לָא יִפֵּל וְיִסְגֻּד בַּהּ־שַׁעֲתָא יִתְרְמֵא לְגוֹא־אַתּוּן נוּרָא יָקִדְתָּא: (BHS)

Table #10: Dan. 3:10

"You, O king, have made a decree that every man who hears the sound of the horn, flute, lyre, trigon, psaltery, and bagpipe and all kinds of music, is to fall down and worship the golden image" (NASBU).

σὺ βασιλεῦ ἔθηκας δόγμα πάντα ἄνθρωπον ὃς ἂν ἀκούσῃ τῆς φωνῆς τῆς σάλπιγγος σύριγγός τε καὶ κιθάρας σαμβύκης καὶ ψαλτηρίου καὶ συμφωνίας καὶ παντὸς γένους μουσικῶν (GSEPT)

אַנְתָּה מַלְכָּא שָׂמְתָּ טְעֵם דִּי כָל־אֱנָשׁ דִּי־יִשְׁמַע קָל קַרְנָא מַשְׁרֹקִיתָא קַתְרֹס שַׂבְּכָא פְּסַנְתֵּרִין וְסִיפֹּנְיָה וְכֹל זְנֵי זְמָרָא יִפֵּל וְיִסְגֻּד לְצֶלֶם דַּהֲבָא: (BHS)

Table #11: Dan. 3:11

"But whoever does not fall down and worship shall be cast into the midst of a furnace of blazing fire" (NASBU).

καὶ μὴ πεσὼν προσκυνήσῃ τῇ εἰκόνι τῇ χρυσῇ ἐμβληθήσεται εἰς τὴν κάμινον τοῦ πυρὸς τὴν καιομένην (GSEPT)

וּמַן־דִּי־לָא יִפֵּל וְיִסְגֻּד יִתְרְמֵא לְגוֹא־אַתּוּן נוּרָא יָקִדְתָּא:

Table #12: Dan. 3:15

"Now if you are ready, at the moment you hear the sound of the horn, flute, lyre, trigon, psaltery and bagpipe and all kinds of music, to fall down [πεσόντες, תִּפְּלוּן] and worship [προσκυνήσητε, וְתִסְגְּדוּן] the image that I have made, *very well*. But if you do not worship [προσκυνήσητε, תִסְגְּדוּן], you will immediately be cast into the midst of a furnace of blazing fire; and what god is there who can deliver you out of my hands?" (NASBU)

νῦν οὖν εἰ ἔχετε ἑτοίμως ἵνα ὡς ἂν ἀκούσητε τῆς φωνῆς τῆς σάλπιγγος σύριγγός τε καὶ κιθάρας σαμβύκης καὶ ψαλτηρίου καὶ συμφωνίας καὶ παντὸς γένους μουσικῶν πεσόντες προσκυνήσητε τῇ εἰκόνι ᾗ ἐποίησα ἐὰν δὲ μὴ προσκυνήσητε αὐτῇ τῇ ὥρᾳ ἐμβληθήσεσθε εἰς τὴν κάμινον τοῦ πυρὸς τὴν καιομένην καὶ τίς ἐστιν θεός ὃς ἐξελεῖται ὑμᾶς ἐκ τῶν χειρῶν μου; (GSEPT)

כְּעַן הֵן אִיתֵיכוֹן עֲתִידִין דִּי בְעִדָּנָא דִּי־תִשְׁמְעוּן קָל קַרְנָא מַשְׁרוֹקִיתָא קִיתָרֹס שַׂבְּכָא פְּסַנְתֵּרִין וְסוּמְפֹּנְיָה וְכֹל זְנֵי זְמָרָא תִּפְּלוּן וְתִסְגְּדוּן לְצַלְמָא דִי־עַבְדֵת וְהֵן לָא תִסְגְּדוּן בַּהּ־שַׁעֲתָה תִתְרְמוֹן לְגוֹא־אַתּוּן נוּרָא יָקִדְתָּא וּמַן־הוּא אֱלָהּ דִּי יְשֵׁיזְבִנְכוֹן מִן־יְדָי׃ (BHS)

In each instance the GSEPT uses the same two words, πίπτω and προσκυνέω, to translate the Aramaic text. The Aramaic term translated worship is סְגַד. In Daniel, it is used in 2:46; 3:5, 6, 7, 10, 11, 12, 14, 15, 18, and 28. Nebuchadnezzar sends out a command that at the hearing of the instruments, everyone must "fall down [πίπτοντες, תִּפְּלוּן] and worship [προσκυνεῖτε, וְתִסְגְּדוּן] the golden image" (3:5). The command included a warning that anyone who does not fall down and worship the image would be thrown into the furnace. Of course the three Hebrew youths do not obey the command, but notice that when the accusation is brought before Nebuchadnezzar, the accusation does not use the word "fall down": "There are certain Jews whom you have appointed over the administration of the province of Babylon, Shadrach, Meshach and Abed-nego. These men, O king, have disregarded you; they do not serve your gods or worship [προσκυνοῦσιν, סָגְדִין] the golden image which you have set up" (Dan. 3:12, NASBU). The accusation is not that they did not fall down, but that they did not worship the image. If the problem was merely a physical action, then the accusation should have included both the action of falling down and the action of prostration. Rather, it was the religious or spiritual implication of the action of prostration, namely worship, that the Hebrews were unwilling to do. In other words, they would not prostrate themselves before the golden image because they understood the action of prostration as an act of worship.

There is also a similar situation in Dan. 3:15. Here again this is about commanding the three Hebrews to bow down and worship. In the first part of the verse, Nebuchadnezzar gives the three Hebrew youths another opportunity to obey: "Now if you are ready, at the moment . . . fall down and worship the image . . ." This second chance is followed by a warning: "But if you do not worship . . ." Notice that

Nebuchadnezzar does not say, "if you do not fall down and worship," but he says only, "if you do not worship." The three Hebrews are not condemned because they did not fall down, but because they did not worship. If the simple physical act of prostration was the basis of the their condemnation, then they should have been condemned for not falling down and prostrating themselves. The Hebrews knew exactly what Nebuchadnezzar wanted. He did not want them simply to fall down and prostrate themselves. Rather, he wanted them to *worship* the image. Their response to Nebuchadnezzar's second chance makes it clear that Nebuchadnezzar was commanding them to worship the image: "we are not going to serve your gods or worship [προσκυνοῦμεν, *proskunoumen*] the golden image that you have set up" (Dan. 3:18).[25] The physical action was not the issue, and this is clear from the fact that the act of "falling down" is no longer part of the issue.

The second of BeDuhn's principles for an unbiased and accurate translation is the literary context. However, BeDuhn does not actually consider the literary context beyond a few references in Matthew. He does not consider the particular expression, "fall down and worship," in Matt. 2:11 that describes the actions of the magi, nor does he consider how this expression with these particular words is used in both the NT and the OT to describe the act of worship. There is also an interesting parallelism between the testing of Jesus in Matt. 4:9 and the testing of the three Hebrew youths in Daniel 3. As Jesus is tested by Satan, that Satan would give Jesus all the kingdoms of the earth if He would fall down and worship, so the three Hebrew youths are commanded by Nebuchadnezzar, of whom Daniel said, "You, O king, are a king of kings. For the God of heaven has given you a kingdom, power, strength, and glory; and wherever the children of men dwell, or the beasts of the field and the birds of the heaven, He has given them into your hand, and has made you ruler over them all"(Dan. 2:37–38 NKJV), to fall down and worship the image. Also, as Jesus refused to fall down and worship Satan, declaring, "You shall worship the Lord your God, and serve Him only" (Matt. 4:10), so the three Hebrews refuse and declare, "we are not going to serve your gods or worship the golden image that you have set up" (Dan. 3:18 NASBU). The literary context of the account of the magi clearly indicates that the magi fell down and worshiped Jesus. BeDuhn's account fails his second test of unbiased and accurate translation.

Historical and Cultural Environment

The third of BeDuhn's criteria for accurate and unbiased translation is the historical and cultural environment. With reference to this criterion we will consider several sources. First we will present the article on "Wise Men" from the *Baker Encyclopedia of the Bible*:

---

[25] τοῖς θεοῖς σου οὐ λατρεύομεν καὶ τῇ εἰκόνι τῇ χρυσῇ ᾗ ἔστησας οὐ προσκυνοῦμε (Dan. 3:18 — GSEPT)

Wise Men.
Men appearing in Matthew 2:1–12 who, following a star, come to Jerusalem and then Bethlehem to pay homage to the newborn "king of the Jews." While Matthew tells nothing of their personal identity or positions and little of their nationalities, the account forms an appropriate introduction to his Gospel by drawing attention to the true identity of Jesus and by foreshadowing the homage paid by the Gentiles to Jesus throughout that Gospel.

The Role and Position in the Ancient World.
Extrabiblical evidence offers various clues that shed light on the place of origin and positions held by the "wise men" of Matthew 2. The historian Herodotus mentions "magi" as a priestly caste of Media, or Persia, and, as the religion in Persia at the time was Zoroastrinism, Herodotus' magi were probably Zoroastrian priests. Herodotus, together with Plutarch and Strabo, suggests that magi were partly responsible for ritual and cultic life (supervising sacrifices and prayers) and partly responsible as royal advisers to the courts of the East. Believing the affairs of history were reflected in the movements of the stars and other phenomena, Herodotus suggests the rulers of the East commonly utilized the magi's knowledge of astrology and dream interpretation to determine affairs of state. The magi were therefore concerned with what the movement of the stars (as sign and portents) might signify for the future affairs of history. Such an interest could account not only fort the wise men's association with the star in Matthew 2, but also their conclusion, shared with Herod, that the nova's appearance signified the birth of a new ruler of great importance (2:2). Several centuries before Christ a similar correlation was noted between a stellar phenomenon and the birth of Alexander the Great.

Identity in Matthew's Gospel.
Matthew's infancy narrative contains little information concerning the identity of the magi. Matthew states only that the wise men were "from the East" (2:1, 2), an ambiguous point of origin that left room for many subsequent hypotheses. Some church fathers proposed Arabia on the basis of where the gifts (gold, frankincense, and myrrh, 2:11) were likely to have originated. Other suggested Chaldea or Media/Persia, and, although certainty is impossible, Persia did certainly have a caste of priests (magi) which would fit the description in Matthew.

Interestingly, Matthew does not tell how many magi came to honor the infant Jesus. The Eastern church held that there were 12 travelers, although this may simply derive from the biblical penchant for that number (12 tribes of Israel, 12 disciples). The Western church settled on 3 wise men, based presumably on the 3 gifts brought in homage. The exact number is not known.

A similar silence exists in Matthew regarding the names of the wise men. The names Gaspar, Melchior (Melkon), and Balthasar are legendary and do not derive from Matthew. Similarly, the later tradition that Gaspar was a king of India, Melchoir a king of Persia, and Balthasar a king of Arabia has no basis in fact.[26]

In the second paragraph under the heading ***The Role and Position in the Ancient World***, the encyclopedia makes reference to the Zoroastrian faith. The encyclopedia asserts that the magi referred to by Herodotus may have been Zoroastrian priests. According to this encyclopedia, although this could be the magi in Matthew, Matthew's

---

[26] Walter A. Elwell and Barry J. Beitzel, *Baker Encyclopedia of the Bible* (Grand Rapids: Baker Book House, 1988), 2153.

Chapter 2: Worshiping Christ

account "contains little information concerning the identity of the magi. Matthew states only that the wise men were 'from the East' (2:1, 2), an ambiguous point of origin that left room for many subsequent hypotheses."[27]

Leo Oppenheim, author of the book *Ancient Mesopotamia*, makes the following observations about the אָשַׁף (*'āšaph*) which is translated with the Greek word μάγος in the Greek of Daniel, with the English translation "conjurer" in the NASBU.

> Much of what we know of Akkadian anatomic nomenclature, the terminology of the healthy and the morbid body and its functions, comes from texts we have termed omen texts or, to be exact, prognostic omens. The expert who carefully searches for revealing signs is not called a physician (*asû*), but an *āšipu*, which we translate traditionally as "conjurer." The signs observed tell him whether the patient will live or die, how long the illness is to last, and whether it is serious or passing. Exactly as the diviner does not content himself with observing the extra of the sheep slaughtered but to derive additional signs extends his observation to the behavior of the animal before it is killed, so does the *āšipu* in his treatment of the patient. Not only do the symptoms of the sick man convey information but the situation in which he is observed is taken into account. The time of day or night, the date are observed and signs interpreted. But what is the nature of the countermeasures taken by the *āšipu*? In view of what we know of Mesopotamian divination, there is every reason to assume that magic acts — conjurations and rituals — are indicated.[28]

Oppenheim does not connect the term Aramaic term אָשַׁף (μάγος) with Zoroastrianism and in fact depicts this term as referring to a person using magic to practice medicine. In his book, *The History of Magic and the Occult*, Kurt Seligmann has a lengthy discussion of Zoroastrianism, but throughout the discussion he makes no mention of anyone associated with the practice of this religion being referred to as a μάγος or אָשַׁף.

Colin Wilson, in his book *The Occult*, specifically connects the Magi with Zoroastrianism. He says,

> The Magi, from whom the word 'magic' is derived, were the priests of this ancient religion [Zoroastrianism]. I would suggest, then, as a hypothesis that can never be proved or disproved, that the original Magi derived their magic powers from 'positive consciousness' — from the recognition that subjectivity is only good so long as it keeps itself open to the reality of a meaning outside itself. . . . The little we know of the Magi is derived almost entirely from the history of Herodotus, much as our knowledge of Atlantis depends entirely on Plato. Herodotus, writing in the fifth century B.C., a few decades before Plato, was speaking about the latter stages of the Magian religion. . . . All the references in Herodotus are incidental, so we learn only that the Magi are skilled in the interpretation of dreams, and that they were a powerful cast, who continued to dominate Persian life. Even after an attempt

---

[27] Ibid.
[28] A. Leo Oppenheim, *Ancient Mesopotamia: Portrait of a Dead Civilization* (Chicago: The University of Chicago Press, 1964), 294–95.

to seize power lead to mass executions — presumably because daily life was unthinkable without them.[29]

Interestingly, Wilson provides no support for his claim that the Magi were associated with Zoroastrianism. He cites no ancient sources nor any other sources of any kind. He simply makes the assertion. He points out that his information about the magi comes from Herodotus, but Herodotus nowhere refers to Zoroastrianism in his discussion of the magi. Wilson's association of the two is not supported by his appeal to Herodotus, and since, as Wilson himself admits, "the little we know of the Magi is derived almost entirely from the history of Herodotus," Wilson's connection between the Magi and Zoroaster seems to be speculation on his part. Nevertheless, Wilson never connects the Magi of the Zoroastrian faith with the μάγος mentioned in the Bible.

Since the word μάγος does not seem to have any necessary relationship to Zoroastrianism, and since it can refer to other persons than the Zoroastrian priests, and since Matthew's reference to the μάγοι is ambiguous at best, the bare, unsupported claim by BeDuhn that the μάγοι of Matthew are followers of the Zoroastrian faith is shear speculation on BeDuhn's part. According to his own principles, his choice to translate Matt. 2:11 in such a ways as to make the action of the wise men doing something less than worship can be motivated only by his own bias. At the very least BeDuhn has failed to make his case and his translation has failed his own principles, and at worst this demonstrates that he is as biased in his translation as any of those he criticizes. The fact of the matter is, προσκυνέω in Matt. 2:11 can indeed legitimately be translated worship without any inaccuracy or bias.

Literal Meanings

"Worship"

BeDuhn makes some further observations about the Matt. 2:11 passage:

> We can take the other passages in the Gospel according to Matthew where *proskuneō* is used, and see how "worship" works its way into modern translations. If the word is used to refer to the actions of a leper (Matthew 8:2), a local Jewish authority (Matthew 9:18), or women (Matthew 15:25 and 20:20) most translations stick with the literal meaning of kneeling, or bowing (only the AB and LB, along with the KJV, regularly employ "worship" in these passages). But when the disciples of Jesus are the actors, suddenly we see "worship" everywhere.[30]

---

[29] Colin Wilson, *The Occult* (New York: Vintage Books, 1973), 185–86.
[30] BeDuhn, *Translation*, 45.

First of all, BeDuhn falsely characterizes the translation of other passages in Matthew as the word "worship" having "worked" its way into modern translations. In fact, the translation of the Greek word as indicating worship goes back at least to the Latin Vulgate. The Vulgate translates Matt. 4:10 as: *"tunc dicit ei Iesus vade Satanas scriptum est Dominum Deum tuum adorabis* [worship] *et illi soli servies."* The Latin word *adoro* is used to translate the Greek word προσκυνέω, and the Lewis&Short Latin dictionary gives the following meanings: *"to reverence, honor, adore, worship* to gods or objects of nature regarded as gods. more emphatic than *venerari*, and denoting the highest degree of reverence (Gr. προσκυνεῖν);"[31] Also, the *Oxford Latin Dictionary* gives the following meanings: "To approach (the gods, etc.) as a suppliant or worshipper, make petitions or pay homage to, pray to, worship."[32] The fact that Latin translations were made as early as the third century A.D. demonstrates that this is not a "modern" translation. Secondly, although the translations "kneeling" and "bowing" certainly indicate literal meanings of the word προσκυνέω, according to the standard Greek lexicons, the meaning "worship" is also a literal meaning. In fact, the meaning "fall down and worship" is one of the literal meanings of this word as indicated by LSL.[33] Also, the standard NT Greek lexicon lists "worship" as one of the literal meanings: "to express in attitude or gesture one's complete dependence on or submission to a high authority figure, *(fall down and) worship, do obeisance to, prostrate oneself before, do reverence to, welcome respectfully* . . ."[34] For BeDuhn to speak as if the definition "worship" is not literal is simply a biased misrepresentation. In fact, that Matt. 4:10 uses this word with reference to God clearly demonstrates that its meaning is "worship."

"Bowing to Power"

With reference to Matt. 14:33, BeDuhn asserts, "Most translations choose to import the modern meaning of 'worship' into the passage, apparently because of the recognition by the disciples that they are in the presence of 'a son of God.'"[35] He then emphatically declares, "Yes, that's what the Greek says: 'a son of God.'"[36]

The text of verse 33 is set out below with a word-for-word translation:

---

[31] *A Latin Dictionary* (1966), s.v. "*ădōro.*"
[32] *Oxford Latin Dictionary* (2005), s.v. "*adōrō.*"
[33] LSL, s.v. "προσκυ νέω."
[34] BDAG, s.v. "προσκυνέω."
[35] BeDuhn, *Translation*, 46.
[36] Ibid.

Table #13: Matt. 14:33

οἱ	δὲ	ἐν	τῷ
the	but	in	the
πλοίῳ	προσεκύνησαν	αὐτῷ	λέγοντες
boat	?	to him	saying
ἀληθῶς	θεοῦ	υἱὸς	εἶ
truly	of God	son	you are

There is no Greek definite article before the word υἱὸς (son). What BeDuhn neglects to tell his reader is that there is no indefinite article corresponding to the English "a." Greek does not have an indefinite article. So, technically, it is incorrect for BeDuhn to translate this "a son of God." What the text says is, "of God son." Since there is no indefinite article, to add the English indefinite article is inaccurate and reveals BeDuhn's bias. Although this construction could certainly means "a son of God," and since Greek has not indefinite article, this has to be proven, not simply asserted.

Along this same line, BeDuhn looks at Matt. 28:9: "And behold, Jesus met them on their way and greeted them. They approached, embraced his feet, and did him homage." BeDuhn comments, "Struck with amazement and fear at seeing Jesus alive when they thought him dead, the disciples cower at his feet."[37] Interestingly, no Greek lexicon or dictionary, including BeDuhn's favorite, LSL, gives the meaning "cower" as one of the possible meanings of the word προσκυνέω. BeDuhn goes on to say, "I am not going to enter into a debate over interpretation,"[38] and yet anyone who has studied translation theory knows that no translation is possible without some interpretation. To say that he is not going to enter into a debate over interpretation is flatly falsifying what he has been doing all along. The very fact that he is discussing which words in the target language best translate words in the source language is in fact a debate about interpretation. He says, "It is always possible that the interpretation of the significance of the gesture *may be* correct. But the simple translation 'prostrate,' or 'do homage,' or 'do obeisance' is *certainly* correct."[39] However, if by these meanings BeDuhn is implying that "worship" is not correct, then this is indeed a debate about interpretation, and BeDuhn is certainly incorrect. To translate the Greek word προσκυνέω with the English word "worship" is not inaccurate or questionable as BeDuhn implies. His own prejudice against the notion that Jesus is God is evident in his discussion. And to forestall debate amounts to defining one's position into existence and denying others the right to question him or even ask for support for his position. One can infer from his

---

[37] Ibid.
[38] Ibid., 47.
[39] Ibid.

Chapter 2: Worshiping Christ

reluctance to enter into debate that perhaps he is aware that his claims cannot stand up to examination. This is like hitting someone in the face and then saying, "Now I don't want to get into a fight."

In his response to the question of why some translators would translate this word as "worship," BeDuhn says, "the translators seem to feel the need to add to the New Testament support for the idea that Jesus was recognized to be God. But the presence of such an idea cannot be supported by selectively translating a word one way when it refers to Jesus an another way when it refers to someone else."[40] But this is flatly false. The same action performed to God would certainly not mean the same thing when performed to someone who was merely a human king. This is evident in the case of Matt. 4:10 when the Greek word is used with reference to God. A person might certainly do homage to a merely human king as the custom dictates, but when this same action is performed to God it would indicate not merely homage, but worship. So, translations must reflect these distinctions, and if it can be shown that Jesus is in fact God in the flesh, the translation ought to translate the meaning of the action as worship, not merely homage.

Principles of Translation

BeDuhn asserts, "When we observe how these same translators choose 'worship' when the gesture is made to Jesus by certain persons, and choose other English words to translate the very same Greek term when the gesture is directed to someone other than Jesus, or is directed to Jesus by someone whom they regard as not qualifying as a true believer, their inconsistency reveals their bias."[41] But such statements as this betray BeDuhn's own lack of understanding of the nature of translation. Since the words in one language do not have a one-to-one correspondence of meaning to words in another language, translation requires that the same word in the source language be translated by different words in the target language when the meaning is evidently different. The fact that BeDuhn disallows the change of meaning when this action is performed with reference to Jesus and with reference to others reveals BeDuhn's own bias. He argues against the notion that the context of belief "implies that the gesture is more than 'obeisance' or 'homage'" and that this is "not a very good argument, because in most of the passages the people who make the gesture know next to nothing about Jesus, other than that it is obvious or rumored that he has power to help them."[42] Even if this were true it does not address those instances where the persons performing the action do in fact know enough about Jesus to know whether they should worship Him or not. Unfortunately for his readers, BeDuhn assumes that his response absolves him of the

---

[40] Ibid.
[41] Ibid.
[42] Ibid., 48.

responsibility of addressing those instances that do not fall within his characterization of "most" instances. What about those other instances?

One Final Example

One final example BeDuhn gives is from Matt. 28:16–17. Once again the text is set out with a word-for-word translation:

Table #14: Matt. 28:16–17

Οἱ	δὲ	ἕνδεκα	μαθηταὶ
The	but	eleven	disciples
ἐπορεύθησαν	εἰς	τὴν	Γαλιλαίαν
went up	into	the	Galilee
εἰς	τὸ	ὄρος	οὗ
into	the	mountain	which
ἐτάξατο	αὐτοῖς	ὁ	Ἰησοῦς
designated	to them	the	Jesus
καὶ	ἰδόντες	αὐτὸν	προσεκύνησαν
and	beholding	him	they ?
οἱ	δὲ	ἐδίστασαν	
the	but	they were doubting	

In his discussion of this passage BeDuhn's bias is especially evident. He says, "Here all translations except the NW have recourse to 'worship' – a rendering which makes no sense in this context. How can someone worship and doubt at the same time?"[43] BeDuhn's bias is evident by the fact that he reads into the text what simply is not there. The text does not say what they doubted, just simply that they were doubting. But, because BeDuhn is biased against the notion of worshiping Jesus, he has assumed that they were doubting something that has to do with worshiping Jesus. However, as far as the text is concerned, they could have been having doubts about what they were going to do now. The fact that Jesus tells them that He has been given all authority and that they are to go into all the world to make disciples indicates that they were in fact not having doubts about who Jesus is or whether He should be worshiped. Jesus instructs them concerning what they are supposed to do now that He has raised from the dead. For BeDuhn to assume without argument or evidence that their doubt was necessarily

---

[43] Ibid., 48.

Chapter 2: Worshiping Christ

contrary to their worship reveals his bias. It is perfectly reasonable for someone to worship God and yet have doubts, particularly if their doubts are about something other than whether God should be worshiped.

Consider the father who cried out for Jesus to heal his son: "Immediately the boy's father cried out and said, 'I do believe; help my unbelief [πιστεύω· βοήθει μου τῇ ἀπιστίᾳ]'" (Mk. 9:24). He believes, but his faith is not very strong, and he pleads for Jesus to help him have stronger faith. Believing and having doubts are not necessarily mutually exclusive. It is extremely arrogant for BeDuhn to conclude that just because the statement doesn't make sense to him that the statement cannot make sense in itself.

BeDuhn goes on to say, "Notice how all eleven disciples prostrate themselves, but not all believe what they are experiencing (actually, the NAB is the only version to correctly translate the Greek 'but they doubted'; there is nothing in the Greek from which you can get 'some')."[44] But neither is there anything in the Greek from which BeDuhn gets the idea that "not all believe what they are experiencing." And if there is nothing in the Greek from which one can get the notion "some," on what basis does BeDuhn claim that "not all" of the disciples believe? If there is indeed nothing in the Greek from which one can get the notion of "some," then shouldn't BeDuhn have said that *none* of the disciples were believing what they were experienceing? Again BeDuhn's treatment reveals his own bias. He says, "The word can't possibly mean 'worship' as we use that word today, as a mental state of reverence, since 'they doubted.'"[45] But why not? Who says that a person cannot worship and still have doubts? BeDuhn makes this assertion without evidence or support. He declares, "It only refers to the outward physical act of bowing down, which may or may not reflect how the one making the gesture really feels about the person to whom they make it,"[46] but nowhere in any Greek lexicon does the word have anything to do with how anyone feels! And we must state the obvious again. Just because the text said they doubted does not mean they necessarily had doubts about worshiping Jesus. Their doubts could have been about many other things, and the statements of Jesus imply that it is possible that their doubts were about what they were supposed to do now, a doubt that Jesus addressed when He instructs them about their task.

Conclusion about *Proskuneō*

BeDuhn concludes his discussion of προσκυνέω by saying, "In our exploration of the Greek word *proskuneō* in the New Testament, therefore, the NAB and NW receive the highest marks for accuracy, while the others show a tendency to lapse into interpretive judgments guided by their theological biases."[47] However, contrary to

---

[44] Ibid.
[45] Ibid.
[46] Ibid.
[47] Ibid.

BeDuhn's analysis, his discussion has revealed that his grading of the accuracy of translations is propelled by his own theological bias.

BeDuhn further declares,

> It is perfectly legitimate for readers of the Bible to have different opinions about what is implied in a gesture of reverence such as prostration. Some will give it great theological importance; others will find it too broadly used to necessarily have theological import. But this debate of interpretation is the right of readers, and should not be decided for them by translators whose biases lead them to restrict what they will allow the readers to be able to consider.[48]

Since we have seen that the meaning "worship" is just as legitimate and just as literal a translation of the word as the ones BeDuhn advocates, it turns out that for BeDuhn to disallow this translation is every bit as bias as the ones he accuses of being bias. In fact, not only is BeDuhn's bias revealed in his discussion, but the fact that he is being disingenuous by deliberately misrepresenting the situation indicates that he is the most bias of all. Most revealing is his unwillingness to address the statement by Jesus in Matt. 4:10 in which the term προσκυνέω is used of worshiping God and where Jesus declares that such an act should be performed with reference only to God. This one verse at once reveals BeDuhn's own theological bias and the deceitful way in which he handles the evidence.

Apologetic Points

Our study of the evidence gives us at least five points that we can use when dealing with the New World Translation and the claims the Jehovah's Witnesses when they appeal to BeDuhn.

1. The word μάγος, (magos, the singular form), or μάγοι, (magi, the plural form), does not necessarily refer to someone following the Zoroastarian faith. In Acts 13:6, the word μάγος refers to a Jew and a pseudo-prophet, someone who would not be a Zoroastrian.

2. Even the historical background of the word μάγος shows that it does not necessarily refer to someone of the Zoroastrian faith. In order to make this association, this must be proven, not simply asserted.

3. Of the 13 times this word is used in Matthew's Gospel, only 3 are not used of prostrating before Jesus. In Matt. 4:9, Jesus says, "You shall worship

---

[48] Ibid., 48–49.

Chapter 2: Worshiping Christ

[προσκυνήσεις] the Lord your God, and serve Him only." Since Jesus uses this word to refer to worship, it is clear that the word can certain have that meaning.

4. There are only four instances in the NT in which these two verbs πίπτω (*piptō*), "to fall down," and προσκυνέω (*proskuneō*) "to worship" are used together. These are Matt. 2:11 and 4:9, and Rev. 5:14 and 22:8. In each of these instances, the word προσκυνέω (*proskuneō*) must mean "worship."

5. The evidence proves that the word προσκυνέω (*proskuneō*) can mean "worship," and it does mean "worship" in Matt. 2:11.

CHAPTER 3

IN THE FORM OF GOD

Introduction

The statements in Phil. 2:5–6 have been the subject of much debate and discussion through the years. Among the orthodox, the discussion has primarily been an effort precisely to understand the meaning of verse 6. In the NASB, the statement of interest is translated "did not regard equality with God a thing to be grasped." The NIV translates this portion, "did not consider equality with God something to be grasped." Although there has been much debate and controversy over precisely what these words mean, there has never been any question, at least among the orthodox, that this passage indicates that Jesus is God.

Not to be Grasped

Looking at the modern translations of Phil. 2:5–6 is BeDuhn's next effort. The text is set out below with a word-for-word translation.

Table #15: Phil. 2:5–6

Τοῦτο	φρονεῖτε	ἐν	ὑμῖν
This	have in mind	in	you
ὃ	καὶ	ἐν	Χριστῷ
which	also	in	Christ
Ἰησοῦ	ὃς	ἐν	μορφῇ
Jesus	who	in	form

In the Form of God

θεοῦ	ὑπάρχων	οὐχ	ἁρπαγμὸν
of God	existing	not	something to hold on to
ἡγήσατο	τὸ	εἶναι	ἴσα
he considered	the	to be	same as
θεῷ			
God			

Under the guise of assessing the accuracy of translations, BeDuhn is set upon attacking the notion that Jesus is God. He objects to modern translations at several points. His first objection is that modern translations have taken liberties with the translation of the term μορφή (*morphē*). However, his primary focus is on the term ἁρπαγμὸν (*harpagmon*), which is translated "something to hold on to."

BeDuhn takes issue with the way most modern translations render the word ἁρπαγμός (*harpagmos*). BeDuhn points out that LSL "defines *harpagmos* as 'robbery,' 'rape,' and 'prize to be grasped.'"[1] BeDuhn acknowledges that the English word 'grasp' "can mean either grabbing at something one does not have in order to get it, or clinging to something one already has in order to hold on to it."[2] He also points out that a Greek noun ending with the letters *-mos* usually carries a verbal idea. LSL relates the Greek noun *harpagmos* to the Greek verb *harpazō* for which it lists several meanings: "(1) snatch away, carry off; (2) seize hastily, snatch up; (3) seize, overpower, overmaster; (4) seize, adopt; (5) grasp with the senses; (6) captivate, ravish; (7) draw up."[3]

BeDuhn then goes into the various uses of the word *harpagē*, (ἁρπαγή) and others, listing many of these with their possible meanings. On the basis of this investigation, he asserts, "You can see that every one of these related words has to do with the seizure of something not yet one's own. There is not a single word derived from *harpazō* that is used to suggest holding on to something already possessed."[4] But this is a particularly problematic assertion. BeDuhn is willing to accept LSL's reports about meanings when it seems to help his case, but he is unwilling to accept it when it seems to count against him. Regardless of the meanings of these other lexemes, LSL reports that the meaning of the word *harpagmos* in Phil. 2:6 is "a prize to be grasped."[5] BeDuhn says, "But the

---

[1] BeDuhn, *Translation*, 54.
[2] Ibid.
[3] LSL, s.v. "ἁρπάζω."
[4] BeDuhn, *Translation*, 55.
[5] LSL, s.v. "ἁρπαγμός."

third definition is itself based on Philippians 2:6; no other case is given by Liddel & Scott where *harpagmos* means this."[6] But, unless BeDuhn wants to charge LSL with being dishonest, in which case we should not trust it any more, and BeDuhn's assessment of it in his introduction is misplaced, there is no reason to reject this as one of the possible meanings of this word. If LSL is sufficiently trustworthy for BeDuhn to rely on it for meanings of other words in other contexts, why, all of a sudden, is it not to be trusted when it comes to this meaning in this verse in this context?

It is important to follow BeDuhn's reasoning here. He claims that the meaning LSL gives to the word *harpagmos* in Phil. 2:6 is influenced by Phil. 2:6, and because of this, LSL questionable on this point. So, BeDuhn would have us believe that the compilers of LSL already had a meaning in mind for Phil. 2:6, and this influenced their addition of this meaning when they compiled the lexicon. So, if they already had this meaning, from where did they get this meaning? It must have come from their understanding of Phil. 2:6. But isn't that exactly how lexicography works? Don't the lexicographers study the instances of words and compile their lexicons on the basis of how they understand the meanings of words in their various contexts? Rather than showing the reader some bias or error on the part of the compilers of LSL, BeDuhn's comment demonstrates his own bias.

In fact, it is incumbent upon the lexicographers to report a different meaning if they believe that a word does not or cannot not have a certain meaning in a certain context. But in fact, BeDuhn's claim, "There is not a single word derived from *harpazō* that is used to suggest holding on to something already possessed" is in fact inaccurate. For the verb *harpazō* itself LSL reports, "ἁρπάζομαι I *have* her *torn* from my arms,"[7] which certainly indicates something that is already possessed that someone is forcibly taking away. This is a case of selective reporting. BeDuhn reports everything except that which hurts his case. Why is he willing to trust LSL on the other meanings but not on the one in Phil. 2:6? The only reason would seem to be his prior theological bias. Lexicographers are certainly not infallible. But unless BeDuhn has strong arguments from the context, which in fact he does not since his entire argument rests on his claims about the meaning of *harpagmos*, there is no reason to reject LSL on this point.

Besides this, BeDuhn does not seem to be aware of the contradiction he has introduced into his own speculations. Earlier he proposed that the meaning of the term *morphē* might indicate that "Christ possessed that perfect form/image of God that humans originally had, but had lost through doing the opposite of what Christ is reported here to have done."[8] But if the word *harpagmos* cannot refer to something already possessed, how can it be speaking of a form/image which Christ possessed? And, if it is not speaking of something already possessed, then it cannot be speaking of a form/image which Christ possessed. The fact of the matter is, in spite of all of

---

[6] BeDuhn, *Translation*, 54.
[7] LSL, s.v. "ἁρπάζω."
[8] BeDuhn, *Translation*, 53.

In the Form of God

BeDuhn's discussion, there is nothing that indicates that the word *harpagmos* cannot have the meaning and the sense reported by LSL and used by most translations.

The Form of God

There is a much more serious problem with BeDuhn's discussion, and that has to do with the word μορφή (*morphē*). Revealingly, BeDuhn passes over this word with very little discussion. Considering all of the lexical work he put into investigating the word *harpagmos*, one wonders why he did not spend an equal amount of effort on the word *morphē*. And if he did spend an equal amount of time, why did he not show this in his discussion? He says, "What exactly Paul means by 'in the form of God' is part of the interpretive debate about this passage. At least one possibility is that it is meant to echo the characterization of human beings as being made 'in the image of God' in Genesis 1 (in other words, Christ possessed that perfect form/image of God that humans originally had, but had lost through doing the opposite of what Christ is reported here to have done)."[9]

The first problem with BeDuhn's statement is that, with reference to mere humans, nowhere are the words "form" and "image" ever presented in the New Testament as having any relation to one another. It is certainly not the case that human beings are ever said to have had God's form. The following table shows the instance of the use of the word εἰκών ("image") and μορφή ("form") in the New Testament.

Table #16: "Image" and "Form" in the New Testament

εἰκών	μορφή
Matt. 22:20	
Mk. 12:16 Caesar's image on a coin	
	Mk. 16:12 Jesus appearing in a different form
Lk. 20:24	
Rom. 1:23	
Rom. 8:29	
1 Cor. 11:7	
1 Cor. 15:49	
2 Cor. 3:18	

---

[9] Ibid., 53.

εἰκών	μορφή
2 Cor. 4:4	
	Phil. 2:6
	Phil. 2:7
Col. 1:15	
Col. 3:10	
Heb. 10:1	
Rev. 13:14	
Rev. 13:15	
Rev. 14:9	
Rev. 14:11	
Rev. 15:2	
Rev. 16:2	
Rev. 19:20	
Rev. 20:4	

As can be seen from the table, there are no contexts in which the words 'image' and 'form' are used together. Also, in the *Greek-English Lexicon of the New Testament Based on Semantic Domains*, edited by Johannes P. Louw and Eugene A. Nida,[10] the words εἰκών and μορφή do not occur as synonyms. Yet without any argument or evidence, BeDuhn equates form with image as if this is something that is obvious or even possible. But, there is no basis upon which to make such an association. To equate form and image is a theological interpretation that smacks of theological bias. In fact, the question in BeDuhn's book is supposed to be about translation, not about "echos," and to refer an "echo," whatever that means, is decidedly an interpretive issue, an issue in which BeDuhn specifically said he would not become involved.

Understand, we are not saying that Jesus is not the image of God in the sense that the word εἰκών (*eikōn*, "image") might be used to express this. In fact, Jesus is specifically referred to as the image of God in Col. 1:5: "And He is the image [εἰκών, *eikōn*] of the invisible God, the firstborn of all creation." Rather, what we are saying is that the words 'form' (μορφή, *morphē*) and 'image' (εἰκών, *eikōn*) are never equated so

---

[10] *Greek-English Lexicon of the New Testament Based on Semantic Domains*, 2d ed. (1996), s.v. "6.96–6.101."

In the Form of God

that they may be thought to indicate or to be referring to the same thing with reference to mere humans. Whatever else the word 'image' may indicate, it does not indicate the same thing that the word 'form' indicates. The words 'form' and 'image' can certainly be predicated of the same individual, Jesus, for example, but that does not make the meanings of these words synonymous. The words 'son' and 'father' can be predicated of the same person, but that does not make these two words mean the same thing. They are not synonyms.

So, it is perfectly reasonable, and literal, and accurate to conclude that the two terms can be used of Jesus even though they have two different meanings. Jesus is both the image of God and was in the form of God. In fact, in Heb. 1:3 the text declares that Jesus is "the radiance of His glory and the exact representation [χαρακτὴρ, *charaktēr*] of His nature [ὑποστάσεως, *hupostaseōs*]." Concerning this very verse, LSL says, "*real nature, essence*, χαρακτὴρ τῆς ὑ. Ep.Hebr.1.3."[11] Although mere humans might be said to be in the image of God, they could never be said to be in form of God.

One look at LSL will inform the reader why BeDuhn did not want to spend much time with this word. According to LSL, the word *morphē* can be used to indicate "kind, sort."[12] The word is used in this sense in Judg. 8:18:

Table #17: Judg. 8:18

καὶ εἶπεν πρὸς Ζεβεε καὶ Σαλμανα ποῦ οἱ ἄνδρες οὓς ἀπεκτείνατε ἐν Θαβωρ καὶ εἶπαν ὡσεὶ σὺ ὅμοιος σοί ὅμοιος αὐτῶν ὡς εἶδος μορφὴ [כְּתֹאַר] υἱῶν βασιλέων (GSEPT).
וַיֹּאמֶר אֶל־זֶבַח וְאֶל־צַלְמֻנָּע אֵיפֹה הָאֲנָשִׁים אֲשֶׁר הֲרַגְתֶּם בְּתָבוֹר וַיֹּאמְרוּ כָּמוֹךָ כְמוֹהֶם אֶחָד כְּתֹאַר [μορφὴ] בְּנֵי הַמֶּלֶךְ: (BHS)
"Then he said to Zebah and Zalmunna, 'What kind of men *were* they whom you killed at Tabor?' And they said, 'They were like you, each appearing as having the form [μορφὴ, כְּתֹאַר] of the son of the king'" (NASBU).

The context of this verse is the actions of Gideon questioning Zebah and Zalmunna, kings of Midian, having defeated them and captured them. Sir Lancelot Brenton translates the GSEPT as: "And he said to Zebee and Salmana, 'Where are the men whom ye slew in Thabor?' and they said, 'As thou, so *were* they, according to the likeness of the son of a king.'"[13] The expression ποῦ οἱ ἄνδρες, is translated by Brenton as "where are the men." The Hebrew text uses the word אֵיפֹה (*'êfōh*) which can be translated "where."[14] The NASBU opted to translate this, "What kind of men." Neither

---

[11] LSL, s.v. "ὑπόστασις."
[12] LSL, s.v. "μορφή."
[13] Sir Lancelot Charles Lee Brenton, *The Septuagint Version of the Old Testament According to the Vatican Text* (London: Samuel Bagster and Sons, 1844), Judg. 8:18.
[14] KBH, s.v. "אֵיפֹה."

KBH nor Waltke-O'Conner[15] give "what kind" as a possible use of this word. However, from the response to the question it seems more likely that the question concerns the identity of the men they slew, not their location. Gideon is asking Zebee and Zalmunna to give him some sort of description so that he can discover whether the men they slew were related to him.

The response of Zebee and Zalmunna is that the men were the same kind of person as Gideon (כָּמוֹךָ, kāmôkā, "as you"), having the form of (כְּתֹאַר, k^{e}tō'ar) the sons of the king. It may be thought that since the word "sons of" (בְּנֵי, benê) does not have the definite article that it should be translated "sons of" rather than "the sons of." This is a common misunderstanding of Hebrew grammar. Because the word "sons of" (it is one word in Hebrew) is in a construct relation to the following word "the king" (הַמֶּלֶךְ, hammelek), and since this word does have the definite article, that renders definite the word in the construct state. The word in the construct state—in this instance בְּנֵי, (benê)—never takes the definite article but is always definite if the word to which it is related is definite. So, this should be translated, "the sons of the king."

So, the testimony of Zebee and Zalmunna is that these men had the form (μορφή, כְּתֹאַר) of the sons of the king. In other words, they appeared to be sons of the king. They are saying that these men gave this impression of the kind of men they were. So, here, the word 'form' indicates the kind of men. That is to say, by their form they gave the impression of being of a certain kind of man. Since this is a possible meaning, and it is highly probable in this context, then we can argue that this is what is meant in the Phil. 2:6. Paul is saying that Jesus was not holding on to the form that would indicate the kind of Being His is, namely, God.

In fact, the use of the word μορφή to indicate the kind of something is found Plato's *Republic*: "Τί δὲ τὸ τοῦ ἑτέρου εἶδος; οὐ τῶν ἐναντίων δεῖται, πασῶν μὲν ἁρμονιῶν δὲ ῥυθμῶν, εἰ μέλλει αὖ οἰκείως λέγεσθαι, διὰ τὸ παντοδαπὰς μορφὰς τῶν μεταβολῶν ἔχειν;"[16] G. M. A. Grube gives the following translation: "What about the other kind of style [εἶδος]? Doesn't it require the opposite if it is to speak appropriately, namely, all kinds [πασῶν] of musical modes and all kinds of rhythms, because it contains every type [μορφὰς] of variation?"[17] Here the musical modes and rhythms are of all kinds because they contain every type [μορφὰς] of variation. That is a variation is of every kind.

LSL places the Phil. 2:6 use under the definition "generally, form, fashion, appearance, outward form."[18] But any one of these definitions is not inimical to the notion of kind or sort. It is by virtue of the form, fashion, appearance, or outward form that we are able to identify anything according to its kind. As philosophers say, we are able to know the nature or essence of anything through its accidents. This seems to be

---

[15] Bruce K. Waltke and M. O'Connor, *An Introduction to Biblical Hebrew Syntax* (Winona Lake, Indiana: Eisenbrauns, 1990).

[16] Plato, Πολιτεια, in *Platonis Opera* (Oxford: Oxford University Press, 1989), 397c.3–6.

[17] Plato, *Republic*, trans. G. M. A. Grube, rev. C. D. C. Rever, in *Plato Complete Works*, ed. John M. Cooper (Indianapolis: Hackett Publishing Company, 1997), 397c.

[18] LSL, s.v. "μορφή."

In the Form of God

precisely what Judg. 8:18 is saying. The men were able to understand what kind of men these were because they had the form, *morphē*, of the sons of the king.

If Phil. 2:6 is saying that Jesus was not grasping at the form that would indicate that He is the same kind of being as God, it makes no sense to think He did not already have this, since it would be impossible and therefore irrational for anyone to think that he might somehow become the same kind of being that God is. In other words, it is not possible to *become* God, since God is eternal and immutable. Since it is not possible to become God, it is not possible to take on the form of God. Since no one can take on the form of God, why even talk about not grasping something that obviously cannot be acquired anyway. That would be like saying, "I chose not to fly to the Moon using only my arms": "I chose not to become God." This must be something one already has because it cannot be acquired. So the grasping must be a holding on to something Jesus already had. Unless BeDuhn wants us to think that Jesus was irrational, taking this to refer to something Jesus already possessed is just as literal and just as rational and logical as anything BeDuhn proposes. Jesus laid aside the form of God that would show His glory. He veiled the brightness of His glory with His flesh, as Moses hid the shining of his face with a veil.

Now BeDuhn makes an important observation that we must not miss. He says, "Now, the Greek word *morphē* ('form') is fairly generic, and can mean a number of things. But it does not mean 'nature' or 'essence,' nor does it signify that anything 'was' or was 'one with' something else."[19] BeDuhn is exactly correct that *morphē* does not mean "nature" or "essence." This is particularly true if we take the words 'nature' and 'essence' in their strict philosophical sense. However, if we take the word *morphē* to indicate the outward form or shape or appearance of anything—all those characteristics that would fall under the heading of accidents—it is *through* the form or *morphē* of anything that we are able to perceive a thing's essence or nature. Jesus could not divest Himself of the essence of God, but He could lay aside the outward appearance/form/*morphē* and take upon Himself the appearance/form/*morphē* of a servant. But, the point that BeDuhn misses is that the *morphē* **indicates** the kind or nature or essence of anything. It is through the *morphē* that we know what kind of thing anything actually is. Jesus took upon Himself the form of a servant, which is exactly what He was—the Servant of YHWH.

The fact that the word μορφή can be used to indicate "kind," in the sense that the nature of anything is indicated by its *morphē*, is also clear from the fact that the word μορφή is used in Phil. 2:7 to assert that Christ took upon Himself the "form of a servant."

Table #18: Phil. 2:7–8

ἀλλὰ	ἑαυτὸν	ἐκένωσεν	μορφὴν
But	himself	he emptied	form

---

[19] BeDuhn, *Translation*, 53.

δούλου	λαβών	ἐν	ὁμοιώματι
of servant	receiving	in	likeness
ἀνθρώπων	γενόμενος	καὶ	σχήματι
of men	becoming	and	outward appearance
εὑρεθεὶς	ὡς	ἄνθρωπος	ἐταπείνωσεν
having been found	as	man	he humbled
ἑαυτὸν	γενόμενος	ὑπήκοος	μέχρι
himself	having become	obedient	to the extent
θανάτου	θανάτου	δὲ	σταυροῦ
of death	death	even	of cross.

This cannot mean simply that He appeared to look like a servant or that the merely appeared to be a servant but really was not a servant. Rather, this is the kind of position He took upon Himself—He became a servant. In Matt. 20:28 Jesus said, "just as the Son of Man did not come to be served, but to serve, and to give His life a ransom for many."[20] Of course BeDuhn might object that in this verse Jesus is not using the term δοῦλος (*doulos*) but is using rather the word δικονέω (*dikoneō*). However, this objection does not work in light of the previous verses: "It is not this way among you, but whoever wishes to become great among you shall be your servant, and whoever wishes to be first among you shall be your slave" (Matt. 20:26–27).[21] In these verses Jesus uses the word δοῦλος as the one who is doing the work of a διάκονος (*diakonos*). Then He uses the comparative ὥσπερ (*hōsper*) to compare Himself with the requirements He has placed on His disciples. LSL gives one of the possible meanings of ὥσπερ (*hōsper*) as "just exactly as."[22] There are certainly other possible meanings, but this is one of them, and it is perfectly reasonable for Jesus to be telling the disciples to do exactly as He has done, that is, to become a slave/servant (δοῦλος, *doulos*), the term that Paul uses.

So, Jesus did not simply appear to be a servant. By putting on the form of a servant, He made Himself a servant. Likewise, to be in the form of God is not simply to appear

---

[20] ὥσπερ ὁ υἱὸς τοῦ ἀνθρώπου οὐκ ἦλθεν διακονηθῆναι ἀλλὰ διακονῆσαι καὶ δοῦναι τὴν ψυχὴν αὐτοῦ λύτρον ἀντὶ πολλῶν (Matt. 20:28).

[21] οὐχ οὕτως ἔσται ἐν ὑμῖν, ἀλλ' ὃς ἐὰν θέλῃ ἐν ὑμῖν μέγας γενέσθαι ἔσται ὑμῶν διάκονος, καὶ ὃς ἂν θέλῃ ἐν ὑμῖν εἶναι πρῶτος ἔσται ὑμῶν δοῦλος· (Matt. 20:26–27).

[22] LSL, s.v. "ὥσπερ."

In the Form of God

to be like God, but to be God, to have the nature or essence of God that is indicated by the *morphē*. The *morphē* indicates the nature or essence that someone actually possesses. This is not something that someone can obtain. Rather, this is something that someone must already have and be. Jesus was and is God, but He did not grasp at the *morphē* of God, but humbled Himself to become a servant. He did not cease being God. Rather, He laid aside the *morphē* by which His essence could be perceived so that when we look at Him, "He has no *stately* form or majesty that we should look upon Him, nor appearance that we should be attracted to Him" (Isa. 53:2). Having the *morphē* of God is not something that can be acquired. It is irrational to think that Jesus decided not to grasp after a *morphē* that was impossible to acquire. Jesus already possessed the *morphē* of God, but He was willing to lay this aside and take on the *morphē* of a servant.

This may not convince BeDuhn, but it shows that the traditional translations are just as reasonable, and just as literal, and just as accurate as anything BeDuhn proposes, and it is not bias that has produced these translations. In fact, BeDuhn's own theological bias is revealed by his claim that humans lost the image of God. This is a theological point that BeDuhn has imported into the discussion that is the basis upon which he floats his possible understanding of the meaning of the term *morphē*. In fact, this particular theological position is advocated by the Jehovah's Witnesses, which gives the reader a hint to BeDuhn's own theological bias. Nowhere does the Bible say that humans lost the image of God. In fact, Gen. 5:1–3 indicates that the image of God is passed from father to son. The text of these verses is laid out below with the English translation, the Hebrew text, and the Greek text below.

Table #19: Gen. 5:1–3

1	"This is the book of the generations of Adam. In the day when God created man, He made him in the likeness of God" (NASBU).
	זֶה סֵפֶר תּוֹלְדֹת אָדָם בְּיוֹם בְּרֹא אֱלֹהִים אָדָם בִּדְמוּת אֱלֹהִים עָשָׂה אֹתוֹ: (BHS)
	αὕτη ἡ βίβλος γενέσεως ἀνθρώπων ᾗ ἡμέρᾳ ἐποίησεν ὁ θεὸς τὸν Αδαμ κατ' εἰκόνα θεοῦ ἐποίησεν αὐτόν (GSEPT)
2	"He created them male and female, and He blessed them and named them Man in the day when they were created" (NASBU).
	זָכָר וּנְקֵבָה בְּרָאָם וַיְבָרֶךְ אֹתָם וַיִּקְרָא אֶת־שְׁמָם אָדָם בְּיוֹם הִבָּרְאָם: (BHS)
	ἄρσεν καὶ θῆλυ ἐποίησεν αὐτοὺς καὶ εὐλόγησεν αὐτοὺς καὶ ἐπωνόμασεν τὸ ὄνομα αὐτῶν Αδαμ ᾗ ἡμέρᾳ ἐποίησεν αὐτούς (GSEPT)

3	"When Adam had lived one hundred and thirty years, he became the father of a son in his own likeness, according to his image, and named him Seth" (NASBU).
	וַיְחִי אָדָם שְׁלֹשִׁים וּמְאַת שָׁנָה וַיּוֹלֶד בִּדְמוּתוֹ כְּצַלְמוֹ וַיִּקְרָא אֶת־שְׁמוֹ שֵׁת: (BHS)
	ἔζησεν δὲ Αδαμ διακόσια καὶ τριάκοντα ἔτη καὶ ἐγέννησεν κατὰ τὴν ἰδέαν αὐτοῦ καὶ κατὰ τὴν εἰκόνα αὐτοῦ καὶ ἐπωνόμασεν τὸ ὄνομα αὐτοῦ Σηθ (GSEPT)

The clear implication of the passage is that the image of God in which Adam was created was passed on to his son, Seth. Since Adam was created in the image of God, and Seth was created in the image of Adam, it follows that the image of God was passed on to Seth. Certainly the image was marred by the fall; but it was not lost. Even in the account of the fall itself there is no indication that the image of God was somehow lost. In fact, in Gen. 9:6 God told Noah, "Whoever sheds man's blood, by man his blood shall be shed, for in the image of God [בְּצֶלֶם אֱלֹהִים, b^eselem $^{\prime e}l\bar{o}h\hat{\imath}m$] He made man." This could not be a reference simply to Adam since Adam was long dead when God spoke to Noah. It is because man was created in the image of God that the man who kills another man will himself be executed. So, there is simply no basis upon which BeDuhn's proposal can be reasonable, and there is every indication that his argument is theologically motivated. BeDuhn is not so free from theological bias as he would like his readers to think.

Apologetics Points

Our study of the evidence shows that Phil. 2:5–6 is clearly saying that Jesus did not hold on to the form of God, a form which He already possessed, and that He laid aside the form of God and took upon Himself the form of a servant. Out study of the evidence yields these two important apologetic points:

1. The evidence from the standard Greek lexicons, including the Liddell & Scott Greek-English Lexicon shows that ἁρπαγμός (*harpagmos*) can be used to mean "grasping onto something that one already possesses."

2. The evidence from the standard Greek lexicons, including the Liddell & Scott Greek-English Lexicon shows that the word μορφή (*morphē*) can be used to refer to individuals of the same kind. Phil. 2:6 says that Jesus is the same kind of being as God.

CHAPTER 4

BY HIM ALL THINGS WERE CREATED

Introduction

Colossians 1:15–20 is probably one of the most important passages for Jehovah's Witnesses in their efforts to show that Jesus is a created being. Jehovah's Witness missionaries are trained in the use of this passage to argue against Christ's deity. The strength of the orthodox position is the opening statement of verse 16: "For by Him all things were created" (NASB). If Jesus is the Creator of all things, then He is Himself not a created Being. To avoid the obvious implication of this statement, the New World Translation adds the word 'other' so that the passage reads: "because by means of him all [other] things were created." The New World Translation adds the word 'other' after the word 'all' to indicate that Jesus is the creator of all the other created things, making Jesus a created being. Only the New World Translation does this, and modern commentators argue that there is no justification for this addition.

In the chapter titled "Probing The Implicit Meaning,"[1] BeDuhn discusses the notion that there are implicit meanings that translators sometimes make explicit in their translations and sometimes do not. He focuses in on Col. 1:15–20 concerning which he says, "It is a tricky passage where every translation does and must 'add words.'"[2] Once again we have set out the passage below, this time with the NASBU translation (I have used the following form rather than the word-for-word form as above due to space constraints):

Table #20: Col. 1:15–20

15	ὅς ἐστιν εἰκὼν τοῦ θεοῦ τοῦ ἀοράτου, πρωτότοκος πάσης κτίσεως,
	And He is the image of the invisible God, the firstborn of all creation.

---

[1] BeDuhn, *Translation*, 75–88.
[2] Ibid., 77.

16	ὅτι ἐν αὐτῷ ἐκτίσθη τὰ πάντα ἐν τοῖς οὐρανοῖς καὶ ἐπὶ τῆς γῆς, τὰ ὁρατὰ καὶ τὰ ἀόρατα, εἴτε θρόνοι εἴτε κυριότητες εἴτε ἀρχαὶ εἴτε ἐξουσίαι· τὰ πάντα δι' αὐτοῦ καὶ εἰς αὐτὸν ἔκτισται·
	For by Him all things were created, *both* in the heavens and on earth, visible and invisible, whether thrones or dominions or rulers or authorities–all things have been created through Him and for Him.
17	καὶ αὐτός ἐστιν πρὸ πάντων καὶ τὰ πάντα ἐν αὐτῷ συνέστηκεν,
	He is before all things, and in Him all things hold together.
18	καὶ αὐτός ἐστιν ἡ κεφαλὴ τοῦ σώματος τῆς ἐκκλησίας· ὅς ἐστιν ἀρχή, πρωτότοκος ἐκ τῶν νεκρῶν, ἵνα γένηται ἐν πᾶσιν αὐτὸς πρωτεύων,
	He is also head of the body, the church; and He is the beginning, the firstborn from the dead, so that He Himself will come to have first place in everything.
19	ὅτι ἐν αὐτῷ εὐδόκησεν πᾶν τὸ πλήρωμα κατοικῆσαι
	For it was the *Father's* good pleasure for all the fullness to dwell in Him,
20	καὶ δι' αὐτοῦ ἀποκαταλλάξαι τὰ πάντα εἰς αὐτόν, εἰρηνοποιήσας διὰ τοῦ αἵματος τοῦ σταυροῦ αὐτοῦ, (δι' αὐτοῦ) εἴτε τὰ ἐπὶ τῆς γῆς εἴτε τὰ ἐν τοῖς οὐρανοῖς.
	and through Him to reconcile all things to Himself, having made peace through the blood of His cross; through Him, *I say*, whether things on earth or things in heaven

Firstborn Over Creation

Use of the Genitive

BeDuhn sets out the passages of various translations and makes observations concerning each. Of the NIV BeDuhn says, "In the NIV, the translators have first of all replaced the 'of' of the phrase 'firstborn of creation' with 'over.' This qualifies as addition because 'over' in no way can be derived from the Greek genitive article meaning 'of.'"[3] The NIV translation is: "He is the image of the invisible God, the firstborn *over* all creation." The Greek phrase of concern is πρωτότοκος πάσης κτίσεως (*prōtotokos pasēs ktiseōs*). It is unclear what BeDuhn means by the expression "Greek Genitive article," since there is no "genitive article" in this phrase.[4] Apparently he is referring to the word "of" which is in fact not even a separate word in the Greek text, and the English word 'of' is not an article. There is a Genitive adjective πάσης, translated "all" or "every." Irrespective of the item to which BeDuhn is referring, he is simply wrong that this notion of "over" can "in no way be derived from the Greek genitive . . ." In fact, Daniel Wallace discusses the use of the Genitive case in which

---

[3] Ibid., 81.
[4] Neither the UBS4 nor the Nestle-Aland 27 indicate a variant here.

there are two possibilities that would justify the addition of the word "over" in the NIV.[5] Also, take for example the statement in Rev. 1:5: "and from Jesus Christ, the faithful witness, the firstborn of the dead, and the ruler of the kings of the earth." The phrase "the ruler of the kings of the earth" is a translation of ὁ ἄρχων τῶν βασιλέων τῆς γῆς. The word "of the kings" is a plural Genitive. It is not difficult to see that the phrase could easily be translated "the one ruling *over* the kings of the earth."

But BeDuhn prefers the grammar of Herbert Weir Smyth.[6] So, let us look at it. First of all, concerning Genitives in general, Smyth points out that Genitives with nouns "is often so loose that it is difficult to include with precision all cases under specific grammatical classes."[7] Nevertheless, when discussing the Genitive of place, Smyth translates πεδίοιο διωκέμεν as *"to chase over the plain."*[8] Now this does not necessarily correspond precisely to the construction in Col. 1:15, but it shows that BeDuhn is simply wrong that the word 'over' can in no way be derived from the Greek Genitive. His own favorite grammar contradicts him.

But notice how BeDuhn characterizes the NIV. He says, "the translators have first of all replaced the 'of' . . . with 'over.'" This may seem like a small matter, but it is tremendously important for the purpose of prejudicing the reader. It is called "poisoning the well." By characterizing the NIV translation as "replacing" something, BeDuhn covertly implies that the word "of" is supposed to be there, and the NIV translators have done something wrong. The fact of the matter is, the word 'over' is just as legitimate as the word 'of,' and the NIV translators have not "replaced" anything. Rather, they have simply translated the passage as they understand it. BeDuhn uses this tactic throughout his book. He covertly attempts to prejudice the reader toward his bias before presenting any evidence in support of his claims.

Getting back to the adverbial use of the Genitive, an adverbial Genitive is one that has the force of an adverb, but may modify either a verb, adjective, or noun. In the case of modifying a noun, there is, as Wallace puts it, "usually an implicit verbal idea in the noun."[9] The noun "creation" certainly has a verbal sense to it. A specific instance of an adverbial use would be the sense of reference. According to Wallace, the Genitive of Reference "usually modifies an adjective (although rarely it will be connected to a noun), and as such its adverbial force is self-evident. The Genitive limits the frame of reference of the adjective" or noun.[10] Wallace cites Matt. 21:21 as an instance of this kind of use: "you shall do not only what [was done] with reference to the fig tree" (οὐ μόνον τὸ τῆς συκῆς ποιήσετε (*ou monon to tēs sukēs poiēsete*). As a Genitive of Reference, the statement in Col. 1:15 could be rendered, "who is the first-born with

---

[5] GGBTB, 104ff.
[6] Herbert Weir Smyth, "Author's Preface," in *Greek Grammar* (Cambridge, Massachusetts: Harvard University Press, 1984).
[7] Ibid., §1295.
[8] Ibid., §1448.
[9] GGBTB, 121.
[10] Ibid., 127.

reference to all creation." So, if this category is legitimately applied to the Colossian passage, the addition of the word 'over' makes perfect sense. The word 'over' is used by the NIV in order to express the notion of "with reference to."

In fact, concerning Col. 1:15 Nigel Turner states, "It is debatable whether we have a partitive gen. in Col. 1^{15} (πρωτότοκος πάσης κτίσεως) and Rev 3^{14} (ἡ ἀρχὴ τῆς κτίσεως) = *among*, or whether the idea is not rather that of rule and supremacy."[11] In other words, if the sense of the Genitive here is that of rule and supremacy, then again the use of the word 'over' makes perfect sense. What this indicates is that the meaning of these words is not as straightforward a matter as BeDuhn would try to make out, and his choice is just as much a function of his own interpretation as any of those he criticizes. BeDuhn's comment, "Whereas 'of' appears to make Jesus part of creation, 'over' sets him apart from it,"[12] is only the case if one already assumes that Jesus is either part of creation or not. As BeDuhn himself admitted, the translation of these verses is tricky, and one's prior assumptions will predispose him to translate them in a certain way. But this is as true of BeDuhn as anyone else, and his pretense of being more objective is a smoke screen. His theological bias is no more evident than in the kind of statement, "'of' appears to make Jesus part of creation . . ." Another tactic of BeDuhn is to try to make his reader think that his own observations are necessitated by the Greek when in fact they are just as much a part of his own interpretative perspective.

Meaning of Πρωτότοκος

TDNT makes the following observations about the term πρωτότοκος:

A. The Word Group outside the New Testament.

1. πρωτότοκος, "firstborn," is rare outside the Bible and does not occur at all prior to the GSEPT. Better attested and earlier (Hom.) is the act. form πρωτοτόκος, "bearing for the first time," of animals and men. Also common in the sense of "firstborn" from Hom. on is πρωτόγονος, which can also mean "first in rank"; in this instance the act. form is rare and late (Polyb.).

B. The Word Group in the New Testament

3. As there is no great emphasis on -τοκος in the πρωτότοκος of R. 8:29, so it is also in Col. 1:18, where Christ is called πρωτότοκος ἐκ τῶν νεκρῶν. The expressions ἀπαρχὴ τῶν κεκοιμημένων in 1 C. 15:20 and πρῶτος ἐξ ἀναστάσεως νεκρων in Ac. 26:23 are close parallels which show that what is denoted here is that Christ is the first to have risen from the dead.

---

[11] Nigel Turner, *Syntax*, vol. 3, *A Grammar of New Testament Greek*, by James Hope Moulton and Nigel Turner (Edinburgh: T. & T. Clark, 1963), 210.

[12] BeDuhn, *Translation*, 81.

5. The description of Christ as πρωτότοκος πάσης κτίσεως in Col. 1:15 obviously finds in the ὅτι clause of v. 16 its more precise basis and explanation: Christ is the Mediator at creation to whom all creatures without exception owe their creation, → V, 894, 28 ff., 37 ff. Hence πρωτότοκος πάσης κτίσεως does not simply denote the priority in time of the pre-existent Lord. If the expression refers to the mediation of creation through Christ, it cannot be saying at the same time that He was created as the first creature. The decisive objection to this view, which sees in the πάση κγίσεως a partitive genitive, is that it would demand emphasis on the -τοκος, whereas with the exception of Lk. 2:7 (→ 876, 6 ff), which refers to literal birth, the -τοκος is never emphasised in the NT in passages which speak of Christ, especially Col. 1:18 (→ 877, 15 ff). A further point is that this view would bring -τοκος into tension with κτίσις (and κτίζεσθαι in 1:16), for creation and birth are different concepts and πρωτότοκος cannot be regarded as simply a synonym for πρωτόκτιστος. The only remaining possibility is to take πρωτότοκος hierarchically (→ line 7 f.). What is meant is the unique supremacy of Christ over all creatures as the Mediator of their creation. The succeeding statement in 1:17a: αὐτός ἐστιν πρὸ πάντων, emphasizes the same supremacy, while 1:17b draws the conclusion from 1:16.[13]

In other words, the term πρωτότοκος can be used to indicate supremacy or priority, and this possibility must be taken into consideration when translating the verse. However, BeDuhn does not even consider this information in his evaluation, but rather launches into a discussion about the word πᾶν, which occurs in the text as πάσης and is translated "all." He declares, "But the Greek *pan*, various forms of which are used in this passage, means simply 'all,' and the phrase could just as well be translated 'all [others].'"[14] But this cannot be the case if the word πρωτότοκος means "supremacy or priority" as TDNT indicates. By not considering this possibility, BeDuhn once again reveals his own theological bias, this time in the form of selective reporting. He simply ignores some of the evidence that is critical in producing an accurate translation, and he reports only that information that supports his own view.

When Does 'All' Actually Mean 'All'?

In fact, he admits that in this sentence Jesus is an exception not included in the word "all": "'All' includes every being and force and substance in the universe, with the exception, of course, of God and, semantically speaking, Jesus, since it is his role in relation to the 'all' that is being discussed."[15] BeDuhn attempts to blunt the force of this point by discussing the hyperbolic use of the word "all."

"All" is commonly used in Greek as a hyperbole, that is, an exaggeration. The "other" is assumed. In one case, Paul takes the trouble to make this perfectly clear. In 1 Corinthians 15, Paul catches himself saying that God will make all things subject to Christ. He stops and clarifies that "of course" when he says "all things" he doesn't mean that God himself will be

---

[13] TDNT, s.v. "πρωτότοκος."
[14] BeDuhn, *Translation*, 84.
[15] Ibid.

subject to Christ, but all other things will be, with Christ himself subject to God. There can be no legitimate objection to "other" in Colossians 1, because here, too, Paul clearly does not mean to include God or Christ in his phrase "all things," when God is the implied subject, and Christ the explicit agent, of the act of creation of these "all things." But since Paul uses "all things" appositively (that is, interchangeably) with "creation," we must still reckon with Christ's place as the firstborn of creation, and the soul of the firstborn of "all things."[16]

But BeDuhn's argument actually argues against his position. He says, "In 1 Corinthians 15, Paul catches himself saying that God will make all things subject to Christ. He stops and clarifies that 'of course' when he says 'all things' he doesn't mean that God himself will be subject to Christ, but all other things will be, with Christ himself subject to God." In other words, Paul realized that without his further explanation, it would have been perfectly legitimate to understand his statement to include God. In order to prevent this understanding, Paul explains that he excepts God in Christ's rule. But in Col. 1:16 Paul does not stop and clarify the use of all because he wants the reader to understand the 'all' as meaning 'all,' not 'all other.' So, contrary to BeDuhn's claim that there can be no legitimate objection to the word 'other' in Colossians 1, BeDuhn's own argument proves that there is in fact no legitimate reason for including 'other.'

BeDuhn considers other examples of how the word 'all' can be used in a hyperbolic sense. But all this, though perhaps interesting, neglects to present the full lexical possibilities for the use of the word. Numerous instances could be cited in which 'all' is not used hyperbolically, but BeDuhn doesn't consider any of this evidence in reference to the question in Colossians 1. How a word *can* be used merely presents the range of possibilities, but it does not directly address how the word *is* being used in a given instance. And by neglecting to present all the evidence, BeDuhn has once again presented a one-sided picture for his reader—selective reporting—revealing his own bias.

Neglect of Contrary Evidence

In his concluding remarks on this chapter, BeDuhn says:

So what exactly are objectors to "other" arguing for as the meaning of the phrase "all things"? That Christ created himself (v. 16)? That Christ is before God and that God was made to exist by means of Christ (v. 17)? That Christ, too, needs to be reconciled to God (v. 20)? When we spell out what is denied by the use of "other" we can see clearly how absurd the objection is. "Other" is implied in "all," and the NW simply makes what is implicit explicit. You can argue whether it is necessary or not to do this. But I think the objections that have been raised to it show that it is, in fact, necessary, because those who object want to negate the meaning of the

---

[16] Ibid.

phrase "firstborn of a creation." If adding "other" prevents this misreading of the biblical text, then it is useful to have it there.[17]

But BeDuhn has omitted the primary objection that others bring against the addition of the word 'other.' The primary objection is that it implies that Jesus is a created being, which is the primary theological motivation for the translators of the NW adding the word. Either BeDuhn is unaware of this point, which means, being uninformed of the issues, he is not as qualified to make these kinds of evaluations as he thinks, or he deliberately omitted this objection, which means that he is once again demonstrating his own theological bias. This, of course, calls into question his own motivation and contradicts his introductory claims about not having a stake in the issue. Also, BeDuhn has attempted to justify his claims by appealing to theological issues, something he specifically denied he was doing. Either BeDuhn is incompetent or disingenuous. Either way his comments do not tell the whole story.

The word 'other' is not implied in the text of Colossians, at least BeDuhn has not made that case, and to claim that the objections are "absurd" flies in the face of centuries of theological debate and argument by competent theologians, linguists, exegetes, etc. BeDuhn's arrogance is more evident here than in his earlier assertions. He has not entered into the full fledged debate but has, instead, given a one-sided presentation with selective evidence, and then he charges others with being absurd. The fact that BeDuhn has employed his own theological perspective in his evaluation is clear from his statement about the meaning of the phrase "firstborn of creation." Earlier he flatly declared, "they [those who object to the addition of the word 'other'] don't want to accept the obvious and clear sense of 'first-born of creation' as identifying Jesus as 'of creation.'"[18] And this is precisely the objection that others have to adding the word 'other,' an objection that BeDuhn conveniently leaves out in his brief survey of to what objectors are objecting.

BeDuhn talks about the "shocking willingness of translators to freely add words and ideas not supported or in any way implied in the Greek,"[19] and yet BeDuhn's analysis has revealed his own shocking willingness to misrepresent the case and to promote a theological bias while denying that this is what he is doing. In fact, contrary to BeDuhn's assertions, many of the words added to the text have as much or more support than the addition of the word 'other,' an addition that can be made only on the basis of a prior theological assumption. There is in fact no grammatical or syntactical reason for adding the word 'other,' since neither God nor Jesus are created beings. Of course this is a theological assumption on my part, but likewise the only reason for adding 'other' is to try to make the text explicitly say what the translators of the NW believe, namely, that Christ is a created being—a theological assumption on their part—and on BeDuhn's part.

---

[17] Ibid., 85.
[18] Ibid., 84.
[19] Ibid., 86.

However, even the bare text with no additions argues against this assumption, and the context makes this clear. Of course the immediate context is another factor that BeDuhn has conveniently neglected to discuss in his analysis of translations, and for good reason. The context militates against his claims. Consider Col. 1:16–17:

> Because by Him all things were created the all in the heavens and upon the earth, the visible and the invisible, whether thrones, whether dominions, whether rulers, whether authorities–the all through Him and by Him have been created, and He is before the all, and the all by Him hold together (Col. 1:16–17).

Table #21: Col. 1:16–17

ὅτι	ἐν	αὐτῷ	ἐκτίσθη
Because	by	Him	were created
τὰ	πάντα	ἐν	τοῖς
the	all	in	the
οὐρανοῖς	καὶ	ἐπὶ	τῆς
heavens	and	upon	the
γῆς	τὰ	ὁρατὰ	καὶ
earth	the	visible	and
τὰ	ἀόρατα	εἴτε	θρόνοι
the	invisible	whether	thrones
εἴτε	κυριότητες	εἴτε	ἀρχαὶ
whether	dominions	whether	rulers
εἴτε	ἐξουσίαι·	τὰ	πάντα
whether	authorities.	The	all
δι'	αὐτοῦ	καὶ	εἰς
through	Him	and	unto
αὐτὸν	ἔκτισται·	καὶ	αὐτός
Him	have been created.	and	He

ἐστιν	πρὸ	πάντων	καὶ
is	before	all	and
τὰ	πάντα	ἐν	αὐτῷ
the	all	by	Him

συνέστηκεν

are held together

An important point in these verses is the fact that the text states in verse 16 that Jesus created "the all" (τὰ πάντα, *ta panta*). A look at every instance in Paul's literature (excluding the Colossians verses which are the point of contention) where he uses the word 'all' with the definite article shows that it would be absurd to add the word 'other' in any of these contexts.

Table #22: Paul's Use of "The All"

Rom. 8:32	"He who did not spare His own Son, but delivered Him over for us all, how will He not also with Him freely give us the all [τὰ πάντα]?"
	ὅς γε τοῦ ἰδίου υἱοῦ οὐκ ἐφείσατο ἀλλὰ ὑπὲρ ἡμῶν πάντων παρέδωκεν αὐτόν, πῶς οὐχὶ καὶ σὺν αὐτῷ τὰ πάντα ἡμῖν χαρίσεται
Rom. 11:32	"For God has shut up the all [τοὺς πάντας] in disobedience so that He may show mercy to all."
	συνέκλεισεν γὰρ ὁ θεὸς τοὺς πάντας εἰς ἀπείθειαν, ἵνα τοὺς πάντας ἐλεήσῃ.
Rom. 11:36	"For from Him and through Him and to Him are the all [τὰ πάντα]. To Him the glory forever. Amen."
	ὅτι ἐξ αὐτοῦ καὶ δι' αὐτοῦ καὶ εἰς αὐτὸν τὰ πάντα· αὐτῷ ἡ δόξα εἰς τοὺς αἰῶνας, ἀμήν.
1 Cor. 8:6	"yet for us there is one God, the Father, from whom are the all [τὰ πάντα] and we for Him; and one Lord, Jesus Christ, by whom are the all [τὰ πάντα], and we through Him."
	ἀλλ' ἡμῖν εἷς θεὸς ὁ πατὴρ ἐξ οὗ τὰ πάντα καὶ ἡμεῖς εἰς αὐτόν, καὶ εἷς κύριος Ἰησοῦς Χριστὸς δι' οὗ τὰ πάντα καὶ ἡμεῖς δι' αὐτοῦ.

1 Cor. 9:22	"To the weak I became weak, that I might win the weak; I have become all [τοῖς πᾶσιν] to all men, so that I may by all means save some."
	ἐγενόμην τοῖς ἀσθενέσιν ἀσθενής, ἵνα τοὺς ἀσθενεῖς κερδήσω· τοῖς πᾶσιν γέγονα πάντα, ἵνα πάντως τινὰς σώσω.
1 Cor. 12:6	"There are varieties of effects, but the same God who works the all [τὰ πάντα] in all."
	καὶ διαιρέσεις ἐνεργημάτων εἰσίν, ὁ δὲ αὐτὸς θεὸς ὁ ἐνεργῶν τὰ πάντα ἐν πᾶσιν,
1 Cor. 12:19	"If they were the all [τὰ πάντα] one member, where would the body be?"
	εἰ δὲ ἦν τὰ πάντα ἓν μέλος, ποῦ τὸ σῶμα
1 Cor. 15:27	"For He has put all things in subjection under His feet. But when He says, 'All things are put in subjection,' it is evident that He is excepted who put all [τὰ πάντα] in subjection to Him,"
	πάντα γὰρ ὑπέταξεν ὑπὸ τοὺς πόδας αὐτοῦ. ὅταν δὲ εἴπῃ ὅτι πάντα ὑποτέτακται, δῆλον ὅτι ἐκτὸς τοῦ ὑποτάξαντος αὐτῷ τὰ πάντα.
1 Cor. 15:28	"When the all [τὰ πάντα] are subjected to Him, then the Son Himself also will be subjected to the One who subjected all [τὰ πάντα] to Him, so that God may be all in all."
	ὅταν δὲ ὑποταγῇ αὐτῷ τὰ πάντα, τότε (καὶ) αὐτὸς ὁ υἱὸς ὑποταγήσεται τῷ ὑποτάξαντι αὐτῷ τὰ πάντα, ἵνα ᾖ ὁ θεὸς πάντα ἐν πᾶσιν.
2 Cor. 5:14	"For the love of Christ controls us, having concluded this, that one died for all, therefore the all [οἱ πάντες] died."
	ἡ γὰρ ἀγάπη τοῦ Χριστοῦ συνέχει ἡμᾶς, κρίναντας τοῦτο, ὅτι εἷς ὑπὲρ πάντων ἀπέθανεν, ἄρα οἱ πάντες ἀπέθανον·
2 Cor. 7:15	"His affection abounds all the more toward you, as he remembers the obedience of you the all [τὴν πάντων], how you received him with fear and trembling."
	καὶ τὰ σπλάγχνα αὐτοῦ περισσοτέρως εἰς ὑμᾶς ἐστιν ἀναμιμνησκομένου τὴν πάντων ὑμῶν ὑπακοήν, ὡς μετὰ φόβου καὶ τρόμου ἐδέξασθε αὐτόν.
Gal. 3:22	"But the Scripture has shut up the all [τὰ πάντα] under sin, so that the promise by faith in Jesus Christ might be given to those who believe."
	ἀλλὰ συνέκλεισεν ἡ γραφὴ τὰ πάντα ὑπὸ ἁμαρτίαν, ἵνα ἡ ἐπαγγελία ἐκ πίστεως Ἰησοῦ Χριστοῦ δοθῇ τοῖς πιστεύουσιν.

Eph. 1:10	"with a view to an administration suitable to the fullness of the times, the summing up of the all [τὰ πάντα] in Christ, things in the heavens and things on the earth in Him."
	εἰς οἰκονομίαν τοῦ πληρώματος τῶν καιρῶν, ἀνακεφαλαιώσασθαι τὰ πάντα ἐν τῷ Χριστῷ, τὰ ἐπὶ τοῖς οὐρανοῖς καὶ τὰ ἐπὶ τῆς γῆς ἐν αὐτῷ
Eph. 1:11	"also we have obtained an inheritance, having been predestined according to His purpose who works the all [τὰ πάντα] after the counsel of His will,"
	Ἐν ᾧ καὶ ἐκληρώθημεν προορισθέντες κατὰ πρόθεσιν τοῦ τὰ πάντα ἐνεργοῦντος κατὰ τὴν βουλὴν τοῦ θελήματος αὐτοῦ
Eph. 1:23	"which is His body, the fullness of Him who fills the all [τὰ πάντα] in all"
	ἥτις ἐστὶν τὸ σῶμα αὐτοῦ, τὸ πλήρωμα τοῦ τὰ πάντα ἐν πᾶσιν πληρουμένου.
Eph. 3:9	"and to bring to light what is the administration of the mystery which for ages has been hidden in God who created the all [τὰ πάντα];"
	καὶ φωτίσαι τίς ἡ οἰκονομία τοῦ μυστηρίου τοῦ ἀποκεκρυμμένου ἀπὸ τῶν αἰώνων ἐν τῷ θεῷ τῷ τὰ πάντα κτίσαντι,
Eph. 4:10	"He who descended is Himself also He who ascended far above all the heavens, so that He might fill the all [τὰ πάντα]."
	ὁ καταβὰς αὐτός ἐστιν καὶ ὁ ἀναβὰς ὑπεράνω πάντων τῶν οὐρανῶν, ἵνα πληρώσῃ τὰ πάντα.
Eph. 4:13	"until we the all [οἱ πάντες] attain to the unity of the faith, and of the knowledge of the Son of God, to a mature man, to the measure of the stature which belongs to the fullness of Christ."
	μέχρι καταντήσωμεν οἱ πάντες εἰς τὴν ἑνότητα τῆς πίστεως καὶ τῆς ἐπιγνώσεως τοῦ υἱοῦ τοῦ θεοῦ, εἰς ἄνδρα τέλειον, εἰς μέτρον ἡλικίας τοῦ πληρώματος τοῦ Χριστοῦ,
Eph. 4:15	"but speaking the truth in love, we are to grow up in the all [τὰ πάντα] into Him who is the head, Christ,"
	ἀληθεύοντες δὲ ἐν ἀγάπῃ αὐξήσωμεν εἰς αὐτὸν τὰ πάντα, ὅς ἐστιν ἡ κεφαλή, Χριστός
Phil. 2:21	"For the all [οἱ πάντες] seek after their own interests, not those of Christ Jesus."
	οἱ πάντες γὰρ τὰ ἑαυτῶν ζητοῦσιν, οὐ τὰ Ἰησοῦ Χριστοῦ.

Phil. 3:8	"More than that, I count all things to be loss in view of the surpassing value of knowing Christ Jesus my Lord, for whom I have suffered the loss of all [τὰ πάντα], and count them but rubbish so that I may gain Christ,"
	ἀλλὰ μενοῦνγε καὶ ἡγοῦμαι πάντα ζημίαν εἶναι διὰ τὸ ὑπερέχον τῆς γνώσεως Χριστοῦ Ἰησοῦ τοῦ κυρίου μου, δι' ὃν τὰ πάντα ἐζημιώθην, καὶ ἡγοῦμαι σκύβαλα, ἵνα Χριστὸν κερδήσω
Phil. 3:21	"who will transform the body of our humble state into conformity with the body of His glory, by the exertion of the power that He has even to subject the all [τὰ πάντα] to Himself."
	ὃς μετασχηματίσει τὸ σῶμα τῆς ταπεινώσεως ἡμῶν σύμμορφον τῷ σώματι τῆς δόξης αὐτοῦ κατὰ τὴν ἐνέργειαν τοῦ δύνασθαι αὐτὸν καὶ ὑποτάξαι αὐτῷ τὰ πάντα.
Col. 3:8	"But now you also, put the all [τὰ πάντα] aside: anger, wrath, malice, slander, abusive speech from your mouth."
	νυνὶ δὲ ἀπόθεσθε καὶ ὑμεῖς τὰ πάντα, ὀργήν, θυμόν, κακίαν, βλασφημίαν, αἰσχρολογίαν ἐκ τοῦ στόματος ὑμῶν·
1 Tim. 6:13	"I charge you in the presence of God, who gives life to the all [τὰ πάντα], and of Christ Jesus, who testified the good confession before Pontius Pilate,"
	παραγγέλλω (σοι) ἐνώπιον τοῦ θεοῦ τοῦ ζῳογονοῦντος τὰ πάντα καὶ Χριστοῦ Ἰησοῦ τοῦ μαρτυρήσαντος ἐπὶ Ποντίου Πιλάτου τὴν καλὴν ὁμολογίαν,

The fact that Col. 1:16 immediately follows 1:15 implies that 1:16 is a further explanation of what is meant in 1:15: "Jesus is the image of the invisible God, the firstborn of all creation because by Him the all were created." And Paul's enumeration of what "the all" includes makes it clear that this includes everything that could possibly have been created. Since Jesus is excluded from this group, as BeDuhn admits, it can be only because He is not a created being. What would it possibly mean to say "the all in the heavens and upon the earth, the visible and the invisible, whether thrones, whether dominions, whether rulers, whether authorities" if Jesus was actually one of the things in heaven or on earth, visible or invisible, thrones, dominions, rulers, or authorities"? Earlier we pointed out that BeDuhn argued that some uses of "all" can be hyperbolic, and we argued that this presents only a possible meaning but does not decide what is the actual meaning. Some may object that we have used a similar argument here. But that would be incorrect. The difference is, though BeDuhn's argument applied only to some uses of the word "all," our argument shows that none of the uses by Paul of the expression "the all" would make sense by the addition of the word 'other.' This is a much stronger argument than simply the fact that some uses of "all" *can* be hyperbolic. Additionally, since verses 16 and 17 are obviously expansions on Paul's statement in verse 15, the only reasonable, clear, and obvious conclusion that one can draw is that BeDuhn's claims are unsupported and unsupportable and ultimately motivated by his own theological bias.

Who Created What?

There is another devastating argument against the theological position BeDuhn promotes, and that is the statement in Eph. 3:9: "and to bring to light what is the administration of the mystery which for ages has been hidden in God who created the all;" (Eph. 3:9). The text with a word-for-word translation is set out below:

Table #23: Eph. 3:9

καὶ	φωτίσαι	τίς	ἡ
and	to bring to light	what	the
οἰκονομία	τοῦ	μυστηρίου	τοῦ
administration	of the	mystery	of the
ἀποκεκρυμμένου	ἀπὸ	τῶν	αἰώνων
having been hidden	from	the	ages
ἐν	τῷ	θεῷ	τῷ
in	the	God	to the
τὰ	πάντα	κτίσαντι	
the	all	having created	

This text states that God is the Creator of "the all," (τὰ πάντα, *ta panta*) whereas Col. 1:16–17 clearly states that Jesus is the Creator of "the all" (τὰ πάντα, *ta panta*). Now, either God created "the all," or Christ created "the all," or Christ is God. The only other option is to assume that Paul has contradicted himself, but this option presents a problem for BeDuhn in two different ways.

First, BeDuhn assured the reader that he was not going to get involved in the theological debates. But, by ignoring the theological implications of his assertions he has interjected himself into the theological debate while maintaining a false impression of not doing so. And, to ignore the theological implications of a translation, and then to pretend that his claims about the translation are somehow theologically neutral is not only to misrepresent what he is doing, but it is also to deceive his readers. The problem is, it is not possible to advocate one translation over another without entering into the theology of the passage, and BeDuhn has advocated a translation that is actually and theologically impossible for those who believe in the inerrancy of Scripture. But, if BeDuhn does not believe the doctrine of inerrancy, then he ought to alert his readers that he will make no attempt to insure that his translations do not contradict the clear statements of other passages. And again, if he does not believe in inerrancy, then he has approached the text with a theological bias concerning which he has not alerted his readers all the while pretending to be theologically neutral. He is far from theologically neutral. By introducing contradiction into the text without the least acknowledgment or explanation, he has, once again, betrayed a theological bias. He has not lived up to the claims he made in his introduction.

Second, even if BeDuhn does not believe in inerrancy, he stated in his introduction that he assumes that an author is not going to be contradictory: "Our use of literary context assumes that an author was relatively consistent and non-contradictory in what he or she said."[20] But, unless BeDuhn wants to modify his assertion to apply only to the immediate context of an assertion or to a single book of an author, his assumption indicates that he cannot legitimately propose his understanding of the Colossians passage without introducing a contradiction into the writings of Paul. And this is particularly the case since most scholars look upon Ephesians and Colossians as sister productions, that is, that Paul gave these two letters to these two churches as interchangeable letters. Most scholars also claim that the topics of these two letters are at least complementary if not overlapping.

Fullness or Fullness?

BeDuhn next attacks the NIV for adding the word 'his' into verse 19: "For *God* was pleased to have all *his* fullness dwell in him."[21] BeDuhn asserts, "Secondly, the NIV adds 'his' to the word 'fullness,' in this way interpreting the ambiguous reference in line with a specific belief about Christ's role in the process being described."[22] He goes on to add, "Whether this is true or not, and whether this is one of the ideas to be found in Paul's letters or not, it certainly is not present in the original Greek wording of this passage."[23] At this point BeDuhn adds an endnote. It is important to provide the whole of this endnote for the purpose of analysis:

To what, exactly, "fullness" is meant to refer here is ambiguous. Those translators who add words to identify the fullness as God's (whatever that may mean) are influenced by Colossians 2:9, where Paul again uses the noun "fullness" in a phrase (not the same as that found in

---

[20] Ibid., xvi.
[21] ὅτι ἐν αὐτῷ εὐδόκησεν πᾶν τὸ πλήρωμα κατοικῆσαι (Col. 1:19).
[22] Ibid., 81.
[23] Ibid.

Colossians 1:19) that can be translated "the fullness of deity" or "the fullness of divinity" (again, leaving aside how that is to be interpreted). But the context of the two statements is quite different, and the assumption that whenever Paul talks about "fullness" he means something divine is baseless (in fact, most of the times he uses "fullness" it is not in reference to God), and illegitimately restricts Paul's possible meaning. The "fullness" that dwells in Christ in Colossians 1:19 *may* refer to the fullness of God, so that Christ stands in for God in the reconciliation process Paul is talking about in parentheses. In this way reflecting back to verse 15's statement that Christ is the "image' [sic] of God). Or it *may* refer to the fullness of creation, so that Christ stands in for creation in the reconciliation process (in this way pointing forward to verse 20's references to Christ's blood and the cross). Or it *may* have been Paul's precise intention to suggest both kinds of fullness, and to indicate that Christ forms a bridge between God and creation in the mediation of reconciliation. By over determining what "fullness" refers to, some translations drain the passage of its richness and subtlety."[24]

First, BeDuhn refers to the statement in Col. 2:9. That statement is set out below:

Table #24: Col. 2:9

ὅτι	ἐν	αὐτῷ	κατοικεῖ
because	in	him	dwells
πᾶν	τὸ	πλήρωμα	τῆς
all	the	fullness	of the
θεότητος	σωματικῶς		
deity	bodily		

BeDuhn asserts, "Those translators who add words to identify the fullness as God's (whatever that may mean) are influenced by Colossians 2:9, where Paul again uses the noun 'fullness' in a phrase (not the same as that found in Colossians 1:19) that can be translated 'the fullness of deity' or 'the fullness of divinity' (again leaving aside how that is to be interpreted)."[25] The problem with BeDuhn's assertion here is that he has not left aside how it is to be interpreted. The use of the translation "fullness of divinity" is calculated to blunt the meaning of the phrase in 2:9. The problem here is not the Greek word, but BeDuhn's selection of an English word. The English word "divinity" can refer to something that relates to or proceeds directly from God or a god without itself being deity. But, the underlying Greek word, "θεότης" does not necessarily indicate merely something or someone that proceeds from God, but of someone that is in fact God, i.e., deity. BeDuhn's choice of words to translate the underlying Greek term again reveals his own prior theological bias. Of course the choice of the term "deity" is also a

---

[24] Ibid., 88.n3 (emphasis in original).
[25] Ibid.

theological decision, but the point is that BeDuhn's choice is just as theologically motivated as those he attacks. He strategically neglects to inform his readers of these possibilities—selective reporting.

He goes on to argue that the contexts of the two passages "are quite different." He does not bother to say what he means by this or how this supposedly militates against taking the latter context to inform the former context. Rather, he suddenly floats a strawman argument: "the assumption that whenever Paul talks about 'fullness' he means something divine is baseless (in fact, most of the times he uses 'fullness' it is not in reference to God), and illegitimately restricts Paul's possible meaning." Of course no one said that whenever Paul talks about fullness he is talking about something divine, and someone does not have to think that Paul is doing this in every instance in order to believe he is doing it in this instance. Also, even if in every other instance Paul uses the term to refer to something other than divine fullness does not mean that he cannot be using it to refer to divine fulness in this particular instance. BeDuhn's argument is simply a *non sequitur*.

BeDuhn then proposes various ways of understanding Paul's statement in Col. 1:19, once again entering into the theological debate which he said he would not do. First he says, "The 'fullness' that dwells in Christ in Colossians 1:19 *may* refer to the fullness of God, so that Christ stands in for God in the reconciliation process Paul is talking about in parentheses." He doesn't bother to explain what it means for Christ to "stand in for God," but it certainly does not seem to mean that Christ is in fact God. Here again BeDuhn is involved in the debate over the interpretation of the passage, something else he said he would not do.

After considering the various translations, BeDuhn declares, "So it is the NIV, NRSV, TEV, and LB – the four Bibles that make no attempt to mark added words – that actually add the most significant, tendentious material. Yet in many public forums on Bible translation, the practice of these four translations is rarely if ever pointed to or criticized, while the NW is attacked for adding the innocuous 'other' in a way that clearly indicates its character as an addition of the translators."[26] BeDuhn's use of the word 'innocuous' is yet another instance of interpretation and theological bias. The addition by the NW of the word 'other' is anything but innocuous, at least from the perspective of orthodoxy. The addition of 'other' is designed to promote a particular theological perspective, the very thing that BeDuhn decries in the practice of others. To add the word 'other' is to make theologically specific what BeDuhn has identified as ambiguous in itself.

But BeDuhn seems to be oblivious to the debate about the translation of what seems to be ambiguous. Some argue that accurate and unbiased translation should not attempt to make specific what in the Greek text is ambiguous. Mark Strauss, an advocate of Functional Equivalence translation, declares, "If the translator, through sound exegesis, has determined the most likely meaning of the text, why should this meaning be withheld from the reader? Intentional ambiguity invites misinterpretation. A translator

---

[26] Ibid., 83–84.

should leave the meaning ambiguous only when (1) the original author was intentionally ambiguous or (2) the meaning of a text is so obscure that any interpretation is highly speculative. In the latter case, marginal notes are usually necessary to alert readers to the difficulty in arriving at a solution."[27] But Moisés Silva, also an advocate of Functional Equivalence, takes the contrary position:

> But there is an additional and serious problem with the argument that Bible versions should be more or less neutral with regard to texts where the interpretation is debatable. Or as it is usually put, "What is ambiguous in the original should be left ambiguous in the translation." The main flaw in this principle (whatever truth it may contain) is the assumption that typical English readers recognize an ambiguity when they see one. Take 1 Corinthians 5:5, which the ESV renders quite literally, "You are to deliver this man to Satan for the destruction of the flesh, so that his spirit may be saved in the day of the Lord." Some people object to the NIV rendering "sinful nature" instead of the literal "flesh" for various reasons, including their concern that the Greek word *sarx* is ambiguous, and that therefore the NIV immediately slants the text in a particular direction. But it would be delusion to think that the literal translation "flesh" does not slant the text for the average reader, who needs a book or a preacher to tell him or her what the options are (of course, a book or a preacher can clarify those options regardless of which version is being read). At least the NIV provides a footnote with the alternate renderings "his body" and "the flesh."[28]

Although the debate still rages, one point on which all sides agree is that to make an ambiguous text specific by one's translation is necessarily to take a theological position on the issue and to promote that position in the translation. So, if the text of Col. 2:9 is ambiguous in itself, as BeDuhn admits, then to make it specific by adding the word 'other' is to take a specific theological position on the issue and to make that theological position explicit. This is hardly innocuous.

In fact, BeDuhn admits this very point: "The reason is that many readers apparently want the passage to mean what the NIV and TEV try to make it mean. That is, they don't want to accept the obvious and clear sense of 'first-born of creation' as identifying Jesus as 'of creation.' 'Other' is obnoxious to them because it draws attention to the fact that the Jesus is 'of creation' and so when Jesus acts with respect to 'all things' he is actually acting with respect to 'all other things.' But the NW is correct."[29] Suddenly what BeDuhn earlier identified as "ambiguous" has become "clear and obvious." But, the NW is not only incorrect, it is heretical. There is an abundance of evidence in the Bible to prove beyond question that Jesus is God in the flesh, so to translate this verse

---

[27] Mark L. Strauss, *Distorting Scripture? The Challenge of Bible Translation and Gender Accuracy* (Downers Grove, Illinois: InterVarsity Press, 1998), 85.

[28] Moisés Silva, "Are Translators Traitors? Some Personal Reflections," in *The Challenge of Bible Translation*, ed. Glen G. Scorgie, Mark L. Strauss, and Steven M. Voth (Grand Rapids: Zondervan Publishing House, 2003), 44.

[29] Ibid., 84.

in such a manner as to make Jesus part "of creation" is a heretical belief and contrary to this body of evidence.

Be that as it may, BeDuhn's own theological bias is out in the open. In the earlier parts of this chapter BeDuhn talked about how obscure and ambiguous this text is, but as soon as it comes to the NW translation that promotes a theology BeDuhn likes, the passage is now clear and obvious. But, even if we leave the Genitive ambiguous, BeDuhn's conclusion is not a necessary conclusion. In fact, to add the word 'other' is just as motivated by a theological bias since the expression itself is ambiguous. An unbiased scholar would have said that the NW translation seems to promote a particular theological position, and to add 'other' would prejudice the reader toward that perspective and prevent the reader from realizing that there may be other options. Instead, BeDuhn, quite apart from the linguistic evidence, gives his imprimatur to the NW translation in the face of the linguistic ambiguities and difficulties. BeDuhn should have remained true to his principle not to get involved in the theological or interpretative debate.

Apologetic Points

The evidence of the standard Greek grammars and the standard Greek lexicons, and from related passages demonstrate that Col. 1:15–16 clearly states that Jesus is God and that He is the Creator, not a created being. These four apologetic points summarize the evidence we have studied in this chapter.

1. According to the grammar from Daniel Wallace and Herbert Smyth, the Genitive case can certainly have the meaning "over."

2. The term πρωτότοκος (*prōtotokos*) can be used to indicate supremacy or priority, and this possibility must be taken into consideration when translating the verse.

3. A look at every instance in Paul's literature where he uses the word 'all' (πᾶς, *pas*) with the definite article shows that it would be absurd to add the word 'other' in any of these contexts. So, adding the word "other" in Col. 1:16 as the New World Translation does is inaccurate.

4. Eph. 3:9 states that God is the Creator of "the all," (τὰ πάντα, *ta panta*) whereas Col. 1:16–17 clearly states that Jesus is the Creator of "the all" (τὰ πάντα, *ta panta*). Now, either God created "the all," or Christ created "the all," or Christ is God.

CHAPTER 5

OUR GOD AND SAVIOR JESUS CHRIST

Introduction

Titus 2:13 is another important passage concerning the deity of Christ.

Table #25: Titus 2:13

προσδεχόμενοι	τὴν	μακαρίαν	ἐλπίδα
waiting for	the	blessed	hope
καὶ	ἐπιφάνειαν	τῆς	δόξης
and	appearance	of the	glory
τοῦ	μεγάλου	θεοῦ	καὶ
of the	great	God	and
σωτῆρος	ἡμῶν	Χριστοῦ	Ἰησοῦ
savior	of us	Christ	Jesus

The statement for our consideration in this verse is, "our great God and Savior, Christ Jesus" (NASBU). The question that arises from this statement is whether the words "great God and Savior" are all modifying "Christ Jesus," or whether the verse should be divided so that it is saying, "our great God, and *our* Savior Christ Jesus." Is this verse saying that Jesus is our "great God" and our "Savior," or is it referring to God as our "great God," and Christ Jesus as our "Savior"? This is a crucial distinction. Some modern translations add a comma after the word 'Savior' indicating that the words 'great God' and 'Savior' are both referring to Jesus. Other translations do not add a comma leaving the passage ambiguous. Modern orthodox theologians argue that this is a declaration that Jesus is "our great God." Understandably, the Jehovah's Witnesses take exception to this argument, and the New World Translation actually adds the word 'the' before 'Savior' to make the passage refer to two different Persons: "while we wait for the happy hope and glorious manifestation of the great God and of [the] Savior of us, Christ Jesus."

In chapter eight of his book, "Words Together and Apart,"[1] BeDuhn says he is going to "turn now to questions of grammar, the rules governing the relation of words."[2] BeDuhn places the word 'our' in a different place than does the NASBU. In this instance, BeDuhn's translation more accurately reflects the placement of the Greek words, as can be seen in Table #25 below. According to BeDuhn, the phrasing is ambiguous, and he proposes two possible ways of understanding the phrase: "It could be read as 'the glory of our great God and Savior, Christ Jesus,' as if the whole phrase was about Jesus only and he is called both 'God' and 'Savior.' Or it could be read as 'the glory of the great God, and of our savior, Christ Jesus,' as if both God and Jesus, as distinct figures, are mentioned."[3]

Similar Passages

After looking at the various translations, BeDuhn proposes a course of action: "When we find ourselves facing an ambiguous passage, frustrated in our attempt to make a decision one way or another about how to translate, it is always a good idea to look for similar passages in order to make a comparison of expression, and so help to clarify the possible meaning of the words we are translating."[4]

Titus 2:13 and Titus 1:4

Figure 1: Titus 2:13 and 1:4

Titus 2:13	τοῦ	μεγάλου	θεοῦ	καὶ	σωτῆρος	ἡμῶν	Ἰησοῦ Χριστοῦ
	the	great	God	and	Savior	of us	Jesus Christ
	article	adjective	noun	conj.	noun	pronoun	noun
Titus 1:4	ἀπὸ	θεοῦ	πατρὸς	καὶ	Χριστοῦ Ἰησοῦ	τοῦ	σωτῆρος	ἡμῶν
	from	God	Father	and	Christ Jesus	the	Savior	of us
	prep.	noun	noun	conj.	noun	article	noun	pronoun

---

[1] BeDuhn, *Translation*, 89–101.
[2] Ibid., 89.
[3] Ibid.
[4] Ibid., 90–91.

According to BeDuhn, "The closest parallel to Titus 2:13 is just a chapter away, in Titus 1:4."[5] The two passages are set out below. BeDuhn declares that the differences between the verses "are entirely incidental."[6] However, as can be seen from the tables above and below, the differences between the passages make all the difference.

The graphic below shows just how disparate these two passages are:

Figure 2: Titus 2:13 and 1:4 Disparity

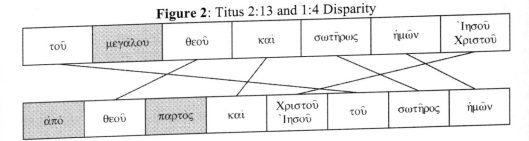

Notice the order of the parts of speech in the respective passages:

Titus 2:13	article	adj.	noun	conj.	noun	pron.	noun	
Titus 1:4	prep.	noun	noun	conj.	noun	article	noun	pron.

The lack of similarity in the order of words is so drastic that the only basis upon which they could be called similar is the fact that they happen to contain similar words. And yet there are elements in each passage that are not contained in the other. These elements are indicated by the shaded blocks. Titus 2:13 is on the top and Titus 1:4 on the bottom. Titus 2:13 has an adjective, and yet no adjective occurs in Titus 1:4. Titus 1:4 has a preposition, and Titus 2:13 does not. Also, after the word "God," Titus 1:4 includes the word 'Father.' Although BeDuhn believes the are entirely incidental, the comparison shows that this claim is not only false, but is in fact misleading.

BeDuhn begins by saying his is going to consider questions of grammar, the rules governing the relation of words, and yet the two passages are not grammatically similar. Since they are not grammatically similar, on what basis does BeDuhn call them similar? Because he believes Titus 1:4 can be used to support his theological bias. But, if the two passages are not similar in arrangement, how can they tell us anything about the meaning? BeDuhn's theological bias is evident in the following assertion: "The word modifying 'God' is changed from 'father' to 'great.' But that does not change the identity of the God spoken of. In fact, it can be said without qualification that if Paul had simply repeated 'father' in Titus 2:13, there would never have been any controversy

---

[5] Ibid., 91.
[6] Ibid.

over the meaning of the passage."[7] But, of course, that's the whole point, isn't it. The fact that Paul does not include the word 'father' may indicate that this does in fact "change the identity" of the one spoken of. It can be argued that the reason Paul does not repeat the word 'father' is because in 1:4 he wants to distinguish the Person of the Father and the Person of the Christ Jesus, and in 2:13 he wants to conjoin the words 'God' and 'savior' as both referring to Jesus. If Paul had meant God the Father, he could simply have said "God the Father" as he had already done in 1:4. The fact that he does not say this indicates that he means some different Person, namely, God the Son, Jesus Christ. For BeDuhn matter-of-factly to assert that this does not change the identity betrays his theological bias, and he makes this claim without argument or evidence. He certainly does not try to account for the difference in terms of the grammar of the "original Greek."

Titus 2:13 and 2 Thess. 1:2

BeDuhn selects another passage he claims is a similar, 2 Thess. 1:2. The passage is set out below:

Table #26: 2 Thess. 1:2

ὅπως	ἐνδοξασθῇ	τὸ	ὄνομα
so that	might be glorified	the	name
τοῦ	κυρίου	ἡμῶν	Ἰησοῦ
the	Lord	of us	Jesus
ἐν	ὑμῖν	καὶ	ὑμεῖς
in	you	also	you
ἐν	αὐτῷ	κατὰ	τὴν
in	Him	according to	the
χάριν	τοῦ	θεοῦ	ἡμῶν
grace	of the	God	of us
καὶ	κυρίου	Ἰησοῦ	Χριστοῦ
and	Lord	Jesus	Christ

The point of focus in 2 Thess. 1:12 is the phrase "the God of us and Lord Jesus Christ" (see **Figure 4** below). The graphic below, **Figure 3**, shows the disparities between these passages:

---

[7] Ibid.

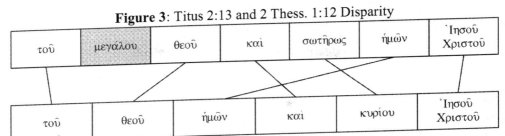

Figure 3: Titus 2:13 and 2 Thess. 1:12 Disparity

Figure 4: Titus 2:13 and 2 Thess. 1:12

Titus 2:13	τοῦ	μεγάλου	θεοῦ	καὶ	σωτῆρος	ἡμῶν	Ἰησοῦ Χριστοῦ
	the	great	God	and	Savior	of us	Jesus Christ
	article	adjective	noun	conj.	noun	pronoun	noun
2 Thess. 1:12	τοῦ	θεοῦ	ἡμῶν	καὶ	κυρίου	Ἰησοῦ Χριστοῦ
	the	God	of us	and	Lord	Jesus Christ
	article	noun	pronoun	conj.	noun	noun

Notice the order of the parts of speech in the respective passages:

Titus 2:13	article	adj.	noun	conj.	noun	pron.	noun
2 Thess. 1:12	article	noun	pron.	conj.	noun	noun	

Although there is a bit more correspondence between these passages, there is still a huge grammatical disparity between them. Once again the shaded box indicates the element that is contained in Titus that is not contained in 2 Thessalonians. Another important distinction is the fact that the possessive pronoun "of us" (ἡμῶν, *hēmōn*) comes before the conjunction καὶ (*kai*, "and"). The fact that the two nouns "God" and "savior" are connected by καὶ in Titus and that following this compound is the possessive pronoun "of us" (ἡμῶν, *hēmōn*) indicates that the two nouns should be taken as one thing belonging to "us," whereas the fact that the nouns are separated by the possessive pronoun in the 2 Thessalonians passage makes this construction critically different in the most important aspects.

Titus 2:13 and 2 Pet. 1:1–2

BeDuhn moves on to attempt a similar correlation between Titus 2:13 and 2 Pet. 1:1–2. Verses 1 and 2 of 2 Peter are set out below with a word-for-word translation:

Table #27: 2 Pet. 1:1–2

Συμεὼν	Πέτρος	δοῦλος	καὶ
Simon	Peter	servant	and
ἀπόστολος	Ἰησοῦ	Χριστοῦ	τοῖς
apostle	of Jesus	Christ	to the
ἰσότιμον	ἡμῖν	λαχοῦσιν	πίστιν
equal	with us	having received	faith
ἐν	δικαιοσύνῃ	τοῦ	θεοῦ
in	righteousness	of the	God
ἡμῶν	καὶ	σωτῆρος	Ἰησοῦ
of us	and	Savior	Jesus
Χριστοῦ	χάρις	ὑμῖν	καὶ
Christ	Grace	to you	and
εἰρήνη	πληθυνθείη	ἐν	ἐπιγνώσει
peace	may be multiplied	in	knowledge
τοῦ	θεοῦ	καὶ	Ἰησοῦ
of the	God	and	Jesus
τοῦ	κυρίου	ἡμῶν	
of the	Lord	of us.	

The portions in 2 Peter that are supposed to be similar to Titus 2:13 are set out below:

Table #28: 2 Pet. 1:1 and 1:2

2 Pet. 1:1	τοῦ	θεοῦ	ἡμῶν	καὶ	σωτῆρος	Ἰησοῦ Χριστοῦ
	of the	God	of us	and	Savior	Jesus Christ
	article	noun	pron.	conj.	noun	noun

2 Pet. 1:2	τοῦ	θεοῦ	καὶ	Ἰησοῦ	τοῦ	κυρίου	ἡμῶν
	of the	God	and	Jesus	of the	Lord	of us
	article	noun	conj.	noun	article	noun	pron.

The disparities between these passages and Titus 2:13 are set out in the figures below:

Figure 5: Titus 2:13 and 2 Pet. 1:2

Figure 6: Titus 2:13 and 2 Pet. 1:1

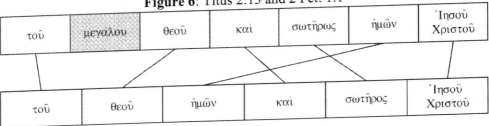

Again notice the order of the parts of speech:

Titus 2:13	article	adj.	noun	conj.	noun	pron.	noun
2 Pet. 1:1	article	noun	pron.	conj.	noun	noun	
2 Pet. 1:2	article	noun	conj.	noun	article	noun	pron.

2 Pet. 1:1 and 1:2 Compared

As has been the case with each of the supposed similar passages, the two instances in 2 Peter are not similar passages either. Of course, BeDuhn's argument is more than simply that the two passages in 2 Peter are similar to Titus 2:13. BeDuhn tries or argue that translators are being inconsistent when they "maintain the distinction between 'God' and 'Jesus, our Lord' in verse 2," and yet ignore this distinction in verse 1, even though, as BeDuhn sees it, "the grammatical structure of the two sentences is identical, making it very doubtful that they should be translated in different ways."[8] But, as we see in the tables above and **Figure 7** below, 2 Peter 1:1, 1:2, and Titus 2:13 are not "identical."

Figure 7: 2 Pet. 1:1 and 2 Pet. 1:2

| τοῦ | θεοῦ | ἡμῶν | καὶ | σωτῆρος | Ἰησοῦ Χριστοῦ |

| τοῦ | θεοῦ | καὶ | Ἰησοῦ | τοῦ | κυρίου | ἡμῶν |

As we pointed out, BeDuhn argues, "All translations we are comparing properly maintain the distinction between 'God' and 'Jesus, our Lord' in verse 2, while most ignore it in verse 1."[9] For example, the NASBU gives the following translations for the two verses:

> Simon Peter, a bond-servant and apostle of Jesus Christ, to those who have received a faith of the same kind as ours, by the righteousness of our God and Savior, Jesus Christ: (2 Pet. 1:1).

> Grace and peace be multiplied to you in the knowledge of God and of Jesus our Lord; (2 Pet. 1:2).

---

[8] Ibid., 92.
[9] Ibid.

The argument is that most translations acknowledge a distinction between "God" and "Jesus" as two distinct individuals while maintaining that "God" and "Jesus" in verse 1 refer to the same individual. First of all, as we have shown the verses are not "identical" in construction. The distinction between "God" and "Jesus" is predicated on the fact that these two are treated as names in verse 2, "God and Jesus," whereas they are treated as designations in verse 1, "God and Savior" both modifying "Jesus Christ." In fact, concerning verse 1, Daniel Wallace argues, "Some grammarians have objected that since ἡμῶν is connected with θεοῦ, two persons are in view. The pronoun seems to 'bracket' the noun, effectively isolating the trailing noun. However in v. 11 of this same chapter (as well as in 2:20 and 3:18), the author writes τοῦ κυρίου ἡμῶν καὶ σωτῆρος, Ἰησοῦ Χριστοῦ [*tou kuriou hēmōn kai sōteros, Iēsou Christou*, "the Lord of us and Savior, Jesus Christ"], and expression which refers to one person, Jesus Christ: 'Why refuse to apply the same rule to 2 Peter 1:1, that all admit . . . to be true of 2 Peter i.11 [not to mention 2:20 and 2:18]?'"[10] Now, compare the similarity of structure between 2 Pet. 1:1 and 1:11.

Figure 8: 2 Pet. 1:1 & 1:11

τοῦ	θεοῦ	ἡμῶν	καὶ	σωτῆρος	Ἰησοῦ	Χριστοῦ
τοῦ	κυρίου	ἡμῶν	καὶ	σωτῆρος	Ἰησοῦ	Χριστοῦ

As Wallace points out, if the words 'Lord' and 'savior' in 2 Pet. 1:11 both refer to Jesus Christ, then why do not the words "God" and 'savior' of 2 Pet. 1:1 both refer to Jesus Christ? Unlike BeDuhn's choices, these verses are actually grammatically identical. Of course, BeDuhn neglects to point this out to his readers.

Sharp's Rule and Smyth's Grammar

BeDuhn argues, "If we turn to the standard work of Greek grammar, that of Smyth, we find no 'Sharp's Rule.'"[11] However, to appeal to Smyth's grammar as a standard for judging the validity of Sharp's rule is illegitimate. Smyth's grammar is a grammar of Attic, literary Greek, not of the Koine Greek of the New Testament. The "Editor's Preface" to the 1956 reprint of Smyth's grammar points out that Smyth deals "almost

---

[10] GGBTB, 276–77.
[11] Ibid., 93.

exclusively" with the "literary use of the Greek language . . ."[12] Additionally, Smyth states in his own Preface, "It has been my purpose to set forth the essential forms of Attic speech, and of the other dialects, as far as they appear in literature . . ."[13] And, as Caragounis points out, "The language of the New Testament is well on its way away from Attic and towards Modern Greek."[14] There would be no reason for Smyth to address a distinctly New Testament, Koine Greek phenomenon since this was not within the scope of Smyth's grammar.

Additionally, the Editor repeatedly points out in his preface that the amount of revision that Smyth's grammar needed in order to bring it up to date and to correct the many errors that inevitably accrue to such a text having been written before more recent advances in the understanding of Greek grammar were too vast to undertake: "Nevertheless, it is only fair to the reader to point out certain features of the original work which called for revision. Smyth spoke in his preface of having 'adopted many of the assured results of comparative linguistics'; inevitably, time has invalidated some of these supposedly assured results, and new discoveries have successively altered existing concepts or added to our fund of information. . . . Moreover, a thorough-going revision which might attempt to take into consideration all the multitudinous pertinent literature in the field of Greek grammar since Smyth's day would run the risk of turning Smyth into a completely different book."[15] Smyth's grammar, although still a valuable reference work, is dated and is not the standard that BeDuhn assumes it to be, and it certainly is not the standard of measure of the validity of grammatical and syntactical features that competent grammarians and linguists have observed and documented in the New Testament.

Why does BeDuhn ballyhoo Smyth's grammar? Because he believes he can use Smyth's grammar to undermine the grammatical and syntactical observations made by grammarians and linguists who have actually studied these aspects of the New Testament. BeDuhn wants to use Smyth's grammar because he thinks it will support his theological bias. But, as we have seen, it does not support his bias, and in fact, as we will see, BeDuhn must selectively report the information from Smyth's grammar in order to make it appear as though it is saying what he wants it to say.

BeDuhn's Misunderstanding of Smyth's Grammar

Not only has BeDuhn appealed to a grammar that is outdated and not directly concerned with the NT, but BeDuhn manages to misunderstand even his own favorite grammar. BeDuhn argues,

---

[12] Gordon M. Messing, "Editor's Preface," in *Greek Grammar*, Herbert Weir Smyth (Cambridge, Massachusetts: Harvard University Press, 1984), iv.

[13] Smyth, "Author's Preface," in *Greek Grammar*, viii.

[14] Caragounis, *Development of Greek*, 103.

[15] Messing, "Editor's Preface," iii–iv.

Smyth, section 1143, says, "A single article, used with the first of two or more nouns connected by *and* produces the effect of a single notion." That sounds an awful lot like "Sharp's Rule," doesn't it? But what exactly is meant by "a single notion"? Smyth gives two examples: "the generals and captains (the commanding officers)"; "the largest and smallest ships (the whole fleet)." You can see from these examples that the two nouns combined by "and" are not identical; the individual words do not represent the same thing. Instead, by being combined, they suggest a larger whole.[16]

But BeDuhn's argument serves only to accentuate his misunderstanding of both Sharp's Rule and Smyth's grammar. First, as Wallace points out, "Smyth tells us that 'a single article, used with the first of two or more nouns connected by and, produces the effect of a single notion . . .' None of his examples involve the same referent, but neither are any of them personal and singular."[17] So, these are not actually counter-examples to Sharp's Rule since Sharp's Rule applies only to singular nouns, not to plural nouns like "officers" or "ships" (we shall see this more clearly when we consider Sharp's Rule under the next heading). Second, even though it may be true that the two nouns combine to suggest a larger whole, as BeDuhn argues, it is still a fact that they refer to the *same larger whole*, not to two or more distinct larger wholes. Notice that Smyth states that the two nouns have the effect of "a single notion,"[18] not *two* notions. Smyth's example of the "largest and smallest ships" shows that the effect is the whole fleet, that is, one single fleet—in fact, the *same* fleet. Both words "largest" and "smallest" refer to the same thing, the fleet. The point of Sharp's Rule is that the two nouns refer to the same thing, whether that thing be a person, inanimate object, or "larger whole," or, as in Smyth's example, the same fleet. So, BeDuhn has not only misunderstood Sharp, he has misunderstood Smyth, and, by his appeal to Smyth, BeDuhn has actually managed to support Sharp rather than contradict him.

BeDuhn's Misunderstanding of Sharp's Rule

BeDuhn has also misrepresented Sharp's rule. BeDuhn's misrepresentation is a common mistake among those who have not studied New Testament Greek grammar. BeDuhn says, "In 1798, the amateur theologian Granville Sharp published a book in which he argued that when there are two nouns of the same form ('case') joined by 'and' (*kai*), only the first of which has the article, the nouns are identified as the same thing."[19] This is a common misunderstanding and misrepresentation of the rule by those who have, as Wallace puts it, "imprecise knowledge" of the rule and its limitations. You will notice that BeDuhn does not bother to quote Sharp's own statements about the rule.

---

[16] BeDuhn, *Translation*, 93.
[17] Daniel B. Wallace, "Sharp Redivivus? A Reexamination of the Granville Sharp Rule," http://www.bible.org/page.php?page_id=1496 (Accessed May 29, 2008).
[18] Smyth, *Greek Grammar*, §1143.
[19] BeDuhn, *Translation*, 92.

This omission is designed to hide the fact that BeDuhn's argument has weight only because of his misrepresentation of it. The rule, as Sharp stated it is as follows:

> *When the copulative* καὶ *connects two nouns of the same case, [viz. nouns (either substantive or adjective, or participles) of personal description, respecting office, dignity, affinity, or connexion, and attributes, properties, or qualities, good or ill], if the article* ὁ, *or any of its cases, precedes the first of the said nouns or participles, and is not repeated before the second noun or participle, the latter always relates to the same person that is expressed or described by the first noun or participle:* i.e. it denotes a farther description of the first-named person.[20]

Wallace goes on to explain the very kind of misunderstanding evident in BeDuhn.

> In other words, in the TSKS construction [article-substantive-καὶ-substantive construction], the second noun refers to the *same* person mentioned with the first noun when:
>
>   (1) neither is *im*personal;
>   (2) neither is *plural*;
>   (3) neither is a *proper* name.
>
> Therefore, according to Sharp, the rule applied absolutely *only* with personal, singular, and non-proper nouns. The significance of these requirements can hardly be overestimated, for those who have misunderstood Sharp's principle have done so almost without exception because they were unaware of the restrictions that Sharp set forth.[21]

That BeDuhn has misunderstood Sharp's Rule is evidenced by the fact that he tries to use Smyth's examples as counter-examples to Sharp's Rule. But, as we noted from Wallace's observation, Smyth's examples are not examples of singular nouns, and Sharp's Rule was never formulated to apply to plural nouns.

BeDuhn's Misrepresentation of Daniel Wallace

Not only has BeDuhn misrepresented Sharp's rule, but he actually misrepresents Wallace's discussion. BeDuhn says, "Daniel Wallace has demonstrated that even that claim is too broad, since he found that 'Sharp's Rule' doesn't work with plural forms of personal titles."[22] But this is not what Wallace says. What Wallace says is that Sharp

---

[20] Granville Sharp, *Remarks on the Uses of the Definite Article* (Philadelphia: B. B. Hopkins, 1807), 2; quoted in GGBTB, 271.
[21] GGBTB, 271–72.
[22] BeDuhn, *Translation*, 92–93.

never intended it to refer to personal titles and plural forms. In fact, Daniel Wallace has done extensive study on this principle, and the following quote indicates that not only does Wallace accept its validity, but he shows that grammarians generally also accept its validity:

> The monotonous pattern of personal singular substantives in the TSKS construction indicating an identical referent immediately places such substantives in a different category from proper names, impersonal nouns, or plural nouns. The statistics accentuate this difference: in this construction there are about a dozen personal proper names in the NT (none having an identical referent); close to fifty impersonal nouns (only one unambiguously having the same identical referent); more than seventy plural substantives (little more than a third having an identical referent); and *eighty* TSKS constructions fitting the structural requirements of the rule (the christologically significant texts excepted), *all* of which apparently having an identical referent. It is evident that Sharp's limitation to personal singular substantives does indeed have substance; he seems to have articulated a genuine principle of NT grammar. But is his rule inviolable? C. Kuehne, in his second article of a seven-part series entitled "The Greek Article and the Doctrine of Christ's Deity" [In the *Journal of Theology* 13 (September 1973) 12–28; 13 (December 1973) 14–30; 14 (March 1974) 11–20; 14 (June 1974) 16–25; 14 (September 1974) 21–33; 14 (December 1974) 8–19; 15 (March 1975) 8–22], discusses all the instances in the NT which meet the requirements for the rule. He summarizes his findings by stating that "Sharp claimed that his rule applied uniformly to such passages, and I indeed could not find a single exception" [*JT* 13 (December 1973) 28.]. Kuehne is not alone in his view of these texts. None of Sharp's adversaries was able to produce a single exception to his rule within the pages of the NT. Calvin Winstanley, Sharp's most able opponent, conceded that Sharp's "first rule has a real foundation in the idiom of the language . . ." [C. Winstanley, *A Vindication of Certain Passages in the Common English Version of the New Testament. Addressed to Granvile Sharp, Esq.* (Cambridge: University Press—Hilliard and Metcalf, 1819), 36.]. And later, he declares, "Now, Sir, if your rule and principles of criticism must be permitted to close up every other source of illustration, there is an end of all farther enquiry . . ." [Ibid., 38.]—an obvious concession that, apart from the christologically significant texts, Winstanley could produce no exceptions within the NT corpus. Finally, he admits as much when he writes, "There are, you say, no exceptions in the New Testament, to your rule; that is, I suppose, unless these particular texts [i.e., the ones Sharp used to adduce Christ's deity] be such. . . . it is nothing surprising to find all these particular texts in question appearing as exceptions to your rule, and the sole exceptions . . . in the New Testament . . ." [Ibid., 39–40]. We must conclude, then, that (suspending judgment on the christologically significant texts) Sharp's rule is indeed an inviolable canon of NT syntactical usage.[23]

---

[23] Daniel B. Wallace, "Sharp Redivivus? A Reexamination of the Granville Sharp Rule," http://www.bible.org/page.php?page_id=1496 (Accessed May 29, 2008). Wallace also adds, "There is in fact but one passage which could possibly be taken as constituting a violation to Sharp's principle. In 1 Pet 4:18, "the godless and sinful man" (ὁ ἀσεβὴς καὶ ἁμαρτωλός), if rendered "the godless man and sinner" might suggest more than one referent. But surely that is the English way of looking at the passage, not the Greek. The antecedent in v 17 (τῶν ἀπειθούντων) clearly implies that all disobedient persons are godless and sinful. Nevertheless, since all three terms are generic, this may be a moot point." Ibid.

Sharp's Rule and Extra-Biblical Greek

BeDuhn goes on to argue, "The problem is not with Sharp's honesty or his diligence, but with the premises by which he did his work. He ignored the fact that the Greek language was not confined to the New Testament. The authors of the books of the New Testament did not have their own form of Greek with its own rules. Rather, they were working within a much large Greek linguistic and literary environment."[24] Of course, this kind of argumentation ignores the fact that within a larger linguistic environment there are always sub-environments, if you will, of dialects and localized idioms and modes of expression that can be found in particular groups in which certain principles, practices, and rules may be peculiar to that group without violating the rules of the larger environment. Also, BeDuhn is simply unfamiliar with the larger Greek environment. In Wallace's article on Sharp's Rule quoted above, Wallace documents a large number of scholars of Classical Greek who have validated Sharp's rule outside the Greek NT. The evidence is much too large to reproduce here, but Wallace's summary should suffice to demonstrate that BeDuhn simply does not know what he is talking about: "We have seen that Sharp's rule, when properly understood, is not only supported by decent linguistic rationale, but has overwhelming validity in ancient Greek literature. Further, the few classes of exceptions all seem to be capable of linguistic explanation."[25]

BeDuhn's Neglect of Evidence

The fact is, of the passages to which BeDuhn appeals, there is no precise similarity to the structure of Titus 2:13. When we broaden the scope to include any conjunction rather than only καί, there still is no precise similarity between the passages. We can alter the requirements further to include the following arrangement—article-adjective-noun-conjunction-noun—and we discover the following passages that have this kind of arrangement:

Table #29: Parallels to Titus 2:13

Matt. 24:3	As He was sitting on the Mount of Olives, the disciples came to Him privately, saying, "Tell us, when will these things happen, and what the sign of Your coming, and of the end of the age?"
	Καθημένου δὲ αὐτοῦ ἐπὶ τοῦ ὄρους τῶν ἐλαιῶν προσῆλθον αὐτῷ οἱ μαθηταὶ κατ' ἰδίαν λέγοντες· εἰπὲ ἡμῖν, πότε ταῦτα ἔσται καὶ τί τὸ σημεῖον τῆς σῆς παρουσίας καὶ συντελείας τοῦ αἰῶνος

---

[24] BeDuhn, *Translation*, 93.
[25] Daniel B. Wallace, "Sharp Redivivus? A Reexamination of the Granville Sharp Rule," http://www.bible.org/page.php?page_id=1496 (Accessed May 29, 2008).

Acts 18:23	And having spent some time, he left and passed successively through the Galatian region and Phrygia, strengthening all the disciples.
	Καὶ ποιήσας χρόνον τινὰ ἐξῆλθεν διερχόμενος καθεξῆς τὴν Γαλατικὴν χώραν καὶ Φρυγίαν, ἐπιστηρίζων πάντας τοὺς μαθητάς.
1 Tim. 6:20	O Timothy, guard what has been entrusted to you, avoiding worldly empty chatter the opposing arguments of what is falsely called "knowledge"
	Ὦ Τιμόθεε, τὴν παραθήκην φύλαξον ἐκτρεπόμενος τὰς βεβήλους κενοφωνίας καὶ ἀντιθέσεις τῆς ψευδωνύμου γνώσεως,
Titus 2:13	looking for the blessed hope and the appearing of the glory of our great God and Savior, Christ Jesus,
	προσδεχόμενοι τὴν μακαρίαν ἐλπίδα καὶ ἐπιφάνειαν τῆς δόξης τοῦ μεγάλου θεοῦ καὶ σωτῆρος ἡμῶν Ἰησοῦ Χριστοῦ,
1 Jn. 5:20	And we know that the Son of God has come, and has given us understanding so that we may know Him who is true; and we are in Him who is true, in His Son Jesus Christ. This is the true God and eternal life.
	οἴδαμεν δὲ ὅτι ὁ υἱὸς τοῦ θεοῦ ἥκει καὶ δέδωκεν ἡμῖν διάνοιαν ἵνα γινώσκωμεν τὸν ἀληθινόν, καί ἐσμεν ἐν τῷ ἀληθινῷ, ἐν τῷ υἱῷ αὐτοῦ Ἰησοῦ Χριστῷ. οὗτός ἐστιν ὁ ἀληθινὸς θεὸς καὶ ζωὴ αἰώνιος.
Rev. 11:11	But after the three and a half days, the breath of life from God came into them, and they stood on their feet; and great fear fell upon those who were watching them.
	Καὶ μετὰ τὰς τρεῖς ἡμέρας καὶ ἥμισυ πνεῦμα ζωῆς ἐκ τοῦ θεοῦ εἰσῆλθεν ἐν αὐτοῖς, καὶ ἔστησαν ἐπὶ τοὺς πόδας αὐτῶν, καὶ φόβος μέγας ἐπέπεσεν ἐπὶ τοὺς θεωροῦντας αὐτούς.

Interestingly, not a one of these is considered by BeDuhn, and we will learn why shortly. This arrangement is in the following words of the passages listed above:

Table #30: Parallels with Titus 2:13

	article	adjective	noun	conjunction	noun
Matt. 24:3	τῆς	σῆς	παρουσίας	καὶ	συντελείας
	the	your	coming	and	completion

	article	adjective	noun	conjunction	noun
1 Tim. 6:20	τὰς / the	βεβήλους / vile	κενοφωνίας / talk	καὶ / and	ἀντιθέσεις / contradiction
Titus 2:13a	τὴν / the	μακαρίαν / blessed	ἐλπίδα / hope	καὶ / and	ἐπιφάνειαν / appearing
1 Jn. 5:20	ὁ / the	ἀληθινὸς / true	θεὸς / God	καὶ / and	ζωὴ / life
Rev. 11:11	τὰς / the	τρεῖς / three	ἡμέρας / days	καὶ / and	ἥμισυ / half
Titus 2:13b	τοῦ / the	μεγάλου / great	θεοῦ / God	καὶ / and	σωτῆρος / Savior

A pattern becomes apparent when these passages are compared. In the Matthew passage, the coming and completion both belong to the persons indicated by the possessive adjective σῆς (sēs, "your"). In 1 Tim. 6:20, the "talk and contradiction" are both modified by the adjective "vile." In Titus 2:13a, the "hope and appearing" are both modified by the adjective "blessed." The pattern is that the two nouns connected by καὶ (kai, "and") are treated as two parts or aspects or characteristics that constitute one grammatical unit and are modified by the one adjective. So, in Titus 2:13b, "God and Savior" are likewise two characterizing nouns referring to the one whole modified by the adjective "great." The phrase is saying, "the great God-and-Savior, Jesus Christ," where 'Jesus Christ' is in apposition to the two characterizing nouns. The diagram in **Figure 9** below demonstrates this relationship.

The reason BeDuhn did not consider any of the verses listed above is because their similarity with Titus 2:13 demonstrates that the words 'God' and 'Savior' are both referring to Christ Jesus. In each of the passages, two nouns connected by καί are modified by a single adjective and are treated as one grammatical unit. So, since "God and Savior" are one grammatical unit modified by the adjective "great," the name "Christ Jesus" is in apposition to this grammatical unit indicating that the two nouns, "God and Savior," are referring to the one individual, Christ Jesus.

Figure 9: Titus 2:13 Diagraming

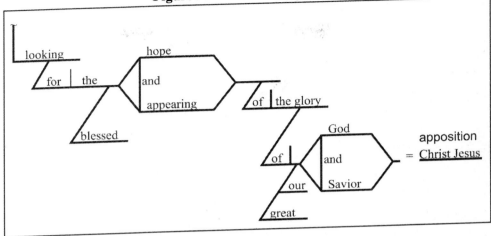

Apologetic Points

Although there is a lot of discussion and study in this chapter, especially showing that the passages that are said to be similar are in fact not similar, we have basically established the following two apologetics points:

1. The evidence from the standard grammars shows that Sharp's Rule is valid and that when applied to Titus 2:13, it proves that Jesus is our great God and Savior.

2. The identical structure of 2 Pet. 1:1 and 1:11 shows that in these verses, Jesus is our God and Savior.

CHAPTER 6

THY THRONE O GOD

Introduction

Heb. 1:8 seems to be a statement in which God is being directly addressed: "Your throne, O God [ὁ θεὸς, *ho theos*], forever and ever, and the righteous scepter is the scepter of your kingdom."[1]

Table #31: Heb. 1:8

πρὸς	δὲ	τὸν	υἱόν
to	but	the	son
ὁ	θρόνος	σου	ὁ
the	throne	of you	the
θεὸς	εἰς	τὸν	αἰῶνα
God	into	the	ages
τοῦ	αἰῶνος	καὶ	ἡ
of the	ages	and	the
ῥάβδος	τῆς	εὐθύτητος	ῥάβδος
septer	of the	righteous	septer

[1] ὁ θρόνος σου ὁ θεὸς εἰς τὸν αἰῶνα τοῦ αἰῶνος, καὶ ἡ ῥάβδος τῆς εὐθύτητος ῥάβδος τῆς βασιλείας σου. (Heb. 1:8).

τῆς	βασιλείας	σου.
of the	kingdom	of you.

The question is, is the use of ὁ θεός ("the God," *ho theos*) a direct address—that is, should this be considered a Vocative of direct address?[2] This is a very important question since verse 8 begins with a reference to the Son as the One Who is being addressed: "But to the Son" (NASBU). If this statement is about the Son, and God is being directly addressed, then the Son is God. The New World Translation is quite different from most modern versions: "But with reference to the Son: 'God is your throne forever and ever, and [the] scepter of your kingdom is the scepter of uprightness.'" Whereas most modern translations make the word 'God' a Vocative of direct address, the New World Translation makes the word 'God' the subject of the verb 'is.' In fact, BeDuhn argues that the whole issue has to do with the placement of the verb 'is.' There is no verb in the Greek sentence, so the translator must decide where is the most likely placement of the verb 'is.' As BeDuhn says, "In English, we know exactly where to place a verb: it goes between the subject and the object of the verb, or, in sentences that use the verb 'to be,' between the subject and the predicate noun or predicate adjective, or some other predicate modifier. The question in Hebrews 1:8 is, what is the subject?"[3]

Translation by Majority Vote

BeDuhn declares, "Since there are a handful of instances in the New Testament where *ho theos* means "O God," rather than 'God,' it is *possible* that in Hebrews 1:8 *ho theos* means 'O God.' But since *ho theos* usually means 'God,' and there are hundreds of examples of this, it is more *probable* that in Hebrews 1:8 *ho theos* means 'God.'"[4] But this is the very poorest of reasoning. This is nothing but meaning by majority vote. This kind of reasoning clearly violates BeDuhn's own principle that "Accuracy in Bible translation has nothing to do with majority votes:"[5] BeDuhn certainly meant this statement in reference to the majority of translations taken as the rule of what is accurate, but it applies equally to the notion that a majority of instances of use cannot be taken as the truth for any given instance. Each instance must be evaluated in its own context.

---

[2] A Vocative of direct address is a construction in which a word, usually a noun, indicates someone or something that is being directly addressed: "Bill, are you going to the store?" A Vocative does not have to occur in a question, but can occur in statements as well.

[3] Ibid., 98.

[4] Ibid., 99.

[5] Ibid., xv.

Heb. 1:8 and Ps. 45:6(H7)

Heb. 1:8 is a quote from Ps. 45:6 (45:7 in the Hebrew text). BeDuhn only briefly discusses the influence of the Hebrew passage that is being quoted. He provides no study of the Hebrew syntax in order to support his claim that the word 'God' (אֱלֹהִים, ʾelōhîm) should not be taken as a Vocative in its own passage.

Table #32: Ps. 45:7

כִּסְאֲךָ	אֱלֹהִים	עוֹלָם	וָעֶד
Your throne	God	forever	and forever
שֵׁבֶט	מִישֹׁר	שֵׁבֶט	מַלְכוּתֶךָ:
scepter of	uprightness	the scepter of[6]	your kingdom.

Waltke-O'Connor describe the Hebrew Vocative: "Vocatives stand in apposition to the second-person pronoun, expressed or unexpressed, and may occur with either verbless or verbal clauses."[7] This is precisely the construction we have here. The second-person pronoun is the pronominal suffix, the final *kaph* (ךָ, *cā*), of the first word of the line כִּסְאֲךָ (*kisʾakā*), "your throne." The word אֱלֹהִים (*ʾelōhîm*, "God") is the Vocative in apposition to the possessive pronoun 'your.' The word אֱלֹהִים (*ʾelōhîm*, "God") is juxtaposed to the pronominal suffix 'your' with no conjunction. In this case, the line should be translated, "Your throne, God, forever and ever." Heb. 1:8 is an exact quote of the GSEPT translation of Ps. 45:6(H7).[8]

Table #33: Ps. 44:7 and Heb. 1:8

Ps. 44:7 (GSEPT)	ὁ θρόνος σου ὁ θεός εἰς τον αἰῶνα τοῦ αἰῶνος
Heb. 1:8	ὁ θρόνος σου ὁ θεος εἰς τον αἰῶνα τοῦ αἰῶνος

---

[6] In a construct relation, the word in the construct state, in this case 'scepter,' is considered definite if it is in a construct relation to a word with a pronominal suffix, in this case 'your kingdom.'

[7] Waltke-O'Connor, *Biblical Hebrew Syntax*, 4.7d. They define apposition as, "the asyndetic [the omission of conjunctions] juxtaposition of two or more nouns with a single extra-linguistic referent." Ibid. 4.4.1b.

[8] When an Old Testament Bible verse is indicated with an 'H' in parentheses, as Ps. 45:6(H7), this indicates that the Hebrew text uses the verse indicated by the number following the 'H.'

Brenton gives the following translation of Ps. 44:7: "Thy throne, O God, is for ever and ever:"[9] Interestingly, George Lamsa's translation of the Syriac text reads: "Thy throne, O God, is for ever and ever."[10] (ܟܘܪܣܝܟ ܐܠܗܐ ܠܥܠܡ ܥܠܡܝܢ).[11] When it comes to an analysis of Ps. 45:6(H7), BeDuhn again violates his own principle of majority votes. He says, "Within the Jewish tradition, Psalm 45 has never been taken to call the king 'God.'"[12] But, so what! So Jewish tradition has never taken it this way! What does that prove other than the fact that BeDuhn has appealed to a majority vote to settle a question of accuracy in translation? He claims, "The modern translation published by the Jewish Bible Society reads, 'Your divine throne is everlasting,'"[13] and BeDuhn accepts this without the least concern that maybe the Jewish translators have their own bias against Christian claims that Jesus is the Messiah, and without the least analysis of their translation. Again this demonstrates BeDuhn's own theological bias at work.

Construct Relation

The Hebrew of Ps. 45:7 does not express the idea of a "divine" throne. To express the notion of "divine," the Hebrew author would use a noun in a construct relation to the word 'God' (אֱלֹהִים, 'elōhîm). An example of this can be found in Gen. 41:38: "Then Pharaoh said to his servants, 'Can we find a man like this, in whom is a divine spirit?'" (NASBU). The Hebrew text with a word-for-word translation is set out below:

Table #34: Gen. 41:38

עֲבָדָיו	אֶל-	פַּרְעֹה	וַיֹּאמֶר
his servants	to	Pharaoh	And said
אֲשֶׁר	אִישׁ	כָזֶה	הֲנִמְצָא
who	man	as this	Can be found
בּוֹ:	אֱלֹהִים		רוּחַ
in him?	gods		spirit of

---

[9] Brenton, *Septuagint*, 596. In Brenton's text, the verse is actually 6, not 7.
[10] George M. Lamsa, *Holy Bible: From the Ancient Eastern Text* (San Francisco: Harper & Row, Publishers, 1968), 609.
[11] *Leiden Peshitta*, Leiden: Peshitta Institute Leiden, 2008. Referring to the Syriac is not a gratuitous task. Since Syriac is a Semitic language, like Hebrew, it can often reflect the Hebrew structure better than Greek does since Greek is an Indo-European language.
[12] BeDuhn, *Translation*, 100.
[13] Ibid.

The word 'spirit' (רוּחַ, *rûach*) is in a construct relation to the word 'gods' (אֱלֹהִים, *ʾelōhîm*). A construct relation involves the juxtaposition of two words so that the first word is in the construct state, and the two words together express a Genitive idea. A word in a construct state is usually a shortened form of the word. Sometimes this shortening involves the dropping of a weak letter or the shortening of a vowel. Many words, however, do not change even when they are in a construct state, and the word 'spirit' (רוּחַ, *rûach*) is one of these. The Genitive idea here indicates the kind of spirit, so the translation "divine spirit" is entirely appropriate. There is, however, no construct relation in Ps. 45:7, so the translation "divine throne" is grammatically incorrect. This means that the word 'God' in Ps. 45:7 must be treated as a Vocative. Therefore, in Heb. 1:8, following both the Hebrew and GSEPT of Ps. 45:7, the word 'God' must be treated as a Vocative also.

GSEPT of Ps. 45:6(GSEPT7)

Concerning the GSEPT translation, BeDuhn floats his own speculation as if this were support for his claims: "The Greek translation of the psalm made before the beginning of Christianity, which reads exactly as the author of Hebrews has quoted it, certainly followed this traditional Jewish understanding of the verse, and its translators thought that by using *ho theos* they were saying 'God is your throne,' not 'Your throne, O God.'"[14] What special powers does BeDuhn suppose he possesses that he is able to divine what the Septuagint translators thought when they were working on their translation of this passage? Earlier in this very chapter BeDuhn admitted, "These facts make it very hard for us to know which way to translate this phrase in Hebrew 1:8."[15] But, now that BeDuhn has miraculously divined what the GSEPT translators were thinking at the time, it is suddenly no longer a problem to declare how Heb. 1:8 must be taken. Again BeDuhn's bias has led him to make claims that cannot be supported by the text or by his speculations.

Another important factor that BeDuhn neglects to observe is the fact that the GSEPT adds the definite article that is not present in the Hebrew.

Table #35: GSEPT and BHS of Ps. 45:7

GSEPT Ps. 45:7	ὁ θρόνος	σου	ὁ θεός
	the throne	of you	the God
BHS Ps. 45:7	אֱלֹהִים		כִּסְאֲךָ
	God		your throne

---

[14] Ibid.
[15] Ibid., 99.

Why would the Greek translators add the definite article before θεός when the Hebrew text does not have the definite article before אֱלֹהִים? Of course we don't have the power to divine what the translators were thinking, but one reason would be to make sure that the Greek readers would take the word 'God' as a Vocative rather than simply a subject. Another reason is that the Greek translators understood this to be a reference to the God of Israel, so they wanted to indicate that by the definite article. So, even though the definite article in the Greek translation is not conclusive, it is another factor that BeDuhn simply avoids.

Vocatives in Hebrews

The fact of the matter is, the Hebrew syntax of Ps. 45:6(H7) indicates that the word "God" is a Vocative, and the Greek translation follows this pattern. The fact that the use of ὁ θεός as a Vocative is infrequent is no argument against taking it this way here. There are at least 9 instances in the New Testament, excluding the Heb. 1:8 passage, in which ὁ θεός is used as a vocative.

Table #36: ὁ θεός as Vocative

Mk. 15:34	At the ninth hour Jesus cried out with a loud voice, "Eloi, Eloi, lama sabachthani?" which is translated, "My God [ὁ θεός μου], My God [ὁ θεός μου], why have You forsaken Me?"
	καὶ τῇ ἐνάτῃ ὥρᾳ ἐβόησεν ὁ Ἰησοῦς φωνῇ μεγάλῃ· ελωι ελωι λεμα σαβαχθανι ὅ ἐστιν μεθερμηνευόμενον· ὁ θεός μου ὁ θεός μου, εἰς τί ἐγκατέλιπές με
Lk. 18:11	"The Pharisee stood and was praying this to himself: 'God [ὁ θεός], I thank You that I am not like other people: swindlers, unjust, adulterers, or even like this tax collector.'"
	ὁ Φαρισαῖος σταθεὶς πρὸς ἑαυτὸν ταῦτα προσηύχετο· ὁ θεός, εὐχαριστῶ σοι ὅτι οὐκ εἰμὶ ὥσπερ οἱ λοιποὶ τῶν ἀνθρώπων, ἅρπαγες, ἄδικοι, μοιχοί, ἢ καὶ ὡς οὗτος ὁ τελώνης·
Lk. 18:13	"But the tax collector, standing some distance away, was even unwilling to lift up his eyes to heaven, but was beating his breast, saying, 'God [ὁ θεός], be merciful to me, the sinner!'"
	ὁ δὲ τελώνης μακρόθεν ἑστὼς οὐκ ἤθελεν οὐδὲ τοὺς ὀφθαλμοὺς ἐπᾶραι εἰς τὸν οὐρανόν, ἀλλ' ἔτυπτεν τὸ στῆθος αὐτοῦ λέγων· ὁ θεός, ἱλάσθητί μοι τῷ ἁμαρτωλῷ.
Jn. 20:28	Thomas answered and said to Him, "My Lord and my God [ὁ θεός]!"
	ἀπεκρίθη Θωμᾶς καὶ εἶπεν αὐτῷ· ὁ κύριός μου καὶ ὁ θεός μου.

Heb. 10:7	"Then I said, 'Behold, I have come (In the scroll of the book it is written of Me) To do Your will, O God [ὁ θεός].'"
	τότε εἶπον· ἰδοὺ ἥκω, ἐν κεφαλίδι βιβλίου γέγραπται περὶ ἐμοῦ, τοῦ ποιῆσαι ὁ θεός τὸ θέλημά σου.
Rev. 4:11	"Worthy are You, our Lord and our God [ὁ θεός], to receive glory and honor and power; for You created all things, and because of Your will they existed, and were created."
	ἄξιος εἶ, ὁ κύριος καὶ ὁ θεός ἡμῶν, λαβεῖν τὴν δόξαν καὶ τὴν τιμὴν καὶ τὴν δύναμιν, ὅτι σὺ ἔκτισας τὰ πάντα καὶ δια τὸ θέλημά σου ἦσαν καὶ ἐκτίσθησαν.
Rev. 11:17	saying, "We give You thanks, O Lord God [ὁ θεός], the Almighty, who are and who were, because You have taken Your great power and have begun to reign."
	λέγοντες· εὐχαριστοῦμέν σοι, κύριε ὁ θεὸς ὁ παντοκράτωρ, ὁ ὢν καὶ ὁ ἦν, ὅτι εἴληφας τὴν δύναμίν σου τὴν μεγάλην καὶ ἐβασίλευσας.
Rev. 15:3	And they sang the song of Moses, the bond-servant of God, and the song of the Lamb, saying, "Great and marvelous are Your works, O Lord God [ὁ θεος], the Almighty; Righteous and true are Your ways, King of the nations!"
	καὶ ᾄδουσιν τὴν ᾠδὴν Μωϋσέως τοῦ δούλου τοῦ θεοῦ καὶ τὴν ᾠδὴν τοῦ ἀρνίου λέγοντες· μεγάλα καὶ θαυμαστὰ τὰ ἔργα σου, κύριε ὁ θεος ὁ παντοκράτωρ· δίκαιαι καὶ ἀληθιναὶ αἱ ὁδοί σου, ὁ βασιλεὺς τῶν ἐθνῶν·
Rev. 16:7	And I heard the altar saying, "Yes, O Lord God [ὁ θεος] the Almighty, true and righteous are Your judgments."
	Καὶ ἤκουσα τοῦ θυσιαστηρίου λέγοντος· ναὶ κύριε ὁ θεος ὁ παντοκράτωρ, ἀληθιναὶ καὶ δίκαιαι αἱ κρίσεις σου.

In this list there is a particularly problematic verse for BeDuhn's thesis that ὁ θεός in Heb. 1:8 should not be taken as a Vocative, and that is Heb. 10:7. Concerning this verse BeDuhn says, "In the latter verse [Heb. 10:7], a quote from Psalm 40 includes the following clause, 'I have come to do your will, O God.' In this verse, 'O God' translates *ho theos*. So it is obvious that the author of this book of the Bible can use *ho theos* to mean 'O God.' At the same time, the same author uses *ho theos* dozens of times to mean 'God,' the usual meaning of the phrase."[16] But BeDuhn lightly dismisses the strong evidence from Heb. 10:7 and opts for a majority vote to decide what must be the most accurate translation. The non-vocative use of ὁ θεός occurs 18 times in the book of

---

[16] Ibid., 99.

Hebrews: (Heb. 1:1, 9; 2:13; 4:4,10; 6:3, 10, 13, 17; 9:20; 11:5, 10, 16, 19; 12:7, 29; 13:4, 16). If we count Heb. 1:8 as a Vocative, then the Vocative use of ὁ θεός in the book of Hebrews occurs twice: Heb. 1:8 and Heb. 10:7.

Heb. 10:7 and Ps. 40:9

Considering the Heb. 10:7 use of ὁ θεός, it is important to look at Ps. 40:9:

Table #37: Ps. 40:9

אֱלֹהָי	רְצוֹנְךָ	-	לַעֲשׂוֹת
O my God	your will	(Meqqeph)	To do
מֵעָי׃	בְּתוֹךְ	וְתוֹרָתְךָ	חָפָצְתִּי
my bowels.	in the midst of	and Your Torah	I delight

Table #38: Ps. 39:9 (GSEPT)

τοῦ	ποιῆσαι	τὸ	θέλημά	σου	ὁ
the	to do	the	will	of you	the
θεός	μου	ἐβουλήθην	καὶ	τὸν	νόμον
God	of me	I desired	and	the	law
σου	ἐν	μέσῳ	τῆς	κοιλίας	μου
of you	in	midst of	the	bosom	of me

Sir Lancelot Brenton gives the following translation of the GSEPT: "I desired to do thy will, O my God, and thy law in the midst of mine heart."[17] Lamsa's translation of the Syriac reads: "I delight to do they will, O my God; yea, thy law is within my heart."[18] Both of these scholars recognize ὁ θεός as a Vocative in this verse. The fact that the author of Hebrews uses ὁ θεός as a Vocative here cannot be so lightly dismissed. BeDuhn needs to do more than simply count votes in order to substantiate his claim as over against the wealth of scholarship through the centuries that takes the traditional understanding of the text.

---

[17] Brenton, *Septuagint*, 594. In Brenton's text the verse number is 8.
[18] Lamsa, *Holy Bible*, 607. This verse is designated Ps. 40:8 in Lamsa's translation.

Table #39: Ps. 39:9 (GSEPT), Ps. 40:9 (BHS), Heb. 10:7

GSEPT Ps. 39:9	τὸ θέλημά	σου	ὁ θεός	μου
	the will	of you	the God	of me
BHS Ps. 40:9		אֱלֹהָי		רְצוֹנְךָ
		my God		your good will
Heb 10:7	ὁ θεὸς		τὸ θέλημά	σου
	the God		the will	of you

BeDuhn concedes, "Let me repeat that both ways of translating Hebrews 1:8 are legitimate readings of the original Greek of the verse. There is no basis for proponents of either translation to claim that the other translation is *certainly* wrong."[19] The evidence shows that BeDuhn is *certainly* wrong.

Apologetic Points

In Heb. 1:8, Jesus is directly addressed as "God." The evidence we examined has yielded two apologetic points:

1. Heb. 1:8 is an exact quote of the Geek Old Testament translation of Ps. 45:6 (44:7 in the GSEPT and 45:7 in the Hebrew text) which clearly shows that the words ὁ θεός (*ho theos*) should be treated as a Vocative of direct address.

2. The Hebrew of Ps. 45:6(H7) in its relation to other passages, such as Gen. 41:38, clearly shows that the word אֱלֹהִים (*ʾelōhîm*) cannot be translated "divine."

---

[19] BeDuhn, *Translation*, 101.

CHAPTER 7

BEFORE ABRAHAM WAS

Introduction

One of the most unusual statements in most modern translations is found in Jn. 8:58: "before Abraham was born, I am." (NASBU). This is not what one would expect. One would perhaps expect the expression to be something like, "before Abraham was born, I was." A word-for-word translation of the whole verse is set out below:

Table #40: Jn. 8:58

εἶπεν	αὐτοῖς	Ἰησοῦς·	ἀμὴν
said	to them	Jesus	Truly
ἀμὴν	λέγω	ὑμῖν	πρὶν
truly	I am saying	to you	before
Ἀβραὰμ	γενέσθαι	ἐγὼ	εἰμί
Abraham	became	I	I am

According to BeDuhn, modern English translations have rendered this verse inaccurately because they have not attempted to render the Greek expression into proper English. Focusing in on the TEV translation, BeDuhn complains, "The TEV of John 8:58 strays from normal English usage in word order and verbal tense complementarity. That is, it puts the subject after the predicate, which is not normal word order of English sentences, and it mixes a present tense verb with a past tense verb in a totally ungrammatical construction. Most other versions have the same problem."[20] BeDuhn

---

[20] Ibid., 104.

claims that this problem arises because modern English translations have not properly rendered the Greek idiom.

Misrepresenting Idioms

BeDuhn has actually misrepresented what constitutes and idiom. He says, "When verb tenses or any other part of grammar is used in a way outside of usual expectations, we call it an 'idiom.'"[21] But this is simply false. An idiom is, "A construction whose meaning cannot be deduced from the meanings of its parts."[22] Zdenek Salzmann gives a similar definition: "An expression whose meaning is not determined by the meaning of its constituents and their syntactic relations is an idiom. The sentence 'My uncle kicked the bucket last week' contains an idiom if what is meant is that he died;"[23] Also, an idiom is a customary expression that has an understandable meaning within the language community. In other words, an idiom is not "outside of usual expectations" if by this BeDuhn means that it is outside the usual way people communicate. As John Beekman and John Callow observe, "A particularly difficult area for translators is that of idioms and figures of speech. In a number of languages of northern Ghana, an expression is commonly used which, literally translated, is 'he ate a woman.' In English this can only mean that he was a cannibal; but in fact, it means 'he got married.'"[24] In other words, the idiom in northern Ghana is a commonly used expression that is readily understood by those in the language community.

BeDuhn characterizes Jesus' statement in 8:58 as "fine, idiomatic Greek."[25] But this is simply false. This is not customary usage. Greek speakers did not customarily use such an expression. Beekman's example of an idiom in northern Ghana noted that it was a commonly used expression, not a unique expression. Silzer and Finley give two commonly used English idioms: "*Fly off the handle*," and "*They spilled the beans about the party.*"[26] Neither one of these expressions is a departure from normal syntax, nor are they "outside usual expectations." What makes these idioms is the meaning of the whole expression that cannot be derived from the collective meanings of the individual parts.

An identifying characteristic of an idiom is that "the meaning of the words of an idiom is obviously not literal; they are used in a figurative way that speakers of the language understand. The meaning of an idiom is not clear from the usual meaning of

---

[21] Ibid., 105.

[22] Peter James Silzer and Thomas John Finley, *How Biblical Languages Work: A Student's Guide to Learning Hebrew and Greek* (Grand Rapids: Kregel Academic & Professional, 2004), 240.

[23] Zdenek Salzmann, *Language, Culture, & Society: An Introduction to Linguistic Anthropology* (Boulder, Colorado: Westview Press, 1993), 68.

[24] John Beekman and John Callow, *Translating the Word of God* (Dallas, Texas: Summer Institute of Linguistics, 1986), 22.

[25] BeDuhn, *Translation*, 104.

[26] Silzer and Finley, *Biblical Languages*, 240.

the words themselves."[27] But this is not the case in Jn. 8:58. The problem with Jesus' statement is not grammatical. We can understand exactly what Jesus is saying form the words He uses. He is saying that before Abraham existed, He exists—He is before Abraham. The combination of His words are not the problem. This statement does not qualify as an idiom because the meaning of the whole *is* the collective meaning of the individual parts.

Why would BeDuhn misrepresent the case? Either he does not understand what an idiom is, or he is using the notion of an idiom to manipulate the text to conform to his prior theological bias. As it turns out, it appears that the latter is BeDuhn's reason for incorrectly identifying Jesus' statement as an idiom.

Misrepresenting Word Order

BeDuhn also attacks modern translations by discussing normal English word order. He says, "On the matter of word order, normal English follows the structure we all learned in elementary school: subject + verb + object or predicate phrase. The order of the Greek in John 8:58 is: predicate phrase + subject + verb. So it is the most basic step of translation to move the predicate phrase 'before Abraham came to be' (*prin Abraam genesthai*) from the beginning of the sentence to the end, after the subject and verb."[28] But what BeDuhn has either failed to realize, or simply failed to tell his readers, is that normal English word order is not a straight jacket that demands all expressions to follow in the normal order. There are many reasons why an author would depart from the normal order. As Beekman and Callow point out, "In English, we can say equally well, 'I didn't go out today, because it was raining,' 'Because it was raining, I didn't go out today,' and 'It was raining today, so I didn't go out.'"[29] So, simply because normal English word order is subject + verb + object or predicate phrase is not a sufficient reason for altering the word order of this unique statement of Jesus. Jesus said it a certain way, not because it was a Greek idiom, but because it was an unusual expression, even in Greek, for saying what Jesus wanted to say.

Another point that BeDuhn neglects to tell his reader is that the normal word order for Greek is the same as English, subject + verb + object or predicate phrase, and deviation from this normal order, though often due to customary or common usage, may be for the purpose of emphasis or to communicate a unique concept, or to grab the attention of an audience. By advocating the change of word order BeDuhn is actually introducing inaccuracy in the translation. BeDuhn says, "Just as we do not say 'John I am' or 'Hungry I am' or 'First in line I am,' so it is not proper English to say 'Before Abraham came to be I am.'"[30] But this is clearly false. There may in fact be good reason

---

[27] Ibid., 178.
[28] BeDuhn, *Translation*, 105.
[29] Beekman and Callow, *Translating*, 225.
[30] BeDuhn, *Translation*, 105.

to say any one of these expressions. It is not unusual for someone enthusiastically relating an experience to say "First in line I was, boy!!!" BeDuhn talks as if normal English word order is compulsory, and to characterize the word order of 8:58 as "mangled" is an egregious misrepresentation. In fact, for each one of the examples BeDuhn presents there can be a proper occasion for its use. Proper is simply not always the normal.

Misrepresenting Verb Tenses

BeDuhn next attacks modern translations on the basis of verbal tenses. He says, "On the subject of verbal tenses, there is a proper way to coordinate verb tenses in English that must be followed regardless of the idioms unique to Greek that provide the raw material for a translation."[31] BeDuhn's characterization of the source language as "raw material" betrays his lack of understanding of the significance of what one is translating. The source language of a text is not "raw material" that must be manipulated in order to be useful. The source language is the standard against which the translator must judge the accuracy of his translation. And it is simply false that the verb tenses of the receptor language must be followed at the expense of the meaning of the source language, and that is precisely what BeDuhn means by saying that the translator must coordinate verb tenses in English "regardless of the idioms unique to Greek." Perhaps Longfellow best expressed the task of translating in his evaluation of his own translation of Dante's *Divina Commedia*:

> The only merit my book has is that it is exactly what Dante says, and not what the translator imagines he might have said if he had been an Englishman. In other words, while making it rhythmic, I have endeavoured to make it also as literal as a prose translation. . . . In translating Dante, something must be relinquished. Shall it be the beautiful rhyme that blossoms all along the line like a honeysuckle on the hedge? It must be, in order to retain something more precious than rhyme, namely, fidelity, truth, — the life of the hedge itself. . . . The business of a translator is to report what the author says, not to explain what he means; that is the work of the commentator. What an author says and how he says it, that is the problem of the translator.[32]

BeDuhn wants to be a commentator, not a translator. And in fact he has departed from his own principles. He frequently decries the actions of translators who supposedly interpret the text rather than translating it, but BeDuhn is doing precisely that with reference to Jn. 8:58. He has already decided what the statement must mean, and he is determined to make an English translation that coincides with his prior theological commitment regardless of what the Greek text says. In fact, he as much as admits this:

---

[31] Ibid.
[32] Henry Wadsworth Longfellow; quoted in Susan Bassnett, *Translation Studies*, 3d ed. (London: Routledge, 2004), 73.

"When verb tenses or any other part of grammar is used in a way outside of usual expectations, we call it an 'idiom.' Because Greek idioms are different from English idioms, translators do not translate these expressions word-for-word, but rather convey the meaning of the Greek idiom in proper, comprehensible English. At least that is what translators are supposed to do."[33] By classifying Jesus' statement as an idiom, BeDuhn seeks to justify his distortion of the Greek and to force upon it what he believes are the requirements of English. But Jesus did not speak English, and the English translation must report what Jesus said in Greek without changing the meaning. We have already shown that this is not an idiom, and an accurate translation must report what Jesus said the way He said it without distorting or changing the meaning. BeDuhn has already decided what the statement must mean, and he is forcing the text into this mold by misidentifying it as an idiom. That's not what translators are supposed to do.

Apologetic Points

In order accurately to translate a text, the translator must understand some basic principles of language. One of these is to know the meaning of various terms, such as 'idiom.' Our study of Jn. 8:58 has shown that the unusual expression in this verse ought to be reflected in the English translation in order to preserve the meaning of the Greek text. This verse speaks to the timelessness of Jesus. We can summarize our study with these three apologetic points:

1. The expression in Jn. 8:58, "Before Abraham was, I am," is not a Greek idiom and should be rendered by English translations precisely as it is found in the Greek text.

2. Normal English word order is not a straightjacket that requires words to be arranged in a certain way. The context must be the determiner of meaning, and word order in an English translation can follow the Greek so long as this does not change the meaning of the Greek text.

3. The business of a translator is to report what an author says, not to explain what he means. The English translation should follow the form of the Greek text as closely as possible without changing what the Greek says.

---

[33] BeDuhn, *Translation*, 105.

CHAPTER 8

THE WORD IS GOD

Introduction

This is probably the most important chapter in this book because it deals with arguably the most important statement in the New Testament about the deity of Jesus Christ, namely, Jn. 1:1: "And the Word was God." The whole verse is set out below with a word-for-word translation:

Table #41: Jn. 1:1

Ἐν	ἀρχῇ	ἦν	ὁ λόγος
In	beginning	was	the word
καὶ	ὁ λόγος	ἦν	πρὸς
and	the word	was	with
τὸν θεόν	καὶ	θεὸς	ἦν
the God	and	God	was
ὁ λόγος			
the word			

Since the discussion will be concerned primarily with the use of the definite article with certain nouns in the verse, for clarity and ease of reference, in the table above I have kept the definite articles with the nouns to which they are related. The third clause on which the argument focuses reads καὶ θεὸς ἦν ὁ λόγος (*kai theos ēn ho logos*). Strictly keeping to the word order of the phrase, the translation would be, "and God was the Word," but this woodenly literal translation actually changes the meaning of the sentence. A more accurate translation would be, "And the Word was God." The fact that Jn. 1:14 identifies Jesus as the Word (Λόγος, *Logos*), this verse seems to be asserting that Jesus is God. The New World Translation renders it, "and the Word was a god."

Anarthrous and Definite

BeDuhn begins his discussion by informing the reader about the Greek definite article: "Greek has only a definite article, like our *the*; it does not have an indefinite article, like our *a* or *an*. So, generally speaking, a Greek definite noun will have a form of the definite article (*ho*), which will become 'the' in English. A Greek indefinite noun will appear without the definite article, and will be properly rendered in English with 'a' or 'an.'"[1] Right away there is a problem with BeDuhn's characterizations. First, a Greek word does not need to have the definite article to be definite. Jn. 1:6 makes reference to God and does not have the definite article, but it certainly is a definite noun:

Table #42: Jn. 1:6

Ἐγένετο	ἄνθρωπος	ἀπεσταλμένος	παρὰ
Became	man	having been sent	from
θεοῦ	ὄνομα	αὐτῷ	Ἰωάννης
God	name	to him	John

It is interesting and revealing that nowhere in this chapter, easily the longest chapter in BeDuhn's book, does he refer to this verse. That may be because it poses a problem that he cannot make fit his thesis. Be that as it may, the point is that the word 'God,' in the second line of the table above, does not have the definite article, and yet there can be no question that this is a definite noun. BeDuhn admits that "anarthrous *theos* in the genitive or dative cases" are "two forms that freely dispense with the article in a number of uses . . ."[2] and in Jn. 1:6 the word θεοῦ is in the Genitive case.

This is not unlike English that can use an indefinite form to refer to something definite. In the statement, "I met a man in the mall yesterday," the word 'man' is certainly indefinite in grammatical form, being preceded by the indefinite article 'a,' but it is certainly definite in meaning. The statement is not saying, "I met an indefinite man," but rather "I met a certain man." This is a case of a noun that is grammatically indefinite actually referring to something definite. The reverse is also common in English, that is, using a definite noun to refer to something indefinite. In the sentence,

---

[1] Ibid., 114.
[2] Ibid., 117.

"When you are severely injured you should go to the hospital," the noun "hospital" is clearly grammatically definite, being preceded by the definite article 'the,' but it is also clearly indefinite in meaning since it is not saying you should go to a definite hospital, but to any hospital. So, a form that is grammatically definite can actually be indefinite in meaning, and a form that is grammatically indefinite can be definite in meaning.

BeDuhn's characterization is in fact wrong and misleading. A Greek noun that is grammatically definite by virtue of the definite article is not necessarily conceptually definite and may not require the definite article when translated into English. Conversely, a Greek noun that is grammatically indefinite may in fact be conceptually definite and might need the definite article in English. So, just because a Greek noun is grammatically indefinite does not mean that it should be "properly rendered in English with 'a' or 'an.'" It is simply not true that we are "obeying the rules of English grammar that tell us we cannot say 'Snoopy is dog,' but must say 'Snoopy is a dog.'"[3] In fact, it entirely depends upon what the word 'dog' means as to whether we can or cannot say "Snoopy is dog." If the word 'dog' is an adjective and identifies a quality that is being predicated of Snoopy, or if 'dog' is a name that is being applied to Snoopy, then it would be proper English to omit the article. For example, we say "Snoopy is tired." We do not say, "Snoopy is a tired." There may not be such uses of the particular word 'dog,' but there are myriads of examples of this kind of construction with other words. For example, one can say "It is a house," where the word 'house' refers to a building, or "It is House," where the word 'House' is a name. Someone may object that this distinction is made evident by capitalization, but Greek did not have such a convention, and although the convention functions with reference to the name 'House' in English, this is not true of every possible construction. Also, if someone is responding to a question like this: "What is a synonym for dwelling?" The answer might be, "It is house." It depends upon the meaning as to whether the indefinite article should be used. BeDuhn simply misrepresents the case.

BeDuhn asserts, "For example, in John 1:1c, the clause we are investigating, *ho logos* is 'the word,' as all translations accurately have it. If it was written simply *logos*, without the definite article *ho*, we would have to translate it as 'a word.'"[4] But this is misleading. For example, in Matt. 8:8 we find the statement, "But the centurion said, 'Lord, I am not worthy for You to come under my roof, but just say *the* word [ἀλλὰ μόνον εἰπὲ λόγῳ, *alla monon eipe logō*], and my servant will be healed'" (NASBU).[5] In this sentence the word λόγῳ, translated "*the* word," does not have the definite article, and yet it can legitimately be translated, "but just say *the* word [λόγῳ, *logō*].'" To translate this, "but just say *a* word" would be awkward and contrary to customary English usage. And the centurion is not asking Jesus to say just any word at all. He is asking Jesus to say the word that would heal his servant. Also, if the word λόγος is used

---

[3] Ibid., 114.
[4] Ibid.
[5] καὶ ἀποκριθεὶς ὁ ἑκατόνταρχος ἔφη· κύριε, οὐκ εἰμὶ ἱκανὸς ἵνα μου ὑπὸ τὴν στέγην εἰσέλθῃς, ἀλλὰ μόνον εἰπὲ λόγῳ, καὶ ἰαθήσεται ὁ παῖς μου. (Matt. 8:8).

The Word is God

to mean 'reason,' which is one of its literal meanings,⁶ and if this were the meaning in Jn. 1:1, even without the definite article it would not only be inappropriate but misleading to add the indefinite article 'a': "In beginning was a reason" would be improper English while "In beginning was reason" would not only be proper English but would be an accurate translation that communicates this meaning. Why would BeDuhn misrepresent the case in this way? If his past course of action can inform our understanding here, it would be to prejudice his readers by setting them up to accept his theological bias.

The fact that BeDuhn has been setting the reader up in order to promote his own theological agenda becomes even more evident in his next assertion: "Similarly, when we have a form of *ho theos*, as we do in John 1:1b and 1:2, we are dealing with a definite noun that we would initially ('lexically') translate as 'the god'; but if it is written simply *theos*, as it is in John 1:1c, it is an indefinite noun that would normally be translated as 'a god.'"⁷ We have already shown that just because a word does not have the definite article does not mean it is indefinite. In addition to Jn. 1:6 there are a number of instances that demonstrate this fact. In the table below there are four examples:

Table #43: Anarthrous Instances of θεός

Matt. 4:4	But He answered and said, "It is written, 'Man shall not live on bread alone, but on every word that proceeds out of the mouth of God.'"
	ὁ δὲ ἀποκριθεὶς εἶπεν· γέγραπται· οὐκ ἐπ' ἄρτῳ μόνῳ ζήσεται ὁ ἄνθρωπος, ἀλλ' ἐπὶ παντὶ ῥήματι ἐκπορευομένῳ διὰ στόματος θεοῦ.
Mk. 11:22	And Jesus answered saying to them, "Have faith in God."
	καὶ ἀποκριθεὶς ὁ Ἰησοῦς λέγει αὐτοῖς· ἔχετε πίστιν θεοῦ.
Jn. 1:18	No one has seen God at any time; the only begotten God who is in the bosom of the Father, He has explained [Him].
	Θεὸν οὐδεὶς ἑώρακεν πώποτε· μονογενὴς υἱὸς ὁ ὢν εἰς τὸν κόλπον τοῦ πατρὸς ἐκεῖνος ἐξηγήσατο.
1 Cor. 8:4	Therefore concerning the eating of things sacrificed to idols, we know that there is no such thing as an idol in the world, and that there is no God but one.
	Περὶ τῆς βρώσεως οὖν τῶν εἰδωλοθύτων, οἴδαμεν ὅτι οὐδὲν εἴδωλον ἐν κόσμῳ καὶ ὅτι οὐδεὶς θεὸς εἰ μὴ εἷς.

The above examples include two instances from the Synoptic Gospels, one instance from the Gospel of John, and one from 1 Cor. 8:4. Not one of these would make sense

---

⁶ See LSL, s.v. "λόγος," III.5. *"reason, ground."*
⁷ BeDuhn, *Translation*, 114–15.

if translated "a God," and yet each one is anarthrous, that is, they do not have a definite article. The 1 Corinthian example is particularly interesting. The phrase in which the anarthrous use of θεός occurs can be translated, "because no God except one." Not only would this make no sense if translated "a God," it would in fact be a contradictory statement to say "because no a god except one." And, this is a case of an anarthrous noun in the Nominative case being used in a definite sense.

The Jn. 1:18 example presents another instance in the Gospel of John in which the anarthrous use of the word θεός must be understood to be a definite use. In fact, this is an instance in which, though clearly definite, it would be awkward English to use the definite article: "No one has seen the God at any time." It is much better English simply to say, "No one has seen God at any time," and yet it is still clear that the use is definite. So, once again BeDuhn's claims are proven not only to be wrong, but misleading and disingenuous. It is particularly disingenuous for BeDuhn to assert, "But what about the indefinite *theos* in John 1:1c? This does not correspond to the English definite proper noun 'God,' but to the indefinite noun 'a god.'" The problem here is that he makes this assertion before he has presented any evidence to substantiate such a claim. BeDuhn starts with his conclusion. This is called poisoning the well. He has stated his conclusion as if it were obviously true in order to prejudice his reader toward his point of view.

Definitely Definite

BeDuhn objects to the claim by some that "*theos* does not require the definite article to be definite, and that there are examples of article-less ('anarthrous') *theos* used definitely in the New Testament."[8] His objection is that there are none of these in the NT:

> While this may be true of the anarthrous *theos* in the genitive or dative cases, two forms that freely dispense with the article in a number of uses, it is not the case for anarthrous *theos* in the nominative case, the format used in John 1:1c. The nominative case is much more dependent than other Greek cases on the definite article to mark definiteness. There is a very limited range of definitizing elements that may make an anarthrous nominative *theos* definite. These include the presence of an attached possessive pronoun (John 8:54; 2 Corinthians 6:16), the use of the noun in direct address (the "vocative" function, Romans. 9:5; 1 Thessalonians 2:5), and the association of the noun with the numeration "one" (1 Corinthians 8:6; Ephesians 4:6; 1 Timothy numeral 2:5). None of these definitizing elements are present in John 1:1c, and it and the remaining eleven examples of anarthrous nominative *theos* in the New Testament are indefinite (Mark 12:27; Luke 20:38; John 1:18; Romans 8:33; 1 Corinthians 8:4; 2 Corinthians 1:3; 2 Corinthians 5:19; collations 6:7; Philippians 2:13; 2 Thessalonians 2:4; Revelation 21:7).[9]

---

[8] Ibid., 117.
[9] Ibid.

But, as has been his practice, BeDuhn has once again misrepresented the situation. First, BeDuhn presents no support and cites no source to substantiate his claim that the Nominative case is "much more dependent than other Greek cases on the definite article to mark definiteness." None of the standard Greek grammars present this as a rule or principle in Greek. If it is simply an observation on BeDuhn's part, then he should make it clear to his reader that this is simply his own observation, not a grammatical or syntactical rule of Greek.

Second, there is also no grammatical rule or principle for talking about "definitizing elements" as BeDuhn calls them. None of the standard Greek grammars talk about definitizing elements. These seem simply to be elements that BeDuhn enumerates in order to try to get around the fact that there are indeed anarthrous Nominative nouns that are definite.

Third, BeDuhn's claim that there are no instances of anarthrous, Nominative *theos* that are definite is simply false. Table 44 below presents 19 instances of anarthrous uses of the Nominative form of θεός, each of which is definite:

Table #44: Anarthrous, Definite Uses of θεός

Mk. 12:27	"He is not *the* God of the dead, but of the living; you are greatly mistaken."
	οὐκ ἔστιν θεὸς νεκρῶν ἀλλὰ ζώντων· πολὺ πλανᾶσθε.
	It would make no sense to say, "He is not *a* God of the dead."
Lk. 20:38	"Now He is not *the* God of the dead but of the living; for all live to Him."
	θεὸς δὲ οὐκ ἔστιν νεκρῶν ἀλλὰ ζώντων, πάντες γὰρ αὐτῷ ζῶσιν.
	This verse is parallel to the one in Mark.
Jn. 1:18	"God no one has seen at any time; the only begotten God who is in the bosom of the Father, He has explained."[10]
	Θεὸν οὐδεὶς ἑώρακεν πώποτε· μονογενὴς θεὸς ὁ ὢν εἰς τὸν κόλπον τοῦ πατρὸς ἐκεῖνος ἐξηγήσατο.
	Assuming the reading adopted in the critical text to be correct (see footnote 10), it would make no sense to say, "an only begotten God."

---

[10] The critical text adopts the reading μονογενὴς θεὸς based on 𝔓⁶⁶, ℵ* B C*L and others. The Majority text adopts the reading μονογενὴς υἱὸς based on A C³ W^supp *Byz* and others.

Jn. 8:54	"Jesus answered, 'If I glorify Myself, My glory is nothing; it is My Father who glorifies Me, of whom you say, "He is our God";'"
	ἀπεκρίθη Ἰησοῦς· ἐὰν ἐγὼ δοξάσω ἐμαυτόν, ἡ δόξα μου οὐδέν ἐστιν· ἔστιν ὁ πατήρ μου ὁ δοξάζων με, ὃν ὑμεῖς λέγετε ὅτι θεὸς ἡμῶν ἐστιν,
	Here is a case of an anarthrous θεός as a predicate nominative. It would make no sense to say, "because He is a god of us." This would indicate that God was merely one of their gods, something particularly unlikely for the Jews to say. Also, here is an example of Nominative use of θεός as a predicate nominative, as in Jn. 1:1c, that is definite and anarthrous.
Rom. 8:33	"Who will bring a charge against God's elect? God is the one who justifies;"
	τίς ἐγκαλέσει κατὰ ἐκλεκτῶν θεοῦ; θεὸς ὁ δικαιῶν·
	Again, it would make no sense to say, "A god is the one who justifies." This has to be a reference to *the* God who elects.
1 Cor. 3:7	"So then neither the one who plants nor the one who waters is anything, but the one causing the growth *is* God."
	ὥστε οὔτε ὁ φυτεύων ἐστίν τι οὔτε ὁ ποτίζων ἀλλ' ὁ αὐξάνων θεός.
	To translate this, "but the one causes the growth is a god," would be absurd.
1 Cor. 8:4	"Therefore concerning the eating of things sacrificed to idols, we know that there is no such thing as an idol in the world, and that there is no God but one."
	Περὶ τῆς βρώσεως οὖν τῶν εἰδωλοθύτων, οἴδαμεν ὅτι οὐδὲν εἴδωλον ἐν κόσμῳ καὶ ὅτι οὐδεὶς θεὸς εἰ μὴ εἷς.
	This is another definite, Nominative, anarthrous use of θεός.
1 Cor. 8:6	"yet for us there is one God, the Father, from whom are all things and we for Him; and one Lord, Jesus Christ, by whom are all things, and we through Him."
	ἀλλ' ἡμῖν εἷς θεὸς ὁ πατὴρ ἐξ οὗ τὰ πάντα καὶ ἡμεῖς εἰς αὐτόν, καὶ εἷς κύριος Ἰησοῦς Χριστὸς δι' οὗ τὰ πάντα καὶ ἡμεῖς δι' αὐτοῦ.
	Even though this includes one of BeDuhn's so-called definitizing elements, it is nevertheless an example of an anarthrous, Nominative form of θεός that is definite and does not have the definite article.

2 Cor. 1:3	"Blessed the God and Father of our Lord Jesus Christ, the Father of mercies and God of all comfort,"
	Εὐλογητὸς ὁ θεὸς καὶ πατὴρ τοῦ κυρίου ἡμῶν Ἰησοῦ Χριστοῦ, ὁ πατὴρ τῶν οἰκτιρμῶν καὶ θεὸς πάσης παρακλήσεως,
	It would make no sense to say "and a god of all comfort."
2 Cor. 1:21	"Now He who establishes us with you in Christ and anointed us is God,"
	ὁ δὲ βεβαιῶν ἡμᾶς σὺν ὑμῖν εἰς Χριστὸν καὶ χρίσας ἡμᾶς θεός,
	Here is another instance of the use of θεός as a definite predicate nominative without the definite article. It would make no sense to say "Now He who establishes us with you in Christ and anointed us is a god."
2 Cor. 5:5	"Now He who prepared us for this very purpose *is* God, who gave to us the Spirit as a pledge."
	ὁ δὲ κατεργασάμενος ἡμᾶς εἰς αὐτὸ τοῦτο θεός, ὁ δοὺς ἡμῖν τὸν ἀρραβῶνα τοῦ πνεύματος.
	This is yet another use of a definite predicate nominative without the definite article, and it makes no sense to translate this, "Now the One who prepared us for this very purpose is a god."
2 Cor. 5:19	"namely, that God was in Christ reconciling the world to Himself, not counting their trespasses against them, and He has committed to us the word of reconciliation."
	ὡς ὅτι θεὸς ἦν ἐν Χριστῷ κόσμον καταλλάσσων ἑαυτῷ, μὴ λογιζόμενος αὐτοῖς τὰ παραπτώματα αὐτῶν καὶ θέμενος ἐν ἡμῖν τὸν λόγον τῆς καταλλαγῆς.
	Here is an instance of an anarthrous use of θεός as a subject. Here again it would be absurd to translate this as "namely, that a god was in Christ . . ."
2 Cor. 6:16	"just as said the God that, "I will dwell in them and I will walk among; and I will be of them God, and they shall be of me people."
	καθὼς εἶπεν ὁ θεὸς ὅτι ἐνοικήσω ἐν αὐτοῖς καὶ ἐμπεριπατήσω καὶ ἔσομαι αὐτῶν θεὸς καὶ αὐτοὶ ἔσονταί μου λαός.
	Notice the second use of *theos*. It would be absurd to say, "and I will be to them a god."

Gal. 6:7	"Do not be deceived, God is not mocked; for whatever a man sows, this he will also reap."
	Μὴ πλανᾶσθε, θεὸς οὐ μυκτηρίζεται. ὃ γὰρ ἐὰν σπείρῃ ἄνθρωπος, τοῦτο καὶ θερίσει·
	Here is another instance of a definite article-less use of θεός as subject. It would be absurd to translate this as, "Do not be deceived, a god is not mocked."
Phil. 2:13	"for the one working in you is God, both to will and to work for the good pleasure."
	θεὸς γάρ ἐστιν ὁ ἐνεργῶν ἐν ὑμῖν καὶ τὸ θέλειν καὶ τὸ ἐνεργεῖν ὑπὲρ τῆς εὐδοκίας.
	Here is yet another instance of a pre-verbal, anarthrous use of θεός as a definite predicate nominative.
1 Thess. 2:5	"For we never came with flattering speech, as you know, nor with a pretext for greed—God is witness—"
	Οὔτε γάρ ποτε ἐν λόγῳ κολακείας ἐγενήθημεν, καθὼς οἴδατε, οὔτε ἐν προφάσει πλεονεξίας, θεὸς μάρτυς,
	This is an example of a definite, anarthrous form of θεός in a verbless clause.
2 Thess. 2:4	"who opposes and exalts himself above every so-called god or object of worship, so that he takes his seat in the temple of God, displaying himself as being God."
	ὁ ἀντικείμενος καὶ ὑπεραιρόμενος ἐπὶ πάντα λεγόμενον θεὸν ἢ σέβασμα, ὥστε αὐτὸν εἰς τὸν ναὸν τοῦ θεοῦ καθίσαι ἀποδεικνύντα ἑαυτὸν ὅτι ἔστιν θεός.
	Here is another instance of a definite, anarthrous use of θεός as a predicate nominative: "that he is God."
Heb. 3:4	"For every house is built by someone, but the builder of all things *is* God."
	πᾶς γὰρ οἶκος κατασκευάζεται ὑπό τινος, ὁ δὲ πάντα κατασκευάσας θεός.
	Here is another definite, anarthrous use of θεός as a predicate nominative.
Rev. 21:7	"He who overcomes will inherit these things, and I will be his God and he will be My son."
	ὁ νικῶν κληρονομήσει ταῦτα καὶ ἔσομαι αὐτῷ θεὸς καὶ αὐτὸς ἔσται μοι υἱός.
	Although this verse has one of BeDuhn's so-called definitizing elements, it is nevertheless an anarthrous, definite use of θεός.

Contrary to BeDuhn's claim, each one of these is an anarthrous, Nominative form of *theos* that is definite. The fact that each is definite is demonstrated by the absurdity of translating any of them as indefinite. Of these 19 instances, there are five that are of particular interest.

Table #45: Anarthrous *theos* as Definite Predicate Nominatives

Jn. 8:54	ὃν ὑμεῖς λέγετε ὅτι θεὸς ἡμῶν ἐστιν,
	whom you say that God of us he is.
2 Cor. 1:21	ὁ δὲ βεβαιῶν ἡμᾶς σὺν ὑμῖν εἰς Χριστὸν καὶ χρίσας ἡμᾶς θεός,
	but the one having established us together with you into Christ and anointed us God
2 Cor. 6:16	τίς δὲ συγκατάθεσις ναῷ θεοῦ μετὰ εἰδώλων; ἡμεῖς γὰρ ναὸς θεοῦ ἐσμεν ζῶντος, καθὼς εἶπεν ὁ θεὸς ὅτι ἐνοικήσω ἐν αὐτοῖς καὶ ἐμπεριπατήσω καὶ ἔσομαι αὐτῶν θεὸς καὶ αὐτοὶ ἔσονταί μου λαός.
	But what agreement temple of God with idols? For we are the temple of God living; just as said the God that, "I will dwell in them and I will walk among; and I will be of them God, and they shall be of me people.
2 Thess. 2:4	ὁ ἀντικείμενος καὶ ὑπεραιρόμενος ἐπὶ πάντα λεγόμενον θεὸν ἢ σέβασμα, ὥστε αὐτὸν εἰς τὸν ναὸν τοῦ θεοῦ καθίσαι ἀποδεικνύντα ἑαυτὸν ὅτι ἔστιν θεός.
	the opposing and exalting above every being called god or object of worship, so that his into the temple of the God to sit, displaying himself as he is God.
Heb. 3:4	ὁ δὲ πάντα κατασκευάσας θεός.
	but the one all having built God.

BeDuhn attempts to blunt the force of the anarthrous uses of θεός by referring to "definitizing elements." We have quoted this above, but we present it again for clarity.

There is a very limited range of definitizing elements that may make an anarthrous nominative *theos* definite. These include the presence of an attached possessive pronoun (John 8:54; 2 Corinthians 6:16), the use of the noun in direct address (the "vocative" function, Romans 9:5; 1 Thessalonians 2:5), and the association of the noun with the numeration "one" (1 Corinthians 8:6; Ephesians 4:6; 1 Timothy 2:5). None of these definitizing elements are present in John 1:1c, and it and the remaining eleven examples of anarthrous nominative *theos* in the New Testament are indefinite (Mark 12:27; Luke 20:38; John 1:18; Romans 8:33; 1

Corinthians 8:4; 2 Corinthians 1:3; 2 Corinthians 5:19; Galatians 6:7; Philippians 2:13; 2 Thessalonians 2:4; Revelation 21:7.[11]

The following table lists the verses from Table 44 above along with the verses BeDuhn gives in the previous quote:

Table #46: Comparative List of Anarthrous Uses of θεός

My List From Table 41	BeDuhn's Lists	
	With Definitizing Elements	Indefinite
Mk. 12:27		Mark 12:27
Lk. 20:38		Luke 20:38
Jn. 1:18		John 1:18
Jn. 8:54	John 8:54	
Rom. 8:33		Romans 8:33
	Romans 9:5	
1 Cor. 3:7		
1 Cor. 8:4		1 Corinthians 8:4
1 Cor. 8:6	1 Corinthians 8:6	
2 Cor. 1:3		2 Corinthians 1:3
2 Cor. 1:21		
2 Cor. 5:5		
2 Cor. 5:19		2 Corinthians 5:19
	2 Corinthians 6:16	
Gal. 6:7		Galatians 6:7
	Ephesians 4:6	
Phil. 2:13		Philippians 2:13
1 The. 2:5	1 Thessalonians 2:5	
2 The. 2:4		2 Thessalonians 2:4
	1 Timothy 2:5	
Heb. 3:4		
Rev. 21:7		Revelation 21:7

---

[11] BeDuhn, *Translation*, 117.

There are a couple of things to notice about the comparative lists above. First, every one of the verses that BeDuhn classifies as indefinite we have already shown to be definite. Second, the shaded boxes indicate verses with definite, anarthrous, Nominative uses of *theos* that BeDuhn conveniently omits from his lists. What is interesting about these omissions is that three of these include anarthrous, Nominative uses of *theos* that are not only definite, but are predicate nominatives, and not one of these has BeDuhn's "definitizing elements":

Table #47: Definite Predicate Nominatives of θεός

2 Cor. 1:21	ὁ δὲ βεβαιῶν ἡμᾶς σὺν ὑμῖν εἰς Χριστὸν καὶ χρίσας ἡμᾶς θεός,
	but the one having established us together with you into Christ and anointed us *is* God
2 Cor. 5:5	ὁ δὲ κατεργασάμενος ἡμᾶς εἰς αὐτὸ τοῦτο θεός,
	but the one having prepared us unto same this *is* God,
Heb. 3:4	ὁ δὲ πάντα κατασκευάσας θεός.
	but the one all having built *is* God.

But BeDuhn's discussion is not only irrelevant, it flatly contradicts his earlier claim about the Nominative case. He says it is not the case that there are "examples of article-less ('anarthrous') *theos* used definitely in the New Testament," and then he points out several instances of anarthrous uses of θεός in the New Testament. Basically what he is saying is, "There aren't any of these. And when I say there aren't any of these, what I mean is there are some of these, and I believe I can explain why there are some of these." But, even if there are certain "definitizing elements," it is still the case that there are anarthrous uses of θεός that are still definite. Additionally, we have shown in the above table several instances of the anarthrous θεός without any of BeDuhn's "difinitizing elements" that are nonetheless Nominative and definite.

Another interesting fact that BeDuhn just happens to omit is that 'the God' does not occur even once in the ASV, KJV, NASB, NIV, NRSV, or TEV translations of the Gospel of John even though ὁ θεός, 'God' with the definite article, occurs 53 times in the Greek text of John.

Table #48: θεός in John With and Without the Definite Article

Greek with no definite article (θεὸς)	Greek with definite article (ὁ θεὸς)	English Translation with no definite article (ASV, KJV, NASB, NIV, NRSV, TEV)
Jn. 1:1	Jn. 1:1	Jn. 1:1 (twice)
	Jn. 1:2	Jn. 1:2

Greek with no definite article (θεός)	Greek with definite article (ὁ θεός)	English Translation with no definite article (ASV, KJV, NASB, NIV, NRSV, TEV)
Jn. 1:6		Jn. 1:6
Jn. 1:12		Jn. 1:12
Jn. 1:13		Jn. 1:13
Jn. 1:18		Jn. 1:18
	Jn. 1:29	Jn. 1:29
	Jn. 1:34	Jn. 1:34
	Jn. 1:36	Jn. 1:36
	Jn. 1:49	Jn. 1:49
	Jn. 1:51	Jn. 1:51
Jn. 3:2	Jn. 3:2	Jn. 3:2 (twice)
	Jn. 3:3	Jn. 3:3
	Jn. 3:5	Jn. 3:5
	Jn. 3:16	Jn. 3:16
	Jn. 3:17	Jn. 3:17
	Jn. 3:18	Jn. 3:18
Jn. 3:21		Jn. 3:21
	Jn. 3:33	Jn. 3:33
	Jn. 3:34	Jn. 3:34
	Jn. 3:36	Jn. 3:36
	Jn. 4:10	Jn. 4:10
	Jn. 4:24	Jn. 4:24
	Jn. 5:18	Jn. 5:18
	Jn. 5:25	Jn. 5:25
	Jn. 5:42	Jn. 5:42
Jn. 5:44		Jn. 5:44
	Jn. 6:27	Jn. 6:27
	Jn. 6:28	Jn. 6:28
	Jn. 6:29	Jn. 6:29
	Jn. 6:33	Jn. 6:33
Jn. 6:45		Jn. 6:45

The Word is God

Greek with no definite article (θεὸς)	Greek with definite article (ὁ θεὸς)	English Translation with no definite article (ASV, KJV, NASB, NIV, NRSV, TEV)
	Jn. 6:46	Jn. 6:46
	Jn. 6:69	Jn. 6:69
	Jn. 7:17	Jn. 7:17
	Jn. 8:40	Jn. 8:40
	Jn. 8:41	Jn. 8:41
	Jn. 8:42	Jn. 8:42
	Jn. 8:47	Jn. 8:47
Jn. 8:54		Jn. 8:54
	Jn. 9:3	Jn. 9:3
Jn. 9:16		Jn. 9:16
	Jn. 9:24	Jn. 9:24
	Jn. 9:29	Jn. 9:29
	Jn. 9:31	Jn. 9:31
Jn. 9:33		Jn. 9:33
Jn. 10:33		Jn. 10:33
	Jn. 10:35	Jn. 10:35
	Jn. 10:36	Jn. 10:36
	Jn. 11:4	Jn. 11:4
	Jn. 11:22	Jn. 11:22
	Jn. 11:27	Jn. 11:27
	Jn. 11:40	Jn. 11:40
	Jn. 11:52	Jn. 11:52
	Jn. 12:43	Jn. 12:43
Jn. 13:3	Jn. 13:3	Jn. 13:3 (twice)
	Jn. 13:31	Jn. 13:31
	Jn. 13:32	Jn. 13:32
	Jn. 14:1	Jn. 14:1
	Jn. 16:2	Jn. 16:2

Greek with no definite article (θεός)	Greek with definite article (ὁ θεός)	English Translation with no definite article (ASV, KJV, NASB, NIV, NRSV, TEV)
	Jn. 16:27	(Translated "Father" in the NASB and ASV, and "God" in the KJV)
Jn. 16:30		Jn. 16:30
Jn. 17:3		Jn. 17:3
Jn. 19:7		Jn. 19:7
Jn. 20:17		Jn. 20:17
	Jn. 20:28	Jn. 20:28
	Jn. 20:31	Jn. 20:31
	Jn. 21:19	Jn. 21:19

In the Gospel of John, θεός, without the definite article, occurs 18 times; ὁ θεός, with the definite article, occurs 53 times; 'God,' without the definite article occurs 71 times (in one instance, τοῦ θεοῦ is translated "Father" in the ASV, NASB, NRSV, and TEV, and "God" in the KJV and NIV); "the God" does not occur in even one instance throughout the Gospel of John in any of these translations. What this shows is that in the Gospel of John one cannot determine that the word θεός is definite or indefinite by the presence or absence of the definite article. This must be determined by the context, and it is going to involve the translator's theological perspective. So, BeDuhn's claim that Jn. 1:1c must be translated "the word was a god" reveals his translation is theologically motivated. However, BeDuhn's translation is less likely because the grammatical and syntactical evidence argues against his translation.

At the end of the paragraph in which he briefly discusses the anarthrous uses of the Nominative form of θεός, BeDuhn identifies several verses of which he says, "and the remaining eleven examples of anarthrous Nominative *theos* in the New Testament are indefinite (Mark 12:27; Luke 20:38; John 1:18; Romans 8:33; 1 Corinthians 8:4; 2 Corinthians 1:3; 2 Corinthians 5:19; Galatians 6:7; Philippians 2:13; 2 Thessalonians 2:4; Revelation 21:7)."[12] These are listed in Table 46 above. At this point BeDuhn notes, "We will come back to these."[13] Rather than wait, we will go ahead at this point and consider what BeDuhn says about these verses.

---

[12] Ibid.
[13] Ibid.

Mk. 12:27 and Lk. 20:38

Because these are parallel verses, BeDuhn treats them together. He starts by considering the Lk. 20:38 passage:

> Luke 20:38 reads: "But he is not a god of the dead" (*theos de ouk estin nekrōn*). Notice that in this verse *theos* is before the verb (*estin*), just as it is in John 1:1. The article is missing not because of "Colwell's Rule," but because *theos* is indefinite. The implied question is: What kind of God is the Christian god? The answer is: He is not a god of the dead, but a god of the living. The word "god" is indefinite because it is speaking of a category to which the subject belongs. Because categories are indefinite, *theos* is written here without the article. The proper translation is "a god." The indefiniteness of "god" is proved by the parallel passage in Mark 12:27 (*ouk estin theos nekrōn*), where *theos* follows the verb, rather than preceding it as it does in Luke 20:38. In such a position, anarthrous *theos* must be indefinite.[14]

BeDuhn completely ignores the literary and historical context of the verse and discusses it as if it were spoken in a complete vacuum. In fact, the notion that the implied question is "What kind of God is the Christian god?" goes beyond being absurd since the statement made in this passage was made before Christianity was even established.[15] In the context, Jesus is being questioned by the Sadducees, and besides the fact that there was no Christian church at this time, the Sadducees would have had no interest in the Christian God. Rather, the question is about the fact that the Sadducees denied life after death and the resurrection. Jesus is responding to their inquisition. The fact that this exchange has to do with the God of Israel, who would have been the God of the Sadducees, and this was the God about whom the question is posed, proves that this cannot be an indefinite use.

The Sadducees are trying to trap Jesus by their scenario, and Jesus responds to them by saying, "But that the dead are raised, even Moses showed, in the bush, where he calls the Lord the God of Abraham [τὸν θεὸν Ἀβραὰμ, *ton theon Abraam*], and the God of Isaac, and the God of Jacob. Now He is not *the* God [θεὸς, *theos*] of the dead but of the living; for all live to Him" (Lk. 20:37–38).[16] In verse 37 Jesus refers to God as "the God [τὸν θεὸν] of Abraham," and then in verse 38 he is referring to the same God as the one He referred to in verse 37. Therefore, this must be a definite use, not an indefinite use. Also, this cannot be a case of a category since the Jews would never have thought in terms of there being a category of "God" into which their God would be classified. All

---

[14] Ibid., 126.

[15] Of course, this reveals BeDuhn's commitment to a critical view that holds that much of what Jesus said was attributed to him by the early church and was not actually spoken by Jesus. This is quite similar to what is being proposed by the Jesus Seminar, and view that has been repudiated by contemporary scholars both evangelical and liberal.

[16] ὅτι δὲ ἐγείρονται οἱ νεκροί, καὶ Μωϋσῆς ἐμήνυσεν ἐπὶ τῆς βάτου, ὡς λέγει κύριον τὸν θεὸν Ἀβραὰμ καὶ θεὸν Ἰσαὰκ καὶ θεὸν Ἰακώβ. θεὸς δὲ οὐκ ἔστιν νεκρῶν ἀλλὰ ζώντων, πάντες γὰρ αὐτῷ ζῶσιν. (Lk. 20:37–38).

Israelites, whether Pharisees, scribes, or Sadducees, or the run-of-the-mill Jew believed that there was and could be only one true God: שְׁמַע יִשְׂרָאֵל יְהוָה אֱלֹהֵינוּ יְהוָה אֶחָד: "Hear Israel, the LORD our God, the LORD one." Jesus quoted this in Mk. 12:29: "Hear, O Israel; The Lord our God, the Lord is one:" (ἄκουε, Ἰσραήλ, κύριος ὁ θεὸς ἡμῶν κύριος εἷς ἐστιν,). If Jesus was using *theos* as a category, this would have been all the proof the Sadducees would need to accuse Him of blasphemy.

BeDuhn tries to appeal to Mk. 12:27 as evidence that the word is indefinite because "*theos* follows the verb, rather than preceding it as it does in Luke 20:38. In such a position, anarthrous *theos* must be indefinite."[17] But where did he get this rule? Not only has BeDuhn presented this as a rule of grammar when it is not, but he has also, again, not given the whole story. The portion to which BeDuhn is referring is the first part of verse 27. In **Figure 10** I have put together the information from Swanson's *New Testament Greek Manuscripts: Mark*.[18] Notice how many manuscripts have the definite article in the place where BeDuhn says it "must be indefinite."

Figure 10: Textual Variants of Mk. 12:27

ΚΑΤΑ ΜΑΡΚΟΝ							12.26-28
27 οὐκ ἔστιν	θεὸς	νεκρῶν ἀλλὰ	ζώντων·		πολὺ	πλανᾶσθε.	B L W Δ u[w]
27	....	....	....			........νᾶσθε.	𝔓45
27 οὐκ ἔστιν	ὁ θεὸς	νεκρῶν ἀλλὰ	ζώντων·		πολὺ	πλανᾶσθε.	א C Ψ [w]
27 οὐκ ἔστιν	ὁ θεὸς	νεκρῶν ἀλλὰ	ζώντων· ὑμεῖς οὖν		πολὺ	πλανᾶσθε.	A 157* 1424
27 οὐκ ἔστιν	ὁ θεὸς	νεκρῶν ἀλλὰ	ζώντων· ὑμεῖς οὖν		πολὺ	πλανᾶσθε.	D K Mᶜ U Π 28 1071
27 οὐκ ἔστιν	ὁ θεὸς	νεκρῶν ἀλλὰ θεὸς	ζώντων· ὑμεῖς οὖν		πολὺ	πλανᾶσθε.	E Γ 157ᶜ τ
27 οὐκ ἔστιν	ὁ θεὸς	νεκρῶν ἀλλὰ	ζώντων· ὑμεῖς οὖν	πολλοὶ		πλανᾶσθε.	F
27 οὐκ ἔστιν	ὁ θεὸς	νεκρῶν ἀλλὰ θεὸς	ζώντων· ὑμεῖς δὲ			πλανᾶσθε.	G
27 οὐκ ἔστιν	ὁ θεὸς	νεκρῶν ἀλλὰ	ζώντων· ὑμεῖς οὖν	πολλοὶ		πλανᾶσθε.	H S 2
27 οὐκ ἔστιν	θεὸς	νεκρῶν ἀλλὰ θεὸς	ζώντων·		πολὺ	πλανᾶσθε.	Y
27 οὐκ ἔστιν	ὁ θεὸς θεὸς	νεκρῶν ἀλλὰ θεὸς	ζώντων· ὑμεῖς οὖν		πολὺ	πλανᾶσθε.	M*
27 οὐκ ἔστιν	ὁ θεὸς θεὸς	νεκρῶν ἀλλὰ	ζώντων· ὑμεῖς οὖν		πολὺ	πλανᾶσθε.	Θ f¹³
27 οὐκ ἔστιν	ὁ θεὸς	νεκρῶν ἀλλὰ θεὸς	ζώντων· ὑμεῖς οὖν	πολλὰ		πλανᾶσθε.	Ω
27 οὐκ ἔστιν	ὁ θεὸς	νεκρῶν ἀλλὰ	ζώντων· ὑμεῖς δὲ		πολὺ	πλανᾶσθε.	1 1582* 118 565 700
27 οὐκ ἔστιν	ὁ θεὸς θεὸς	νεκρῶν ἀλλὰ	ζώντων· ὑμεῖς δὲ		πολὺ	πλανᾶσθε.	1582ᶜ
27 οὐκ ἔστιν	ὁ θεὸς	νεκρῶν ἀλλὰ θεὸς	ζώντων· ὑμεῖς οὖν		πολὺ	πλανᾶσθε.	33
27 οὐκ ἔστιν	θεὸς	νεκρῶν ἀλλὰ	ζώντων· ὑμεῖς οὖν	πολλοὶ		πλανᾶσθαι.	579

Depending on how you count, there are approximately 25 mss listed that have the definite article after ἔστιν (*estin*, "he is") and before θεός. There are 13 mss that do not have the definite article. In line 12 at the far right, one can see the designation f^{13}. This is the designation for the Family 13 group of manuscripts which accounts for and additional 9 manuscripts bringing the total of manuscripts that have ὁ θεός to 34. The fact that these mss have the definite article after ἔστιν and before θεός clearly shows

---

[17] BeDuhn, *Translation*, 126.

[18] Reuben Swanson, ed. *New Testament Greek Manuscripts: Mark* (Sheffield, England: Sheffield Academic Press, 1995), 200. The underlining indicates a variant. For example, while the first line does not have the definite article after ἔστιν, the third line does, and the underlining of the definite article indicates this difference.

that BeDuhn's claim, "In such a position, anarthrous *theos* must be indefinite,"[19] is not only not a rule, but it also clearly shows that in this instance θεός should be understood to be definite whether or not it has the article.

Table #49: Mk. 12:27 and Lk. 20:38

Mk. 12:27	not	he is	God		of dead	but	of living.
	οὐκ	ἔστιν	θεὸς		νεκρῶν	ἀλλὰ	ζώντων·
Lk. 20:38	θεὸς	δὲ	οὐκ	ἔστιν	νεκρῶν	ἀλλὰ	ζώντων
	God	but	not	he is	of dead	but	of living

The fact that the two passages are parallel, and the fact that θεός is definite in Luke, proves that it is also definite in Mark, and vice versa. It seems that whenever the evidence is against him, BeDuhn makes up some "rule" as an excuse to try to explain away the facts. To claim that because *theos* follows the verb it must be indefinite is the very point at issue. It is circular to use your conclusion as part of the proof for your conclusion.

2 Cor. 1:3

Next BeDuhn looks at 2 Cor. 1:3:

> In 2 Corinthians 1:3, Paul refers to the Christian god (the being called "God") as "a god of every consolation" (*theos pasēs paraklēseōs*). He is characterizing the subject, and so uses the indefinite form of theos in the predicate. The question is once again: What kind of god is the Christian god? He is a god of every consolation.[20]

This extremely brief treatment is not an argument but is merely a restatement of his claim. He presents no supporting argumentation. He simply states his belief. He may be presupposing an earlier claim about a Greek way of expressing the nature or character of something. He says,

> Based on his [John Harner] investigation, he concludes that, "anarthrous predicate nouns preceding the verb may function primarily to express the nature or character of the subject, and this qualitative significance may be more important than the question whether the predicate noun itself should be regarded as definite or indefinite" (Harner 1973, page 75). In

---

[19] BeDuhn, *Translation*, 126.
[20] Ibid.

other words, Greek has a particular way of expressing the nature or character of something that employs predicate nouns before the verb and without the article, just as in John 1:1. The nature or character of *ho logos* ("the Word") is *theos* ("divine"). . . . Generally speaking, the function of indefinite predicate nouns, before or after the verb, is to identify the class or category to which the subject belongs.[21]

Besides the fact that Greek has a word that means "divine," namely θεῖος, that is not used in Jn. 1:1, another point that BeDuhn conveniently omits to tell his readers, BeDuhn's claims about predicating nature or character, or that the function of indefinite predicate nouns is to identify the class or category of the subject, is not the whole story (something that we ought to be used to by now). In logic, a simple subject-copula-predicate statement, regardless of Greek word order, can be of two types, regardless of whether the predicate nouns are definite or indefinite, before or after the verb: 1) The first is referred to as the *is* of predication, 2) and the second is referred to as the *is* of identity. In the first type, character, nature, and category as characteristics or accidents can be predicated of a subject. In the second type, the simple subject-copula-predicate proposition can be used to express a subject's identity in which the subject and the predicate are referring to the same thing. This distinction, although not in these specific terms, can be found as early as the writings of Aristotle. For example, Aristotle says, "if it is true to say that something is a man, it must be a two-footed animal, for this is what the term man signifies."[22] Later Aristotle says, "For those things whose matter is one in species [εἴδει] or in number, and those whose substance [ὕλη] is one, are said to be the same. Hence it is evident that sameness is a kind of unity of the being of many things or of one thing taken as many; for example, when a person says that something is the same as itself, he uses the same thing as though it were two."[23] Concerning these statements, Robert W. Schmidt asserts, "Every affirmative predication asserts an identity of the thing signified as the subject and that signified as the predicate; for whatever is predicated of another is signified as identical with it."[24] He goes on to say, "If things represented by subject and predicate are united in reality, there is a real identity between them."[25]

In other words, a simple subject-predicate proposition, regardless of the Greek word order, asserts that the subject and the predicate are the same thing as a kind of assertion

---

[21] Ibid., 120–21.

[22] Aristotelis, Μετα Τα Φυσικα, in *Opera Omnia* (Parisiis: Ambrosio Firmin-Didot, 1927), IV.1006a.29–30. "εἴ τί ἐστιν ἀληθὲς εἰπεῖν ὅτι ἄνθρωπος, ζῷον εἶναι δίπον· τοῦτο γὰρ ἦν ὃ ἐσήμαινε τὸ ἄνθρωπος."

[23] Ibid., V.1018a. "καὶ γὰρ ὧν ἡ ὕλη μία ἢ εἴδει ἢ ἀριθμῷ ταὐτὰ λέγεται, καὶ ὧν ἡ οὐσία μία· ὥστε φανερὸν ὅτι ἡ ταυτότης ἑνότης τίς ἐστιν ἢ πλειόνων τοῦ εἶναι, ἢ ὅταν χρῆται ὡς πλείοσιν, οἷον ὅταν λέγῃ αὐτὸ αὑτῷ ταὐτόν· ὡς δυσὶ γὰρ χρῆται αὐτῷ."

[24] Robert W. Schmidt, *The Domain of Logic According to Saint Thomas Aquinas* (The Hague: Martinus Nijhoff, 1966), 228.

[25] Ibid., 231.

distinct from the predication of a thing as being in a category. Francis Parker and Henry Veatch also point out,

> For those who are familiar with, or are interested in, modern mathematical or symbolic logic, it might be well to remark that it is precisely with respect to this matter of propositional identity that classical realistic logic, as derived from Aristotle, differs most profoundly from symbolic logic, as developed, say, in the *Principia Mathematica* of Whitehead and Russell. In the latter sort of logic, no regard is paid to the peculiar and distinctive relation of identity that holds between the subject and predicate terms of a proposition; . . . This is not to say that Aristotle himself explicitly recognized the relation between subject and predicate as being a relation of identity in just this sense. And even among the logicians of the Middle Ages the distinctive character of this relationship would appear to have been more hinted at than fully developed."[26]

What is being said by Parker and Veatch is that a simple subject-predicate proposition was employed by Aristotle to assert not only predication of nature, character, or quality, but was also used to assert identity even though Aristotle did not necessarily develop the full sense of this relation of identity as has been done in later developments of classical logic. So, the fact is, neither Harner nor BeDuhn have discovered the way Greek expresses nature or character, and they have completely ignored the function of subject-predicate statements as statements of identity. It is also interesting that whereas Harner said the verb "may" function to express the nature or character, and that this qualitative significance "may" be more important, BeDuhn ignores these qualifications and continues making his claims as if Harner had said these were necessarily the case. So, if BeDuhn is resting on this earlier assertion, he is sitting on thin air.

Rev. 21:7

BeDuhn next sets his sights on Rev. 21:7:

> In Revelation 21:7, God promises, "I will be a god to him, and he will be a son to me" (*esomai autōi theos kai autos estai moi huios*). Since "god" (and "son") is a predicate nominative and follows the verb, it *must* be indefinite. God is characterizing the kind of relationship he will have with the one of whom he is speaking. How will that person relate to God? He will act towards him as to "a god" (in other words, will act toward him with worship and service). God, likewise, will act towards that one as towards "a son." Characterization is achieved through categorization, and "god" and "son" function here as such categories. Therefore, they are indefinite.[27]

---

[26] Francis H. Parker and Henry B. Veatch, *Logic as a Human Instrument* (New York: Harper & Brothers, Publishers, 1959), 113.n1.
[27] BeDuhn, *Translation*, 127.

It is astounding how BeDuhn can discuss a verse of the Bible while completely ignoring the context in which the verse occurs. This is especially astounding since one of the three areas on which BeDuhn declares a translation must be based to be accurate is literary context. As with Lk. 20:38, BeDuhn completely ignores the context of the statement in Revelation 21:

> And He who sits on the throne said, "Behold, I am making all things new." And He said, "Write, for these words are faithful and true." Then He said to me, "It is done. I am the Alpha and the Omega, the beginning and the end. I will give to the one who thirsts from the spring of the water of life without cost. He who overcomes will inherit these things, and I will be his God and he will be My son. But for the cowardly and unbelieving and abominable and murderers and immoral persons and sorcerers and idolaters and all liars, their part in the lake that burns with fire and brimstone, which is the second death" (Rev. 21:5–8).[28]

This passage comes at the end of the Revelation and concerns the end of the work and the point at which the eternal state is about to be established. Those who have been saved will have eternal life. Those who are unbelieving will have eternal separation from God. The promise of life spoken of in terms of the water of life is given to those who believe. Those who overcome will inherit what God has promised to all who believe. Then God says, "I will be his God . . ." (ἔσομαι αὐτῷ θεός). To translate this as "I will be to him as a God" is patently absurd. And BeDuhn's claim that it "must be indefinite" because it follows the verb is apparently made on the basis of his earlier discussion of the predications of nature and character or category, an hypothesis that we have already shown to be false.

Since this is the only true and living God making this statement, it would perhaps be helpful to express it this way: "I will be God to him." What is being said is that God will be that person's only God. He will have no other gods. This is, of course, one of the primary concepts in the whole of the Bible, that is, that there is no God but God, and that if anyone would come to God, he must acknowledge that there is no other God. This has been the bane of Israel's existence throughout their history, namely, their constant tendency to go after others that pretended to be gods. As God said, "Turn to Me and be saved, all the ends of the earth; For I am God, and there is no other" (Isa. 45:22). God is not a category, nor is there a category into which God can be classified. If there is a Being who is completely unique so that there is no other being like Him, then the notion of a category disappears into the reality of the Being: "Remember the former things long past, for I am God, and there is no other; God, and there is no one like Me" (Isa. 46:9).

---

[28] Καὶ εἶπεν ὁ καθήμενος ἐπὶ τῷ θρόνῳ· ἰδοὺ καινὰ ποιῶ πάντα καὶ λέγει· γράψον, ὅτι οὗτοι οἱ λόγοι πιστοὶ καὶ ἀληθινοί εἰσιν. καὶ εἶπέν μοι· γέγοναν. ἐγώ (εἰμι) τὸ ἄλφα καὶ τὸ ὦ, ἡ ἀρχὴ καὶ τὸ τέλος. ἐγὼ τῷ διψῶντι δώσω ἐκ τῆς πηγῆς τοῦ ὕδατος τῆς ζωῆς δωρεάν. ὁ νικῶν κληρονομήσει ταῦτα καὶ ἔσομαι αὐτῷ θεὸς καὶ αὐτὸς ἔσται μοι υἱός. τοῖς δὲ δειλοῖς καὶ ἀπίστοις καὶ ἐβδελυγμένοις καὶ φονεῦσιν καὶ πόρνοις καὶ φαρμάκοις καὶ εἰδωλολάτραις καὶ πᾶσιν τοῖς ψευδέσιν τὸ μέρος αὐτῶν ἐν τῇ λίμνῃ τῇ καιομένῃ πυρὶ καὶ θείῳ, ὅ ἐστιν ὁ θάνατος ὁ δεύτερος (Rev. 21:5–8).

BeDuhn's claims are not based on any syntax or grammar of the Greek language. They are based on his own theological predisposition.

Phil. 2:13

BeDuhn next considers Phil. 2:13:

Table #50: Phil. 2:13

θεὸς	γάρ	ἐστιν	ὁ ἐνεργῶν
God	for	is	the One working
ἐν	ὑμῖν	καὶ	τὸ
in	you	and	the
θέλειν	καὶ	τὸ	ἐνεργεῖν
to will	and	the	to work
ὑπὲρ	τῆς εὐδοκίας		
concerning	the good will		

Concerning this verse BeDuhn says, "The implied question is: What sort of thing is working in/among us? Paul's answer is that it is not a human force, or a demonic one, but a divine one. He is stating the character of the experience, the category to which the agency acting in these peoples' lives belongs. Therefore the indefinite is used."[29] Of course, it is utterly ridiculous to translate this as "For it is a god that is working in you . . ." This is clearly an interpretive and theologically biased choice that BeDuhn has made in these assertions. All of the translations have got it. It is BeDuhn who has "missed this," to use his own words. In fact, BeDuhn's own favorite translation does not support his claim. The NW translations reads, "for God is the one that, for the sake of [his] good pleasure, is acting within YOU in order for YOU both to will and to act."

It is important to consider the fact that Paul says God is at work in them concerning "the good will" or "the good pleasure" (τῆς εὐδοκίας, *tēs eudokias*). Many translations add the word "His" before "the good will" to indicate that the good will is God's good will. That is no doubt true, but it is not necessary to add this word. Paul uses the term "good will" (εὐδοκία) only one other time in Philippians, in 1:15: "Some, to be sure, are preaching Christ even from envy and strife, but some also from good will [εὐδοκίαν];"[30]

---

[29] Ibid.
[30] τινὲς μὲν καὶ διὰ φθόνον καὶ ἔριν, τινὲς δὲ καὶ δι᾽ εὐδοκίαν τὸν Χριστὸν κηρύσσουσιν· (Phil. 1:15).

The term "good will" is used in conjunction with two other words in this context: "love" (ἀγάπης) and "truth" (ἀληθεία,). It is also used in contrast to three other concepts: "envy" (φθόνον), "strife" (ἔριν), and "pretense" (προφάσει). Some were preaching in order to promote good will, love, and truth among the brethren, while others were preaching because they thought this would cause envy and strife for Paul in his imprisonment, and their preaching was out of a pretense of understanding the truth when their actions revealed a real lack of understanding the truth. The "good will" to which Paul is referring in 2:13 is the "good will" that many were promoting by their preaching. The definite article (τῆς) preceding the word "good will" (εὐδοκίας) is referred to as an anaphoric use of the definite article. This is the use of the definite article to refer back to a previous reference in which the term or concept is introduced. As Wallace points out, "The first mention of the substantive [the first use of the noun] is usually anarthrous because it is merely being introduced. But subsequent mentions of it use the article, for the article is now pointing back to *the* substantive previously mentioned."[31]

How does this help us with the question of whether the term θεός is definite? The "the good will" that some are promoting is presented by Paul as a motive for action and a reason for performing some deed. In this case, it is the good will, love, and truth that some are promoting among the brethren during Paul's imprisonment. One might wonder why it is that some are promoting good will while others are promoting envy and strife. In 2:13 Paul assures them that this is evidence that God is at work in their lives. They are able to promote good will, love, and truth because it is God who is working in them to promote these very things. But, good will, love, and truth are characteristics of persons, not inanimate forces. Paul is not encouraging them by telling them that some impersonal "divine force" is working in them to promote good will. NO! God is the one who promotes these kind of virtues in the lives of His people. Others have rebelled against God's working in order to promote envy and strife. To relegate this to an impersonal "divine force" drains Paul's statement of all of its encouragement and instruction. Once again, BeDuhn reveals his theological bias in his interpretation. He makes these comments, not because the grammar dictates this, but because he has an already present theological bias that he reads into the text, and this is evident by the fact that he completely ignores the literary context. This is not translation. This is interpretation, something BeDuhn said he would not do, but something he continues to do while presenting it as if it was a grammatical and syntactical necessity. This, sounds to me, like pretense.

2 Thess. 2:4

BeDuhn says, "The actions of the 'Antichrist' in 2 Thessalonians culminate in chapter 2, verse 4, when he seats himself in the Temple and puts forward the claim 'that he is a god' (*hoti estin theos*). The noun 'god' is an anarthrous predicate nominative

---

[31] GGBTB, 217–18.

following the verb, and so can *only* be indefinite. The Antichrist claims (falsely) to belong to the 'god' category of beings. The NW and NAB accurately translate 'a god.' The other translations erroneously translate 'God.'"[32]

Table #51: 2 Thess. 2:4

ὁ ἀντικείμενος	καὶ	ὑπεραιρόμενος	ἐπὶ
the one opposing	and	exalting himself	above
πάντα	λεγόμενον	θεὸν	ἢ
all	being called	god	or
σέβασμα	ὥστε	αὐτὸν	εἰς
object of worship	so that	him	unto
τὸν ναὸν	τοῦ θεοῦ	καθίσαι	ἀποδεικνύντα
the temple	of the God	to sit	proclaiming
ἑαυτὸν	ὅτι	ἔστιν	θεός
himself	that	he is	God

There are some syntactical features of this text that should perhaps be addressed. First, the two participles, ἀντικείμενος (*antikeimenos*, "opposing") and ὑπεραιρόμενος (*huperairomenos*, "exalting"), are both middle voice. The first is what is called a deponent form. A deponent form is one that has a middle or passive form but an active meaning. The second is not a deponent, and being in the middle voice indicates that it should be taken to refer to a reciprocal action, that is, an action that someone does to or for himself. That is why some translations read "exalting himself." He is doing this action for his own benefit.

Second, the pronoun αὐτὸν is in the Accusative case because this person is doing the action indicated by the infinitive, καθίσαι (*kathisai*, "to sit"). The person or thing that is performing the action indicated by an infinite preceded by the preposition εἰς will be in the Accusative case. Since this person is the one doing the action indicated by the infinitive, this is usually rendered in English as the subject of a finite verb, in this case, "he takes his seat" or "he sits."

Having dealt with these peculiarities of Greek grammar and syntax, we can now consider BeDuhn's comments. Once again BeDuhn has ignored one of his own criteria for accurate and unbiased translation, namely, the literary context. For Antichrist to claim that he is "a god" is of little consequence. An untold number of antichrists, and

---

[32] BeDuhn, *Translation*, 127.

others who would not necessarily be called antichrists, have made this kind of claim as John points out in 1 Jn. 2:18: "Children, it is the last hour; and just as you heard that antichrist is coming, even now many antichrists [ἀντίχριστοι, *antichristoi*] have appeared; from this we know that it is the last hour."[33] What makes this person Antichrist instead of simply another of the billions of antichrists is that he claims to be the one, true God.

Notice that the Antichrist does not sit in "a temple" of "a god," but he sits in "the Temple" (τὸν ναὸν, *ton naon*) of "the God" (τοῦ θεοῦ, *tou theou*). The very reason for sitting in "the Temple" of "the God" would not be merely to claim that he is "a god," but that he is "the God" in whose temple he is sitting. Also, notice that he exalts himself "above *everything* being called god or an object of worship."[34] It is clearly absurd and theologically motived to ignore this context in order to claim that Antichrist is declaring himself to be "a god." If Antichrist is claiming to be "a god" in the "category of beings," then he is not exalting himself above everything that is being called god or everything that is an object of worship. BeDuhn's conclusion is not predicated on the anarthrous form of the word θεός, but is predicated on his prior theological commitment. Again someone may claim that my understanding is also theologically biased, and that may be true. But, I'm not the one claiming that I am theologically neutral and translating only on the basis of the grammar and syntax. BeDuhn claims this but he doesn't do it. The literary context of the passage is too strong to give BeDuhn's conclusion any credence whatsoever.

Smyth on Omitting the Article

After his mishandling of these verses, BeDuhn asserts, "In his grammar, Smyth specifically cites 'god' as an example of a noun that omits the article when used of a class (section 1129: 'Words denoting persons, when they are used of a class, may omit the article.')"[35] But, once again BeDuhn presents only that evidence that supports his claim and not all of the evidence from his source. What Smyth actually says is: "Words denoting persons, when they are used of a class, may omit the article. So, ἄνθρωπος, στρατηγός, θεός *divinity, god* (ὁ θεός the particular god). Thus, πάντων μέτρον ἄνθρωπός ἐστιν *man is the measure of all things*. P.Th. 178 b."[36]

Notice a couple of things about what Smyth actually says. He says the use of θεός as "*god*" is equivalent to "ὁ θεός the particular god." Someone may argue that this is not what Smyth means by putting "ὁ θεός the particular god" in parentheses. That may be true, but this is an equally possible way of understanding what he is saying.

---

[33] Παιδία, ἐσχάτη ὥρα ἐστίν, καὶ καθὼς ἠκούσατε ὅτι ἀντίχριστος ἔρχεται, καὶ νῦν ἀντίχριστοι πολλοὶ γεγόνασιν, ὅθεν γινώσκομεν ὅτι ἐσχάτη ὥρα ἐστίν. (1 Jn. 2:18).
[34] ἐπὶ πάντα λεγόμενον θεὸν ἢ σέβασμα (2 Thess. 2:4b).
[35] BeDuhn, *Translation*, 127.
[36] Smyth, *Greek Grammar*, §1129.

Consequently, BeDuhn's effort to use Smyth to support his claim about the anarthrous use of θεός as referring to "a god" is not as clear as he would like his readers to think. Either deliberately or by ignorance BeDuhn has misrepresented the evidence... again!

Also, notice how Smyth translates the anarthrous use of μέτον in the phrase πάντων μέτρον ἄνθρωπός ἐστιν. He translates it "the measure." Here is an anarthrous predicate noun, that is actually a noun this time, preceding the copula, but is translated as a definite noun by the very authority that BeDuhn cites in the very section he is trying to use as support for his contrary claim. This is powerful evidence that BeDuhn's conclusions are theologically biased and in fact not supported by the grammatical and syntactical evidence.

Notice also that Smyth says, "Words denoting persons, when they are used of a class, *may* omit the article . . . ." He doesn't say they *must* omit the article, nor does he say that every word denoting persons and omitting the article necessarily falls within the scope of his principle. BeDuhn has actually committed the fallacy of an illicit conversion. He has taken Smyth's statement: "Words denoting persons, when they are used of a class, may omit the article," and illicitly converted it to say, "Every word denoting persons that omits the article is used of a class." Just because a word denoting a person omits the article does not mean that it is being used of a class. This is a blatant misuse of Smyth's statement and the logical fallacy of illicit conversion.

But if BeDuhn insists on using a grammar that is concerned primarily with what is popularly called Classical Greek, let us refer to another grammar of this sort. BeDuhn claims, "Generally speaking, the function of indefinite predicate nouns, before or after the verb, is to identify the class or category to which the subject belongs."[37] However, according to the *Oxford Grammar of Classical Greek*, "The [definite] article is used with nouns or adjectives which describe whole classes. We call this usage **generic**:"[38] In other words, contrary to BeDuhn's claim, words used to identify the class or category are not generally anarthrous, but usually have the definite article. Since the *Oxford Grammar* has the benefit of the years of research that have been done since the publishing of Smyth's grammar, even the edited version was published in 1925, one would tend to differ to the newer grammar. However, it is not necessary to differ to the newer grammar since Smyth says the same thing. In his section on the uses of the definite article as "The Particular Article," Smyth states that the definite article is used with "Objects representative of their class."[39] Once again it shows that BeDuhn employs the logical fallacy of selective reporting in order to misrepresent the evidence to make it support his claims.

---

[37] BeDuhn, *Translation*, 121.
[38] James Morwood, *Oxford Grammar of Classical Greek* (Oxford: Oxford University Press, 2001), 123.
[39] Smyth, *Grammar*, §1119.f.

Jn. 10:34

Concerning this verse BeDuhn asserts, "In John 10:34, Jesus even quotes a passage from the Old Testament in which God tells the recipients of his commands, 'You are gods' (theoi este). The term clearly is used broadly, both of 'true' gods and of 'false' gods, and even of individuals who may be entitled to some characteristic associated with the popular notion of a 'god,' while not necessarily fully 'divine' by a stricter standard. This is all theoretical speech, the rhetoric of explanation used by the authors of the New Testament to help their readers understand new ideas."[40] Jn. 10:34 along with the OT reference are set out below:

Table #52: Jn. 10:34

ἀπεκρίθη	αὐτοῖς	(ὁ) Ἰησοῦς	οὐκ
answered	to them	(the) Jesus	that
ἔστιν	γεγραμμένον	ἐν	τῷ νόμῳ
it is	having been written	in	the law
ὑμῶν	ὅτι	ἐγὼ	εἶπα
of you	that	I	I said
θεοί	ἐστὲ		
gods	you are		

The passage that forms the background of Jesus' statement in Jn. 10:34 is Ps. 82:6, or 81:6 in the GSEPT.

Table #53: Ps. 81:6 GSEPT

ἐγὼ	εἶπα	θεοί	ἐστε
I	I said	gods	you are
καὶ	υἱοὶ	ὑψίστου	πάντες
and	sons	of Most High	all
ὑμεῖς			
you			

---

[40] BeDuhn, *Translation*, 128.

The Word is God

Table #54: Ps. 82:6 BHS

אֲנִי־	אָמַרְתִּי	אֱלֹהִים	אַתֶּם
I	I said	gods	you
וּבְנֵי	עֶלְיוֹן	כֻּלְּכֶם׃	
and sons of	Most High	all of you.	

This Psalm starts off, "ὁ θεὸς ἔστη ἐν συναγωγῇ θεῶν ἐν μέσῳ δὲ θεοὺς διακρίνει," which can be translated, "The God stands in the synagogue of gods and in the midst of gods He judges" (Ps. 82:1(GSEPT81:1). Brenton translates the GSEPT passage: "God stands in the assembly of gods; and in the midst *of them* will judge gods."[41] Interestingly, Lamsa translates the Syriac of this verse, "God stands in the congregation of angels; he judges among the angels."[42] According to the Smith's *Compendious Syriac Dictionary*, the Syriac word {ܐܠܗ} (*'lh'*) is the word for *"God, the Supreme Deity."*[43] Although the historical context of the Psalm is in dispute, the message of the Psalm seems to be clear. The rulers of Israel are unjust judges who show partiality to the wicked. In two passages in Exodus, the judges of Israel are referred to with the word "gods," (אֱלֹהִים, *'elōhîm*) Ex. 22:8 and 9(H7–8).

> If the thief is not caught, then the owner of the house shall appear before the judges [τοῦ θεοῦ, הָאֱלֹהִים], determine whether he laid his hands on his neighbor's property. (Ex. 22:8)
> For every breach of trust, for ox, for donkey, for sheep, for clothing, for any lost thing about which one says, "This is it," the case of both parties shall come before the judges [τοῦ θεοῦ, הָאֱלֹהִים]; he whom the judges [τοῦ θεοῦ, אֱלֹהִים] condemn shall pay double to his neighbor. (Ex. 22:9)[44]

The judges of Israel were supposed to judge with righteous judgment, but they were actually judging with partiality. This is precisely the problem that Jesus pointed out in 7:24 when He told them not to judge on the basis of appearance, but to judge righteously, and in 8:15 when He accused them of judging according to the flesh. The judges of Israel were called gods in the sense that they sat in the judgment seat as God's

---

[41] Brenton, *Septuagint*, 615.
[42] Lamsa, *Holy Bible*, 627. ܐܠܗܐ܂ ܘܒܓܘ ܐܠܗܐ ܢܕܘܢ܂ ܐܠܗܐ ܩܡ ܒܟܢܘܫܬܐ ܕܐܠܗܐ
[43] CSD (1990), s.v. "ܐܠܗ."
[44] אִם־לֹא יִמָּצֵא הַגַּנָּב וְנִקְרַב בַּעַל־הַבַּיִת אֶל־הָאֱלֹהִים אִם־לֹא שָׁלַח יָדוֹ בִּמְלֶאכֶת רֵעֵהוּ׃ (Ex. 22:7)
עַל־כָּל־דְּבַר־פֶּשַׁע עַל־שׁוֹר עַל־חֲמוֹר עַל־שֶׂה עַל־שַׂלְמָה עַל־כָּל־אֲבֵדָה אֲשֶׁר יֹאמַר כִּי־הוּא זֶה עַד הָאֱלֹהִים יָבֹא דְּבַר־שְׁנֵיהֶם אֲשֶׁר יַרְשִׁיעֻן אֱלֹהִים יְשַׁלֵּם שְׁנַיִם לְרֵעֵהוּ׃ (Ex. 22:8)

representatives and instruments of justice. But, because they had perverted justice, they would be held accountable for misrepresented the justice of God. Their exalted position would not protect them from the judgment of God upon their unrighteousness. They would die like men.

There is a very interesting statement in the second, Ex. 22:8–9(H7–8), of these two verses. In each case, there is no question that the references are to the judges of Israel who were God's representatives to administer justice in Israel. Once in verse 8(H7) and once in verse 9(H8) the judges are referred to as "the gods" (הָאֱלֹהִים, ha'ᵉlohîm). In both of these instances the word "God" (אֱלֹהִים) has the definite article (הָ). But, in the latter part of verse 9(H8) the phrase that reads "he whom the judges condemn," actually does not uses הָאֱלֹהִים (ha'ᵉlohîm) with the definite article, but actually uses simply אֱלֹהִים without the definite article. Nevertheless, there can be no question that this is referring to "the judges" and should be translated as "the gods." This is another example that BeDuhn is simply wrong about a word without the definite article not being definite. Sometimes a word without the definite article is in fact definite, as these verses indicate. And in fact, this is a good argument for taking the Psalm passage as meaning "the gods" because it is clearly referring to the judges in Israel, the judges that are referred to in Ex. 22:8–9(H7–8) as "the gods." Simply because the Psalm passage does not use the definite article is no argument for the word being indefinite because the very same word in Ex. 22:9(H8), "gods," does not have the definite article but is clearly definite.

BeDuhn says, the word 'god' is used "even of individuals who may be entitled to some characteristic associated with the popular notion of a 'god,' while not necessarily fully 'divine' by a stricter standard."[45] But this is totally contrary to the literary context of the passages and to the beliefs of the Jews at the time. First, the texts are not saying that these judges have characteristics associated with 'a god.' The texts are saying that these judges are the representatives of the God of Israel, and as God's representatives they were supposed to judge righteously. Their condemnation is precisely because they have misrepresented God, not because they have not acted like gods, but because they have perverted God's justice.

A good example of this kind of use is in Ex. 7:1 where God sends Moses to Egypt to confront Pharaoh and to release Israel from captivity.

Table #55: Ex. 7:1

NASB	"Then the Lord said to Moses, 'See, I make you God to Pharaoh, and your brother Aaron shall be your prophet.'"
BHS	וַיֹּאמֶר יְהוָה אֶל־מֹשֶׁה רְאֵה נְתַתִּיךָ אֱלֹהִים לְפַרְעֹה וְאַהֲרֹן אָחִיךָ יִהְיֶה נְבִיאֶךָ:

---

[45] BeDuhn, *Translation*, 128.

GSEPT	καὶ εἶπεν κύριος πρὸς Μωυσῆν λέγων ἰδοὺ δέδωκά σε θεὸν Φαραω καὶ Ααρων ὁ ἀδελφός σου ἔσται σου προφήτης

In this passage, God tells Moses that he will be "God to Pharaoh" (אֱלֹהִים לְפַרְעֹה, θεὸν Φαραω). God cannot be saying "a god to Pharaoh," because simply being a god would not have mattered much to Pharaoh since there were many gods in Egypt. Moses will be the representative of the only true God. This is clear from how in 7:16 Moses is instructed to address Pharaoh:

Table #56: Ex. 7:16

NASB	"You shall say to him, 'The Lord, the God of the Hebrews, sent me to you . . .'"
BHS	וְאָמַרְתָּ אֵלָיו יְהוָה אֱלֹהֵי הָעִבְרִים שְׁלָחַנִי אֵלֶיךָ
GSEPT	καὶ ἐρεῖς πρὸς αὐτόν κύριος ὁ θεὸς τῶν Εβραίων ἀπέσταλκέν με πρὸς σὲ

Notice that the Greek text of the GSEPT renders אֱלֹהֵי with ὁ θεὸς ("the God"). Since God send Moses to be "God to Pharaoh," it is clear that by this He meant "the Lord, the God of the Hebrews." So, once again BeDuhn's claims do not stand up to scrutiny.

Second, Jews would not have even thought in terms of people having characteristics associated with a popular notion of a god. For the Jew, there was only one God. Those who paraded themselves as gods were in fact not gods at all.

Table #57: Jer. 16:20

NASB	"Can man make gods for himself? Yet they are not gods!'"
BHS	הֲיַעֲשֶׂה־לּוֹ אָדָם אֱלֹהִים וְהֵמָּה לֹא אֱלֹהִים׃
GSEPT	εἰ ποιήσει ἑαυτῷ ἄνθρωπος θεούς καὶ οὗτοι οὐκ εἰσιν θεοί

To suppose that these references are to popular notions of gods is absurd and ignores the historical context of these statements, another of BeDuhn's violations of his own translation principles.

BeDuhn asserts, "Both Greek and English put the word 'god' to dual use, sometimes as an indefinite common noun and sometimes as a definite proper noun. But while the Greek-speaking authors of the New Testament were very careful to keep the two uses always distinct through the use or non-use of the definite article, English-speaking translators of the Bible have hopelessly muddled the distinct uses by neglect of the indefinite article and careless use of the capital 'G.'"[46] But notice how the Greek translators of Ex. 22:8–9 translate the particular use of "the gods."

Table #58: Ex. 22:8–9

	Ex. 22:8 - BHS/GSEPT 7	Ex. 22:9 - BHS/GSEPT 8	
		First Instance	Second Instance
GSEPT	τοῦ θεοῦ	τοῦ θεοῦ	τοῦ θεοῦ
BHS	הָאֱלֹהִים	הָאֱלֹהִים	אֱלֹהִים
NASBU	the judges	the judges	the judges

Notice that although the Hebrew text omits the definite article in the second instance in verse 9(H/ GSEPT 8), the Greek translators nevertheless used the definite article with θεοῦ in translating that instance. According to BeDuhn's reasoning, they should have left off the definite article since the definite article was omitted in the Hebrew original. This again proves that the Greek language can indeed recognize a word that does not have the definite article as nevertheless definite. If they can do it with reference to translating an anarthrous word from Hebrew, it shows that BeDuhn's claim that they "kept the two uses always distinct" is simply false.

Some may argue that this actually supports BeDuhn's claim about the authors of the NT keeping the two uses distinct. However, that would be to misunderstand BeDuhn's argument. BeDuhn's argument is a grammatical and syntactical argument, not a conceptual argument. What this shows is that the translation is conceptual, not grammatical or syntactical. Then you may say, "But this is the Greek translators of the OT, not the NT authors." Again this misses the point. The point is, the use of the definite article is not strictly a grammatical or syntactical matter of the Greek language regardless of whether the person is a translator or author. It is often a conceptual matter. What this instance shows is that the use of the definite article is not always dictated by Greek grammar or syntax. If was is not dictated by Greek grammar for the Greek translators of the OT, then it is not dictated by Greek grammar for the NT authors, since both the Greek of the GSEPT and the NT is Koine Greek. In other words, the use or non-use of the definite article is a conceptual matter for the NT authors as well as for the Greek translators of the OT. BeDuhn was trying to use the GSEPT translation to support his view. We are using the GSEPT translation to show that he is wrong. This instance shows that BeDuhn's understanding of Greek grammar is flawed, and his claims about the use of the definite article are motivated by a prior theological bias, not the dictates of Greek grammar or syntax.

Although these arguments would probably not convince BeDuhn, that is not really the point. The point is, the passage is not as clear cut as BeDuhn makes out, and, again,

---

[46] Ibid.

he neglects to present all the evidence. He does not give his readers a true picture of the passages involved, nor even of Greek grammar generally. As a result, BeDuhn's appeal to having "some characteristic associated with the popular notion of a 'god,' while not necessarily being fully 'divine' by a stricter standard" is simply a smoke screen to avoid the real issue. BeDuhn hopes to side-step the fact that the evidence simply does not support his claims.

Colwell and Smyth

BeDuhn dismisses Colwell's rule that many use to support the traditional translation of Jn. 1:1. According to BeDuhn, Colwell's rule is, "A definite predicate nominative has the article when it follows the verb; it does not have the article when it precedes the verb."[47] So, Colwell's rule supposedly speaks to two situations. The first part of the rule is, when a definite predicate nominative follows the connecting verb, also called a copula, such as the verb "to be," it will have the article. An example of this is found in Jn. 1:4:

Figure 11: Definite Predicate Nominative After the Verb

conjunction	definite article	noun	verb	definite article	noun
καὶ	ἡ	ζωὴ	ἦν	τὸ	φῶς
and	the	life	was	the	light
conjunction	subject		copula	predicate nominative	

The other part of the rule is, when a definite predicate nominative precedes the verb, it will not have the definite article. We will use the Jn. 1:1c to illustrate the claim, but remember that whether this is the case is the very point that BeDuhn is contesting:

Figure 12: Definite Predicate Nominative Before the Verb

preposition	noun	verb	definite article	noun
καὶ	θεὸς	ἦν	ὁ	λόγος
and	god	was	the	light
conjunction	predicate nominative	copula	subject	

---

[47] Ibid., 117.

BeDuhn's criticism is that there is no such rule in Greek and that this is proven by the abundance of exceptions. BeDuhn asserts, "We've all heard the expression, 'the exception that proves the rule.' But, generally speaking, exceptions *disprove* rules."[48] Of course this is simply false. If there were no rule, then there would be nothing of which to be an exception. The only way anything is recognized as an exception is if there is a rule that can be excepted. If there is no rule, then there is nothing that can be called an exception. You can have an exception only if you have a rule. BeDuhn actually misunderstands the expression. The expression is not saying that exceptions prove that the rule is true. Rather, what this expression is saying is that the fact that there are some things that are recognized as exceptions verifies that there is a rule to which these are exceptions. So, exceptions cannot "disprove" a rule since they would not be exceptions if there was no rule. Exceptions can be exceptions only if there is a rule.

Be that as it may, BeDuhn has misunderstood the rule in the first place. As Daniel Wallace points out, "Colwell stated that a definite PN [predicate nominative] that precedes the verb is usually anarthrous. He did *not* say the *converse*, namely, an anarthrous PN that precedes the verb is usually definite."[49] In fact, BeDuhn has committed this very error in his comment, "The first problem is that the rule does nothing to establish the definiteness of a noun."[50] The fact is, it was never formulated to do such a thing. The observations of Colwell were concerning nouns that were already believed to be definite in order to see how they are presented in the text.

Another indicator that BeDuhn has misunderstood the rule is his criticism of Colwell's method: "Colwell's mistake, as so often is the case in research, is rooted in a misguided method. He began by collecting all of the predicate nouns in the New Testament that he considered to be definite in meaning, and then, when some of them turned out to look indefinite in Greek, he refused to reconsider his view that they were definite, but instead made up a rule to explain why his subjective understanding of them remained true, even though the known rules of Greek grammar suggested otherwise."[51] But this criticism is valid only if Colwell was trying to establish the definiteness or indefiniteness of these nouns. But, that is not what he was trying to do. He was simply studying how words that appear to be definite nouns are presented in the text. He was not trying to develop a rule to determine when pre-copula predicate nominatives were definite. It is not a "misguided method" to decide what it is you want to study. Perhaps some of the nouns that Colwell thought were definite were in fact not definite, but that is beside the point. He was not trying to prove definiteness. He was only trying to discover if there was a pattern to the way definite nouns before copulas appear in the text. As Daniel Wallace explains:

---

[48] Ibid., 119.
[49] GGBTB, 260.
[50] BeDuhn, *Translation*, 118.
[51] Ibid., 119.

Colwell restricted his study to anarthrous pre-verbal predicate nominatives, which were, as far as he could tell, determined as definite *by the context*. He did not deal with *any* other anarthrous pre-verbal predicate nominatives. However, the misunderstanding has arisen because scholars have not recognized that Colwell only tested these constructions. In other words, Colwell started off with a *semantic* category rather than a *structural* category. He did *not* begin by asking the question, What does the anarthrous pre-verbal PN construction mean? Rather, he began by asking, Will a definite PN be articular or anarthrous? And will it follow or precede the verb? In his initial question, he *assumed* a particular meaning (i.e., definiteness) and sought the particular constructions involved.[52]

What BeDuhn has criticized as a "misguided method" was actually only the parameters of Colwell's study. Any researcher is free to set the parameters of his own study. BeDuhn's argument is not with Colwell but with the many persons who have, like himself, misunderstood what Colwell was doing. Many orthodox Christians illegitimately try to employ Colwell's rule to prove that the word "God" in Jn. 1:1c is definite, and that is precisely what BeDuhn thinks Colwell was trying to do. But that is not what he was trying to do. BeDuhn's criticisms are completely misplaced. Nevertheless, he is correct that Colwell's rule does not prove that θεός is a definite noun.

However, in his discussion of the use of the definite article, Herbert Smyth (BeDuhn calls Smyth's grammar "the standard work of Greek grammar"[53]) makes some observations that contradict the claims of BeDuhn. First, Smyth says, "The article is often omitted . . . (2) when a word is sufficiently definite by itself;"[54] What this means is that the indefiniteness of the word θεός cannot be maintained simply because there is no definite article, and we have already shown that BeDuhn's claim about the Nominative form of θεός is false. Whether the word θεός is definite or indefinite "by itself" must be demonstrated on other grounds. Although BeDuhn pretends that he is arguing on the basis of the grammar, he is actually arguing on the basis of his theological presuppositions. Like Colwell, BeDuhn has already made his decision about the definiteness of the word, but unlike Colwell, BeDuhn is using the structural matters to determine the semantic question. He accuses Colwell of doing this when in fact that was not what Colwell was doing, and then, to support his own claims, BeDuhn employs the very "misguided method" that he tries to foist upon Colwell.

Smyth also says, "Names of deities omit the article, except when emphatic . . ."[55] Of course, some have tried to argue that because of the position of the word in the sentence, θεός is emphatic, and that may or may not be the case. Nevertheless, what this shows is that according to what BeDuhn calls "the standard Greek grammar," the definiteness or indefiniteness of θεός cannot be decided simply because there is no definite article. The question of whether this is an instance of the name of a deity and

---

[52] GGBTB, 260.
[53] BeDuhn, *Translation*, 93.
[54] Smyth, *Greek Grammar*, §1126.
[55] Ibid., §1137.

whether it is emphatic must be decided first. Since it certainly seems to be the name of God, one would expect it to be anarthrous, unless it is emphatic, and that is something that must be debated. But, this is not a purely grammatical question. It is also a conceptual question, and again this demonstrates BeDuhn's own theological bias and the disingenuous way in which he presents the evidence.

Another "rule" given by Smyth is, "A predicate noun has no article, and is thus distinguished from the subject."[56] When these are put together, one could argue (1) the word θεός is sufficiently definite by itself, since the Bible repeatedly declares that there is only one God; (2) θεός is the name of the Jewish and Christian deity and therefore omits the article. However, the question of emphasis must be addressed here. (3) since θεός is a predicate nominative, the lack of the article is to distinguish it from the subject and not to make it indefinite. Consequently, even if it is emphatic, the article is omitted in order to distinguish it from the subject. Once again these arguments probably will not convince BeDuhn, but they demonstrate that BeDuhn has not presented all the evidence and he has distorted the evidence he does present.

Smyth does present another rule that *prima facie* seems to be pertinent to this passage: "Names of *persons* and *places* are individual and therefore omit the article unless previously mentioned (§1120b) or specially marked as well known."[57] But this doesn't apply to this situation. Section 1120b to which Smyth refers explains the circumstances in which this rule obtains: "The particular article defines . . . Objects already mentioned or in the mind of the speaker or writer . . ."[58] Smyth is referring to the fact that the name of a person or place may omit the article unless the author wants to alert the reader to the fact that he is still talking about the same person or place mentioned earlier in the context. But this rule does not apply here because it is designed to address the question of why a noun has the definite article, not why it doesn't.

So, when we look at all the evidence, and not simply the evidence that BeDuhn wants his readers to see, we discover that BeDuhn has misrepresented the case and that his arguments do not work. BeDuhn has on the one hand misunderstood Colwell's rule, and then has employed the very methodology he condemned and tried to attribute to Colwell, and he has not interacted with the actual rules of Smyth's "standard Greek grammar." BeDuhn is wrong on all counts.

Actually Understanding Jn. 1:1 Accurately

In the section of his book titled "Understanding John 1:1 accurately," BeDuhn endeavors to show the reader how to understand Jn. 1:1 accurately. To this end, he first takes a look at Jn. 4:19:

---

[56] Ibid., §1150.
[57] Ibid., §1136.
[58] Ibid., §1120b.

Table #59: Jn. 4:19

λέγει	αὐτῷ	ἡ	γυνή·
says	to Him	the	woman
κύριε	θεωρῶ	ὅτι	προφήτης
Lord	I perceive	that	prophet
εἶ	σύ.		
you are	you.		

BeDuhn says, "For example, in John 4:19 we must translate 'You are a prophet,' not 'You are the prophet.'" He makes a similar claim about Jn. 8:48: "it is 'You are a Samaritan,' not 'You are the Samaritan.'" Again with reference to Jn. 9:24 he states, "the translation is 'This man is a sinner,' not 'This man is the sinner.'" He says the same thing about Jn. 12:6 that it "must be 'He was a thief,' not 'He was the thief.'" Of course BeDuhn is certainly correct, but these observations are also certainly irrelevant. He can go through every instance in the New Testament and show how each one of them must be translated in the same way and that still does not prove that the statement in Jn. 1:1 must be translated this way. [59]

He refers to the fact that Harner "states that the anarthrous predicate noun before the verb cannot be definite in John 1:14; 2:9; 3:4 (twice); 4:9; 6:63; 7:12; 8:31; 8:44 (twice); 8:48; 9:8; 9:24–31 (5 times [sic]); 10:1; 10:8; 10:33–34 (twice); 12:6; 12:36; 18:26; 18:35." BeDuhn appeals to these as parallel with Jn. 1:1. We will look at each one of these references to see whether they really do present parallels to Jn. 1:1.

Table #60: Supposed Parallels with Jn. 1:1

Jn. 1:14	"And the Word became flesh, and dwelt among us, and we saw His glory, glory as of the only begotten from the Father, full of grace and truth."
	Καὶ ὁ λόγος σὰρξ ἐγένετο καὶ ἐσκήνωσεν ἐν ἡμῖν, καὶ ἐθεασάμεθα τὴν δόξαν αὐτοῦ, δόξαν ὡς μονογενοῦς παρὰ πατρός, πλήρης χάριτος καὶ ἀληθείας.
	In this verse, BeDuhn is referring to the predicate nominative σὰρξ which occurs before the verb ἐγένετο. This is an aorist form of the verb γίνομαι, which often functions as a copula. However, this verse does nor form a parallel with Jn. 1:1 since the word σὰρξ would not be translated "a flesh" as BeDuhn claims about Jn. 1:1. It would be absurd to translate this, "And the Word became a flesh." Apparently the point BeDuhn hopes to make is that this is the same kind of translation as would be found in Jn. 1:1 were it translated "and the Word was divine." But, we have already shown that there is no basis upon which to make this translation since Greek has a word for "divine," and John did not use it.

---

[59] All of the quotes in this paragraph come from BeDuhn, *Translation*, 121.

Jn. 2:9	"When the headwaiter tasted the water which had become wine, and did not know where it came from (but the servants who had drawn the water knew), the headwaiter called the bridegroom,"
	ὡς δὲ ἐγεύσατο ὁ ἀρχιτρίκλινος τὸ ὕδωρ οἶνον γεγενημένον καὶ οὐκ ᾔδει πόθεν ἐστίν, οἱ δὲ διάκονοι ᾔδεισαν οἱ ἠντληκότες τὸ ὕδωρ, φωνεῖ τὸν νυμφίον ὁ ἀρχιτρίκλινος
	Here BeDuhn has the same problem as the above verse. It would absurd to translate this "it is a where" (πόθεν ἐστίν).
Jn. 3:4	"Nicodemus said to Him, 'How can a man be born when he is old? He cannot enter a second time into his mother's womb and be born, can he?'"
	λέγει πρὸς αὐτὸν (ὁ) Νικόδημος· πῶς δύναται ἄνθρωπος γεννηθῆναι γέρων ὢν μὴ δύναται εἰς τὴν κοιλίαν τῆς μητρὸς αὐτοῦ δεύτερον εἰσελθεῖν καὶ γεννηθῆναι
	Here again BeDuhn has the same problem. As before, translating this as "a man to be an old." Here the supposed predicate nominative is not ἄνθρωπος ("man"), but γέρων ("old"). Not only is this not a parallel to Jn. 1:1 because it could not be translated "an old," but it is also not a parallel because the word "old" is an adjective, not a noun. So, although someone might translate this as "an old man," The word "man" is not present, and the word that is present is not even a noun. This is simply not parallel and therefore not a support for BeDuhn's claim.
Jn. 3:6	"That which is born of the flesh is flesh, and that which is born of the spirit is spirit."
	τὸ γεγεννημένον ἐκ τῆς σαρκὸς σάρξ ἐστιν, καὶ τὸ γεγεννημένον ἐκ τοῦ πνεύματος πνεῦμά ἐστιν.
	Again, it would be absurd to translate this "That which is born of the flesh is a flesh." Someone might argue that it does make sense to translate this, "that which is born of the spirit is a spirit," but that is not a viable translation since these two statements are contrasting parallels. The terms "flesh" and "spirit" are categories or kinds. The "flesh" category is contrasted with the "spirit" category, so it would be contrary to the parallelism and the point that is being made to translate this "a spirit." But, even though they are kinds or categories, they are not any indefinite kinds, but particular kings, namely, flesh and spirit kinds. So, there are definite kinds or categories, not indefinite things. Once again this is not parallel to Jn. 1:1 and does not support BeDuhn's claim
Jn. 4:9	"Therefore the Samaritan woman said to Him, 'How is it that You, being a Jew, ask me for a drink since I am a Samaritan woman?' (For Jews have no dealings with Samaritans.)"
	λέγει οὖν αὐτῷ ἡ γυνὴ ἡ Σαμαρῖτις· πῶς σὺ Ἰουδαῖος ὢν παρ' ἐμοῦ πεῖν αἰτεῖς γυναικὸς Σαμαρίτιδος οὔσης οὐ γὰρ συγχρῶνται Ἰουδαῖοι Σαμαρίταις.
	This is another instance of the predicate nominative, in this case Ἰουδαῖος following a participial form of εἰμί (ὤν) identifies a kind or category. And again, this is not an indefinite category, but a definite category, namely "Jew." So, again this is not parallel to Jn. 1:1 and does not support BeDuhn's claim.

The Word is God 151

Jn. 6:63	"It is the Spirit who gives life; the flesh profits nothing; the words that I have spoken to you are spirit and are life."
	τὸ πνεῦμά ἐστιν τὸ ζῳοποιοῦν, ἡ σὰρξ οὐκ ὠφελεῖ οὐδέν· τὰ ῥήματα ἃ ἐγὼ λελάληκα ὑμῖν πνεῦμά ἐστιν καὶ ζωή ἐστιν.
	Here again the predicate nominatives "spirit" (πνεῦμά) and "life" (ζωή) are identifying definite categories or kinds. It would be absurd to translate this, "the words that I have spoken are . . . a life," and because the words "spirit" and "life" are comparative terms, they should be understood as parallels. So, even though the translation, "a spirit" may sound correct, since it is referring to a category or kind, that would actually be improper English. Again, this is not a parallel to Jn. 1:1 and does not support BeDuhn's position.
Jn. 7:12	There was much grumbling among the crowds concerning Him; some were saying, 'He is a good man'; others were saying, 'No, on the contrary, He leads the people astray.'"
	καὶ γογγυσμὸς περὶ αὐτοῦ ἦν πολὺς ἐν τοῖς ὄχλοις· οἱ μὲν ἔλεγον ὅτι ἀγαθός ἐστιν, ἄλλοι (δὲ) ἔλεγον· οὔ, ἀλλὰ πλανᾷ τὸν ὄχλον.
	Here again the predicate nominative is actually an adjective (ἀγαθός), not a noun, and does not provide a parallel to Jn. 1:1. Of course it would be perfectly legitimate to translate this "He is a good man," but because this is not using the same part of speech, it does not provide any evidence for BeDuhn's claim.
Jn. 8:31	"So Jesus was saying to those Jews who had believed Him, 'If you continue in My word, you are truly disciples of Mine;'"
	ἔλεγεν οὖν ὁ Ἰησοῦς πρὸς τοὺς πεπιστευκότας αὐτῷ Ἰουδαίους· ἐὰν ὑμεῖς μείνητε ἐν τῷ λόγῳ τῷ ἐμῷ, ἀληθῶς μαθηταί μού ἐστε
	Again the predicate nominative has to do with a kind or category, "disciple" (μαθηταί). Also, in this case the word "disciples" happens to be plural, and it would be really stupid to translate this "you are a disciples of Me."
Jn. 8:44	"You are of father the devil, and you want to do the desires of your father. He was a murderer from the beginning, and does not stand in the truth because there is no truth in him. Whenever he speaks a lie, he speaks from his own, for he is a liar and the father of lies."
	ὑμεῖς ἐκ τοῦ πατρὸς τοῦ διαβόλου ἐστὲ καὶ τὰς ἐπιθυμίας τοῦ πατρὸς ὑμῶν θέλετε ποιεῖν. ἐκεῖνος ἀνθρωποκτόνος ἦν ἀπ' ἀρχῆς καὶ ἐν τῇ ἀληθείᾳ οὐκ ἔστηκεν, ὅτι οὐκ ἔστιν ἀλήθεια ἐν αὐτῷ. ὅταν λαλῇ τὸ ψεῦδος, ἐκ τῶν ἰδίων λαλεῖ, ὅτι ψεύστης ἐστὶν καὶ ὁ πατὴρ αὐτοῦ.

Jn. 8:44 contd.	The two instances to which BeDuhn appeals in this verse are: 1) "that one a murderer he was" (ἀνθρωποκτόνος); and 2) "because liar he is" (ὅτι ψεύστης ἐστίν). These two instances actually seem to be closer parallels to the Jn. 1:1 passage, but looks are deceiving. In neither one of these is there a separate subject with a definite article. The subjects in both cases are contained in the verbs "ἐστίν." Since a critical part of the question in Jn. 1:1 is the relation of the predicate nominative, "God" that does not have the definite article, and the subject, "the Word" that has the definite article, to appeal to this verse in which the subjects are not even separate words and do not have the definite articles, these are not actually parallels to the Jn. 1:1 passage.
Jn. 8:48	"The Jews answered and said to Him, 'Do we not say rightly that You are a Samaritan and have a demon?'"
	Ἀπεκρίθησαν οἱ Ἰουδαῖοι καὶ εἶπαν αὐτῷ· οὐ καλῶς λέγομεν ἡμεῖς ὅτι Σαμαρίτης εἶ σὺ καὶ δαιμόνιον ἔχεις
	Here again the predicate nominative is actually a class or kind (Σαμαρίτης) and as such is not a parallel to Jn. 1:1.
Jn. 9:8	"Therefore the neighbors, and those who previously saw him as a beggar, were saying, 'Is not this the one who used to sit and beg?'"
	Οἱ οὖν γείτονες καὶ οἱ θεωροῦντες αὐτὸν τὸ πρότερον ὅτι προσαίτης ἦν ἔλεγον· οὐχ οὗτός ἐστιν ὁ καθήμενος καὶ προσαιτῶν
	Apparently the construction to which BeDuhn is appealing in this verse is ὅτι προσαίτης ἦν "that a beggar he was," but once again this is not a parallel to the Jn. 1:1 passage. First, the predicate nominative indicates a kind or class, and there is no separate subject that has a definite article.
Jn. 9:24	24 "So a second time they called the man who had been blind, and said to him, 'Give glory to God; we know that this man is a sinner.'
	24 Ἐφώνησαν οὖν τὸν ἄνθρωπον ἐκ δευτέρου ὃς ἦν τυφλὸς καὶ εἶπαν αὐτῷ· δὸς δόξαν τῷ θεῷ· ἡμεῖς οἴδαμεν ὅτι οὗτος ὁ ἄνθρωπος ἁμαρτωλός ἐστιν.
	BeDuhn notes that in verses 24–31 there are five instances in these verses. We will treat these as separate instances. The first is in verse 24: "this the man a sinner he is." (οὗτος ὁ ἄνθρωπος ἁμαρτωλός ἐστιν.). BeDuhn faces the same problem here. Neither the word "this" (οὗτος) nor "the man" (ὁ ἄνθρωπος) is the subject of the verb. These are Nominatives of apposition to the implied subject "he" contained in the verb ἐστιν. So, this instance does not provide a parallel to Jn. 1:1 because there is no subject with a definite article.
Jn. 9:25	25 He then answered, 'Whether He is a sinner, I do not know; one thing I do know, that though I was blind, now I see.'
	25 ἀπεκρίθη οὖν ἐκεῖνος· εἰ ἁμαρτωλός ἐστιν οὐκ οἶδα· ἓν οἶδα ὅτι τυφλὸς ὢν ἄρτι βλέπω.
	This instance is like the previous one in which there is no separate subject with a definite article: εἰ ἁμαρτωλός ἐστιν "if a sinner he is"

The Word is God 153

Jn 9:27	27 He answered them, 'I told you already and you did not listen; why do you want to hear again? You do not want to become His disciples too, do you?'
	27 ἀπεκρίθη αὐτοῖς· εἶπον ὑμῖν ἤδη καὶ οὐκ ἠκούσατε· τί πάλιν θέλετε ἀκούειν μὴ καὶ ὑμεῖς θέλετε αὐτοῦ μαθηταὶ γενέσθαι
	Another instance may be the use of the verb γίνομαι in the phrase, αὐτοῦ μαθηταὶ γενέσθαι "of him disciples to become," but this is a great stretch even for BeDuhn.
Jn. 9:29	29 We know that God has spoken to Moses, but as for this man, we do not know where He is from.'
	29 ἡμεῖς οἴδαμεν ὅτι Μωϋσεῖ λελάληκεν ὁ θεός, τοῦτον δὲ οὐκ οἴδαμεν πόθεν ἐστίν.
	The phrase οἴδαμεν πόθεν ἐστίν "we know from where he is" is similar to the one in Jn. 2:9 and is not a parallel to Jn. 1:1.
Jn. 9:30	30 The man answered and said to them, 'Well, here is an amazing thing, that you do not know where He is from, and He opened my eyes.
	30 ἀπεκρίθη ὁ ἄνθρωπος καὶ εἶπεν αὐτοῖς· ἐν τούτῳ γὰρ τὸ θαυμαστόν ἐστιν, ὅτι ὑμεῖς οὐκ οἴδατε πόθεν ἐστίν, καὶ ἤνοιξέν μου τοὺς ὀφθαλμούς.
	This is the only other possible one, but it is like the one above and in 2:9: οἴδατε πόθεν ἐστίν "you know from where he is." This is not a parallel to Jn. 1:1
Jn. 10:1	"Truly, truly, I say to you, he who does not enter by the door into the fold of the sheep, but climbs up some other way, he is a thief and a robber."
	Ἀμὴν ἀμὴν λέγω ὑμῖν, ὁ μὴ εἰσερχόμενος διὰ τῆς θύρας εἰς τὴν αὐλὴν τῶν προβάτων ἀλλὰ ἀναβαίνων ἀλλαχόθεν ἐκεῖνος κλέπτης ἐστὶν καὶ λῃστής·
	Here again, although there is a separate subject, ἐκεῖνος ("that one"), there is no definite article with the subject: ἐκεῖνος κλέπτης ἐστὶν καὶ λῃστής· "that one a thief he is an a robber." This is not parallel to Jn 1:1
Jn. 10:8	"All who came before Me are thieves and robbers, but the sheep did not hear them."
	πάντες ὅσοι ἦλθον (πρὸ ἐμοῦ) κλέπται εἰσὶν καὶ λῃσταί, ἀλλ' οὐκ ἤκουσαν αὐτῶν τὰ πρόβατα.
	This one is also a stretch. The predicate nominatives in this instance are both plurals, and the subject "all" (πάντες) does not have a definite article.
Jn. 10:33	"The Jews answered Him, 'For a good work we do not stone You, but for blasphemy; and because You, being a man, make Yourself out God.'"
	ἀπεκρίθησαν αὐτῷ οἱ Ἰουδαῖοι· περὶ καλοῦ ἔργου οὐ λιθάζομέν σε ἀλλὰ περὶ βλασφημίας, καὶ ὅτι σὺ ἄνθρωπος ὢν ποιεῖς σεαυτὸν θεόν.
	Here again the copula is a present participle, and the subject is a pronoun without a definite article.

Jn. 10:34	"Jesus answered them, 'Has it not been written in your Law, "I said, you are gods"?'"
	ἀπεκρίθη αὐτοῖς (ὁ) Ἰησοῦς· οὐκ ἔστιν γεγραμμένον ἐν τῷ νόμῳ ὑμῶν ὅτι ἐγὼ εἶπα· θεοί ἐστε
	This one, θεοί ἐστε ("gods you are") does not have a separate subject with a definite article, and the predicate nominative is plural.
Jn. 12:6	"Now he said this, not because he was concerned about the poor, but because he was a thief, and as he had the money box, he used to pilfer what was put into it."
	εἶπεν δὲ τοῦτο οὐχ ὅτι περὶ τῶν πτωχῶν ἔμελεν αὐτῷ, ἀλλ' ὅτι κλέπτης ἦν καὶ τὸ γλωσσόκομον ἔχων τὰ βαλλόμενα ἐβάσταζεν.
	Here again there is no separate subject with a definite article: ὅτι κλέπτης ἦν "that a thief he was."
Jn. 12:36	"While you have the Light, believe in the Light, so that you may become sons of Light."
	ὡς τὸ φῶς ἔχετε, πιστεύετε εἰς τὸ φῶς, ἵνα υἱοὶ φωτὸς γένησθε. ταῦτα ἐλάλησεν Ἰησοῦς, καὶ ἀπελθὼν ἐκρύβη ἀπ' αὐτῶν.
	Here the use of γινομαι is the only copula. Again there is no separate subject with a definite article, and the predicate nominative, "sons" (υἱοὶ), is plural.
Jn. 18:26	"One of the slaves of the high priest, being a relative of the one whose ear Peter cut off, said, 'Did I not see you in the garden with Him?'"
	λέγει εἷς ἐκ τῶν δούλων τοῦ ἀρχιερέως, συγγενὴς ὢν οὗ ἀπέκοψεν Πέτρος τὸ ὠτίον· οὐκ ἐγώ σε εἶδον ἐν τῷ κήπῳ μετ' αὐτοῦ
	This one is not even close. The copula is a participle (ὢν), and there is no subject with a definite article. In fact, grammatically, participles do not even have subjects.
Jn. 18:35	"Pilate answered, 'I am not a Jew, am I? Your own nation and the chief priests delivered You to me; what have You done?'"
	ἀπεκρίθη ὁ Πιλᾶτος· μήτι ἐγὼ Ἰουδαῖός εἰμι τὸ ἔθνος τὸ σὸν καὶ οἱ ἀρχιερεῖς παρέδωκάν σε ἐμοί· τί ἐποίησας
	Here again, although there is a separate subject, it does not have a definite article (ἐγώ), and the predicate nominative is a class or kind ("Jew").

Contrary to BeDuhn's claim, not a single one of these passages is an actual parallel to the statement in Jn. 1:1. So not a single one lends any support to BeDuhn's claim. Nevertheless, BeDuhn draws attention to Jn. 18:35. He says, "The very last verse in this long list is a good place for us to start in exploring sentences structured like John 1:1c and the meaning they are meant to convey."[60] But, as can be clearly seen by looking at each one of the passages in this long list, not a single one is "structured like John 1:1c." BeDuhn asserts, "The setting is Pilate's exchange with Jesus. In John 18, verse 35, Pilate asks, 'Am I a Jew (*ego Ioudaios eimi*)?' The predicate noun here appears before the verb and without the article, as it does in John 1:1c, and clearly is indefinite in meaning, 'a Jew.'"[61]

Table #61: Jn. 1:1c and Jn. 18:35[62]

		Predicate Nominative	verb	Subject
Jn. 1:1c	and	God	was	the Word
	καὶ	θεὸς	ἦν	ὁ λόγος.
Jn. 18:35	μήτι Not	ἐγώ I Subject	Ἰουδαῖός Jew Predicate Nominative	εἰμι; I am? Verb

But, as has been BeDuhn's mode of operation, he does not present all the evidence. First, the subject of 18:35 is a pronoun, unlike 1:1c, and the subject as well as the predicate nominative of 18:35 precede the verb, unlike 1:1c. Also, the term "Jew" is a class or kind, not a thing or person, and would not have the definite article anyway. God is not a class or kind. Since the Jn. 1:1c passage cannot be translated "the Word was divine," these two verses are in fact not structured alike.

He goes on to say, "Two verses later [Jn. 18:37], he asks Jesus, 'Are you a king (*basileus ei su*)?' Here is the exact same syntax as John 1:1 – the predicate noun

---

[60] BeDuhn, *Translation*, 122.
[61] Ibid.
[62] The entire verse of Jn. 18:35 reads: ἀπεκρίθη ὁ Πιλᾶτος· μήτι ἐγὼ Ἰουδαῖός εἰμι; τὸ ἔθνος τὸ σὸν καὶ οἱ ἀρχιερεῖς παρέδωκάν σε ἐμοί· τί ἐποίησας;. The only portion to which BeDuhn is refering is that portion appear in Table #61.

precedes the verb, the subject follows it, and the predicate noun lacks the definite article."[63] But, as is his custom, he leaves out important details.

Table #62: Jn. 1:1 and Jn. 18:37

		Predicate Nominative	Verb	Subject
Jn. 1:1	and καὶ	God θεὸς	was ἦν	the Word. ὁ λόγος.
Jn. 18:37	οὐκοῦν so	βασιλεὺς king | Predicate Nominative	εἶ you are | Verb	σύ; you? | Subject

Unlike Jn. 1:1, the subject of the phrase "so king you are you?" does not have the definite article, and the subject is a pronoun, also unlike Jn. 1:1. And in fact, it could be argued that the word 'king' should be taken as definite, "are you the king?" Consider two other verses in this same context, one before and one after the verses BeDuhn discusses. In both of these verses, Pilate uses the definite article with the word 'king.'

Table #63: Jn. 18:33 and Jn. 18:39

Jn. 18:33	"Therefore Pilate entered again into the Praetorium, and summoned Jesus and said to Him, 'Are You the King [ὁ βασιλεὺς, *ho basileus*] of the Jews?'"
	Εἰσῆλθεν οὖν πάλιν εἰς τὸ πραιτώριον ὁ Πιλᾶτος καὶ ἐφώνησεν τὸν Ἰησοῦν καὶ εἶπεν αὐτῷ· σὺ εἶ ὁ βασιλεὺς τῶν Ἰουδαίων;
Jn. 18:39	"But you have a custom that I release someone for you at the Passover; do you wish then that I release for you the King [τὸν βασιλέα, *ton basilea*] of the Jews?"
	ἔστιν δὲ συνήθεια ὑμῖν ἵνα ἕνα ἀπολύσω ὑμῖν ἐν τῷ πάσχα· βούλεσθε οὖν ἀπολύσω ὑμῖν τὸν βασιλέα τῶν Ἰουδαίων;

---

[63] Ibid.

It is contrary to the context for Pilate to be saying "So, you are a king?" Pilate is mocking Jesus: "Are your really the king of the Jews?" So, not only is the syntax not exactly the same, as BeDuhn claims, but its translation has just the same kind of questions as the Jn. 1:1 passage. Is the predicate nominative definite or not? The context seems to indicate that we should take the word 'king' in 18:37 as definite. In fact, in the middle portion of this verse Jesus says, ἐγὼ εἰς τοῦτο γεγέννημαι καὶ εἰς τοῦτο ἐλήλυθα εἰς τὸν κόσμον, ἵνα μαρτυρήσω τῇ ἀληθείᾳ· ("unto this I have been born, and unto this I have come into the world, in order to testify to the truth"). Jesus was not born to be merely *a* king, but to be *the* King. Jesus did not come into the world to be merely *a* king, but to be *the* King. BeDuhn has ignored the context even of this verse. Again he has violated his own principle for accurate and unbiased translation. BeDuhn cannot settle this question by simply asserting it. He has not presented any supporting evidence as to why anyone should take this as an indefinite. He claims that it is indefinite because he has a prior commitment. In other words, his translation reveals his bias. It is neither syntactically, grammatically, or contextually required to be indefinite. And his reference to Jesus' response has the same issues. Jesus could be saying "You say that I am the king."

Jn. 19:21

Also his account of the placard, Jn. 19:21, does not present the "basic lesson in the distinction between definite and indefinite constructions in Greek"[64] as BeDuhn characterizes it. He claims, "As the story continues, the opponents of Jesus provide, through John's report, a basic lesson in the distinction between definite and indefinite constructions in Greek. Seeing the placard placed over the crucified Jesus, they tell Pilate: 'Do not write "*The* king of the Jews," but that this one said, "I am *a* king of the Jews"' (John 19:21)."[65] In order to consider his claims, we need to set the verse out with word-for-word translation.

Table #64: Jn. 19:21

μὴ	γράφε	ὁ βασιλεὺς	τῶν Ἰουδαίων
Not	you write	The king	of the Jews
ἀλλ'	ὅτι	ἐκεῖνος	εἶπεν
but	that	that one	said

[64] Ibid.
[65] Ibid.

βασιλεύς	εἰμι	τῶν Ἰουδαίων
King	I am	of the Jews

Now it is simply wrong to propose that Jesus was claiming to be "a king of the Jews." Jesus was not claiming to be *a* king of the Jews, but to be King of the Jews. He was claiming to be *the* king, not simply *a* king. This is more a lesson in the lengths to which some will go to promote their own bias than it is a lesson in Greek syntax. The distinction that the Jews are making here is not between "the king" and "a king," but between what the placard says Jesus *is*, and the fact that the Jews wanted to placard to say that He only *claimed* to be King, not that He was in fact King. It is just as syntactically appropriate to take the word 'king' in the second phrase as definite as it is to take it as indefinite. In fact, Smyth says, "Several appellatives, treated like proper names, may omit the article," and then he gives the example, "βασιλεύς the king of Persia."[66] Even BeDuhn's favorite grammar doesn't seem to agree with him. Simply by declaring that it is indefinite does not make it so. BeDuhn has presented no syntactical evidence to support his claim. Rather, he resorts to interpretation, something he said he would not do.

BeDuhn says, "They try to distance Jesus from the royal title by two moves: first by making it clear that it is merely a claim, and second by changing the title itself from 'the king' (*ho basileus*) to 'a king' (*basileus* without the article, before the be-verb)."[67] BeDuhn's argument here makes no sense at all. If Jesus really did claim to be only "a king," then there was never any "royal title" involved, and there would be no reason to try to "distance" Him from it. Besides the fact that this is interpretation on BeDuhn's part, not translation, he has gotten his interpretation all wrong. And, as we said, just because BeDuhn thinks that the second phrase is saying "a king" does not prove that it is. It is not uncommon to say "King of the Jews" when referring to a definite "king." In fact, one such instance is in Jn. 1:49. Here Nathanael realized who Jesus is and he declares, "Rabbi, You are the Son of God; You are the King of Israel." Let use set this out with the Greek as we have been doing:

Table #65: Jn. 1:49

ῥαββί			
Rabbi			

σύ	εἶ	ὁ υἱὸς	τοῦ θεοῦ
you	you are	the Son	of the God

---

[66] Smyth, *Greek Grammar*, §1140.
[67] Ibid.

σὺ	βασιλεὺς	εἶ	τοῦ Ἰσραήλ
you	King	you are	of the Israel

Notice how Nathanael associates the Son of God with King of Israel. In Nathanael's mind, these are linked. Messiah, the prophesied King of Israel, was to be the very Son of God. Remember, when Jesus sees Nathanael coming to Him he says, "Behold, truly an Israelite in whom there is no deceit!" (Jn. 1:47). To supposes that one who is truly an Israelite would say, "you are the Son of God, a King of Israel," would be to ignore the historical and cultural context in which this declaration is made, one of the three criteria that BeDuhn laid down as the basis of an accurate and unbiased translation. Of course someone will say that this is just interpretation on my part, not translation, and that may be correct. But, it is also equally true that BeDuhn is doing interpretation. The problem for BeDuhn is that he offers no grammatical or syntactical support for his claims, and he resorts to interpretation to try to fabricate support. In addition, the grammar and syntax actually contradict his claim. His interpretation serves only to reveal his own theological bias. He is just as bias as any of the translations he charges with bias.

Jn. 6:20 (6:60)

BeDuhn claims that Jn. 6:20 is "set up exactly like John 1:1c which even has *ho logos* (here meaning simply 'the saying' or 'the teaching') as the subject *skleros estin ho logos houtos*, 'This word is a hard one (word-for-word: a hard one is the word this).'"[68] The passage to which BeDuhn is referring is actually Jn. 6:60, not 6:20.

BeDuhn says, "Notice how closely this resembles John 1:1c. The subject is *ho logos*, with the article, following the be-verb, just as in John 1:1c. The predicate noun precedes the verb, and lacks the article just as in John 1:1c."[69] One problem with BeDuhn's claim is that the word σκληρός (*skleros*, "difficult") is not a noun. It is an adjective. And in fact, it could be argued that ὁ λόγος is not the subject. In this instance, ὁ λόγος could be a Nominative of apposition, not the subject of the verb. Now BeDuhn might not agree with this analysis, but what it shows is that this is not an unambiguous parallel to Jn. 1:1c. The dissimilarity is especially acute by the fact that the predicate nominative is not even a predicate noun, but a predicate adjective.

---

[68] Ibid.
[69] Ibid.

Table #66: Jn. 6:60 and Jn. 1:1c

	Predicate Nominative (Adjective)	Verb	Subject	Demonstrative Pronoun
Jn. 6:60	| difficult | σκληρός	| is | ἐστιν	| the word | ὁ λόγος	| this. | οὗτος·
Jn. 1:1c	καὶ | and | Conjunction	θεὸς | God | Predicate Nominative (Noun)	ἦν | was | Verb	ὁ λόγος | the Word | Subject

Now BeDuhn will probably charge me with not understanding Greek grammar, because in his Greek grammar, Smyth subsumes the designation "predicate adjective" under the broad heading "Predicate Nouns," (see Smyth, §910b, page 256). Even though Smyth puts the category "predicate adjective" under the heading "Predicate Nouns," he still makes the distinction between predicate substantives, which would be the classification of the word θεός, and predicate adjective, which would be the classification of the word σκληρός. However, this is not something that the average reader would know. BeDuhn should have made this distinction clear to the reader so as not to mislead. But, he could not do this without compromising his claim that these two passages are "set up exactly" alike. The fact that BeDuhn does not inform his reader about these distinctions once again reveals his theological bias that predisposes him to commit the fallacy of selective reporting.

Again BeDuhn has misrepresented the situation, and he has either failed or deliberately omitted addressing the question of the relationship of ὁ λόγος to οὗτος in Jn. 6:60, a question that must be decided in order to make the case that ὁ λόγος is the subject. Compare the diagraming of the two passages:

The diagraming in **Figure 13** below is a plausible and grammatically acceptable arrangement. Although this might not be the only way to explain the syntax of the passage, it shows that there are other reasonable and grammatically acceptable options that BeDuhn simply does not bother to address. And from the diagraming, if this arrangement is accepted, you can see that there is a considerable difference between the two passages. Jn. 6:60 is in fact not "set up exactly like John 1:1c" as BeDuhn claims, and he has not dealt with some of the grammatical and syntactical issues that account for the difference. Even if he wants to object to this arrangement, he must make his case and present his evidence. He has done neither of these, and he has presented the passage as if his analysis is the only correct one. He makes his claims as if his claims are sufficient to settle the case. But that is simply misleading and disingenuous. If he wants to use Jn. 6:60 as a parallel to Jn. 1:1c, then he needs to explain to the reader why there are these differences.

Figure 13: Jn. 6:0 and 1:1c Diagraming

Jn. 6:60	nominative of apposition ὁ λόγος =	subject οὗτος·	copula ἐστιν	predicate adjective σκληρός
Jn. 1:1c		subject ὁ λόγος	copula ἦν	predicate noun θεὸς

The biggest problem BeDuhn has with reference to Jn. 6:60 is his misrepresentation that σκληρός is a noun when in fact it is an adjective. Someone might complain that this is a minor difference, but that would be to misunderstand the significance of the difference—this difference makes all the difference. Because σκληρός is a predicate adjective, the reason it does not have a definite article is different from the reason why θεὸς does not have the definite article. Simply put, the reason σκληρός does not have the definite article is because adjectives do not take definite articles when functioning predicatively. Smyth says, "Adjectives and participles used substantively have no article when the reference is general."[70] For an adjective to be used substantively means that it is used as a noun. Since in this case the adjective is a predicate nominative, it is being used as a noun would be used. So, according to Smyth, it is not supposed to have the definite article. Adjectives may take the article when functioning attributively, but not when functioning predicatively as in Jn. 6:60.[71] In fact, one of the indicators that an adjective is functioning as a predicate adjective is the fact that it does not have the definite article. In other words, the reason the predicate adjective does not have the article is because it is a predicate adjective. The reason θεὸς does not have the article is a whole different question. In fact, this is the question that BeDuhn's chapter is about. But that question cannot be answered by posing inaccurate parallels as if they were "exactly" alike. The fact is, Jn. 6:60 and Jn. 1:1c are not "set up exactly alike."

---

[70] Smyth, *Greek Grammar*, §1130.
[71] See William D. Mounce, *Basics of Biblical Greek* (Grand Rapids: Zondervan Publishing House, 1999), 9.12. Of course BeDuhn will dismiss this reference as another biased Christian, but that becomes a very convenient way to eliminate all opposition to your point of view. If you don't like what they say, just accuse them of being bias. This seems to be another of BeDuhn's tactics. William D. Mounce is a well qualified grammarian even though he is a Christian.

It is also interesting that BeDuhn again appeals to his interpretation of the passage to support his claims. He says, "In meaning, the predicate noun is indefinite. We know this both from its lack of a definite article, and form the larger contextual meaning of the sentence."[72] First of all, we have already shown that a word does not need a definite article to be definite. Second, we have shown that one reason the predicate adjective does not have a definite article is because it is a predicate adjective. Thirdly, as soon as BeDuhn begins to talk about "meaning," he has passed over from a grammatical and syntactical analysis to interpretation, something he said he would not do because interpretation introduces bias, which is precisely what happens here with BeDuhn's analysis.

Because of the critical differences between Jn. 6:60 and Jn. 1:1c, BeDuhn's claims that because the "hard saying" is only one of the hard sayings of Jesus, not the one-and-only hard saying, therefore, "the Word is not the one-and-only God, but is *a* god, or divine being" simply do not stand up to analysis. Before he can make this connection, if it can be made at all, he must deal with the grammatical and syntactical differences in the two passages. But also, the claim that Jesus is "not the one-and-only God, but is *a* god, or divine being" again is a matter of interpretation. Even if you take the word θεός as indefinite so that it could legitimately be translated "the Word was a divine being," you cannot automatically conclude that the Word is *a* God. A divine being is a Divine Being. And, unless you have already decided that there can be more than one of these, to say that the Word is a Divine Being is to say that He is God, the one and only God. BeDuhn's conclusion about what the Word is cannot be a function of the grammar and syntax. It is a prior theological commitment that leads him to interpret the passage in a way that corresponds to his theological bias. Now, it may be true that other translations are doing this too. But, BeDuhn misleads his readers into thinking that his own theological conclusions are necessarily required by the grammar and syntax, when this is in fact flatly false. He is just as bias as anyone else, and he has already decided that there can be more than one divine being—in other words, he has already committed himself to the possibility of there being more than one god—polytheism. But this is a theological position that could never be attributed to John or any other biblical writer.

Jn. 4:24

Concerning Jn. 4:24, BeDuhn asserts, "John 4:24 provides another example of the same construction as John 1:1c, with the sole exception that the be-verb is omitted as unnecessary: *pneuma ho theos*, 'God (is) a spirit.'"[73]

The texts of Jn. 4:24 and Jn. 1:1c are set out below:

---

[72] BeDuhn, *Translation*, 122.
[73] Ibid., 123.

Table #67: Jn. 1:1 and 4:24

		Predicate Nominative	Implied Verb	Subject
Jn. 4:24		| is | πνεῦμα	| [ἐστιν]	| this. | ὁ θεός
Jn. 1:1c	καὶ and | Conjunction	θεὸς God | Predicate Nominative (Noun)	ἦν was | Verb	ὁ λόγος the Word | Subject

BeDuhn states, "Greek writers frequently omit the be-verb for succinctness, as John does here."[74] For those who know Hebrew and the New Testament, they know that this is not why John omits the verb. Verbless clauses are a common form of expression in Semitic languages, especially when the to-be verb is a simple copula, and John, whose native language was Aramaic, a cognate language of Hebrew, writes his Greek as a Semitic thinker. Consequently, this verbless clause is actually a Semitism, an expression that is the result of the influence of Semitic language on the Greek of the NT.

BeDuhn goes on to argue, "the subject is marked with the article, and the predicate noun appears before the verb without the article in a clearly *indefinite* sense."[75] Of course, this is not "clearly" an indefinite use of this word. There are instances in which the word πνεῦμα appears without the definite article but is nevertheless definite. There are at least two examples of this in John's Gospel:

Table #68: Jn. 7:39 and Jn. 20:22

Jn. 7:39	"But this He spoke of the Spirit, whom those who believed in Him were to receive; for *the* Spirit was not yet *given*, because Jesus was not yet glorified."
	τοῦτο δὲ εἶπεν περὶ τοῦ πνεύματος ὃ ἔμελλον λαμβάνειν οἱ πιστεύσαντες εἰς αὐτόν· οὔπω γὰρ ἦν πνεῦμα, ὅτι Ἰησοῦς οὐδέπω ἐδοξάσθη.
	It would make no sense to say "for a spirit was not *given*" since the beginning of the verse refers to "the Spirit."

---

[74] Ibid.
[75] Ibid.

Jn. 20:22	"And when He had said this, He breathed on them and said to them, 'Receive *the* Holy Spirit.'"
	καὶ τοῦτο εἰπὼν ἐνεφύσησεν καὶ λέγει αὐτοῖς· λάβετε πνεῦμα ἅγιον·
	Again, it would make no sense for Jesus to say, "Receive a Holy Spirit" since there is only one Holy Spirit.

In both of the above verses, the word 'Spirit' must be definite even though there is no definite article in either instance. The context clearly shows this.

Acts 8:39 is another example:

Table #69: Acts 8:39

Acts 8:39	And when they came up out of the water, *the* Spirit of the Lord [πνεῦμα κυρίου] caught away Philip; and the eunuch saw him no more, for he went on his way rejoicing.
	ὅτε δὲ ἀνέβησαν ἐκ τοῦ ὕδατος, πνεῦμα κυρίου ἥρπασεν τὸν Φίλιππον καὶ οὐκ εἶδεν αὐτὸν οὐκέτι ὁ εὐνοῦχος, ἐπορεύετο γὰρ τὴν ὁδὸν αὐτοῦ χαίρων.
	It would certainly make no sense to translate this, "a Spirit of the Lord."

Another example is Rom. 8:11:

Table #70: Rom. 8:11

Rom. 8:11	But if the Spirit of him that raised up Jesus from *the* dead dwells in you, he that raised up Christ Jesus from *the* dead shall give life also to your mortal bodies through his Spirit [αὐτοῦ πνεύματος] that dwells in you.
	εἰ δὲ τὸ πνεῦμα τοῦ ἐγείραντος τὸν Ἰησοῦν ἐκ νεκρῶν οἰκεῖ ἐν ὑμῖν, ὁ ἐγείρας Χριστὸν ἐκ νεκρῶν ζωοποιήσει καὶ τὰ θνητὰ σώματα ὑμῶν διὰ τοῦ ἐνοικοῦντος αὐτοῦ πνεύματος ἐν ὑμῖν.

This is a particularly interesting example. In the first part of the verse Paul refers to "the Spirit the one having raised the Jesus out of dead." In the latter part of the verse Paul is referring to the same Spirit, but this time he leaves off the definite article. However, this is clearly a definite use of the word 'Spirit' since earlier he referred to this same Spirit with the definite article. Some may want to argue that the definite article τοῦ is the definite article for πνεύματος, but this is not the case. This definite article actually goes with the participle ἐνοικοῦντος. This is clearly a case of the use of the word πνεῦμα without the definite article that is nevertheless definite. Other examples of the use of the word πνεύμα without the definite article that are nevertheless definite include Rom. 8:13, 14; 15:19; 1 Cor. 2:13; 7:40; 2 Cor. 3:3, and others.

What is the Word? The Word is God!

BeDuhn starts this section of the chapter, "What is the Word?" beginning on page 128, by arguing that the reader must "keep in mind that when John says 'God' he means 'God the Father.' The heavy concentration of 'Father' and 'Son' language in the gospel helps us to understand this."[76] But as true as it may be that there is a "heavy concentration of 'Father' and 'Son' language in the gospel," that cannot apply to Jn. 1:1 for at least three reasons. First, this is the very first verse of the Gospel, so John could not have expected his readers to understand such a distinction before they have even read his Gospel. Second, the association of ὁ λόγος with creation in Jn. 1:3 precludes the notion that John is employing a Father/Son distinction in these opening verses. Verse 3 states, "All things came into being through Him, and apart from Him nothing came into being that has come into being." (πάντα δι᾽ αὐτοῦ ἐγένετο, καὶ χωρὶς αὐτοῦ ἐγένετο οὐδὲ ἕν ὃ γέγονεν).[77] The text of John clearly depicts ὁ λόγος as the agent of creation. The OT account of creation depicts the creation as the act of God אֱלֹהִים (GSEPT ὁ θεός). Now, unless BeDuhn and his JW friends are willing to admit the existence of the Trinity in these OT references, the fact that God is depicted as the Creator in Genesis and ὁ λόγος is presented as the Creator in Jn. 1:3, there is no basis upon which arbitrarily to make the claim that John is making a distinction between Father and Son in these opening verses. Third, the fact that John makes the distinction between Father and Son in many places in his Gospel does not prove that he is doing so here. This must be demonstrated by argument and evidence, not simply by assertion.

Son Near the Father?

BeDuhn thinks he has support for his Father/Son distinction in Jn. 1:1b by the fact that the text states, "and the word was with God" (καὶ ὁ λόγος ἦν πρὸς τὸν θεόν). He says, "In the immediate literary context, we see how carefully John differentiates between the Word and God (the Father). The Word is 'with' or 'near' God (the Father) (John 1:1–2). The Word becomes flesh and is seen; God (the Father) cannot be seen (John 1:18)."[78] Using one of BeDuhn's own arguments, if John had wanted to make a

---

[76] Ibid., 128.
[77] Although the critical text, UBS and Nestle-Aland, place a period before ὃ γέγονεν, effectively altering the translation to read: "... and apart from Him became not even one. Which has become ⁴ in Him was life ..." only a few mss support this reading: 𝔓⁷⁵ᶜ, C, L, W and a few others, the second corrector of ℵ Θ Ψ and the *Byz* support the period at the end of verse 3. See Swanson, *New Testament Greek Manuscripts: John*, 5, for a fuller account.
[78] BeDuhn, *Translation*, 129.

distinction between Father and Son, why didn't he simply use these terms—πατήρ ("Father") and υἱός ("Son")? He uses the word 'father' in 1:14: Καὶ ὁ λόγος σὰρξ ἐγένετο καὶ ἐσκήνωσεν ἐν ἡμῖν, καὶ ἐθεασάμεθα τὴν δόξαν αὐτοῦ, δόξαν ὡς μονογενοῦς παρὰ πατρός ["Father"], πλήρης χάριτος καὶ ἀληθείας.; and 1:18: μονογενὴς υἱὸς ὁ ὢν εἰς τὸν κόλπον τοῦ πατρός ["Father"].[79] Also, given the fact that ὁ λόγος is presented as the Creator, the only basis upon which BeDuhn could make this claim is on the basis of a Trinitarian assumption. But, if BeDuhn is interpreting this statement from a Trinitarian theological bias, then why the problem with claiming that the text of Jn. 1:1c cannot be saying that ὁ λόγος is God? Of course BeDuhn would probably say, "That's the point I've been trying to make! I'm not arguing from a theological bias. I'm arguing from a purely grammatical basis. Since I do not have a theological bias either for or against the notion of the Trinity, I can argue the distinction of Father and Son in verses 1 and 2 and that 'the word was a god' or 'the word was divine' in verse 3."

But this argument doesn't work. We have already shown that the use or non-use of the definite article is not a purely grammatical or syntactical issue, but is rather a conceptual issue. So either BeDuhn has entangled himself in a contradiction, or one of his claims is false. Of course a third option is that he simply does not grasp Greek grammar and syntax. Either the Jn. 1:1c passage should be translated "the Word was God" on the basis of the a Trinitarian theology, or there is no distinction between Father and Son in Jn. 1:1–2. If there is a Father/Son distinction in verses 1 and 2, then ὁ λόγος is God the Son, and there is no problem with understanding 1:1c to be saying "and the Word was God." However, if Jn. 1:1c is saying "the Word was *a* god," but not "*the* God," then there can be no distinction in 1–2 between God the Father and God the Son. He can't have it both ways. The reason he can't have it both ways is because in the introduction to his book he stated that one of his assumptions is that "an author is relatively consistent and non-contradictory in what he or she said."[80] Either John is contradicting himself or BeDuhn is contradicting himself. I would opt for the latter.

Of course there is one way that he *could* have it both ways, and that is if when BeDuhn talks about the Father/Son distinction, he is not using these terms according to the traditional, Trinitarian categories. In other words, he may be using the term "Son" to refer to a being who is in fact not God, but still designated "Son." And that is precisely what he does:

> What then is the *logos* ("Word")? John says it was the agent through which God (the Father) made the world. He starts his gospel "In the beginning..." to remind us of Genesis 1. How does God create in Genesis? He speaks words that make things come into existence. So the Word is God's creative power and plan and activity. It is not God (the Father) himself, but it is not really something separate from God either. It occupies a kind of ambiguous status. That

---

[79] I am aware of the variant reading in this verse that has μονογενὴς θεός rather than μονογενὴς υἱός, but I believe the manuscript evidence does not support that reading.

[80] BeDuhn, *Translation*, xvi.

is why a monotheist like John can get away with calling it 'a god' or 'divine' without becoming a polytheist. This divine thing or being acts, takes on a kind of distinct identity, and in 'becoming flesh' brings God's will and plan right down face to face with humans.[81]

Of course, all of this is a declaration of BeDuhn's theological bias, a bias which he has tried to hide from his readers, but one that has been operative from the very beginning. This kind of theological position does not grow out of the grammar or syntax of the passage as we have repeatedly shown. In fact, BeDuhn is not reading this *out of* the passage. Rather, he is reading it *into* the passage. So, basically, what all of this amounts to is simply another theological treatise by another person who does not believe that Jesus is God. Only this time, the author, BeDuhn, parades his theology as if it is Greek grammar and syntax. But, when it comes to explaining his theological bias, he ends up make contradictory and nonsensical statements that could not possibly have been John's meaning. To say that ὁ λόγος, who presents all the characteristics of a Personal being—He faces God, He creates, He has life, He came to His own but they rejected Him, He became flesh, He explains the Father—is some ambiguous something that is neither God nor man nor angel is nonsensical. Also, the Genesis account of creation gives no hint that there is some *tertium quid* (although I guess it would be a *quartum quid*) involved in the creation of the universe. Of course someone will say that there is no hint that the Logos was involved in creation either, but that's not correct. The fact that God is the creator, and the fact that the Logos is God, there is not merely a hint that He is involved in creation, there is an outright declaration that He did it.

A Class of Divine Things? What's That?

BeDuhn says he believes that the Word "has a divine character, or belongs to the class of divine things, however that is to be worked out technically."[82] But what would a "class of divine things" be? If by the word "divine" BeDuhn means something that is equal with God in being and essence and is responsible for creating the universe, then there is no "class of divine things" because there can be only one Divine Being or Divine Thing who is the same in being and essence and is the Creator of the universe. For there to be two Divine Beings, they would have to differ by some difference. But, they could not differ by being, because that is the very aspect in which they are the same. But, they cannot differ by non-being, because non-being is nothing, and to differ by nothing is not to differ. So, since two Divine beings cannot differ, then there are not two, but only one. So, there cannot be a class of "divine things" if by "divine" he means Divine or God. However if by "divine" he means something less than God, then he is simply promoting a theology that is anti-Trinitarian, a theology that he is imposing upon the text.

---

[81] Ibid., 129.
[82] Ibid.

BeDuhn tries to argue that the notion of the Messiah as merely a chosen human being is what John is trying to combat. He says that the Jews expected their Messiah to be exactly this.[83] He goes on, "Whatever the other New Testament authors intended, it was and is still possible to read their language about Christ in this more limited way."[84] But for someone actually to read the Gospel of Matthew, for example, and come away with the notion that Jesus the Messiah is not God in the flesh would need utterly to ignore the clear statements of the text. Matthew unquestionably presents Jesus as the Messiah, the King of Israel, God in the flesh. In fact, Isaiah declares that the Son Who is to be given will carry the government of Israel upon His shoulders: "For a child will be born to us, a son will be given to us; and the government will rest on His shoulders;" (Isa. 9:6). Later Isaiah declares, "For the Lord is our judge, the Lord is our lawgiver, the Lord [יְהוָה, *yehwāh*] is our King;"[85] (Isa. 33:22), specifically declaring that God is "our King." If the government of Israel will rest on the shoulders of the Messiah, the Son who is given, and if God is their King, then this clearly means that the Messiah is God, the King of Israel. Even the very descriptions of the Son in Isa. 9:6 depict Messiah as God, as Craig L. Blomberg points out, "Here, in [Isa.] 9:6 another description of the birth of a wonderful child appears, one who can be called 'Almighty God, 'Eternal Father,' and 'Prince of Peace,' who will rule from David's throne and establish universal justice forever—prophecies that scarcely could have been fulfilled in a mere earthly king."[86] Actually, the Hebrew text should be translated, "Father of eternity," (אֲבִיעַד, *ᵃbî'ad*), not "Eternal Father." Regardless of what the average Jew would have believed about the Messiah, it would hardly be possible, either then or now, to read Matthew's Gospel and come away with any other notion than the fact that Matthew presents Messiah as the King of Israel, God in the flesh.

John and the Trinity

Earlier in this analysis I pointed out a statement in his introduction that BeDuhn makes that reveals his theological bias. BeDuhn asserts, "Accuracy in Bible translation has nothing to do with majority votes; it has to do with . . . strictly excluding bias towards later developments of Christian thought."[87] What was only a hint in the introduction becomes here a full-fledged assertion. BeDuhn summarily dismisses all talk about the Trinity as a "later development" in Christian theology. He says,

---

[83] Ibid.
[84] Ibid.
[85] (Isa. 33:22): כִּי יְהוָה שֹׁפְטֵנוּ יְהוָה מְחֹקְקֵנוּ יְהוָה מַלְכֵּנוּ הוּא יוֹשִׁיעֵנוּ
[86] Craig L. Blomberg, "Matthew," in *Commentary on the New Testament Use of the Old Testament*, ed. G. K. Beale and D. A. Carson (Grand Rapids: Baker Academic, 2007), 4.
[87] BeDuhn, *Translation*, xv.

Of course, once you make the move of saying the Word belongs to that category [the god category], you have to count up how many gods Christians are willing to have, and start to do some philosophical hair-splitting about what exactly you mean by "god." As Christians chewed on this problem in the decades and centuries after John, some of them developed the idea of the Trinity, and you can see how a line can be drawn from John 1:1 to the later Trinity explanation as a logical development. But John himself has not formulated a Trinity concept in his gospel. Instead, he uses more fluid, ambiguous, mystical language of oneness, without letting himself get held down to technical definitions.[88]

Of course such speculations are absurd. The fact that the church may have developed the terminology and expressly determined definitions in later years does not mean that the theology was not there in the writings of John. There is an abundance of literature on this topic and the arguments against BeDuhn's position are too well known to rehearse them here.[89] What is important is that BeDuhn's theological bias is, once again, out there in the open for all to see. For the careful reader, BeDuhn hinted in his introduction at this theological bias on the basis of which he would draw his conclusions. Now he states it as if this is a conclusion that has grown out of the text. If BeDuhn wants to hold to a anti-Trinitarian theology, that is his right. But to present his study as if he is an unbiased investigator is disingenuous, misleading, and wrong. As John Hannah points out,

> Jehovah's Witnesses assert that Trinity is not a biblical term, having been first used in the third century, and that the doctrine of the Trinity was not set forth until the fourth century; that is, church leaders invented the doctrine.... The error of the Jehovah's Witness teaching is rooted in at least one historical miscue. They assume that the early church invented the teaching on the Trinity, which conflicts with the Bible. That is, what the church wrote much later in a creed to describe the nature of God is a perversion of the original scriptural teachings. My reply is that the church did compose creeds but that these creeds were explanations of, not errant additions to, what the Bible teaches.... The proclamation of the deity of Christ is integral to the gospel message.[90]

BeDuhn goes on to espouse a doctrine that was popular in the early 1900s but has sense lost any serious support from scholars. Ronald Nash has demonstrated that this

---

[88] Ibid., 130.

[89] Two such examples are Larry W. Hurtado, *Lord Jesus Christ: Devotion to Jesus in Earliest Christianity* (Grand Rapids: William B. Eerdmans Publishing Company, 2003). In this book Hurtado argues that Jesus was acknowledged to be God from the very earliest periods, conservatively within the first two decades, from 30 to 50 A.D. according to Hurtado on page 2. Also see Larry W. Hurtado, *The Earliest Christian Artifacts: Manuscripts and Christian Origins* (Grand Rapids: William B. Eerdmans Publishing Company, 2006). In this book Hurtado examines the New Testament documents in which he shows that the documents as artifacts demonstrate an acknowledgment of Jesus as God in the flesh.

[90] John Hannah, *Our Legacy: The History of Christian Doctrine* (Colorado Springs, Colorado: NavPress, 2001), 71–72.

view is not only out of date, but it is also out of steam. In fact, Nash points out that "most contemporary New Testament scholars see no need to postulate a conscious relationship between Alexandrian Judaism and the New Testament use of *logos*."[91] He continues, "Many scholars prefer a different hypothesis in their search for a non-Philonic source for John's use of *logos*. They note that the phrases 'The Word of God' and 'The Word of the Lord [Yahweh]' are used throughout the Old Testament in ways that suggest an independent existence and personification (see Pss. 33:6; 107:20; 147:15, 18; Isa. 9:8; 55:10ff.).... It is a mistake, then, to assume that the early Christian use of *logos* had to be derived from Alexandrian Judaism. There are at least two separate Old Testament traditions that could have given rise to the teaching found in the Prologue to the Fourth Gospel."[92] BeDuhn's claims about the Logos are not only wrong grammatically, but they are wrong historically, culturally, and theologically.

Conclusions

BeDuhn's theological bias that predisposes him to understand John's text in the way he does is expressed by him in his section titled "What is the Word?" It is clear that his theological position expressed in this section could not have grown out of only this one verse, or in fact this one phrase—or for that matter from the New Testament. BeDuhn in fact discusses his understanding of early Christian belief, his view on John's references to Jesus and God the Father elsewhere in the Gospel, and his own understanding of John's presentation of Jesus as Messiah. All of this forms the background and basis of his position on Jn. 1:1c—not the outcome of his understanding of this one phrase.

But against BeDuhn's claims is a wealth of scholarship and the majority of the scholarly community. As just a single example, in his massive commentary on John's Gospel, Craig Keener makes the following observations about the phrase:

> Many commentators doubt that the anarthrous construction signifies anything theologically at all. It certainly cannot connote "a God," as in "one among many," given Jesus' unique titles, roll, and relationship with the Father later in the Gospel. Nor should it mean "divine" in a weaker sense distinct from God's own divine nature, for example, in the sense in which Philo can apply it to Moses. Had John meant merely "divine" in a more general sense, the common but more ambiguous expression τὸ θεῖον was already available; thus, for example, Philo repeatedly refers to the divine word and Aristeas refers to "the divine law" (τοῦ θείου νόμου).
>
> The anarthrous construction cannot be pressed to produce the weaker sense of merely "divine" in a sense distinct from the character of the Father's deity. In one study of about 250 definite predicative nominatives in the NT, 90 percent were articular when following the verb, but a comparable 87 percent were anarthrous when before the verb, as here. Grammatically, one would thus expect John's predicate nominative "θεός" to be anarthrous, regardless of the

---

[91] Nash, *Christianity and the Hellenistic World*, 85 (emphasis in original).
[92] Ibid., 85–87.

point he was making. Further, John omits the article for God the Father elsewhere in the Gospel, even elsewhere in the chapter (e.g., 1: 6, 12, 13, 18). The same pattern of inconsistent usage appears in early patristic texts, and apparently Greek literature in general. And in a context where absolute identification with the Father would be less of a danger, John does not balk at using the articular form to call Jesus ὁ θεός (20: 28).[93]

With reference to the statistics reported by Keener, he includes the following footnote: "It should be noted, of course, that a writer who wished to *emphasize* that a predicate noun was definite was free to insert the article (Harner, "Nouns," 87); and the pattern does not always obtain even in the context (John 1:8–9)."[94] What this shows is that, contrary to BeDuhn's claims, the grammatical construction does not demand that the translator take the approach BeDuhn has proposed. BeDuhn's choice is theologically motivated, not grammatically or syntactically based. His choice is not only not grammatically or syntactically based, it is in fact the weaker and less likely way to understand the syntax. Keener also notes a comment from F. F. Bruce in his book, *Books and Parchments*: "those who translate 'a god' here 'prove nothing thereby save their ignorance of Greek grammar.'"[95]

BeDuhn's disingenuous selective reporting betrays his theological bias in his account of why he chooses to translate Jn. 1:1c as "the Word was a god." Just as he charges translators with employing their own theological bias, since we have shown that BeDuhn's claims about the grammar and syntax are either incorrect or only partially correct, the same charge can be made against BeDuhn with much greater accuracy. The NW translation is not the better or even the more likely translation of this verse.

Apologetic Points

This extensive study of Jn. 1:1 and related passages has conclusively demonstrated that this phrase, "and the Word was God," coupled with the statement in Jn. 1:14, is undoubtedly a reference to Jesus as God in the flesh. From this study we can glean the following apologetic points:

1. Words do not need to have a definite article in order to be definite, and just because a word does have a definite article does not necessarily mean it is

---

[93] Craig S. Keener, *The Gospel of John: A Commentary* (Peabody, Massachusetts: Hendrickson Publishers, 2003), 372–73. Keener does include the following footnote for clarification with reference to the statistics: "It should be noted, of course, that a writer who wished to *emphasize* that a predicate noun was definite was free to insert the article (Harner, 'Nouns,' 87); and the pattern does not always obtain even in the context (John 1:8–9)." Keener, *Gospel of John*, 373.n90 (emphasis in original).
[94] Ibid., 373.n90.
[95] Ibid., 373.n85.

definite. So, just because θεός in Jn. 1:1 does not have the definite article does not mean it is indefinite.

2. Throughout the Gospel of John the ASV, KJV, NASB, NIV, NRSV, and TEV never translate ὁ θεός as "the God" shows that the translation of Jn. 1:1 as "and the word was a god" is theologically motivated. But the grammatical and syntactical evidence does not support this translation.

3. Jn. 1:1c and Jn. 6:60 are not set up exactly alike, so Jn. 6:60 does not provide a parallel structure to Jn. 1:1c.

4. Even if you take the word θεός as indefinite so that it could legitimately be translated "the Word was a divine being," you cannot automatically conclude that the Word is *a* God. A divine being is a Divine Being. And, unless you have already decided that there can be more than one of these, to say that the Word is a Divine Being is to say that He is God, the one and only God.

5. There are several examples of the word 'Spirit' without the definite article that are nevertheless definite: Jn. 7:39; 20:22; Acts 8:39; Rom. 8:13, 14; 15:19; 1 Cor. 2:13; 7:40; 2 Cor. 3:3, and others.

6. The Father and Son distinction in John's Gospel cannot apply to Jn. 1:1 for at least three reasons. First, this is the very first verse of the Gospel, so John could not have expected his readers to understand such a distinction before they have even read his Gospel. Second, the association of ὁ λόγος with creation in Jn. 1:3 precludes the notion that John is employing a Father/Son distinction in these opening verses. Third, the fact that John makes the distinction between Father and Son in many places in his Gospel does not prove that he is doing so here.

7. The Word is not some third or fourth thing that is the instrument of creation. The Word is God who created the heavens and the earth. It is not accidental that in Genesis God creates by His Word and that John calls Jesus the Word of God. The Word is the creator, the very Word of God.

8. Matthew's Gospel clearly presents Jesus Christ as the Messiah, the King of Israel, God in the flesh. Also, Nathanael makes this same connection in Jn. 1:49.

9. The doctrine of the Trinity was not a later development in Christianity. The doctrine of the Trinity is clearly taught in the New Testament, and this doctrine,

as expressed in Jn. 1:1 has grown out of the implications of many Old Testament passages, including but not limited to Ps. 33:6; 107:20; 147:15, 18; Isa. 9:8; 55:10ff.

CHAPTER 9

THE SPIRIT AND THE TRINITY

Introduction

According to the Jehovah's Witnesses, the Holy Spirit is not the third Person of the Trinity. In fact, the Holy Spirit, according to the JWs, is not a Person at all. Rather, they believe that the Holy Spirit is "the invisible active force of the Almighty God."[1] They argue, "There is no basis for concluding that the Holy Spirit is a Person."[2] In lockstep with the Jehovah's Witnesses, BeDuhn attempts to show that the Holy Spirit is an "it." He calls his chapter on this topic, "The Spirit Writ Large."[3] Appealing to an account of the history of Christian doctrine, BeDuhn asserts, "Later Christian theology also applied technical status of a 'person' on the Holy Spirit, which has led modern translators and readers to think of the Holy Spirit in human terms as a 'who,' even a 'he,' rather than an 'it' that transcends human measures of personhood."[4] Once again BeDuhn incorrectly assumes that because later Christian theologians began to formulate and develop the terminology about the Holy Spirit, that this amounts to creating the doctrine. This is a common misunderstanding about the history of Christian doctrine. The doctrine of the Holy Spirit was already present in the Word of God. The formation of a doctrinal statement about the Holy Spirit did not create the doctrine. Rather it merely articulated the doctrine that was already taught by Scripture.

---

[1] Watch Tower Bible and Tract Society, *Let God Be True* (n.p.: Watch Tower Bible and Tract Society, 1952), 108; quoted in Walter Martin, *The Kingdom of the Cults* (Minneapolis: Bethany Fellowship, 1977), 47.
[2] Watch Tower Bible and Tract Society, "Watch Tower" (January 1, 1952): 24; quoted in Martin, *Kingdom of Cults*, 47.
[3] BeDuhn, *Translation*, 135–60.
[4] Ibid., 136.

"A Holy Spirit?"

BeDuhn supposedly considers all the instances in the NT that contain the words "holy spirit" or "spirit holy" with and without the definite article(s). Of the eighty-seven instances, BeDuhn concludes that seven instances should be viewed as indefinite: Acts 8:15; Acts 8:17–19; Acts 10:38; Acts 19:2; Lk. 2:25; 11:13; and Jn. 20:22. We will examine BeDuhn's claims about each of these instances in the order in which he treats them. But before we look at the specific verses, it is important to point out that, according to Smyth, "Names of deities omit the article, except when emphatic."[5] Traditionally, "Holy Spirit" has been treated as a name for the third Person of the Trinity. Now, this is certainly a theological position, but it cannot be simply ignored by BeDuhn. BeDuhn has already assumed that "Holy Spirit" is not a name for the third Person of the Trinity. But this cannot be merely assumed either; it must be proven. That is, it must be proven either way. If "Holy Spirit" is a name for the third Person of the Trinity, then this must be proven by those who hold that position. But, likewise, those who hold the opposite position must prove their view also. There is no "neutral" position since the words appear both with and without the definite article. What this means is, the presence or absence of the definite article is not sufficient to determine whether the reference to "Holy Spirit" is definite or indefinite, or whether the Holy Spirit is a Person or a non-person. That must be demonstrated on other grounds. He has already admitted that under various circumstances the anarthrous use can still be definite. So, BeDuhn's whole thesis is irrelevant.

Acts 8:15

The Accusative Case and Definiteness

When BeDuhn begins his consideration of Acts 8:15, he asserts, "Because the phrase is in the accusative form, the absence of the article suggests indefiniteness."[6] However, just because an Accusative word does not have the definite article does not prove that it is indefinite. Take for example the following statement in Heb. 7:5:

Table #71: Heb. 7:5

Heb. 7:5	"And those indeed of the sons of Levi who receive the priest's office have commandment [ἐντολὴν ἔχουσιν] in the Law to collect a tenth from the people, that is, from their brethren, although these are descended from Abraham."
	καὶ οἱ μὲν ἐκ τῶν υἱῶν Λευὶ τὴν ἱερατείαν λαμβάνοντες ἐντολὴν ἔχουσιν ἀποδεκατοῦν τὸν λαὸν κατὰ τὸν νόμον, τοῦτ' ἔστιν τοὺς ἀδελφοὺς αὐτῶν, καίπερ ἐξεληλυθότας ἐκ τῆς ὀσφύος Ἀβραάμ·

---

[5] Smyth, *Grammar*, §1137.
[6] BeDuhn, *Translation*, 137.

The relevant portion is the statement in the last part of the first line of the English translation and the first part of the second line: "have commandment" (ἐντολὴν ἔχουσιν, *entolēn echousin*). Here the word "commandment" (ἐντολὴν, *entolēn*) is an Accusative direct object of the verb "have" (ἔχουσιν, *echousin*). The word "commandment" is anarthrous, but it is hardly referring to an indefinite commandment. It is, rather, referring to a definite commandment given to the sons of Levi who have received the priest's office. Paul Ellingworth comments, " Ἐντολή . . . is usually plural in the GSEPT; but even in the singular, it may refer to the Mosaic law as a whole (as in v. 18; cf. Jos. 22:3; Lk. 23:56). Here, however, as in 9:19, it must mean a specific commandment (Bauer 2aγ), in this case the one relating to tithing (Nu. 18:21–24)."[7] In English, we can say, "they have the commandment," or "they have commandment," and each expression can be referring to the same definite commandment —the one referring to the commandment itself; the second referring to the commandment but with the added of nuance of focusing on the fact that it is a commandment, not just a statement or recommendation. There are many examples of Accusative words functioning as direct objects of verbs that are anarthrous yet definite. Matt. 1:21 says, "She will bear a Son [τέξεται δὲ υἱόν]; and you shall call His name Jesus, for He will save His people from their sins." Here the word "Son" is indefinite, but this is certainly not referring to an indefinite Son, but to the definite Son to whom she would give birth. Another example is found in Matt. 4:7: "Jesus said to him, 'On the other hand, it is written, 'You shall not put the Lord your God to the test.''" The relevant portion in this verse is the quote from Deut. 6:16.

Table #72: Matt. 4:7c

οὐκ	ἐκπειράσεις	κύριον	τὸν	θεόν	σου.
Not	you will test	Lord	the	God	of you.

What is particularly interesting about this verse is the fact that it is a quote from Deut. 6:16 in which the word "Lord" (κύριον, *kurion*) is the translation of the Divine Name:

Table #73: Deut. 6:16 (BHS)

אֱלֹהֵיכֶם	יְהוָה	־אֶת	תְנַסּוּ	לֹא
your God	Lord		you will test	Not

---

[7] Paul Ellingworth, *The Epistle to the Hebrews: A Commentary on the Greek Text* (Grand Rapids: William B. Eerdmans Publishing Company, 1993), 363. In the quote, Ellingworth makes reference to the Bauer-Arndt-Gingrich Lexicon, section 2aγ. In the third edition, this reference is now found under section 2bα.

Table #74: Deut. 6:16 (GSEPT)

οὐκ	ἐκπειράσεις	κύριον	τὸν θεόν	σου
not	you will put to the test	Lord	the God	of you

It can hardly be claimed that the word "Lord" in Matt. 4:7 is indefinite simply because it is Accusative and does not have the definite article. Of course, this is one of those instances covered by Smyth's rule that the definite article is omitted before names of deity.[8] However, the word κύριος ("lord") is not necessarily a name for deity. It is used in various places to refer to someone who is not God. What this means is, whether the word is a proper name or not cannot be determined simply by the presence or absence of the definite article, and a word in the Accusative case does not need to have the definite article to be definite.

Now, this would probably not convince BeDuhn, but that is not really the point. The point is that BeDuhn has not presented all the evidence to his readers. He has distorted the grammatical facts of the case, and he has made his decision about whether the words "Holy Spirit" are definite or indefinite based on a prior theological bias that this is not a proper name or the third Person of the Trinity. Whether it is or not is not the point. The point is, BeDuhn presents his point of view as if this is simply a matter of grammar, and it is not. It is a matter of his prior theological bias, right or wrong, but nevertheless a bias that he attempts to disguise as grammar. His treatment of the text and of the grammar is disingenuous at best and deliberately misleading at worst.

Considering Acts 8:15 Specifically

The passage is set out below with a word-for-word translation:

Table #75: Acts 8:15

οἵτινες	καταβάντες	προσηύξαντο
who	after having come down	they prayed
περὶ	αὐτῶν	ὅπως
concerning	them	that
λάβωσιν	πνεῦμα	ἅγιον
they might receive	spirit	holy

Concerning the verse, BeDuhn asserts,

---

[8] Smyth, *Grammar*, §1137.

Because the phrase is in the accusative form, the absence of the article suggests indefiniteness. The NW translation ("to get holy spirit") is indefinite in meaning, even though the indefinite article is not used. In this, as in the following cases, the NW seems to be employing the form of English expression used of material or substance ("The jar is pewter"), where the indefinite article is not used, just as several translations do in John 4:24 (mentioned in chapter eleven). All other translations use the definite article in Acts 8:15, even though it is not found in the original Greek.[9]

BeDuhn presents no other argumentation as to why this instance should be taken as indefinite other than the fact that it does not have the definite article. As seems to be his *modus operandi*, BeDuhn does not give his reader all the evidence. There are several factors that BeDuhn does not even consider. For example, he does not consider the literary context, one of BeDuhn's own principles for accurate translation. Acts 8:16 says, "For not yet upon none of them having fallen [ἦν ἐπιπεπτωκός]; they had simply been baptized in the name of the Lord Jesus."[10] There are five other instances where the verb "fall" (ἐπιπίπτω, *epipiptō*) occur in Acts.

Table #76: ἐπιπίπτω in Acts

Acts 10:44	"While Peter was still speaking these words, fell [ἐπέπεσεν] the Holy Spirit [τὸ πνεῦμα τὸ ἅγιον] upon all those who were listening to the message."
	Ἔτι λαλοῦντος τοῦ Πέτρου τὰ ῥήματα ταῦτα ἐπέπεσεν τὸ πνεῦμα τὸ ἅγιον ἐπὶ πάντας τοὺς ἀκούοντας τὸν λόγον.
Acts 11:15	"And as I began to speak, fell [ἐπέπεσεν] the Holy Spirit [τὸ πνεῦμα τὸ ἅγιον] upon them just as upon us at the beginning."
	ἐν δὲ τῷ ἄρξασθαί με λαλεῖν ἐπέπεσεν τὸ πνεῦμα τὸ ἅγιον ἐπ' αὐτοὺς ὥσπερ καὶ ἐφ' ἡμᾶς ἐν ἀρχῇ.
Acts 19:17	"This became known to all, both Jews and Greeks, who lived in Ephesus; and fear fell [ἐπέπεσεν] upon them all and the name of the Lord Jesus was being magnified."
	τοῦτο δὲ ἐγένετο γνωστὸν πᾶσιν Ἰουδαίοις τε καὶ Ἕλλησιν τοῖς κατοικοῦσιν τὴν Ἔφεσον καὶ ἐπέπεσεν φόβος ἐπὶ πάντας αὐτοὺς καὶ ἐμεγαλύνετο τὸ ὄνομα τοῦ κυρίου Ἰησοῦ.
Acts 20:10	"But Paul went down and fell [ἐπέπεσεν] upon him, and after embracing him, he said, 'Do not be troubled, for his life is in him.'"
	καταβὰς δὲ ὁ Παῦλος ἐπέπεσεν αὐτῷ καὶ συμπεριλαβὼν εἶπεν· μὴ θορυβεῖσθε, ἡ γὰρ ψυχὴ αὐτοῦ ἐν αὐτῷ ἐστιν.

---

[9] BeDuhn, *Translation*, 137–38.
[10] οὐδέπω γὰρ ἦν ἐπ' οὐδενὶ αὐτῶν ἐπιπεπτωκός, μόνον δὲ βεβαπτισμένοι ὑπῆρχον εἰς τὸ ὄνομα τοῦ κυρίου Ἰησοῦ. (Acts 8:16).

Acts 20:37	"And they began to weep aloud and fell [ἐπιπεσόντες] upon the neck of Paul, and repeatedly kissed him,"
	ἱκανὸς δὲ κλαυθμὸς ἐγένετο πάντων καὶ ἐπιπεσόντες ἐπὶ τὸν τράχηλον τοῦ Παύλου κατεφίλουν αὐτόν,

Acts 19:17 refers to the fear that fell upon the people at Ephesus because of what they heard. Acts 20:10 seems to indicate that Paul actually fell down or lay down upon the young man. Acts 20:37 uses the word "fell" in the idiom "fell upon the neck," which means to embrace someone. The remaining two instances, Acts 10:44 and 11:15 refer to the Holy Spirit falling upon people. In these two instance the reference to the Holy Spirit is literally "the Spirit (τὸ πνεῦμα, to pneuma) the Holy" (τὸ ἅγιον, to hagion). Acts 8:16 states that "Holy Spirit" had not yet fallen on them. The literary context argues that even though there is no definite article in 8:15, that this is talking about the Holy Spirit that fell upon those who believe. Additionally, Acts 11:15 refers to the fact that the Holy Spirit falling on them was "just as also upon us at the beginning" (ὥσπερ καὶ ἐφ' ἡμᾶς ἐν ἀρχῇ, hōsper kai eph hēmas en archē). What is interesting about this statement is that the event to which Peter is referring is the Acts 2 event in which those who were waiting were "filled" with "the Holy Spirit," as is stated in Acts 2:4: "And they were all filled with the Holy Spirit [πνεύματος ἁγίου] and began to speak with other tongues, as the Spirit was giving them utterance."[11] Now, this instance the words "Holy Spirit" do not have the definite article. However, BeDuhn has already admitted that instances in which there is an expression "to be filled with" are nevertheless definite: "'Holy spirit' also appears in verbal phrases where characteristics of the verb may cause the article to be dropped. The expression 'fill with holy spirit' occurs fourteen times in the New Testament. The verb 'fill' has objects in the genitive form, a form which does not need the article to establish definiteness as much as the Nominative or Accusative forms do. The lack of the article in these cases does not necessarily make the expression indefinite."[12] Coupled with the fact that this event is foretold by Jesus in which He specifically uses the definite article to refer to the Holy Spirit: "but you will receive power when the Holy Spirit [τοῦ ἁγίου πνεύματος, tou hagiou pneumatos] has come upon you; and you shall be My witnesses both in Jerusalem, and in all Judea and Samaria, and even to the remotest part of the earth" (Acts 1:8)[13]—these passages connect the "falling upon" in Acts 8:16; 11:15, with the "filling of" the Holy Spirit in Acts 2:4ff. Since in Acts 11:15 Peter refers to the "falling upon" as the same kind of event that occurred in Acts 2:4ff, this indicates that the

---

[11] καὶ ἐπλήσθησαν πάντες πνεύματος ἁγίου καὶ ἤρξαντο λαλεῖν ἑτέραις γλώσσαις καθὼς τὸ πνεῦμα ἐδίδου ἀποφθέγγεσθαι αὐτοῖς. (Acts 2:4).

[12] BeDuhn, *Translation*, 137.

[13] ἀλλὰ λήμψεσθε δύναμιν ἐπελθόντος τοῦ ἁγίου πνεύματος ἐφ' ὑμᾶς καὶ ἔσεσθέ μου μάρτυρες ἔν τε Ἰερουσαλὴμ καὶ (ἐν) πάσῃ τῇ Ἰουδαίᾳ καὶ Σαμαρείᾳ καὶ ἕως ἐσχάτου τῆς γῆς. (Acts 1:8).

"falling upon" in Acts 8:16 is also the same kind of event as occurred in Acts 2:4ff, which involved "the Holy Spirit." (τοῦ ἁγίου πνεύματος, *tou hagiou pneumatos*). The literary context, then, indicates that the statement in Acts 8:15 should in fact be translated "the Holy Spirit."

Acts 8:17–19

This passage is too long to[14] set out with a word-for-word translation as before. The passage is, however, set out with the NASBU translation for each verse with the Greek text below.

Table #77: Acts 8:17–19

Acts 8:17	"Then they were laying their hands on them, and they were receiving *the* Holy Spirit [πνεῦμα ἅγιον]."
	τότε ἐπετίθεσαν τὰς χεῖρας ἐπ᾽ αὐτοὺς καὶ ἐλάμβανον πνεῦμα ἅγιον.
Acts 8:18	"Now when Simon saw that the Spirit [τὸ πνεῦμα] was bestowed through the laying on of the apostles' hands, he offered them money,"
	ἰδὼν δὲ ὁ Σίμων ὅτι διὰ τῆς ἐπιθέσεως τῶν χειρῶν τῶν ἀποστόλων δίδοται τὸ πνεῦμα, προσήνεγκεν αὐτοῖς χρήματα
Acts 8:19	"saying, 'Give this authority to me as well, so that everyone on whom I lay my hands may receive *the* Holy Spirit [πνεῦμα ἅγιον].'"
	λέγων· δότε κἀμοὶ τὴν ἐξουσίαν ταύτην ἵνα ᾧ ἐὰν ἐπιθῶ τὰς χεῖρας λαμβάνῃ πνεῦμα ἅγιον.

Concerning these verses, BeDuhn asserts: "The missing article here makes the phrase indefinite. Here, too, the NW follows the Greek in not making 'holy spirit' definite ('receive holy spirit'), although it doesn't actually use the indefinite article. The other translations again add the definite article."[15] We have already shown that this is a reference to the Holy Spirit by its connection with the event in Acts 2:4ff. Also, Acts 8:17 refers to "receiving Holy Spirit" (ἐλάμβανον πνεῦμα ἅγιον, *elambanon pneuma hagion*). Acts 2:38 states: "Peter to them, 'Repent, and each of you be baptized in the name of Jesus Christ for the forgiveness of your sins; and you will receive the gift of the Holy Spirit." This last part is set out below:

14

[15] BeDun, *Translation*, 138.

Table #78: Acts 2:38c

καὶ	λήμψεσθε	τὴν	δωρεὰν
and	you will receive	the	gift

τοῦ	ἁγίου	πνεύματος
of the	Holy	Spirit

In this verse, the same verb is used, λήμψεσθε (*lēmpsesthe*, "you will receive") as is used in 8:17, ἐλάμβανον (*elambanon*, "receiving"). The people of Samaria were receiving the gift of the Holy Spirit. As verse 16 stated, the Holy Spirit had not fallen upon them, so Peter and John lay hands on them so that they can receive the Holy Spirit. Once again the literary context indicates that this is the Holy Spirit and it should be translated as such. BeDuhn has ignored his own principle of literary context.

Acts 10:38

Again, this passage is too long to set out in a word-for-word format, but the NASBU translation and the Greek text are set out in the following table:

Table #79: Acts 10:38

Acts 10:38	"Jesus of Nazareth, how God anointed Him with Holy Spirit [πνεύματι ἁγίῳ] and with power, and He went about doing good and healing all who were oppressed by the devil, for God was with Him."
	Ἰησοῦν τὸν ἀπὸ Ναζαρέθ, ὡς ἔχρισεν αὐτὸν ὁ θεὸς πνεύματι ἁγίῳ καὶ δυνάμει, ὃς διῆλθεν εὐεργετῶν καὶ ἰώμενος πάντας τοὺς καταδυναστευομένους ὑπὸ τοῦ διαβόλου, ὅτι ὁ θεὸς ἦν μετ' αὐτοῦ.

BeDuhn says, "'Holy spirit' is coordinated with 'power,' and both terms are indefinite here. The NW has, accordingly, 'anointed him with holy spirit.' The other translations ignore the original Greek and add 'the' to 'holy spirit.'"[16] Once again BeDuhn has ignored the literary context. In Acts 1:38 Jesus told the disciples that they would receive power (δύναμιν, *dunamin*, the same word used in Acts 10:38) when the Holy Spirit (τοῦ ἁγίου πνεύματος, *tou hagiou pneumatos*) would come upon them.

---

[16] Ibid.

Table #80: Acts 1:8

Acts 1:8	"but you will receive power when the Holy Spirit has come upon you; and you shall be My witnesses both in Jerusalem, and in all Judea and Samaria, and even to the remotest part of the earth."
	ἀλλὰ λήμψεσθε δύναμιν ἐπελθόντος τοῦ ἁγίου πνεύματος ἐφ' ὑμᾶς καὶ ἔσεσθέ μου μάρτυρες ἔν τε Ἰερουσαλὴμ καὶ (ἐν) πάσῃ τῇ Ἰουδαίᾳ καὶ Σαμαρείᾳ καὶ ἕως ἐσχάτου τῆς γῆς.

Contrary to BeDuhn's claim, the translators have not ignored the "original Greek." Rather, BeDuhn has ignored his own principle of literary context by thinking that this reference is indefinite. The translators have gotten it right. BeDuhn and the NW have gotten it wrong — again.

Acts 19:2

Table #81: Acts 19:2

Acts 19:2	"He said to them, 'Did you receive Holy Spirit [πνεῦμα ἅγιον] when you believed?' And they to him, 'No, we have not even heard whether there is a Holy Spirit [πνεῦμα ἅγιον].'"
	εἶπέν τε πρὸς αὐτούς· εἰ πνεῦμα ἅγιον ἐλάβετε πιστεύσαντες; οἱ δὲ πρὸς αὐτόν· ἀλλ' οὐδ' εἰ πνεῦμα ἅγιον ἔστιν ἠκούσαμεν.

BeDuhn has a bit more to say with reference to this verse:

In this example, the first sentence involves "holy spirit" in the accusative form. The absence of the article suggests indefiniteness here. This suspicion is confirmed by the second occurrence of "holy spirit," this time with the verb "is," a combination (similar to that discussed in chapter eleven) that leaves no room for doubt that "holy spirit" is meant to be indefinite. So the NW has "receive holy spirit" and "a holy spirit." The other translations obey the rules of Greek grammar in the second sentence, and all print "a Holy Spirit." By having both the indefinite article and capitalized "Holy Spirit," they are entangled in a contradiction. How can the definite, singular "Holy Spirit" be indefinite? None of these translators seem to have noticed the contradiction built into their translations. In the first sentence they all add the definite article.[17]

One begins to wonder whether BeDuhn has ever actually considered how language works. It is no contradiction to refer to "the Holy Spirit" in one verse and use the anarthrous reference in the next while capitalizing the words "Holy Spirit." This kind

---

[17] Ibid.

The Spirit and the Trinity

of expression is a daily occurrence in common parlance. Someone comes up to you and says, "Did you see the President of Druistan today?" And you respond, "I didn't even know there was a 'President of Druistan.'" Here the second use employs an indefinite article, but is nevertheless talking about the one President of Druistan. So also, those believers had not heard that the Holy Spirit was being received, so they ask a similar kind of question. The only contradiction is between BeDuhn's pretense of understanding language and the kinds of naive charges he makes here. Again BeDuhn employs his practice of selective reporting by not providing his reader with all the necessary evidence. The expression, "whether Holy Spirit you received" is set out below:

Table #82: Acts 19:2b

εἰ	πνεῦμα	ἅγιον	ἐλάβετε
whether	holy	spirit	you received
πιστεύσαντες;			
having believed?			

We have already come across the phrase expressing "receiving the Holy Spirit," and we have already shown how this is connected with the statement in Acts 1:8 that uses the definite article, and with the event in Acts 2:4ff that also uses the definite article. The literary context indicates that the statement in Acts 19:2b should be taken as definite. Also, of the fifty-one times that Luke-Acts uses the verb "receive" (λαμβάνω, *lambanō*), he uses it with reference to the Holy Spirit only in the book of Acts.

Table #83: "Receiving the Holy Spirit" in Luke-Acts

Acts 1:8	"but you will receive power [ἐπελθόντος] when the Holy Spirit [τοῦ ἁγίου πνεύματος] has come upon you; and you shall be My witnesses both in Jerusalem, and in all Judea and Samaria, and even to the remotest part of the earth."
	ἀλλὰ λήμψεσθε δύναμιν ἐπελθόντος τοῦ ἁγίου πνεύματος ἐφ᾽ ὑμᾶς καὶ ἔσεσθέ μου μάρτυρες ἔν τε Ἰερουσαλὴμ καὶ (ἐν) πάσῃ τῇ Ἰουδαίᾳ καὶ Σαμαρείᾳ καὶ ἕως ἐσχάτου τῆς γῆς.
Acts 2:38	"Peter to them, 'Repent, and each of you be baptized in the name of Jesus Christ for the forgiveness of your sins; and you will receive [λήμψεσθε] the gift of the Holy Spirit [τοῦ ἁγίου πνεύματος].'"
	Πέτρος δὲ πρὸς αὐτούς· μετανοήσατε, (φησίν,) καὶ βαπτισθήτω ἕκαστος ὑμῶν ἐπὶ τῷ ὀνόματι Ἰησοῦ Χριστοῦ εἰς ἄφεσιν τῶν ἁμαρτιῶν ὑμῶν καὶ λήμψεσθε τὴν δωρεὰν τοῦ ἁγίου πνεύματος.

Acts 8:15	"who came down and prayed for them that they might receive [λάβωσιν] *the* Holy Spirit [πνεῦμα ἅγιον]."
	οἵτινες καταβάντες προσηύξαντο περὶ αὐτῶν ὅπως λάβωσιν πνεῦμα ἅγιον·
Acts 8:17	"Then they began laying their hands on them, and they were receiving [ἐλάμβανον] *the* Holy Spirit [πνεῦμα ἅγιον]."
	τότε ἐπετίθεσαν τὰς χεῖρας ἐπ' αὐτοὺς καὶ ἐλάμβανον πνεῦμα ἅγιον.
Acts 8:19	"saying, 'Give this authority to me as well, so that everyone on whom I lay my hands may receive [λαμβάνῃ] *the* Holy Spirit [πνεῦμα ἅγιον].'"
	λέγων· δότε κἀμοὶ τὴν ἐξουσίαν ταύτην ἵνα ᾧ ἐὰν ἐπιθῶ τὰς χεῖρας λαμβάνῃ πνεῦμα ἅγιον.

Of the 23 instances where Luke uses the verb "receive" followed by an Accusative direct object, only 6 of these occur with the definite article, while 17 occur without the definite article. Now there are a number of reasons why an Accusative direct object will occur without the definite article, but it is not simply a matter of the presence or absence of the article that determines whether it is definite or indefinite. BeDuhn has either not thoroughly studied the issue, or he is deliberately leaving out pertinent information when presenting the evidence to his reader. The literary context demonstrates that determining whether "Holy Spirit" is definite or indefinite is not a matter of simply seeing whether it has the definite article.

Table #84: Λαμβάνω in Luke-Acts

1	Luke 9:16 With	"Then He took [λαβὼν] the five loaves [τοὺς πέντε ἄρτους] and the two fish [τοὺς δύο ἰχθύας], and looking up to heaven, He blessed them, and broke them, and kept giving them to the disciples to set before the people."
		λαβὼν δὲ τοὺς πέντε ἄρτους καὶ τοὺς δύο ἰχθύας ἀναβλέψας εἰς τὸν οὐρανὸν εὐλόγησεν αὐτοὺς καὶ κατέκλασεν καὶ ἐδίδου τοῖς μαθηταῖς παραθεῖναι τῷ ὄχλῳ.
2	Luke 13:19 Without	"It is like a mustard seed, which [ὃν] a man took [λαβὼν] and threw into his own garden; and it grew and became a tree, and the birds of the air nested in its branches."
		ὁμοία ἐστὶν κόκκῳ σινάπεως, ὃν λαβὼν ἄνθρωπος ἔβαλεν εἰς κῆπον ἑαυτοῦ, καὶ ηὔξησεν καὶ ἐγένετο εἰς δένδρον, καὶ τὰ πετεινὰ τοῦ οὐρανοῦ κατεσκήνωσεν ἐν τοῖς κλάδοις αὐτοῦ.

3	Luke 19:12 Without	"So He said, 'A nobleman went to a distant country to receive [λαβεῖν] a kingdom [βασιλείαν] for himself, and return.'"
		εἶπεν οὖν· ἄνθρωπός τις εὐγενὴς ἐπορεύθη εἰς χώραν μακρὰν λαβεῖν ἑαυτῷ βασιλείαν καὶ ὑποστρέψαι.
4	Luke 19:15 With	"When he returned, after receiving [λαβόντα] the kingdom [τὴν βασιλείαν], he ordered that these slaves, to whom he had given the money, be called to him so that he might know what business they had done."
		καὶ ἐγένετο ἐν τῷ ἐπανελθεῖν αὐτὸν λαβόντα τὴν βασιλείαν καὶ εἶπεν φωνηθῆναι αὐτῷ τοὺς δούλους τούτους οἷς δεδώκει τὸ ἀργύριον, ἵνα γνοῖ τί διεπραγματεύσαντο.
5	Luke 20:21 Without	"They questioned Him, saying, 'Teacher, we know that You speak and teach correctly, and You are not partial [λαμβάνεις πρόσωπον] to any, but teach the way of God in truth.'" (The expression "receiving the face" is an idiom for showing partiality—treating someone special on the basis of superficial characteristics or for superficial reasons.)
		καὶ ἐπηρώτησαν αὐτὸν λέγοντες· διδάσκαλε, οἴδαμεν ὅτι ὀρθῶς λέγεις καὶ διδάσκεις καὶ οὐ λαμβάνεις πρόσωπον, ἀλλ' ἐπ' ἀληθείας τὴν ὁδὸν τοῦ θεοῦ διδάσκεις·
6	Luke 20:29 Without	"Now there were seven brothers; and the first took [λαβὼν] a wife [γυναῖκα] and died childless;"
		ἑπτὰ οὖν ἀδελφοὶ ἦσαν· καὶ ὁ πρῶτος λαβὼν γυναῖκα ἀπέθανεν ἄτεκνος·
7	Luke 20:47 Without	"who devour widows' houses, and for appearance's sake offer long prayers. These will receive [λήμψονται] greater condemnation [κρίμα]."
		οἳ κατεσθίουσιν τὰς οἰκίας τῶν χηρῶν καὶ προφάσει μακρὰ προσεύχονται· οὗτοι λήμψονται περισσότερον κρίμα.
8	Luke 22:19 Without	"And when He had taken [λαβὼν] bread [ἄρτον] after having given thanks, He broke it and gave it to them, saying, 'This is My body which is given for you; do this in remembrance of Me.'"
		καὶ λαβὼν ἄρτον εὐχαριστήσας ἔκλασεν καὶ ἔδωκεν αὐτοῖς λέγων· τοῦτό ἐστιν τὸ σῶμά μου τὸ ὑπὲρ ὑμῶν διδόμενον· τοῦτο ποιεῖτε εἰς τὴν ἐμὴν ἀνάμνησιν.
9	Luke 24:30 With	"When He had reclined with them, taking [λαβὼν] the bread [τὸν ἄρτον] and blessed, and breaking, He gives to them."
		καὶ ἐγένετο ἐν τῷ κατακλιθῆναι αὐτὸν μετ' αὐτῶν λαβὼν τὸν ἄρτον εὐλόγησεν καὶ κλάσας ἐπεδίδου αὐτοῖς,

10	Acts 1:8 Without	"but you will receive [λήμψεσθε] power [δύναμιν] when the Holy Spirit has come upon you; and you shall be My witnesses both in Jerusalem, and in all Judea and Samaria, and even to the remotest part of the earth."
		ἀλλὰ λήμψεσθε δύναμιν ἐπελθόντος τοῦ ἁγίου πνεύματος ἐφ' ὑμᾶς καὶ ἔσεσθέ μου μάρτυρες ἔν τε Ἰερουσαλὴμ καὶ (ἐν) πάσῃ τῇ Ἰουδαίᾳ καὶ Σαμαρείᾳ καὶ ἕως ἐσχάτου τῆς γῆς.
11	Acts 1:25 With	"to occupy [λαβεῖν] this ministry [τὸν τόπον τῆς διακονίας ταύτης, lit. "the place of this service"] and apostleship from which Judas turned aside to go to his own place."
		λαβεῖν τὸν τόπον τῆς διακονίας ταύτης καὶ ἀποστολῆς ἀφ' ἧς παρέβη Ἰούδας πορευθῆναι εἰς τὸν τόπον τὸν ἴδιον.
12	Acts 2:38 With	"Peter to them, 'Repent, and each of you be baptized in the name of Jesus Christ for the forgiveness of your sins; and you will receive [λήμψεσθε] the gift [τὴν δωρεὰν] of the Holy Spirit.'"
		Πέτρος δὲ πρὸς αὐτούς· μετανοήσατε, (φησίν,) καὶ βαπτισθήτω ἕκαστος ὑμῶν ἐπὶ τῷ ὀνόματι Ἰησοῦ Χριστοῦ εἰς ἄφεσιν τῶν ἁμαρτιῶν ὑμῶν καὶ λήμψεσθε τὴν δωρεὰν τοῦ ἁγίου πνεύματος.
13	Acts 7:53 With	"you who received [ἐλάβετε] the law [τὸν νόμον] as ordained by angels, and did not keep it."
		οἵτινες ἐλάβετε τὸν νόμον εἰς διαταγὰς ἀγγέλων καὶ οὐκ ἐφυλάξατε.
14	Acts 8:15 Without	"who came down and prayed for them that they might receive [λάβωσιν] the Holy Spirit [πνεῦμα ἅγιον]."
		οἵτινες καταβάντες προσηύξαντο περὶ αὐτῶν ὅπως λάβωσιν πνεῦμα ἅγιον·
15	Acts 8:17 Without	"Then they were laying their hands on them, and they were receiving [ἐλάμβανον] Holy Spirit [πνεῦμα ἅγιον]."
		τότε ἐπετίθεσαν τὰς χεῖρας ἐπ' αὐτοὺς καὶ ἐλάμβανον πνεῦμα ἅγιον.
16	Acts 8:19 Without	"saying, 'Give this authority to me as well, so that everyone on whom I lay my hands may receive [λαμβάνῃ] Holy Spirit [πνεῦμα ἅγιον].'"
		λέγων· δότε κἀμοὶ τὴν ἐξουσίαν ταύτην ἵνα ᾧ ἐὰν ἐπιθῶ τὰς χεῖρας λαμβάνῃ πνεῦμα ἅγιον.
17	Acts 9:19 Without	"and he took [λαβὼν] food [τροφὴν] and was strengthened. Now for several days he was with the disciples who were at Damascus,"
		καὶ λαβὼν τροφὴν ἐνίσχυσεν. Ἐγένετο δὲ μετὰ τῶν ἐν Δαμασκῷ μαθητῶν ἡμέρας τινὰς

18	Acts 15:14 Without	"Simeon has related how God first concerned Himself about taking [λαβεῖν] from among the Gentiles a people [λαὸν] for His name."
		Συμεὼν ἐξηγήσατο καθὼς πρῶτον ὁ θεὸς ἐπεσκέψατο λαβεῖν ἐξ ἐθνῶν λαὸν τῷ ὀνόματι αὐτοῦ.
19	Acts 17:15 Without	"Now those who escorted Paul brought him as far as Athens; and receiving [λαβόντες] a command [ἐντολὴν] for Silas and Timothy to come to him as soon as possible, they left."
		οἱ δὲ καθιστάνοντες τὸν Παῦλον ἤγαγον ἕως Ἀθηνῶν, καὶ λαβόντες ἐντολὴν πρὸς τὸν Σιλᾶν καὶ τὸν Τιμόθεον ἵνα ὡς τάχιστα ἔλθωσιν πρὸς αὐτὸν ἐξῄεσαν.
20	Acts 24:27 Without	"But after two years had passed, Felix was succeeded by [ἔλαβεν διάδοχον] Porcius Festus, and wishing to do the Jews a favor, Felix left Paul imprisoned."
		Διετίας δὲ πληρωθείσης ἔλαβεν διάδοχον ὁ Φῆλιξ Πόρκιον Φῆστον, θέλων τε χάριτα καταθέσθαι τοῖς Ἰουδαίοις ὁ Φῆλιξ κατέλιπε τὸν Παῦλον δεδεμένον.
21	Acts 26:18 Without	"to open their eyes so that they may turn from darkness to light and from the dominion of Satan to God, that they may receive [λαβεῖν] forgiveness [ἄφεσιν] of sins and an inheritance among those who have been sanctified by faith in Me."
		ἀνοῖξαι ὀφθαλμοὺς αὐτῶν, τοῦ ἐπιστρέψαι ἀπὸ σκότους εἰς φῶς καὶ τῆς ἐξουσίας τοῦ σατανᾶ ἐπὶ τὸν θεόν, τοῦ λαβεῖν αὐτοὺς ἄφεσιν ἁμαρτιῶν καὶ κλῆρον ἐν τοῖς ἡγιασμένοις πίστει τῇ εἰς ἐμέ.
22	Acts 27:35 Without	"Having said this, he took [λαβὼν] bread [ἄρτον] and gave thanks to God in the presence of all, and he broke it and began to eat."
		εἴπας δὲ ταῦτα καὶ λαβὼν ἄρτον εὐχαρίστησεν τῷ θεῷ ἐνώπιον πάντων καὶ κλάσας ἤρξατο ἐσθίειν.
23	Acts 28:15 Without	"And the brethren, when they heard about us, came from there as far as the Market of Appius and Three Inns to meet us; and when Paul saw them, he thanked God and took [ἔλαβε] courage [θάρσος]."
		κἀκεῖθεν οἱ ἀδελφοὶ ἀκούσαντες τὰ περὶ ἡμῶν ἦλθαν εἰς ἀπάντησιν ἡμῖν ἄχρι Ἀππίου φόρου καὶ Τριῶν ταβερνῶν, οὓς ἰδὼν ὁ Παῦλος εὐχαριστήσας τῷ θεῷ ἔλαβε θάρσος.

Lk. 2:25

Again we will quote BeDuhn's comments regarding this verse:

> As the subject of the verb "was," "spirit" would normally have the definite article. Therefore, the fact that it does not shows that the author wanted it to be understood in the generic, indefinite sense. The NW prints accordingly "and holy spirit was upon him." The other translations ignore the rules of Greek grammar and add the article "the."[18]

Table #85: Lk. 2:25

Lk. 2:25	And there was a man in Jerusalem whose name was Simeon; and this man was righteous and devout, looking for the consolation of Israel; and the Holy Spirit was [πνεῦμα ἦν ἅγιον] upon him.
	Καὶ ἰδοὺ ἄνθρωπος ἦν ἐν Ἰερουσαλὴμ ᾧ ὄνομα Συμεὼν καὶ ὁ ἄνθρωπος οὗτος δίκαιος καὶ εὐλαβὴς προσδεχόμενος παράκλησιν τοῦ Ἰσραήλ, καὶ πνεῦμα ἦν ἅγιον ἐπ᾽ αὐτόν·

Again BeDuhn does not present all the evidence. In this instance, he fails to look at verses 26 and 27: "And it had been revealed to him by the Holy Spirit that he would not see death before he had seen the Lord's Christ. And he came in the Spirit into the temple; and when the parents brought in the child Jesus, to carry out for Him the custom of the Law,"[19] In the first phrase of verse 26 we find the reference to "the Spirit the Holy" (τοῦ πνεύματος τοῦ ἁγίου, *tou pneumatos tou hagiou*). This is undoubtedly a reference to the Holy Spirit that was "upon him" in verse 25, and here the definite articles are used:

Table #86: Lk. 2:26a

καὶ	ἦν	αὐτῷ	κεχρηματισμένον
and	was	to him	having been revealed
ὑπὸ	τοῦ πνεύματος	τοῦ ἁγίου	
by	the Spirit	the Holy	

---

[18] Ibid., 139.

[19] καὶ ἦν αὐτῷ κεχρηματισμένον ὑπὸ τοῦ πνεύματος τοῦ ἁγίου μὴ ἰδεῖν θάνατον πρὶν (ἢ) ἂν ἴδῃ τὸν χριστὸν κυρίου. καὶ ἦλθεν ἐν τῷ πνεύματι εἰς τὸ ἱερόν· καὶ ἐν τῷ εἰσαγαγεῖν τοὺς γονεῖς τὸ παιδίον Ἰησοῦν τοῦ ποιῆσαι αὐτοὺς κατὰ τὸ εἰθισμένον τοῦ νόμου περὶ αὐτοῦ (Lk. 2:26–27).

Once again BeDuhn makes a judgment based on partial evidence. Also, notice that in this case his argument is not grammatical, but interpretive. He is arguing about what he thinks the author must surely have meant by not using the definite article. But, this is not a grammatical argument. This is speculation on BeDuhn's part about what the author might have meant. This is the very kind of argument he condemns in the modern translations.

Lk. 11:13

Table #87: Lk. 11:13

Lk. 11:13	"If you then, being evil, know how to give good gifts to your children, how much more will the heavenly Father give *the* Holy Spirit [πνεῦμα ἅγιον] to those who ask Him?"
	εἰ οὖν ὑμεῖς πονηροὶ ὑπάρχοντες οἴδατε δόματα ἀγαθὰ διδόναι τοῖς τέκνοις ὑμῶν, πόσῳ μᾶλλον ὁ πατὴρ (ὁ) ἐξ οὐρανοῦ δώσει πνεῦμα ἅγιον τοῖς αἰτοῦσιν αὐτόν.

Concerning this verse, BeDuhn says, "If Luke meant a specific 'holy spirit,' he would have been obligated to use the definite article here. He does not. So the NW translates 'will give holy spirit.' The other translations add 'the' without justification in the original Greek."[20] Of course, there is no rule in Greek that says an author is "obligated" to use the definite article, and we have already shown several instances in which Luke omits the definite article even though it is a reference to the one Holy Spirit. BeDuhn's theological bias is again at work here. He has already assumed that this cannot be a reference to the Holy Spirit, so he invents this "rule" without justification.

Luke uses the words πνεῦμα ἅγιον ("Spirit Holy") in this order 11 times in the Gospel (Lk. 1:15; 1:35; 1:41; 1:67; 2:25; 2:26; 3:16; 3:22; 4:1; 10:21; 11:13), and 33 times in the book of Acts (1:2; 1:5; 1:16; 2:4; 2:33; 4:8; 4:25; 5:3; 5:32; 6:5; 7:51; 7:55; 8:15; 8:17; 8:19; 9:17; 10:38; 10:44; 10:47; 11:15; 11:16; 11:24; 13:2; 13:9; 13:52; 15:8; 15:28; 19:2; 19:6; 20:23; 20:28; 21:11; 28:25); 19 times with the definite article(s), or 43% of the time, 25 times without, or 57% of the time. Of these, we have already shown that some, which occur without the definite article, should still be considered definite. Interestingly, Luke uses the phrase "the Holy Spirit," in which the word "holy" precedes the word "spirit," only 9 times in the Gospel and the book of Acts, and in every instance the phrase includes the definite article. Only two of these occurrences are in the Gospel, and the rest occur in Acts. Also, every one of the occurrences in Acts is in the Genitive case (τοῦ ἁγίου πνεύματος, *tou hatiou pneumatos*). So, Luke does in fact refer to the Holy Spirit by the expression "Spirit

---

[20] BeDuhn, *Translation*, 139.

Holy," without the definite article, and this does not necessarily mean that the references are indefinite. BeDuhn simply has not done his homework.

Table #88: τοῦ ἁγίου πνεύματος in Luke Acts

Lk. 12:10	"And everyone who speaks a word against the Son of Man, it will be forgiven him; but he who blasphemes against the Holy Spirit [τὸ ἅγιον πνεῦμα], it will not be forgiven him."
	Καὶ πᾶς ὃς ἐρεῖ λόγον εἰς τὸν υἱὸν τοῦ ἀνθρώπου, ἀφεθήσεται αὐτῷ· τῷ δὲ εἰς τὸ ἅγιον πνεῦμα βλασφημήσαντι οὐκ ἀφεθήσεται.
Lk. 12:12	"for the Holy Spirit [τὸ γὰρ ἅγιον πνεῦμα] will teach you in that very hour what you ought to say."
	τὸ γὰρ ἅγιον πνεῦμα διδάξει ὑμᾶς ἐν αὐτῇ τῇ ὥρᾳ ἃ δεῖ εἰπεῖν.
Acts 1:8	"but you will receive power when the Holy Spirit [τοῦ ἁγίου πνεύματος] has come upon you; and you shall be My witnesses both in Jerusalem, and in all Judea and Samaria, and even to the remotest part of the earth."
	ἀλλὰ λήμψεσθε δύναμιν ἐπελθόντος τοῦ ἁγίου πνεύματος ἐφ' ὑμᾶς καὶ ἔσεσθέ μου μάρτυρες ἔν τε Ἰερουσαλὴμ καὶ (ἐν) πάσῃ τῇ Ἰουδαίᾳ καὶ Σαμαρείᾳ καὶ ἕως ἐσχάτου τῆς γῆς.
Acts 2:38	"Peter to them, 'Repent, and each of you be baptized in the name of Jesus Christ for the forgiveness of your sins; and you will receive the gift of the Holy Spirit [τοῦ ἁγίου πνεύματος].'"
	Πέτρος δὲ πρὸς αὐτούς· μετανοήσατε, (φησίν,) καὶ βαπτισθήτω ἕκαστος ὑμῶν ἐπὶ τῷ ὀνόματι Ἰησοῦ Χριστοῦ εἰς ἄφεσιν τῶν ἁμαρτιῶν ὑμῶν καὶ λήμψεσθε τὴν δωρεὰν τοῦ ἁγίου πνεύματος.
Acts 4:31	"And when they had prayed, the place where they had gathered together was shaken, and they were all filled with the Holy Spirit [τοῦ ἁγίου πνεύματος] and began to speak the word of God with boldness."
	καὶ δεηθέντων αὐτῶν ἐσαλεύθη ὁ τόπος ἐν ᾧ ἦσαν συνηγμένοι, καὶ ἐπλήσθησαν ἅπαντες τοῦ ἁγίου πνεύματος καὶ ἐλάλουν τὸν λόγον τοῦ θεοῦ μετὰ παρρησίας.
Acts 9:31	"So the church throughout all Judea and Galilee and Samaria enjoyed peace, being built up; and going on in the fear of the Lord and in the comfort of the Holy Spirit [τοῦ ἁγίου πνεύματος], it continued to increase."
	Ἡ μὲν οὖν ἐκκλησία καθ' ὅλης τῆς Ἰουδαίας καὶ Γαλιλαίας καὶ Σαμαρείας εἶχεν εἰρήνην οἰκοδομουμένη καὶ πορευομένη τῷ φόβῳ τοῦ κυρίου καὶ τῇ παρακλήσει τοῦ ἁγίου πνεύματος ἐπληθύνετο.
Acts 10:45	"All the circumcised believers who came with Peter were amazed, because the gift of the Holy Spirit [τοῦ ἁγίου πνεύματος] had been poured out on the Gentiles also."
	καὶ ἐξέστησαν οἱ ἐκ περιτομῆς πιστοὶ ὅσοι συνῆλθαν τῷ Πέτρῳ, ὅτι καὶ ἐπὶ τὰ ἔθνη ἡ δωρεὰ τοῦ ἁγίου πνεύματος ἐκκέχυται·

Acts 13:4	"So, being sent out by the Holy Spirit [τοῦ ἁγίου πνεύματος], they went down to Seleucia and from there they sailed to Cyprus."
	Αὐτοὶ μὲν οὖν ἐκπεμφθέντες ὑπὸ τοῦ ἁγίου πνεύματος κατῆλθον εἰς Σελεύκειαν, ἐκεῖθέν τε ἀπέπλευσαν εἰς Κύπρον
Acts 16:6	They passed through the Phrygian and Galatian region, having been forbidden by the Holy Spirit [τοῦ ἁγίου πνεύματος] to speak the word in Asia;
	Διῆλθον δὲ τὴν Φρυγίαν καὶ Γαλατικὴν χώραν κωλυθέντες ὑπὸ τοῦ ἁγίου πνεύματος λαλῆσαι τὸν λόγον ἐν τῇ Ἀσίᾳ·

Jn. 20:22

Table #89: Jn. 20:22

Jn. 20:22	"And when He had said this, He breathed on them and said to them, 'Receive the Holy Spirit.'"
	καὶ τοῦτο εἰπὼν ἐνεφύσησεν καὶ λέγει αὐτοῖς· λάβετε πνεῦμα ἅγιον·

With reference to this verse, BeDuhn says, "We would fully expect 'holy spirit' to be definite here, but the Greek grammar does not cooperate. With an object in the Accusative form, we are constrained to take 'holy spirit' indefinitely. All translations other than the NW, of course, make it definite despite this grammatical obstacle."[21] However, as has been his pattern, BeDuhn simply does not give evidence of having done his homework, and he strategically omits to give all of the pertinent evidence. John uses the expression "spirit holy" only three times:

Table #90: "Spirit Holy" in John

Jn. 1:33	"I did not recognize Him, but He who sent me to baptize in water said to me, 'He upon whom you see the Spirit descending and remaining upon Him, this is the One who baptizes in *the* Holy Spirit [πνεύματι ἁγίῳ].'"
	κἀγὼ οὐκ ᾔδειν αὐτόν, ἀλλ᾽ ὁ πέμψας με βαπτίζειν ἐν ὕδατι ἐκεῖνός μοι εἶπεν· ἐφ᾽ ὃν ἂν ἴδῃς τὸ πνεῦμα καταβαῖνον καὶ μένον ἐπ᾽ αὐτόν, οὗτός ἐστιν ὁ βαπτίζων ἐν πνεύματι ἁγίῳ.

[21] Ibid.

Jn. 14:26	"But the Helper, the Holy Spirit [τὸ πνεῦμα τὸ ἅγιον], whom the Father will send in My name, He will teach you all things, and bring to your remembrance all that I said to you."
	ὁ δὲ παράκλητος, τὸ πνεῦμα τὸ ἅγιον, ὃ πέμψει ὁ πατὴρ ἐν τῷ ὀνόματί μου, ἐκεῖνος ὑμᾶς διδάξει πάντα καὶ ὑπομνήσει ὑμᾶς πάντα ἃ εἶπον ὑμῖν (ἐγώ).
Jn. 20:22	"And when He had said this, He breathed on them and said to them, 'Receive *the* Holy Spirit [πνεῦμα ἅγιον].'"
	καὶ τοῦτο εἰπὼν ἐνεφύσησεν καὶ λέγει αὐτοῖς· λάβετε πνεῦμα ἅγιον·

John does not use the expression "holy spirit" where the word "holy" precedes the word "spirit." Of the three instances in which John uses "spirit holy," two are anarthrous, 1:33 and 20:22, and one is articular, 14:26. BeDuhn has once again ignored the literary context of the statement upon which he is commenting. Although John uses the expression "Spirit Holy" only three times, he refers to "the Spirit," with the definite article, 14 times in 13 verses in his Gospel. The breathing of the Holy Spirit in 20:22 is connected with the notion of the indwelling of the Holy Spirit to which John has already made reference in 7:39 and 14:17:

Table #91: Jn. 7:39 & 14:17

Jn. 7:39	"But this He spoke of the Spirit [τοῦ πνεύματος], whom those who believed in Him were to receive; for the Spirit was not yet *given*, because Jesus was not yet glorified."
	τοῦτο δὲ εἶπεν περὶ τοῦ πνεύματος ὃ ἔμελλον λαμβάνειν οἱ πιστεύσαντες εἰς αὐτόν· οὔπω γὰρ ἦν πνεῦμα, ὅτι Ἰησοῦς οὐδέπω ἐδοξάσθη.
Jn. 14:17	"the Spirit [τὸ πνεῦμα] of truth, whom the world cannot receive, because it does not see Him or know Him, you know Him because He abides with you and will be in you."
	τὸ πνεῦμα τῆς ἀληθείας, ὃ ὁ κόσμος οὐ δύναται λαβεῖν, ὅτι οὐ θεωρεῖ αὐτὸ οὐδὲ γινώσκει· ὑμεῖς γινώσκετε αὐτό, ὅτι παρ' ὑμῖν μένει καὶ ἐν ὑμῖν ἔσται.

As Keener explains, "Jesus as the giver of the Spirit is a recurrent theme in the Gospel, starting in 1:33 and climaxing here (e.g., 3:5; 7:37–39; 19:30, 34). This emphasis serves an important christological function (cf. 3:34) because, as the giver of God's Spirit, Jesus himself is divine (especially here [Jn. 20:22], where his action evokes God's creative work of breathing life into Adam). In biblical imagery, only God would baptize in his Spirit (as in 1:33; 3:5) or pour out his Spirit (Isa 42:1; 44:3; 61:11; Ezek 36:27; 37:15; 39:29; Joel 2:28–29; Hag 2:5; Zech 4:6; 12:10)."[22]

Of course BeDuhn will object that this is interpretation, not strictly translation. However, BeDuhn's own statements are just a much interpretation. In his introduction he states that one of the principles for accurate translation is the literary context. Concerning this literary context he says, "Our use of literary context assumes that an author was relatively consistent and non-contradictory in what he or she said."[23] How can a translator know whether an author is consistent and non-contradictory in what he says without being able to interpret what the author says? This assumption of consistency and non-contradictory writing necessarily involves interpreting what the author says to grasp that consistency and to know that what he says is non-contradictory. John would be contradicting himself if, in Jn. 20:22, he is referring to some indistinct "holy spirit" and not the Holy Spirit concerning which he has declared that this Spirit would be given after Jesus' glorification.

And, should someone want to attempt to capitalize on the expression in 7:39—"for the Spirit was not yet" (γὰρ ἦν πνεῦμα, *gar ēn pneuma*)—as if this implies that the Spirit did not yet exist, this would be contradictory with the statement in Jn. 14:17, which, before Jesus breathed on them, says of this Spirit that "He abides with you and will be in you" (παρ᾽ ὑμῖν μένει καὶ ἐν ὑμῖν ἔσται, *par humin menei kai en humin estai*). According to BeDuhn's own principle of literary context, a principle he consistently ignores, the reference must be taken as definite in Jn. 20:22 in order for John's writing to be consistent and non-contradictory.

Another aspect of this to which Keener points is the connection between Jesus' action in 20:22 and Gen. 2:7:

Table #92: Gen. 2:7

אֶת־הָאָדָם	אֱלֹהִים	יְהוָה	וַיִּיצֶר
τὸν ἄνθρωπον	ὁ θεὸς		καὶ ἔπλασεν
the man	God	YHWH	And formed
וַיִּפַּח	הָאֲדָמָה	מִן	עָפָר
καὶ ἐνεφύσησεν	τῆς γῆς	ἀπὸ	χοῦν
and He breathed	the ground	from	dust
וַיְהִי	חַיִּים	נִשְׁמַת	בְּאַפָּיו
καὶ ἐγένετο	ζωῆς	πνοὴν	εἰς τὸ πρόσωπον αὐτοῦ
and He was	the life	breath of	in his nostrils

---

[22] Keener, *Gospel of John*, 1205.
[23] BeDuhn, *Translation*, xvi.

הָאָדָם	לְנֶפֶשׁ	חַיָּה:
ὁ ἄνθρωπος	εἰς ψυχὴν	ζῶσα
the man	to a soul	living.

As Keener points out, "This passage [Jn. 20:22] combines two of the central aspects of the Spirit's work that appear elsewhere in John and various early Jewish sources, both purification or rebirth (Gen 2:7) and empowerment. Most scholars concur that when Jesus breathes on the disciples, John is alluding to the creative, life-imparting act of God in Gen 2:7; Jesus is creating a new humanity, a new creation."[24] It is important to note that Keener, in the above quote and in his subsequent discussion, refers to the historical and cultural background of John's statement in 20:22, another of BeDuhn's principles for accuracy in translation. Keener goes on to say, "But despite the value of these other images to suggest language that was 'in the air,' such sources shared with John, his audience, and early Judaism in general a thorough knowledge of the language of Genesis in Greek."[25] It is also significant that in Jn. 20:22 John uses the verb "breath" (ἐνεφύσησεν, *enephusēsen* from ἐμφυσάω, *emphusaō*), which Keener characterizes as "a rare one," which is the same verb used in the GSEPT translation of Gen. 2:7 (ἐνεφύσησεν, *enephusēsen*). In fact, this verb is used only once in the entire NT, and that is here in Jn. 20:22. This verb is used only six times in the GSEPT. One of those instances is Ezek. 37:9 in which God commands Ezekiel to prophecy to the wind that it would breath upon the slain so that they will come to life.

Table #93: Ezek. 37:9

	"Then He said to me, 'Prophesy to the breath, prophesy, son of man, and say to the breath, "Thus says the Lord God, 'Come from the four winds, O breath, and breathe [ἐμφύσησον, וּפְחִי] on these slain, that they come to life."""
Ezek. 37:9	וַיֹּאמֶר אֵלַי הִנָּבֵא אֶל־הָרוּחַ הִנָּבֵא בֶן־אָדָם וְאָמַרְתָּ אֶל־הָרוּחַ כֹּה־אָמַר אֲדֹנָי יְהוִה מֵאַרְבַּע רוּחוֹת בֹּאִי הָרוּחַ וּפְחִי בַּהֲרוּגִים הָאֵלֶּה וְיִחְיוּ׃
	καὶ εἶπεν πρός με προφήτευσον υἱὲ ἀνθρώπου προφήτευσον ἐπὶ τὸ πνεῦμα καὶ εἰπὸν τῷ πνεύματι τάδε λέγει κύριος ἐκ τῶν τεσσάρων πνευμάτων ἐλθὲ καὶ ἐμφύσησον εἰς τοὺς νεκροὺς τούτους καὶ ζησάτωσαν.

Keener points out that "Genesis 2:7 was naturally connected with Ezek 37:9 in later midrash and Jewish artwork, and Ezek 37:9 was explicitly understood to refer to the

---

[24] Keener, *Gospel of John*, 1204.
[25] Ibid., 1205.

resurrection of the dead. Given John's earlier treatment of rebirth imagery (3:3–5) and his linking of water (3:6) and wind (3:8) images for the Spirit (cf. Ezek 36–37), it is likely that he recalls here [Jn. 20:22] the regenerating aspect of the Spirit of purification. Jesus had promised that his return to them alive would bring them new life as well (14:19)."[26] To ignore this historical, cultural, and theological background as well as the literary context is not to translate accurately. To translate Jn. 20:22 as "a holy spirit" is to dismiss the context in which John both lived and wrote and to makes John's text unintelligible and inconsistent.

BeDuhn's third principle of historical and cultural environment also requires interpretation. Concerning this principle BeDuhn states, "Our attention to the historical and cultural environment presumes that an author worked with images and ideas available in his or her world (even if working to redefine or transform them), and that a contemporaneous audience was the intended readership. If the books of the New Testament were written in a way that was incomprehensible to the earliest Christians, they never would have been valued, preserved, and collected into scripture."[27] According to this principle, to translate Jn. 20:22 as "a holy spirit" would have been unintelligible to John's audience and would have been inconsistent with the prevailing images and ideas of his day. BeDuhn's own principle demands that the reference in Jn. 20:22 be understood as definite—"the Holy Spirit."

Gender and Theology

In one of his arguments about the non-Personhood of the Holy Spirit, BeDuhn asserts, "Now it turns out that both 'masculine' and 'feminine' Greek nouns can be used for impersonal things as well as persons. But 'neuter' nouns are used only for impersonal things, such as objects, animals, forces, abstract principles, and so on."[28] Of course this is the fallacy of begging the question. BeDuhn assumes that the Holy Spirit is not a Person, and because the word "spirit" in Greek is neuter, he tries to use this to prove that the Holy Spirit is not a Person. But, if the Holy Spirit is a Person, then it is simply not true that neuter nouns are used "only for impersonal things." In other words, BeDuhn has assumed what must be proven. He is arguing in a circle, and as such his argument is false. It takes only a single counter-example to demonstrate the falsity of BeDuhn's assumption.

In fact, it is simply not true that the neuter gender is used "only for impersonal things." The word 'spirit' is often used of sentient, intelligent beings that give evidence of being not only alive, but thinking, reasoning, and speaking beings. For example, in Matt. 12:43–45 Jesus describes unclean spirits as beings that think, reason, and speak.

---

[26] Ibid., 1205.
[27] BeDuhn, *Translation*, xvi.
[28] Ibid., 140.

Table #94: Matt. 12:43–45

Matt. 12:43–45	Now when the unclean spirit goes out of a man, it passes through waterless places seeking rest, and does not find. Then it says, "I will return to my house from which I came"; and when it comes, it finds unoccupied, swept, and put in order. Then it goes and takes along with it seven other spirits more wicked than itself, and they go in and live there; and the last state of that man becomes worse than the first. That is the way it will also be with this evil generation.
	Ὅταν δὲ τὸ ἀκάθαρτον πνεῦμα ἐξέλθῃ ἀπὸ τοῦ ἀνθρώπου, διέρχεται δι' ἀνύδρων τόπων ζητοῦν ἀνάπαυσιν καὶ οὐχ εὑρίσκει. τότε λέγει· εἰς τὸν οἶκόν μου ἐπιστρέψω ὅθεν ἐξῆλθον· καὶ ἐλθὸν εὑρίσκει σχολάζοντα σεσαρωμένον καὶ κεκοσμημένον. τότε πορεύεται καὶ παραλαμβάνει μεθ' ἑαυτοῦ ἑπτὰ ἕτερα πνεύματα πονηρότερα ἑαυτοῦ καὶ εἰσελθόντα κατοικεῖ ἐκεῖ· καὶ γίνεται τὰ ἔσχατα τοῦ ἀνθρώπου ἐκείνου χείρονα τῶν πρώτων. οὕτως ἔσται καὶ τῇ γενεᾷ ταύτῃ τῇ πονηρᾷ.

Additionally, it is simply false that the neuter gender refers to "objects, animals, forces, abstract principles, and so on," and not to people. The following is a list of neuter nouns that refer either to individual persons or groups of people:

Table #95: Neuter Nouns Referring to Persons

γένος	race, descendant(s), family, nation, class - Use 20 times in the NT - twice used of human beings, translated "family"
	"On the second *visit* Joseph made himself known to his brothers, and Joseph's family was disclosed to Pharaoh" (Acts 7:13).
	καὶ ἐν τῷ δευτέρῳ ἀνεγνωρίσθη Ἰωσὴφ τοῖς ἀδελφοῖς αὐτοῦ καὶ φανερὸν ἐγένετο τῷ Φαραὼ τὸ γένος (τοῦ) Ἰωσήφ.
	"Brethren, sons of Abraham's family, and those among you who fear God, to us the message of this salvation has been sent." (Acts 13:26).
	Ἄνδρες ἀδελφοί, υἱοὶ γένους Ἀβραὰμ καὶ οἱ ἐν ὑμῖν φοβούμενοι τὸν θεόν, ἡμῖν ὁ λόγος τῆς σωτηρίας ταύτης ἐξαπεστάλη.
	Using this word to refer to the families of Joseph and Abraham hardly constitutes a use of this neuter noun as an impersonal thing, objects, animals, forces, abstract principles, or a "so on."

γυναικάριον	idle or silly woman - 1 time in the NT
	"For among them are those who enter into households and captivate weak women weighed down with sins, led on by various impulses" (2 Tim. 3:6).
	ἐκ τούτων γάρ εἰσιν οἱ ἐνδύνοντες εἰς τὰς οἰκίας καὶ αἰχμαλωτίζοντες γυναικάρια σεσωρευμένα ἁμαρτίαις, ἀγόμενα ἐπιθυμίαις ποικίλαις,
	This is clearly a reference to persons, human beings.
δωδεκάφυλον	the twelve tribes - 1 time in the NT
	"[the promise] to which our twelve tribes hope to attain, as they earnestly serve God night and day" (Acts 26:7).
	εἰς ἣν τὸ δωδεκάφυλον ἡμῶν ἐν ἐκτενείᾳ νύκτα καὶ ἡμέραν λατρεῦον ἐλπίζει καταντῆσαι
	This is not an abstract concept or principle since the text states that these persons "hope" and "serve." These are not actions of a principle or abstract concept.
ἔθνος	nation, people, Gentile, heathen (pl.) - 150 times in the NT
	"For the Gentiles eagerly seek all these things; for your heavenly Father knows that you need all these things" (Matt. 6:32)
	πάντα γὰρ ταῦτα τὰ ἔθνη ἐπιζητοῦσιν· οἶδεν γὰρ ὁ πατὴρ ὑμῶν ὁ οὐράνιος ὅτι χρῄζετε τούτων ἁπάντων.
	This term is not an abstract concept since abstract concepts do not seek things to eat, drink, or wear.
παιδάριον	boy, youth, young slave - 1 time in the NT
	"There is a lad here who has five barley loaves and two fish, but what are these for so many people?" (Jn. 6:9)
	ἔστιν παιδάριον ὧδε ὃς ἔχει πέντε ἄρτους κριθίνους καὶ δύο ὀψάρια· ἀλλὰ ταῦτα τί ἐστιν εἰς τοσούτους;
	This is clearly a reference to a person.

παιδίον	child, infant - 52 times in the NT
	"And he sent them to Bethlehem and said, 'Go and search carefully for the Child; and when you have found, report to me, so that I too may come and worship Him'" (Matt. 2:8).
	καὶ πέμψας αὐτοὺς εἰς Βηθλέεμ εἶπεν· πορευθέντες ἐξετάσατε ἀκριβῶς περὶ τοῦ παιδίου· ἐπὰν δὲ εὕρητε, ἀπαγγείλατέ μοι, ὅπως κἀγὼ ἐλθὼν προσκυνήσω αὐτῷ.
	The important thing to note about this instances is that the neuter noun παιδίον is used of Jesus.
σπέρμα	seed, survivors, descendants, children, nature - Used 34 times in the NT to refer to human descendants, seed, or children
	"Remember Jesus Christ, risen from the dead, descendant of David, according to my gospel" (2 Tim 2:8)
	Μνημόνευε Ἰησοῦν Χριστὸν ἐγηγερμένον ἐκ νεκρῶν, ἐκ σπέρματος Δαυίδ, κατὰ τὸ εὐαγγέλιόν μου,
	The word σπέρμα in this instance is referring to Jesus Christ, hardly an inanimate object, impersonal thing, anima, force, abstract principle, or even a "so on."
τεκνίον	little child - 8 times in the NT
	"Little children, I am with you a little while longer" (Jn. 13:33).
	τεκνία, ἔτι μικρὸν μεθ' ὑμῶν εἰμι·
	Here Jesus is talking to His disciples, hardly inanimate objects, animals, forces, abstract principles or "so on."

There are some few other neuter words that are used to refer to persons, but these are sufficient to demonstrate that BeDuhn's claim is simply false. Neuter nouns can and indeed are used to refer to persons. BeDuhn asserts, "But even though the 'personal' category is larger in Greek than in English, the 'Holy Spirit' is referred to by a 'neuter' noun in Greek. Consequently, it is never spoken of with personal pronouns in Greek. It is a 'which,' not a 'who.' It is an 'it,' not a 'he.'"[29] Simply because the word 'Spirit' is neuter does not mean that the Holy Spirit is an "it," in the same way that the neuter nouns translated 'child' (τεκνίον, παιδίον, et al.) do not indicate that human children

---

[29] Ibid.

are "it"s. BeDuhn's basic mistake is his lack of understanding an elementary principle of linguistics. Grammatical gender does not have a necessary relation to actual gender. Just because a word has a certain grammatical gender does not mean that this indicates either actual gender or personhood.

Besides the fact that we have already shown BeDuhn's claims about the neuter gender to be false, it is simply not true that the Holy Spirit is not referred to with a personal pronoun. In the Gospel of John, Jesus instructs His disciples about the sending of the Holy Spirit. In the instruction in Jn. 14:16, Jesus refers to the Holy Spirit as the "Helper" (παράκλητος, *paraklētos*). In 14:26 Jesus identifies the "Helper" as "the Holy Spirit" (τὸ πνεῦμα τὸ ἅγιον, *to pneuma to hagion*) Whom the Father will send. In 16:7 Jesus says, "But I tell you the truth, it is to your advantage that I go away; for if I do not go away, the Helper [ὁ παράκλητος, *ho paraklētos*] will not come to you; but if I go, I will send Him [αὐτόν, *auton*] to you." Here Jesus uses the third person, personal pronoun to refer to the Helper, the Παράκλητος, Who is the Holy Spirit. And, it should be pointed out that this is a masculine personal pronoun, not a neuter form. It must be masculine because it must agree in gender with the word 'Helper,' which is masculine. So, it is simply false for BeDuhn to claim that the Holy Spirit is never referred to with a personal pronoun.

Table #96: Παράκλητος

Jn. 14:16	"I will ask the Father, and He will give you another Helper, that He may be with you forever;"
	κἀγὼ ἐρωτήσω τὸν πατέρα καὶ ἄλλον παράκλητον δώσει ὑμῖν, ἵνα μεθ᾽ ὑμῶν εἰς τὸν αἰῶνα ᾖ,
Jn. 14:26	"But the Helper, the Holy Spirit, whom the Father will send in My name, He will teach you all things, and bring to your remembrance all that I said to you."
	ὁ δὲ παράκλητος, τὸ πνεῦμα τὸ ἅγιον, ὃ πέμψει ὁ πατὴρ ἐν τῷ ὀνόματί μου, ἐκεῖνος ὑμᾶς διδάξει πάντα καὶ ὑπομνήσει ὑμᾶς πάντα ἃ εἶπον ὑμῖν (ἐγώ).
Jn. 15:26	"When the Helper comes, whom I will send to you from the Father, the Spirit of truth who proceeds from the Father, He will testify about Me,"
	Ὅταν ἔλθῃ ὁ παράκλητος ὃν ἐγὼ πέμψω ὑμῖν παρὰ τοῦ πατρός, τὸ πνεῦμα τῆς ἀληθείας ὃ παρὰ τοῦ πατρὸς ἐκπορεύεται, ἐκεῖνος μαρτυρήσει περὶ ἐμοῦ·
Jn. 16:7	"But I tell you the truth, it is to your advantage that I go away; for if I do not go away, the Helper will not come to you; but if I go, I will send Him to you."
	ἀλλ᾽ ἐγὼ τὴν ἀλήθειαν λέγω ὑμῖν, συμφέρει ὑμῖν ἵνα ἐγὼ ἀπέλθω. ἐὰν γὰρ μὴ ἀπέλθω, ὁ παράκλητος οὐκ ἐλεύσεται πρὸς ὑμᾶς· ἐὰν δὲ πορευθῶ, πέμψω αὐτὸν πρὸς ὑμᾶς.

After having drawn conclusions that are wrong based on a principle that is wrong, BeDuhn attempts to apply his conclusions to certain passages.

Acts 5:32

Table #97: Acts 5:32

Acts 5:32	"And we are witnesses of these things; and the Holy Spirit, whom [ὅ, *ho*] God has given to those who obey Him."
	καὶ ἡμεῖς ἐσμεν μάρτυρες τῶν ῥημάτων τούτων καὶ τὸ πνεῦμα τὸ ἅγιον ὃ ἔδωκεν ὁ θεὸς τοῖς πειθαρχοῦσιν αὐτῷ.

BeDuhn claims, "In Acts 5:32 it is said, 'We are witnesses of these things, and (so is) the holy spirit, which (*ho*) God has given to those who obey him.' The NW has 'which,' the NAB uses 'that.' Both are accurate renderings of the relative pronoun ho. But the KJV, NASB, NIV, NRSV, and AB all change the word to 'whom,' the TEV and LB to 'who,' guided in this choice solely by a theological bias about the nature or character of the 'Holy Spirit' that overrides accurate translation."[30] Of course, since we have shown that BeDuhn's assumptions about the neuter gender nouns is both false and inaccurate, this shows that BeDuhn's own claim is theologically motivated. It is not a matter of grammatical accuracy since a neuter noun can refer to a person. Since we have shown that a Greek neuter noun can refer to a person, and since we have also shown that the Holy Spirit is a Person, it would in fact change the meaning of the statement in Acts to use "which" or "that" since these English words would communicate the wrong meaning to English readers. Both BeDuhn and NW have got it wrong.

Eph. 4:30

Table #98: Eph. 4:30

Eph. 4:30	"Do not grieve the Holy Spirit of God, by whom [ᾧ, *hō*] you were sealed for the day of redemption."
	καὶ μὴ λυπεῖτε τὸ πνεῦμα τὸ ἅγιον τοῦ θεοῦ, ἐν ᾧ ἐσφραγίσθητε εἰς ἡμέραν ἀπολυτρώσεως.

Concerning this verse BeDuhn states, "In Ephesians 4:30, Paul writes, 'And do not cause grief to the holy spirit of God, by which you are sealed for a day of redemption.' How do our translators handle the relative pronoun 'which' in the phrase en *hōi*? The

---

[30] Ibid., 140–41.

NRSV, NAB, and NW translate literally 'with which'; the KJV offers 'whereby.' But the NASB, NIV, and AB change the expression to 'by/with whom.' The LB has 'he is the one who.' The TEV restructures the sentence to avoid the relative pronoun."[31] As before, "which" is actually an inaccurate translation since it would give the English reader the wrong idea about the fact that the Holy Spirit is a person. And, as before, BeDuhn parades his theologically bias evaluation as if it is translation.

What is particularly absurd about BeDuhn's translation is that he ignores the literary context again. He does not even try to deal with the question of how the Holy Spirit can be 'grieved' if He is merely a force? Being grieved is an emotion. The verb 'grieve' (λυπέω, *lupeō*) occurs 26 times in the New Testament, and in each one of these it refers to a person.

Table #99: "Grieve" in the New Testament

Matt. 14:9	"Although he was grieved, the king commanded *it* to be given because of his oaths, and because of his dinner guests."
	καὶ λυπηθεὶς ὁ βασιλεὺς διὰ τοὺς ὅρκους καὶ τοὺς συνανακειμένους ἐκέλευσεν δοθῆναι,
Matt. 17:23	"'. . . and they will kill Him, and He will be raised on the third day.' And they were deeply grieved."
	καὶ ἀποκτενοῦσιν αὐτόν, καὶ τῇ τρίτῃ ἡμέρᾳ ἐγερθήσεται. καὶ ἐλυπήθησαν σφόδρα.
Matt. 18:31	"So when his fellow slaves saw what had happened, they were deeply grieved and came and reported to their lord all that had happened."
	ἰδόντες οὖν οἱ σύνδουλοι αὐτοῦ τὰ γενόμενα ἐλυπήθησαν σφόδρα καὶ ἐλθόντες διεσάφησαν τῷ κυρίῳ ἑαυτῶν πάντα τὰ γενόμενα.
Matt. 19:22	"But when the young man heard this statement, he went away grieving; for he was one who owned much property."
	ἀκούσας δὲ ὁ νεανίσκος τὸν λόγον ἀπῆλθεν λυπούμενος· ἦν γὰρ ἔχων κτήματα πολλά.
Matt. 26:22	"Being deeply grieved, they each one began to say to Him, 'Surely not I, Lord?'"
	καὶ λυπούμενοι σφόδρα ἤρξαντο λέγειν αὐτῷ εἷς ἕκαστος· μήτι ἐγώ εἰμι, κύριε;

---

[31] Ibid., 141.

Matt. 26:37	"And He took with Him Peter and the two sons of Zebedee, and began to be grieved and distressed."
	καὶ παραλαβὼν τὸν Πέτρον καὶ τοὺς δύο υἱοὺς Ζεβεδαίου ἤρξατο λυπεῖσθαι καὶ ἀδημονεῖν.
Mk. 10:22	"But at these words he was saddened, and he went away grieving, for he was one who owned much property."
	ὁ δὲ στυγνάσας ἐπὶ τῷ λόγῳ ἀπῆλθεν λυπούμενος· ἦν γὰρ ἔχων κτήματα πολλά.
Mk. 14:19	"They began to be grieved and to say to Him one by one, 'Surely not I?'"
	ἤρξαντο λυπεῖσθαι καὶ λέγειν αὐτῷ εἷς κατὰ εἷς· μήτι ἐγώ;
Jn. 16:20	"Truly, truly, I say to you, that you will weep and lament, but the world will rejoice; you will grieve, but your grief will be turned into joy."
	ἀμὴν ἀμὴν λέγω ὑμῖν ὅτι κλαύσετε καὶ θρηνήσετε ὑμεῖς, ὁ δὲ κόσμος χαρήσεται· ὑμεῖς λυπηθήσεσθε, ἀλλ' ἡ λύπη ὑμῶν εἰς χαρὰν γενήσεται.
Jn. 21:17	"He said to him the third time, 'Simon, *son* of John, do you love Me?' Peter was grieved because He said to him the third time, 'Do you love Me?' And he said to Him, 'Lord, You know all things; You know that I love You.' Jesus said to him, 'Tend My sheep.'"
	λέγει αὐτῷ τὸ τρίτον· Σίμων Ἰωάννου, φιλεῖς με; ἐλυπήθη ὁ Πέτρος ὅτι εἶπεν αὐτῷ τὸ τρίτον· φιλεῖς με; καὶ λέγει αὐτῷ· κύριε, πάντα σὺ οἶδας, σὺ γινώσκεις ὅτι φιλῶ σε. λέγει αὐτῷ (ὁ Ἰησοῦς)· βόσκε τὰ πρόβατά μου.
Rom. 14:15	"For if because of food your brother is grieved, you are no longer walking according to love. Do not destroy with your food him for whom Christ died."
	εἰ γὰρ διὰ βρῶμα ὁ ἀδελφός σου λυπεῖται, οὐκέτι κατὰ ἀγάπην περιπατεῖς· μὴ τῷ βρώματί σου ἐκεῖνον ἀπόλλυε ὑπὲρ οὗ Χριστὸς ἀπέθανεν.
2 Cor. 2:2	"For if I grieve you, who then makes me glad but the one whom I made sorrowful?"
	εἰ γὰρ ἐγὼ λυπῶ ὑμᾶς, καὶ τίς ὁ εὐφραίνων με εἰ μὴ ὁ λυπούμενος ἐξ ἐμοῦ;

2 Cor. 2:4	"For out of much affliction and anguish of heart I wrote to you with many tears; not so that you would be grieved, but that you might know the love which I have especially for you."
	ἐκ γὰρ πολλῆς θλίψεως καὶ συνοχῆς καρδίας ἔγραψα ὑμῖν διὰ πολλῶν δακρύων, οὐχ ἵνα λυπηθῆτε ἀλλὰ τὴν ἀγάπην ἵνα γνῶτε ἣν ἔχω περισσοτέρως εἰς ὑμᾶς.
2 Cor. 2:5	"But if anyone grieved, he has not grieved me, but in some degree—in order not to say too much—to all of you."
	Εἰ δέ τις λελύπηκεν, οὐκ ἐμὲ λελύπηκεν, ἀλλὰ ἀπὸ μέρους, ἵνα μὴ ἐπιβαρῶ, πάντας ὑμᾶς.
2 Cor. 6:10	". . . as being grieved yet always rejoicing, as poor yet making many rich, as having nothing yet possessing all things."
	ὡς λυπούμενοι ἀεὶ δὲ χαίροντες, ὡς πτωχοὶ πολλοὺς δὲ πλουτίζοντες, ὡς μηδὲν ἔχοντες καὶ πάντα κατέχοντες.
2 Cor. 7:8	"For though I grieved you by my letter, I do not regret it; though I did regret it—*for* I see that that letter grieved you, though only for a while . . ."
	Ὅτι εἰ καὶ ἐλύπησα ὑμᾶς ἐν τῇ ἐπιστολῇ, οὐ μεταμέλομαι· εἰ καὶ μετεμελόμην, βλέπω (γὰρ) ὅτι ἡ ἐπιστολὴ ἐκείνη εἰ καὶ πρὸς ὥραν ἐλύπησεν ὑμᾶς,
2 Cor. 7:9	"I now rejoice, not that you were grieved, but that you were grieved to *the point of* repentance; for you were grieved according to *the will of* God, so that you might not suffer loss in anything through us."
	νῦν χαίρω, οὐχ ὅτι ἐλυπήθητε ἀλλ' ὅτι ἐλυπήθητε εἰς μετάνοιαν· ἐλυπήθητε γὰρ κατὰ θεόν, ἵνα ἐν μηδενὶ ζημιωθῆτε ἐξ ἡμῶν.
2 Cor. 7:11	"For behold what earnestness this very thing, this godly grief, has produced in you: what vindication of yourselves, what indignation, what fear, what longing, what zeal, what avenging of wrong! In everything you demonstrated yourselves to be innocent in the matter."
	ἰδοὺ γὰρ αὐτὸ τοῦτο τὸ κατὰ θεὸν λυπηθῆναι πόσην κατειργάσατο ὑμῖν σπουδήν, ἀλλὰ ἀπολογίαν, ἀλλὰ ἀγανάκτησιν, ἀλλὰ φόβον, ἀλλὰ ἐπιπόθησιν, ἀλλὰ ζῆλον, ἀλλὰ ἐκδίκησιν. ἐν παντὶ συνεστήσατε ἑαυτοὺς ἁγνοὺς εἶναι τῷ πράγματι.

Eph. 4:30	"Do not grieve the Holy Spirit of God, by whom you were sealed for the day of redemption."
	καὶ μὴ λυπεῖτε τὸ πνεῦμα τὸ ἅγιον τοῦ θεοῦ, ἐν ᾧ ἐσφραγίσθητε εἰς ἡμέραν ἀπολυτρώσεως.
1 Thess. 4:13	"But we do not want you to be uninformed, brethren, about those who are asleep, so that you will not grieve as do the rest who have no hope."
	Οὐ θέλομεν δὲ ὑμᾶς ἀγνοεῖν, ἀδελφοί, περὶ τῶν κοιμωμένων, ἵνα μὴ λυπῆσθε καθὼς καὶ οἱ λοιποὶ οἱ μὴ ἔχοντες ἐλπίδα.
1 Pet. 1:6	"In this you greatly rejoice, even though now for a little while, if necessary, you have been grieved by various trials . . ."
	ἐν ᾧ ἀγαλλιᾶσθε, ὀλίγον ἄρτι εἰ δέον (ἐστὶν) λυπηθέντες ἐν ποικίλοις πειρασμοῖς.

The verb occurs 26 times in the GSEPT (Gen. 4:5; 45:5; Deut. 15:10: 1 Kgs. 29:4; 2 Kgs. 13:21; 19:3; 4 Kgs 13:19; 2 Esd. 15:6; Esth. 1:12; 2:21; 6:12; Ps. 54:3; Prov. 25:20; Job 31:39; Micah 6:3; Jonah 4:1; 4:4; 4:9; Isa. 8:21; 15:2; 19:10; 32:11; 57:17; Jer. 15:18; Lam. 1:22; Ezek. 16:43; Dan. 3:50, 6:15, 19),[32] and in every instance it refers to a person. All the definitions and reference in LSL are to persons.[33] To grieve or to be grieved is something that can happen only to a person, not to a thing or object. Now BeDuhn might try to make some argument, but the fact that he does not even attempt to deal with that question here indicates his unwillingness actually to prove his case to his readers. He merely floats his assumptions and makes his erroneous claims without presenting any argument or evidence.

1 Cor. 6:19

Table #100: 1 Cor. 6:19

1 Cor. 6:19	"Or do you not know that your body is a temple of the Holy Spirit who is in you, whom you have from God, and that you are not your own?"
	ἢ οὐκ οἴδατε ὅτι τὸ σῶμα ὑμῶν ναὸς τοῦ ἐν ὑμῖν ἁγίου πνεύματός ἐστιν οὗ ἔχετε ἀπὸ θεοῦ, καὶ οὐκ ἐστὲ ἑαυτῶν;

BeDuhn offers a bit more discussion with reference to this verse:

---

[32] In the GSEPT, 1 and 2 Samuel, and 1 and 2 Kings are all referred to as Kings, 1, 2, 3, and 4 Kings. Also, the versification is different in the GSEPT version of Daniel from what we have in our English translations.

[33] LSL, s.v. "λυπέω."

The Spirit and the Trinity 205

In 1 Corinthians 6:19, Paul asks "Don't you know that your body is a temple of the holy spirit in you, which you have from God?" The Greek relative pronoun is used here at the beginning of the clause "which you have from God." It appears in the genitive ("of") form because it refers back to "of the holy spirit," which is also in the genitive form. Both the personal, masculine relative pronoun *hos* ("who/whom") and the impersonal, neuter relative pronoun *ho* ("which") become *hou* in the genitive form, and that is the form that appears in 1 Corinthians 6:19: *hou*. For translators to decide whether to translate *hou* as "who/whom" or "which," they have to see whether the antecedent (the noun it refers back to) is masculine or neuter. The antecedent in this verse is *to hagion pneuma*, which is neuter. Therefore, the relative pronoun *hou* should be translated "which."

Once again BeDuhn has made the elementary mistake of violating the linguistic principle that there is no necessary relationship between grammatical gender and actual gender. Even though the relative pronoun is neuter, this says nothing about whether the Holy Spirit is a person. As we have shown in Table #95, there are many instances of neuter words that refer to persons.

Another principle that BeDuhn conveniently ignores is his own principle of the literary context, and the historical and cultural environment. As we have already demonstrated, the literary context requires that the translation be "who/whom," not "which," since "which" would give the English reader the incorrect idea. Also we have shown that the historical and cultural environment requires the understanding of the Holy Spirit as a Person. So, this principle also requires the translation "who/whom." Because we have shown BeDuhn's claims to be false and inaccurate, it is not necessary to respond to his subsequent reasoning on this verse.

Jn. 14:26

Table #101: Jn. 14:26

Jn. 14:26	"But the Helper, the Holy Spirit, whom the Father will send in My name, He will teach you all things, and bring to your remembrance all that I said to you."
	ὁ δὲ παράκλητος, τὸ πνεῦμα τὸ ἅγιον, ὃ πέμψει ὁ πατὴρ ἐν τῷ ὀνόματί μου, ἐκεῖνος ὑμᾶς διδάξει πάντα καὶ ὑπομνήσει ὑμᾶς πάντα ἃ εἶπον ὑμῖν (ἐγώ).

Concerning this verse, BeDuhn says:

In John 14:26, Jesus says, "But the defender (*parakletos*) – the holy spirit, which the Father will send in my name – that one will teach you everything." Here a relative pronoun and a demonstrative pronoun are involved in the sentence. The demonstrative pronoun "that one" (*ekeinos*) refers back to the word "defender" (*parakletos*), a masculine noun meaning a defense attorney or supporter, a role thought appropriate only for males in the male-dominated society in which the Greek language was formed. Since Greek grammar requires gender agreement between a pronoun and the noun it refers back to, "that one" is in the masculine form, like "defender." The relative pronoun "which" (*ho*) refers back to the phrase "holy spirit," which as always appears in the neuter form. So, the neuter pronoun "which" (*ho*) is used rather than the masculine form (*hos*).[34]

Besides the fact that he continues to violate the linguistic principle of grammatical and actual gender, BeDuhn does not even attempt to deal with the question of why an impersonal force could be said to "teach you everything," or why, since the role of the defender (*paraklētos*) was "a role thought appropriate only for males in the male-dominated society" would refer to the Holy Spirit? Being a defender and teaching are an actions of persons, not of things or inanimate objects. Even tools, such as a written text, is said to "teach" only in an analogical sense. Persons create the texts that are then used as tools to teach other persons. Texts are said to teach only in the sense that they are employed by persons in the process of teaching. This is true of any tools, even those used today, such as computers, blackboards, machines of any kind. It is much easier to say "the text teaches" than to say "by means of the text the person teaches." Abbreviation of expression is one reason analogical predication is frequently employed in common parlance. But, whether or not BeDuhn has a response, he simply ignores this issue. However, as we keep pointing out, we have already demonstrated BeDuhn's thesis about the neuter words to be false.

BeDuhn asserts, "As always, it is not the theology of the translators to which I object, but the habit of imposing that theology on the biblical text."[35] But this is both false and disingenuous. BeDuhn's own translation practices are driven by his prior theological bias, and this is precisely the point of his contention. Since the basic principle of linguistics dictates that there is no necessary relation between grammatical gender and actual gender, the only reason BeDuhn could have made the statement, "It is a 'which,' not a 'who.' It is an 'it,' not a 'he,'"[36] is a theological one. If his motive was purely grammatical, he should have said, "The words to use are 'which' and 'it,' not 'who' and 'he.'" Instead, he makes a theological declaration about the nature of the Holy Spirit based on the gender of the words. His objection is in fact theologically motivated. He advocates the use of the English relative pronoun 'that' since, according to BeDuhn, "its use in translations of the New Testament would not foreclose the issue of the character of the 'holy spirit,' but would allow both personal and impersonal interpretations of it."[37] But, if the Bible is the authoritative source, as BeDuhn suggests, then to allow for an impersonal interpretation would be to distort what the Bible clearly presents. It is simply a fact of Greek grammar that a neuter words does not necessarily indicate an impersonal object. Neuter words can refer to persons, and since we have shown that both the biblical presentation and the historical and cultural environment require an understanding of the Holy Spirit as a Person, to use the relative pronoun 'that' would be misleading to English audiences.

---

[34] Ibid., 141–42.
[35] Ibid., 142.
[36] Ibid., 140.
[37] Ibid., 143.

BeDuhn's Misunderstanding of Misunderstood Passages

Misunderstanding 'Breath' or 'Life-Spirit' for the Holy Spirit

In the section titled "Misunderstood references to 'breath' or 'life spirit,'" BeDuhn gives a brief discussion of the fact that words do not always have the same meaning in every use. He then turns to address what he believes are misunderstood passages. The thrust of this section is explained: "Because we don't use language of a 'life-spirit' every day, and because the tendency of modern Christians is to think of only one, 'holy' spirit whenever 'spirit' is mentioned, modern translators sometimes misunderstand that a New Testament author is employing this idea of the individual's life-giving spirit."[38] The first passage he considers is Jn. 6:63:

Table #102: Jn. 6:63

Jn. 6:63	"It is the Spirit who gives life; the flesh profits nothing; the words that I have spoken to you are spirit and are life."
	τὸ πνεῦμά ἐστιν τὸ ζωοποιοῦν, ἡ σὰρξ οὐκ ὠφελεῖ οὐδέν· τὰ ῥήματα ἃ ἐγὼ λελάληκα ὑμῖν πνεῦμά ἐστιν καὶ ζωή ἐστιν.

Before looking at BeDuhn's comments on this verse, it must be pointed out that BeDuhn's claim that, "The Greek word translated 'spirit' is *pneuma*, the most basic meaning of which is 'wind,' the movement of air."[39] Although this may have been the case in Classical, Attic Greek, it is not the case in the GSEPT or the NT. As Blass-Debrunner point out, "Τὸ ἅγιον πνεῦμα ["the Holy Spirit] sometimes with article as more or less a person; sometimes without article as a divine spirit entering into man. Occassional anarthrous ἐκκλησία ["assembly"] in Paul also has the character of a proper name . . ."[40] Simply because a definition occurs first in the list in a lexicon does not necessarily mean that this is the basic meaning. The overwhelming use of the word πνεῦμα in the New Testament is with reference to the Holy Spirit, not to wind. The translation 'wind' occurs 27 times in the the NASB, 26 times in the KJV, 41 times in the TEV, 36 times in the NRSV, 26 times in the NIV, 36 times in the ESV, 40 times in the ASV, yet the word πνεῦμα occurs 379 times in the NT.

---

[38] Ibid., 145.

[39] Ibid., 144.

[40] F. Blass and A. DeBrunner, *A Greek Grammar of the New Testament and Other Early Christian Literature* (Chicago: The University of Chicago Press, 1961), §257(2). By the expression "more or less a person," Blass-DeBrunner are indicating that sometimes the reference is not absolutely clear, but tends toward the notion of person.

Concerning Jn. 6:63 BeDuhn asserts, "Starting with the basic idea that the breath/spirit is what gives life to a body, Jesus equates 'spirit' with 'life,' and goes on to equate both of these with his words. His words are for the hearer like what 'breath' and 'life' are for the lifeless body. Jesus makes his point by an analogy that builds on the general understanding of 'spirit' or breath as life-giving. The basic, unspecialized meaning of 'spirit' in this verse is accurately translated by the KJV, NRSV, NAB, and NW, none of which capitalize 'spirit.'"[41] In this instance, BeDuhn undisguisedly engages in interpretation to justify his translation, something that he has been doing covertly. And, once again, it is BeDuhn who has misunderstood.

It must be remembered that John uses the single word πνευμα for the Holy Spirit more than any other expression. John uses "the Spirit," (τὸ πνεῦμα, *to pneuma*) with the definite article, 14 times in 13 verses in his Gospel, while he uses "Holy Spirit" only three times. John uses the anarthrous form πνεῦμα six times in his Gospel (John 3:5; 4:24, twice; 6:63, twice; 7:39. Of the 14 instances of the use of τὸ πνεῦμα ("the Spirit") in John's Gospel, only 4 of these unquestionably do not speak of the Holy Spirit. This kind of literary context does more than bring BeDuhn's assertions into doubt. In the context of Jn. 6:63, Jesus is talking about spiritual life, not the life-giving force of one's body. It is the Holy Spirit—in John's words, τὸ πνεῦμά ἐστιν (*to pneuma estin*)—who gives life (Jn. 6:63a).

Table #103: The Spirit Gives Life

τὸ πνεῦμά	ἐστιν	τὸ ζῳοποιοῦν
the Spirit	is	the one giving life

When Jesus says His words are "spirit and they are life," He uses the anarthrous πνεῦμα. In fact, BeDuhn has made the very mistake that those disciples made who said, "This is a difficult statement; who can listen to it?" They thought Jesus was talking about literally eating His flesh and drinking His blood. They did not understand that He was talking about the Spirit. As Keener puts it, "It is in 6:63 that Jesus explains the nature of his metaphors, explicitly defining the character of 'the words I spoke to you.' Others consistently misinterpret Jesus' figurative pronouncements literally (3:4; 6:52; 11:12). It is not the *literal* flesh (cf. 6:51) that brings life, but the Spirit, a point also underlined in 3:6. The Spirit thus joins the Father and Son (5:21; cf. Rom 4:17; 1 Cor 15:22) in giving life (6:63; cf. Rom 8:11; 2 Cor 3:6; 1 Pet. 3:18; perhaps 1 Cor 15:45."[42] Once again the image is of the giving of life by the Breath/Spirit of God in Gen. 2:7 and Ezek. 37:9 as discussed above.

---

[41] Ibid., 146.
[42] Keener, *Gospel of John*, 694.

Table #104: John's Use of τὸ πνεῦμα

Jn. 1:32	"John testified saying, 'I have seen the Spirit [τὸ πνεῦμα] descending as a dove out of heaven, and He remained upon Him.'"
	Καὶ ἐμαρτύρησεν Ἰωάννης λέγων ὅτι τεθέαμαι τὸ πνεῦμα καταβαῖνον ὡς περιστερὰν ἐξ οὐρανοῦ καὶ ἔμεινεν ἐπ᾽ αὐτόν.
Jn. 1:33	"I did not recognize Him, but He who sent me to baptize in water said to me, 'He upon whom you see the Spirit [τὸ πνεῦμα] descending and remaining upon Him, this is the One who baptizes in the Holy Spirit.'"
	κἀγὼ οὐκ ᾔδειν αὐτόν, ἀλλ᾽ ὁ πέμψας με βαπτίζειν ἐν ὕδατι ἐκεῖνός μοι εἶπεν· ἐφ᾽ ὃν ἂν ἴδῃς τὸ πνεῦμα καταβαῖνον καὶ μένον ἐπ᾽ αὐτόν, οὗτός ἐστιν ὁ βαπτίζων ἐν πνεύματι ἁγίῳ.
Jn. 3:6	"That which is born of the flesh is flesh, and that which is born of the Spirit [τοῦ πνεύματος] is spirit."
	τὸ γεγεννημένον ἐκ τῆς σαρκὸς σάρξ ἐστιν, καὶ τὸ γεγεννημένον ἐκ τοῦ πνεύματος πνεῦμά ἐστιν.
Jn. 3:8	"The wind [τὸ πνεῦμα] blows where it wishes and you hear the sound of it, but do not know where it comes from and where it is going; so is everyone who is born of the Spirit [τοῦ πνεύματος]."
	τὸ πνεῦμα ὅπου θέλει πνεῖ καὶ τὴν φωνὴν αὐτοῦ ἀκούεις, ἀλλ᾽ οὐκ οἶδας πόθεν ἔρχεται καὶ ποῦ ὑπάγει· οὕτως ἐστὶν πᾶς ὁ γεγεννημένος ἐκ τοῦ πνεύματος.
Jn. 3:34	"For He whom God has sent speaks the words of God; for He gives the Spirit [τὸ πνεῦμα] without measure."
	ὃν γὰρ ἀπέστειλεν ὁ θεὸς τὰ ῥήματα τοῦ θεοῦ λαλεῖ, οὐ γὰρ ἐκ μέτρου δίδωσιν τὸ πνεῦμα.
Jn. 6:63	"It is the Spirit [τὸ πνεῦμά] who gives life; the flesh profits nothing; the words that I have spoken to you are spirit and are life."
	τὸ πνεῦμά ἐστιν τὸ ζῳοποιοῦν, ἡ σὰρξ οὐκ ὠφελεῖ οὐδέν· τὰ ῥήματα ἃ ἐγὼ λελάληκα ὑμῖν πνεῦμά ἐστιν καὶ ζωή ἐστιν.
Jn. 7:39	"But this He spoke of the Spirit [τοῦ πνεύματος], whom those who believed in Him were to receive; for the Spirit was not yet *given*, because Jesus was not yet glorified."
	τοῦτο δὲ εἶπεν περὶ τοῦ πνεύματος ὃ ἔμελλον λαμβάνειν οἱ πιστεύσαντες εἰς αὐτόν· οὔπω γὰρ ἦν πνεῦμα, ὅτι Ἰησοῦς οὐδέπω ἐδοξάσθη.

Jn. 11:33	"When Jesus therefore saw her weeping, and the Jews who came with her weeping, He was deeply moved in spirit [τῷ πνεύματι] and was troubled,"
	Ἰησοῦς οὖν ὡς εἶδεν αὐτὴν κλαίουσαν καὶ τοὺς συνελθόντας αὐτῇ Ἰουδαίους κλαίοντας, ἐνεβριμήσατο τῷ πνεύματι καὶ ἐτάραξεν ἑαυτὸν
Jn. 13:21	"When Jesus had said this, He became troubled in spirit [τῷ πνεύματι], and testified and said, 'Truly, truly, I say to you, that one of you will betray Me.'"
	Ταῦτα εἰπὼν (ὁ) Ἰησοῦς ἐταράχθη τῷ πνεύματι καὶ ἐμαρτύρησεν καὶ εἶπεν· ἀμὴν ἀμὴν λέγω ὑμῖν ὅτι εἷς ἐξ ὑμῶν παραδώσει με.
Jn. 14:17	"the Spirit [τὸ πνεῦμα] of truth, whom the world cannot receive, because it does not see Him or know Him, you know Him because He abides with you and will be in you."
	τὸ πνεῦμα τῆς ἀληθείας, ὃ ὁ κόσμος οὐ δύναται λαβεῖν, ὅτι οὐ θεωρεῖ αὐτὸ οὐδὲ γινώσκει· ὑμεῖς γινώσκετε αὐτό, ὅτι παρ' ὑμῖν μένει καὶ ἐν ὑμῖν ἔσται.
Jn. 15:26	"When the Helper comes, whom I will send to you from the Father, the Spirit [τὸ πνεῦμα] of truth who proceeds from the Father, He will testify about Me,"
	Ὅταν ἔλθῃ ὁ παράκλητος ὃν ἐγὼ πέμψω ὑμῖν παρὰ τοῦ πατρός, τὸ πνεῦμα τῆς ἀληθείας ὃ παρὰ τοῦ πατρὸς ἐκπορεύεται, ἐκεῖνος μαρτυρήσει περὶ ἐμοῦ·
Jn. 16:13	"But when He, the Spirit [τὸ πνεῦμα] of truth, comes, He will guide you into all the truth; for He will not speak on His own initiative, but whatever He hears, He will speak; and He will disclose to you what is to come."
	ὅταν δὲ ἔλθῃ ἐκεῖνος, τὸ πνεῦμα τῆς ἀληθείας, ὁδηγήσει ὑμᾶς ἐν τῇ ἀληθείᾳ πάσῃ· οὐ γὰρ λαλήσει ἀφ' ἑαυτοῦ, ἀλλ' ὅσα ἀκούσει λαλήσει καὶ τὰ ἐρχόμενα ἀναγγελεῖ ὑμῖν.
Jn. 19:30	"Therefore when Jesus had received the sour wine, He said, 'It is finished!' And He bowed His head and gave up the spirit [τὸ πνεῦμα]."
	ὅτε οὖν ἔλαβεν τὸ ὄξος (ὁ) Ἰησοῦς εἶπεν· τετέλεσται, καὶ κλίνας τὴν κεφαλὴν παρέδωκεν τὸ πνεῦμα.

Misunderstanding References to One's Own Spirit

BeDuhn next investigates what he believes are misunderstood references to a person's own individual spirit. Under this heading he considers Rom. 12:10–11; Col. 1:8; Eph. 6:18; 1 Cor. 14:2; and 1 Cor. 14:14–16. In each of these discussions BeDuhn argues that the reference is not to the Holy Spirit, but to a person's own individual spirit.

The Spirit and the Trinity

These discussions are relatively innocuous and in some instances even correct. In some instances BeDuhn's conclusions are debatable and not as straightforward as he wants his readers to think, but even here his conclusions are at least plausible. None of these passages has anything to say one way or another about the Holy Spirit, whether He is a Person, or the third Person of the Trinity, or any of the other controversial topics that characterize his discussion up to this point. Therefore, we will pass over these discussions with no additional comment.

Misunderstanding References to a Spiritual Domain

In this section BeDuhn considers some passages that he believes are using the word 'spirit' "to refer to a level of reality."[43] He looks at 1 Pet. 3:18–10; 1 Tim. 3:16; Eph. 2:20–22; and Jn. 4:23–24. Again his comments on most of these passages is fairly innocuous. However, his discussion of Jn. 4:23–24 requires our examination.

Table #105: Jn. 4:23–24

Jn. 4:23–24	"But an hour is coming, and now is, when the true worshipers will worship the Father in spirit and truth; for such people the Father seeks to be His worshipers. God is spirit, and those who worship Him must worship in spirit and truth."
	ἀλλὰ ἔρχεται ὥρα καὶ νῦν ἐστιν, ὅτε οἱ ἀληθινοὶ προσκυνηταὶ προσκυνήσουσιν τῷ πατρὶ ἐν πνεύματι καὶ ἀληθείᾳ· καὶ γὰρ ὁ πατὴρ τοιούτους ζητεῖ τοὺς προσκυνοῦντας αὐτόν. πνεῦμα ὁ θεός, καὶ τοὺς προσκυνοῦντας αὐτὸν ἐν πνεύματι καὶ ἀληθείᾳ δεῖ προσκυνεῖν.

Concerning these verses, BeDuhn asserts, "To worship 'in spirit' seems to mean to worship 'spiritually,' just as to worship 'in truth,' means to worship 'truly.'"[44] Most of BeDuhn's discussion concerns what he believes to be a misunderstanding of the concepts in the quote just given. In his translation of Jn. 4:24, however, he gives the following: "God (is) a spirit."[45] At the end of this section he says, "I have already discussed the clause 'God (is) a spirit' in chapter eleven."[46] We have already dealt with BeDuhn's claims concerning this verse, and we do not need to restate that material. We will add a few thoughts, however.

BeDuhn is heavily engaged in interpretation in these sections, and his theological and philosophical assumptions are certainly guiding his understanding of the passages he is discussing. The reader gets a peek at BeDuhn's concept of God with his translation

---

[43] BeDuhn, *Translation*, 150.
[44] Ibid., 153.
[45] Ibid.
[46] Ibid.

of the phrase πνεῦμα ὁ θεός (*pneuma ho theos*) as "God (is) a spirit." There is no grammatical or syntactical rule that states that a word without the definite article must be taken as indefinite. Several times BeDuhn has made reference to his rule that a Nominative subject must have the definite article. Coupled with the fact that Smyth says, "Its [the article's] presence or absence is often determined by the need of distinguishing subject from predicate," and "A predicate noun has no article, and is thus distinguished from the subject,"[47] the absence of the definite article with the word πνεῦμα in the phrase πνεῦμα ὁ θεός (*pneuma ho theos*), does not necessarily mean that the word is indefinite.

However, to hold to the notion that God is *a* spirit implies that God is one spirit in the category of spirits, and that there either are or could be other beings that could be spirits like God is a spirit. But, such a notion is both theologically and philosophically irrational. It is theologically irrational because God had declared that there is none like Him: "Thus says the Lord, 'The products of Egypt and the merchandise of Cush and the Sabeans, men of stature, will come over to you and will be yours; They will walk behind you, they will come over in chains and will bow down to you; They will make supplication to you: "Surely, God is with you, and there is none else, No other God."'" (Isa. 45:14); "For thus says the Lord, who created the heavens (He is the God who formed the earth and made it, He established it [and] did not create it a waste place, formed it in order to be inhabited), 'I am the Lord, and there is none else'" (Isa. 45:18); "Turn to Me and be saved, all the ends of the earth; For I am God, and there is no other" (Isa. 45:22). It is theologically irrational to translate this "God is a spirit." Since there is no God but God, there cannot be another like God or of this kind. God is not *a* spirit. Rather, He is Spirit. Whereas other beings *have* spirits, God *is* Spirit.

This translation is also philosophically irrational. There can be only one infinite, eternal God. There cannot be two Gods. We have already demonstrated this earlier. However, it bears repeating. Two Gods would have to differ by some difference. But, two Gods that are infinite and eternal can have no differences. They cannot differ by the kinds of beings they are, because this is the very aspect in which they are the same. And, they cannot differ by non-being, because non-being is nothing, and to differ by nothing is not to differ. So, there cannot be two Gods. Consequently, God cannot be *a* spirit. Rather, God is Spirit. BeDuhn's translation is propelled by his interpretation, and his interpretation is grounded in his theology and philosophy, both of which are in error about the nature of God.

Spirit of Truth

In the section titled "Inspired Spirits," BeDuhn discusses references that he thinks concern spirits, good or evil. He says, "But that does not mean that the Holy Spirit is

---

[47] Smyth, *Greek Grammar*, §1126, §1150.

necessarily involved every time one speaks of an inspiring spirit."[48] His discussion of many of these instances are certainly correct. He then makes the following observations: "According to 1 Corinthians 15:45, Jesus becomes a 'life-giving spirit,' an image that draws on the same basic meaning of *pneuma* we have seen underlying all applications of the word. Other examples of spirits with important positive attributes are: 'the spirit of truth' (John 14:17; John 15:26; John 16:13; 1 John 4:6), in other words, the force that enables Christians to know rightly;"[49]

It is important to point out that BeDuhn makes no comment about how the fact that Jesus becomes a "life-giving spirit" relates to his earlier claim that neuter nouns can refer only to impersonal objects.

Table #106: Jesus Life-Giving Spirit

ὁ ἔσχατος	Ἀδὰμ	εἰς	πνεῦμα	ζῳοποιοῦν.
the last	Adam	unto	Spirit	life-giving

The reader is left in the dark about how BeDuhn would attempt to reconcile these notions. Is Jesus, after His resurrection, an impersonal object? a force? an animal? How can the Bible use the neuter noun πνεῦμα to refer to Jesus if neuter nouns cannot refer to persons?

Table #107: "The Spirit of Truth"

Jn. 14:16–17	"I will ask the Father, and He will give you another Helper, that He may be with you forever; the Spirit [τὸ πνεῦμα] of truth, whom the world cannot receive, because it does not see Him or know Him, you know Him because He abides with you and will be in you."
	κἀγὼ ἐρωτήσω τὸν πατέρα καὶ ἄλλον παράκλητον δώσει ὑμῖν, ἵνα μεθ' ὑμῶν εἰς τὸν αἰῶνα ᾖ, τὸ πνεῦμα τῆς ἀληθείας, ὃ ὁ κόσμος οὐ δύναται λαβεῖν, ὅτι οὐ θεωρεῖ αὐτὸ οὐδὲ γινώσκει· ὑμεῖς γινώσκετε αὐτό, ὅτι παρ' ὑμῖν μένει καὶ ἐν ὑμῖν ἔσται.
Jn. 14:26	"But the Helper, the Holy Spirit [τὸ πνεῦμα τὸ ἅγιον], whom the Father will send in My name, He will teach you all things, and bring to your remembrance all that I said to you."
	ὁ δὲ παράκλητος, τὸ πνεῦμα τὸ ἅγιον, ὃ πέμψει ὁ πατὴρ ἐν τῷ ὀνόματί μου, ἐκεῖνος ὑμᾶς διδάξει πάντα καὶ ὑπομνήσει ὑμᾶς πάντα ἃ εἶπον ὑμῖν (ἐγώ).

---

[48] BeDuhn, *Translation*, 154.
[49] Ibid.

Jn. 15:26	"When the Helper comes, whom I will send to you from the Father, the Spirit [τὸ πνεῦμα] of truth who proceeds from the Father, He will testify about Me,"	
	Ὅταν ἔλθῃ ὁ παράκλητος ὃν ἐγὼ πέμψω ὑμῖν παρὰ τοῦ πατρός, τὸ πνεῦμα τῆς ἀληθείας ὃ παρὰ τοῦ πατρὸς ἐκπορεύεται, ἐκεῖνος μαρτυρήσει περὶ ἐμοῦ·	
Jn. 16:13	"But when He, the Spirit [τὸ πνεῦμα] of truth, comes, He will guide you into all the truth; for He will not speak on His own initiative, but whatever He hears, He will speak; and He will disclose to you what is to come."	
	ὅταν δὲ ἔλθῃ ἐκεῖνος, τὸ πνεῦμα τῆς ἀληθείας, ὁδηγήσει ὑμᾶς ἐν τῇ ἀληθείᾳ πάσῃ· οὐ γὰρ λαλήσει ἀφ' ἑαυτοῦ, ἀλλ' ὅσα ἀκούσει λαλήσει καὶ τὰ ἐρχόμενα ἀναγγελεῖ ὑμῖν.	

One problem with BeDuhn's assessment is that, according to John, "the Spirit of Truth" is "the Holy Spirit." Follow John's reasoning: 1) Jesus say He will ask the Father, and the Father will send the Παράκλητος (14:16); 2) Jesus identifies the Παράκλητος as "the Holy Spirit" (τὸ πνεῦμα τὸ ἅγιον) (14:26); 3) Jesus identifies the Παράκλητος as "the Spirit of Truth." Two things that are equal to a third thing are equal to each other.

The Παράκλητος is The Holy Spirit   A
The Spirit of Truth is the Παράκλητος   A
∴ The Holy Spirit is The Spirit of Truth   A

For BeDuhn to ignore this literary context is, again, to violate the second of his principles for accurate translation, and in this instance, interpretation. The Spirit of Truth is not "the force that enables Christians to know rightly,"[50] as BeDuhn asserts. BeDuhn claims, "As I have mentioned, the trend in the history of Christian theology has been to consolidate all of these references to spirit within the concept of the Holy Spirit. But it would be rash to impose the result of this interpretive development onto the source documents of the Christian faith. One cannot assume that every positive spiritual force mentioned in the Bible is the Holy Spirit."[51] But by the same token, one cannot assume that any particular reference to πνεῦμα is not a reference to the Holy Spirit. BeDuhn is imposing his own later interpretive development upon the text in the same manner as he is accusing Christian theologians in the early years of the Church. Both Christian theology and BeDuhn claim that their interpretations of the text are what the original source documents are actually saying. The difference is, BeDuhn tries to

---

[50] Ibid.
[51] Ibid.

disguise his interpretive later development as simply grammatical demands when in fact they are as much interpretive conclusions as those he accuses.

Conclusion

In concluding this chapter, BeDuhn claims, "But I hope I have demonstrated that close attention to grammar, syntax, literary context, and cultural environment is necessary to figure out exactly how the word is used in a specific verse."[52] What BeDuhn has certainly demonstrated is that considering grammar, syntax, literary context, and cultural environment does not guarantee accurate exegesis of a specific verse. We have shown that on several occasions BeDuhn's interpretation, guided by his prior theological and philosophical commitments, is quite wrong. Now BeDuhn would certainly say that our own interpretation is guided by our prior theological and philosophical commitments, and that would certainly be true. However, unlike BeDuhn, we are not attempting to mask our prior theological and philosophical commitments behind the pretense of simply doing grammatical and syntactical analysis. BeDuhn consistently attempts to present his interpretive conclusions as if they are the demands of grammar and syntax, and he dismisses competing interpretive conclusions as "later developments" that are being imposed upon the source documents, and yet this is precisely what he is doing. BeDuhn "allowed theological bias to interfere with"[53] his accuracy just as much as the translators he is critiquing. Whereas BeDuhn claims that all translations "imported the 'Holy Spirit' into passages where 'spirit' is being used in a different sense,"[54] BeDuhn imposed his own position upon these very passages to deport the Holy Spirit from passages in which He is clearly referenced. BeDuhn's "opinions should not masquerade as Bible translations."[55] And contrary to his claim, BeDuhn consistently ignores the grammar, syntax, literary context, and cultural environment when it serves his purpose.

Apologetic Points

BeDuhn set out in this chapter to show that the Holy Spirit is not the third Person of the Trinity but is rather a force. Even though he disguised his goal behind the pretense of grammar and syntax, BeDuhn already had a theological and philosophical bias, and it is this bias that guides his analyses. From this study, we can glean the following apologetic points:

---

[52] Ibid., 158.
[53] Ibid., 159.
[54] Ibid.
[55] Ibid.

1. Just because is in the Accusative case and does not have the definite article does not mean that the word must be taken as indefinite. We have already shown that words without the definite article in grammar can still be definite in concept. An example of this is Heb. 7:5. The fact that Heb. 7:5 is a quote from Deut. 9:16 shows that the word 'Lord,' though Accusative and without the definite article, must still be taken as definite.

2. The absence of the definite article before the words 'Holy Spirit' in Acts 8:17 and 19 does not mean that this is to be taken as indefinite. We have already shown that this is a reference to the Holy Spirit by its connection with the event in Acts 2:4ff, which is clearly a reference to "the Holy Spirit."

3. Acts 8:17 refers to "receiving Holy Spirit" (ἐλάμβανον πνεῦμα ἅγιον, *elambanon pneuma hagion*). Acts 2:38 states: "Peter to them, 'Repent, and each of you be baptized in the name of Jesus Christ for the forgiveness of your sins; and you will receive the gift of the Holy Spirit." As Acts 8:16 stated, the Holy Spirit had not fallen upon them, so Peter and John lay hands on them so that they can receive the Holy Spirit. The literary context indicates that this is the Holy Spirit and it should be translated as such. So, the receiving of Holy Spirit in Acts 8:17 must be taken as definite.

4. Acts 10:38 refers to how God anointed Jesus with Holy Spirit [πνεύματι ἁγίῳ] and with power. In Acts 1:38 Jesus told the disciples that they would receive power (δύναμιν, *dunamin*, the same word used in Acts 10:38) when the Holy Spirit (τοῦ ἁγίου πνεύματος, *tou hagiou pneumatos*) would come upon them. The words 'Holy Spirit' in Acts 10:38 should be taken as definite even though they do not have the definite article.

5. Whether the words 'Holy Spirit' should be taken as definite cannot be determined only on whether there is or is not a definite article. Although this is important, it is not the whole story. The literary context must be taken into consideration also, and one's prior theological commitment will necessarily be a part of this process.

6. John uses the expression "spirit holy" only three times: Jn. 1:33; 14:26; 20:22. Of the three instances in which John uses "spirit holy," two are anarthrous, 1:33 and 20:22, and one is articular, 14:26. This shows that just because John uses "spirit holy" without the article does not prove that these should be taken as indefinite.

7. In biblical evidence shows that only God would baptize in his Spirit, as is stated in 1:33; 3:5, or pour out God's Spirit as indicated in Isa 42:1; 44:3; 61:11; Ezek 36:27; 37:15; 39:29; Joel 2:28–29; Hag 2:5; Zech 4:6; and 12:10, and as stated in Jn. 20:22.

8. Among the Jewish community, Gen. 2:7 was naturally connected with Ezek. 37:9, and Ezek 37:9 was explicitly understood to refer to the resurrection of the dead. John uses the rebirth imagery in 3:3–5, and he links water in 3:6 with wind in 3:8. These are images of the Holy Spirit. This is related to Jn. 20:22 indicating the regenerating aspect of the Spirit of purification. To translate Jn. 20:22 as "a holy spirit" would have been unintelligible to John's audience, would have been inconsistent with the prevailing images and ideas of his day, and ignores this historical, cultural, and theological background as well as the literary context.

9. The neuter gender is used of persons as well as things. An example of this is Matt. 2:43–45 in which Jesus describes unclean spirits as beings that think, reason, and speak. Other neuter words used to refer to persons include, γένος ("family") in Acts 7:13 and Acts 13:26; γυναικάριον ("idle" or "silly woman") in 2 Tim. 3:6; δωδεκάφυλον ("twelve tribes") in Acts 26:7; ἔθνος ("nation," "people," "Gentile," or "heathen") 150 times in the NT, for example Matt. 6:32; παιδάριον ("boy," "youth," "young slave") in Jn. 6:9; παιδίον ("child," "infant") 52 times in the NT, for example in Matt. 2:8; σπέρμα ("seed," "survivors," "descendants," "children," "nature") 34 times in the NT to refer to human descendants, seed, or children, for example in 2 Tim 2:8; and τεκνίον ("little child") 8 times in the NT, for example in Jn. 13:33.

10. The Holy Spirit is referred to with a personal pronoun. Jesus refers to the Holy Spirit as the "Helper" (παράκλητος, *paraklētos*). In 14:26 Jesus identifies the "Helper" as "the Holy Spirit" (τὸ πνεῦμα τὸ ἅγιον, *to pneuma to hagion*) Whom the Father will send. In 16:7 Jesus says, "But I tell you the truth, it is to your advantage that I go away; for if I do not go away, the Helper [ὁ παράκλητος, *ho paraklētos*] will not come to you; but if I go, I will send Him [αὐτὸν, *auton*] to you." Here Jesus uses the third person, personal pronoun to refer to the Helper, the Παράκλητος, Who is the Holy Spirit.

11. The verb 'grieve' occurs 26 times in the New Testament (Matt. 14:9; 17:23; 18:31; 19:22; 26:22; 26:37; 10:22; 14:19; Jn. 16:20; 21:17; Rom. 14:15; 2 Cor. 2:2; 2:4, 5; 2 Cor. 6:10; 7:8, 9; 7:11; Eph. 4:30; 1 Thess. 4:13; 1 Pet. 1:6) and 26 times in the GSEPT (Gen. 4:5; 45:5; Deut. 15:10: 1 Kgs. 29:4; 2 Kgs. 13:21; 19:3; 4 Kgs 13:19; 2 Esd. 15:6; Esth. 1:12; 2:21; 6:12; Ps. 54:3; Prov. 25:20;

Job 31:39; Micah 6:3; Jonah 4:1; 4:4; 4:9; Isa. 8:21; 15:2; 19:10; 32:11; 57:17; Jer. 15:18; Lam. 1:22; Ezek. 16:43; Dan. 3:50, 6:15, 19). In every instance it refers to a person, not to a thing. Also, in the Liddell & Scott Greek-English Lexicon, the meanings refer only to persons. Because the Holy Spirit can be grieved, this means that He is a Person.

CHAPTER 10

THE FINAL WORD

Introduction

Chapter thirteen of BeDuhn's book is titled "A Final Word."[1] Although followed by an appendix, this chapter constitutes the summary and conclusion of his arguments throughout his book. BeDuhn reminds the reader that he "made it clear that every translation has been created by vested interests, and that none of the translations represent the ideal of a scholarly, neutral project."[2] Unfortunately, BeDuhn seems oblivious to the fact that all translation necessarily involves interpretation, and although a translator may endeavor to be as objective as possible, it is extremely difficult, and in some instances not even desirable, to set aside one's own theological and philosophical bias in order to translate.

In the transcript of a debate between BeDuhn and Robert Bowman, BeDuhn exhibits a consistent lack of understanding of *ad hominem* argumentation. He says, "For one thing, ad honinem [*sic*] is a technical term in logic that refers to a close analysis of an argument for the technical weakness of conflating things about the source of an argument with the argument itself."[3] There are in fact, three different kinds of *ad hominem* argumentation, two that are fallacies and one that is not. As we have already noted, Howard Kahane points out that not all *ad hominem* arguments are fallacious: "But *ad hominem* arguments are not always fallacious. For instance, a lawyer who

---

[1] BeDuhn, *Translation*, 161–68.
[2] Ibid., 161.
[3] BeDuhn, "JASON #16 – 10/19 – #15797," in *John 8:58: The BeDuhn—Bowman Debate* <http://www.forananswer.org/Mars_Jw/John%208-58%20Debate%20-%20Part%20 One.pdf> [Onlilne]: Available: April 11, 2008.

219

attacks the testimony of a witness by questioning his moral character argues *ad hominem*, but does not commit a fallacy."[4] Kahane goes on to explain,

> The question of when an *ad hominem* argument is fallacious, and when not, is quite complex. In general, it can be said that such an argument is *not* fallacious when the man argued against is or claims to be an *expert* on the question at issue. Courtroom witnesses, doctors, auto mechanics, lawyers, etc., often present arguments against which we, as nonexperts, may be unable to argue directly. In such cases, information about the *character* of an expert may well be an important kind of evidence in deciding whether to accept or reject his opinion.
>
> But in these cases, we certainly do not prove by *ad hominem* arguments that the expert testimony or advice is incorrect. At best, *ad hominem* arguments only provide grounds for *cancelling* or *disregarding* the testimony or advice of an expert. They do not provide good grounds for assuming that his opinion is incorrect. For instance, if a doctor who advises operating on a particular patient turns out to be a charlatan, it is rash to conclude that no operation is necessary.[5]

So, *ad hominem* argumentation is not always a fallacy. But, there are two instances in which *ad hominem* argumentation is fallacious—*ad hominem* abusive, and *ad hominem* circumstantial. The *ad hominem* abusive fallacy consists of attacking your opponent on a personal level when this personal level is not relevant to the issue. The second kind of fallacious *ad hominem* argument is *argumentum ad hominem* circumstantial. In this fallacy, the attack is not directed toward one's character, but toward one's circumstances which are again irrelevant to the issue. This fallacy can be both positive and negative. It may be an attempt to urge someone to accept a position because of their circumstances, or it may be an attempt to persuade others to reject an argument because of the circumstances of the proponent of the argument. An example of this fallacy is to argue that someone is certainly going to believe in higher wages for teachers since he is a teacher! But, simply because someone is a teacher does not mean his arguments for higher wages are unsupported or false. In other words, simply because someone has a vested interest does not mean her arguments are invalid, or false. But this is precisely the kind of argument BeDuhn is using. He assumes that simply because translators have a vested interest, their translations cannot be unbiased. But this is the *ad hominem* circumstantial argument, and it is clearly a fallacy. Not only does BeDuhn not understand what an *ad hominem* argument is, he does not recognize one when he is using one—and in this case, a fallacious one.[6]

---

[4] Kahane, *Logic and Philosophy*, 240.

[5] Ibid.

[6] For more information on *ad hominem* fallacies, see Norman L. Geisler and Ronald M. Brooks, *Come Let Us Reason* (Grand Rapids: Baker Academic, 1990).

Catalog of Confusion

BeDuhn provides a summary of several chapters as a "review of the outcome of our investigation."[7] We will present BeDuhn's summary and this comment on each. The headings beginning with "Chapter Four" refer to the chapters in BeDuhn's book.

Chapter Four

In chapter Four, we saw that the NW and NAB handle the Greek word *proskuneō* most consistently, accurately translating it as "give homage" or "do obeisance" rather than switching to "worship" when Jesus is the recipient of the gesture.[8]

Actually, what we found in BeDuhn's analysis is a practice of selective reporting and bias interpretation. Focusing mostly on the text of Matthew's Gospel, we showed how BeDuhn strategically ignored the statement by Jesus that the act of προσκυνέω (*proskuneō*) should be performed only to God. Since Jesus willingly accepted the act of προσκυνέω from others, this implies that Jesus understood their actions not to be contrary to His declaration—in other words, Jesus willingly accepted the action of προσκυνέω toward Him as an act of worship. Therefore, it is completely inaccurate and biased not to translate these instances as worship. BeDuhn is reading back into the source documents the subsequent development of his own theological bias.

Chapter Five

In chapter Five, the NW was shown to have the most accurate translation of *harpagmos*, offering "seizure" consistent with its handling of other words derived from the verb *harpazō*. The NAB and NASB offer the acceptable "grasp." None of these three translations deviate from the accurate meaning of *morphē* ("form"). But the other translations altered one or other of these words to make the passage more palatable to their views.[9]

What we have shown with respect to BeDuhn's claims, however, is that he conveniently ignores the possible meanings of the word ἁρπαγμός (*harpagmos*) when it suits him or seems to support his case. As we pointed out in our Chapter Three — "In The Form of God," BeDuhn's characterization that "not a single word derived from *harpazō* that is used to suggest holding on to something already possessed"[10] is in fact inaccurate. For the verb *harpazō* itself LSL says, "ἁρπάζομαι I *have* her *torn* from my

---

[7] BeDuhn, *Translation*, 161.
[8] Ibid., 161–62.
[9] Ibid., 162.
[10] Ibid., 55.

arms,"[11] which certainly seems to indicate something that is already possessed. Something cannot be torn from someone's arms if that person does not actually possess it. We also showed that BeDuhn is willing to trust LSL on all these other meanings but not on the one in Phil. 2:6. The only reason for doing this is a prior theological bias.

Chapter Six

In chapter Six, the NAB and NRSV (with the TEV not too far behind) emerged as the most conscientious translations when it comes to avoiding the inherent male bias of may habits of English, allowing the more gender-neutral characteristics of the original Greek to come through. They even go a bit further to remove some of male bias to be found also in Greek, when such removal does not alter the basic meaning of a passage.[12]

We did not comment on this chapter because BeDuhn's analysis in this chapter is largely correct. However, it is curious that BeDuhn advocates changing the gender of particular Greek words when translating, that is, making the English more gender neutral than the Greek text, and yet when it contradicts his own theological bias he berates translators for making other reasonable and grammatically acceptable changes.

Chapter Seven

Concerning chapter seven of his book, "Probing the Implicit Meaning," BeDuhn has this to say:

In chapter Seven, it could be seen that the NW, NAB, KJV, and NASB refrain from adding material to Colossians 1:15–20 that changes its meaning or interprets its ambiguities. The other translations, which (along with the NAB) do not indicate additions to the text in any way, slip interpretations and glosses into the text.[13]

We deal with this chapter in Chapter Four "By Him All Things Were Created." In our analysis of BeDuhn's claims, we have shown that the evidence of the standard Greek grammars and the standard Greek lexicons, and of related passages demonstrates that Col. 1:15–16 clearly states that Jesus is God and that He is the Creator, not a created being. We demonstrated that BeDuhn's claims about the Genitive case are not correct, and that BeDuhn ignores any evidence that is contrary to his own position. We also showed that when one considers the relationship between Eph. 3:9 and Col. 1:16–17, the only conclusion is that Christ is God. Eph. 3:9 states that God is the Creator of "the all," (τὰ πάντα, *ta panta*). Col. 1:16–17 clearly states that Jesus is the

---

[11] LSL, s.v. "ἁρπάζω."
[12] BeDuhn, *Translation*, 162.
[13] Ibid.

Creator of "the all" (τὰ πάντα, *ta panta*). Now, either God created "the all," or Christ created "the all," or Christ is God.

Chapters Eight and Nine

In his summary, BeDuhn treats these two chapters together.

> In chapter Eight and Nine, no translation could be judged inaccurate, since either way of translating the passages is possible. But the weight of probability in chapter Nine favored NW's way of handling the verses discussed there.[14]

Although BeDuhn summarizes chapters eight and nine of his book together, we dealt with these in two chapters; Chapter Five, "Our God and Savior Jesus Christ," and Chapter Six, "Thy Throne O God." In Chapter Five we demonstrated that none of the passages that BeDuhn claimed were parallel to Titus 2:13 were in fact parallel. We also showed that a comparison of 2 Pet. 1:1 and 1:11 are clearly identical in structure, and since the words 'Lord' and 'savior' in 2 Pet. 1:11 both refer to Jesus Christ, then why do not the words "God" and 'savior' of 2 Pet. 1:1 both refer to Jesus Christ. In this chapter we also showed how BeDuhn completely misunderstands Sharp's Rule, and how even Smyth's grammar supports the conclusions of Sharp's Rule.

In Chapter Six we dealt with BeDuhn's arguments in his chapter Nine concerning Heb. 1:8. We argued that BeDuhn is actually determining meaning by majority vote, and that the relationship between Heb. 1:8 and the Ps. 45:6(H7) clearly show that the word 'God' should be treated as a Vocative of direct address in both passages. Because of this, Heb. 1:8 is clearly addressing Jesus the Son as God.

Chapter Ten

Chapter Ten of BeDuhn's book is titled "Tampering With Tenses." This is a short chapter in which BeDuhn tries to argue that the statement in Jn. 8:58, "before Abraham was, I am," should not be translated this way. Concerning this chapter, BeDuhn comments,

> In chapter Ten, it was revealed that only the NW and LB render the verbal expression *egō eimi* into a coherent part of its larger context in John 8:58, accurately following the Greek idiom. The other translations distort the obvious sense of the verb under the influence of an unfortunate interpretive mistake.[15]

---

[14] Ibid.
[15] Ibid.

As a matter of fact, BeDuhn's conclusions are actually a distortion of the text since he wants to change the tenses from what the Greek text actually says. Also, we showed in our analysis that BeDuhn has actually misunderstood and misrepresented the nature of an idiom, and because of this, BeDuhn has illegitimately concluded that Jn. 8:58 ought not to be translated literally. In fact, our analysis shows that BeDuhn is acting as a commentator, not as a translator.

Chapter Eleven

Chapter Eleven of his book, titled "And the Word was . . . What?" arguably the longest chapter in his book, BeDuhn attacks the statement in Jn. 1:1c, "and the Word was God." He sought to show that this should be translated, "and the word was a god."

> In chapter Eleven, I demonstrated at length that only the NW adheres exactly to the literal meaning of the Greek clause *theos ēn ho logos* in John 1:1. The other translations have followed an interpretive tradition that ignores the nuance in John's choice of expression.[16]

Once again, having considered every passage that BeDuhn discusses, we showed that not one of these passages is an actual parallel to Jn. 1:1. We demonstrated that BeDuhn's claims about the Nominative case were actually false and contradicted by the textual variants in Matt. 12:27 and by Smyth's grammar. We also demonstrated BeDuhn's misunderstanding of Colwell's Rule and how, contra BeDuhn, Smyth's grammar actually supports the conclusions of Colwell's Rule. Because of the length of the chapter, it would be too much to try to summarize it all here. Suffice to say that once again BeDuhn has misrepresented the evidence or neglected the evidence and that he has thereby distorted the case. Our analysis shows that Jn. 1:1 should in fact be translated "and the Word was God."

Chapter Twelve

Chapter Twelve of BeDuhn's book is another long one, and one that deals with a very important topic, namely, whether the Holy Spirit is a Person, or merely a force as the JWs claim. Concerning this chapter BeDuhn says,

> In chapter Twelve, no translation emerged with a perfectly consistent and accurate handlilng of the many uses and nuances of "spirit" and "holy spirit." The NW scored highest in using correct impersonal forms of the relative and demonstrative pronouns consistently with the neuter noun "holy Spirit," and in adhering to the indefinite expression "holy spirit" in those few instances when it was used by the biblical authors. Avoidance of reading the "holy spirit"

---

[16] Ibid.

into passages where "spirit" is used in other ways was managed best, if imperfectly, by the NW, NAB, NRSV, NASB, and KJV.[17]

Once again the length of the chapter makes it difficult to summarize all of the material into this small space. In our Chapter Nine, we responded to all of BeDuhn's arguments and to every passage to which he appeals. We demonstrated how BeDuhn's lack of understanding of the basic rule of linguistics that there is no necessary relation between grammatical gender and actual gender has led him to make illegitimate claims about the neuter gender in Greek. We also showed how BeDuhn is actually the one who has imposed his prior theology and philosophy on the text.

As a result of our analyses, we have clearly demonstrated that BeDuhn's claim "that the NW emerges as the most accurate of the translations compared," is both false and based on BeDuhn's own theological and philosophical bias. BeDuhn never seems to face the possibility that his own bias has affected his analysis. He consistently argues as if he is the only one who is capable of corralling his bias and bringing it under control, but his misunderstanding of the evidence, his neglect of evidence, his selective reporting, and his many logical fallacies in reasoning demonstrate that his claims are motivated by his own theological and philosophical bias. It appears as if he is completely unaware of this fact.

The Scientific Standard

BeDuhn attempts to use science as a standard of measure for acceptable methodology in translating. He says, "In science, we recognize that an investigation can only have a valid outcome if the observations and results are honestly recorded, unshaped by desired outcomes. It is illegitimate to decide beforehand what results you will accept for an experiment."[18] BeDuhn is obviously not familiar with the debate in philosophy of science concerning the problem of scientific observation. First of all, it is impossible for a scientist to observe everything that may have some impact on his results. Selection of what to count as results is essential to the scientific process, whatever that is (there is, in fact, an ongoing debate on whether there even is such a thing as a "scientific process"), else the scientific process could not be conducted. A scientist would be hopelessly entangled in looking at an infinite number of facts to explain an outcome. This problem is usually discussed in terms of the theoryladenness of observation. Scientists must have a theory that limits what is observed and what can count as results. The argument is that this prior theory necessarily predisposes a scientist toward a specific set of acceptable results. But, this seems to be the only practical way of conducting experimentation. There are, of course, others who argue that the presence of a theory is not prejudicial to the conclusions, and many scientific discoveries are

---

[17] Ibid., 162–63.
[18] Ibid., 166.

completely accidental and outside the theory with which the scientist was originally working. Be that as it may, BeDuhn's lack of familiarity with what is happening in science and the philosophy of science leads him to make this faulty analogy.[19]

BeDuhn uses his analogy to claim, "Likewise, in Bible translation, the only legitimate results are those that are based on neutral, sound, academically rigorous methods, not those prejudiced by a desired conclusion."[20] But BeDuhn has completely missed the self-contradictory nature of his own claim. He dictates that legitimate results must be based on "neutral" methods, but then he dictates what these methods must be—"sound, academically rigorous methods" not "prejudiced by a desired conclusion." But, his own conclusion is precisely a "desired" conclusion. He desires a conclusion that results from a supposedly "sound, academically rigorous" method. But, who decides what is a "sound, academically rigorous" method? BeDuhn's notion of what this is may not be the same as what others think, but BeDuhn has offered no means by which

---

[19] For some additional reading in the philosophy of science, consider these texts: Baggott, Jim. *Beyond Measure: Modern Physics, Philosophy and the Meaning of Quantum Theory*. Oxford: Oxford University Press, 2004: Brown, Harold I. *Perception, Theory, and Commitment: The New Philosophy of Science*. Chicago: The University of Chicago Press, 1979: Brown, Harold I. *Observation and Objectivity*. New York: Oxford University Press, 1987: Burtt, E. A. *The Metaphysical Foundations of Modern Science*. Mineola: Dover Publications, 2003: Cantore, Enrico. *Atomic Order: An Introduction to the Philosophy of Microphysics*. Cambridge: The MIT Press, 1969: Couvalis, George. *The Philosophy of Science: Science and Objectivity*. London: SAGE Publications, 1997. (This is an especially good introduction to the philosophy of science): Feyerabend, Paul. *Against Method*. London: Verso, 1993: Hempel, Carl G. *Philosophy of Natural Science*. Englewood Cliffs: Prentice-Hall, 1966: Klee, Robert. *Introduction to the Philosophy of Science: Cutting Nature at its Seams*. Oxford: Oxford University Press, 1997: Klemke, E. D., and Robert Hollinger. *Introductory Readings in the Philosophy of Science*. Buffalo: Prometheus Books, 1980: Korner, S. *Observation and Interpretation in the Philosophy of Physics: A Symposium*. New York: Dover Publications, 1957: Kosso, Peter. *Appearance and Reality: An Introduction to the Philosophy of Physics*. New York: Oxford University Press, 1998. (This is another very good introduction from a scientific realist): Kuhn, Thomas S. *The Structure of Scientific Revolutions*. Chicago: The University of Chicago Press, 1970: Leon, Jeffrey C. *Science and Philosophy in the West*. Upper Saddle River: Prentice Hall, 1999: Losee, John. *A Historical Introduction to the Philosophy of Science*. Oxford: Oxford University Press, 1993: Moreland, James Porter. *Christianity and the Nature of Science*. Grand Rapids: Baker Book House, 1989. (This is a very good survey of the relationship between science and Christianity. It also serves as an introduction to many issues in the philosophy of science from an evangelical perspective): Norris, Christopher. *Against Relativism: Philosophy of Science, Deconstruction, and Critical Theory*. Oxford: Blackwell Publishers, 1997: Ratzsch, Del. *Philosophy of Science: The Natural Sciences in Christian Perspective*. Downers Grove: InterVarsity Press, 1986: Rosenberg, Alex. *Philosophy of Science: A Contemporary Introduction*. London: Routledge, 2000: Stove, David. *Scientific Irrationalism: Origins of a Postmodern Cult*. New Brunswick: Transaction Publishers, 2001. (This is an excellent presentation of the influence of Postmodernism on science and the philosophy of science.): Trigg, Roger. *Reality at Risk: A Defense of Realism in Philosophy and the Sciences*. Lanham: Rowman & Littlefield Publishing, 1980.

[20] Ibid.

anyone can adjudicate between competing methods. The very translators with whom BeDuhn takes exception would claim that their methods are in fact "sound, academically rigorous," and the charge of "vested interest," as we have seen, is an *ad hominem* fallacy on BeDuhn's part.

BeDuhn admits that one's own bias "can be a tricky thing, and by definition is overlooked by those who are affected by it."[21] Of course, this is simply false. Some people not only recognize their bias, they glory in it. Bias is *not* overlooked by definition. In fact, sometimes, for purposes of deceit, a person will purposely overlook his own bias in hopes that his audience will not be able to detect it or will choose to overlook it. Bias is certainly frequently overlooked, that is to say, persons are frequently unaware of their own biases, but this is not true by definition. In fact, BeDuhn is a perfect example of a person who has overlooked his own bias. He seems either to be unaware of them, or he has intentionally overlooked them in hopes that his reader will do the same.

One bias that BeDuhn has overlooked is his bias toward a particular concept of the nature of translation. BeDuhn has entered into an area for which he is completely ill equipped. The nature of translation is a philosophical issue involving not only linguistics, but philosophy of language as well as philosophy of translation, and BeDuhn has given evidence throughout his book that he is totally ill equipped to deal with philosophical issues. For example, BeDuhn asserts, "In science, bias is combated by making every piece of data available, every step of reasoning plain, every conclusion testable by other scientists who are free to look at the same evidence and repeat the investigation themselves."[22] Of course, it is totally impossible for any scientist to make "every piece of data available." No scientist can even look at every piece of data, much less make this available to others. In any given scientific experiment there is potentially an infinite set of data. This is, in fact, part of the debate in philosophy of science about the whole notion of a scientific method. But BeDuhn naively makes these philosophical assertions as if this is obviously true.

BeDuhn then uses this as an analogy for Bible translation. He says, "The same approach is necessary in the work of translation . . ."[23] According to the analogy, then, BeDuhn ought to look at "every piece of data," but we have seen that he consistently avoids or "overlooks" the data that contradicts his view, as in the case of προσκυνέω ("worship") and the literary, historical, and cultural context of many biblical passages. He misrepresents the nature of translation as simply a matter of selecting the " most obvious, straightforward, unspecialized understanding of the word or phrase."[24] —most obvious to whom? Who decides what counts as "straightforward"? Why should a translation not be specialized? Using BeDuhn's own analogy, all these terms fall under the heading of the theoryladenness of observation. BeDuhn has a theory that predisposes

---

[21] Ibid.
[22] Ibid.
[23] Ibid.
[24] Ibid., xvi.

him, whether he overlooks it or not, toward accepting certain results. The problem is not so much that this is the case. The real problem is that BeDuhn acts as if he is somehow immune to this difficulty simply because he has a "method"—a method that he does not anywhere defend or justify or adjudicate *vis à vis* competing methods. Then he presents his conclusions as the only reasonable ones. But this isn't the case even with his method, as we have seen. There are other conclusions that result from the application of his method, conclusions that he simply dismisses as "bias."

BeDuhn admits that he has his own biases: "Yes, I have biases of my own, and I struggle to be aware of them. One bias that is present in this book is my bias in favor of history. When I read a passage from the New Testament, I am biased in favor of its 1st century meaning, rather than the meanings that might be claimed for it by 21st century interests."[25] But why does BeDuhn think he is any more capable of escaping his biases than other translators? Doesn't BeDuhn live in the 21st century? Doesn't he have his own "interests"? Why are his 21st century interests better than anyone else's 21st century interests? Does he think that he is the only one who struggles to be aware of his own biases? Does he think he is the only who in favor of history? Does he think that no one else is interested in the 1st century meanings of the text? Time and again he claims that his conclusions are the only reasonable ones, but he does not attempt to adjudicate his method as over against competing methods. And the claim that his book is not the place to do this is simply a red herring. In a book in which he is charging others with inaccuracy and bias, he is required to make his method known and to explain why his method is better than others' methods. He is required to explain who is the judge about what counts as "neutral, sound, academically rigorous" methods. Would not an academically rigorous method about translation involve questions of philosophy of language, translation theory, world view, etc.?

And if a book on translation in which the author is claiming that others have mistranslated, misunderstood, and misrepresented the text of the Bible is not the place to explain these aspects of one's own bias, then what forum is the place to do that? Should not his readers be informed about "every piece of data available" according to the dictates of his own method? And, to claim that this is too academic for his readers is also a red herring. An author is certainly free to select his audience and to write in a way that fits the audience he has selected. However, an author is not free to write about an issue that requires a certain level of justification, avoid this level of justification, and then claim that he has not dealt with it because his audience would not be able to understand the issues. An author is not free to write as if these "academic" issues do not exist or do not apply to him, and then claim that he does this because of the intellectual level of his audience. An author who is writing on such an issue ought either to explain the issues so that his readers can understand it, or he ought to point out that there are such issues and that his own conclusions are subject to question in terms of these issues. BeDuhn has done neither. Not only has he not done this, but he has

---

[25] Ibid., 167.

presented his conclusions as if his are the only "neutral, sound, academically rigorous" conclusions. This is completely disingenuous.

BeDuhn charges 4th, 12th, and 20th century writers with "anachronistically reading" their views back into the biblical text.[26] But, the same charge can be leveled against BeDuhn. Why does he think that he has somehow escaped the reading of his own biases anachronistically back into the text? Why does BeDuhn think that his views are not also "making it [the Bible] an echoing voice of later, and by no means universally accepted doctrine?" Why are "later interpretations" props for creeds? Isn't BeDuhn's own interpretation a "later interpretation"? Why does BeDuhn think that he is a "voice crying in the wilderness" of bias and inaccuracy, or that he is the only one who can "let the Bible have its say, regardless of how well or poorly that say conforms" to his expectations or his supposedly "accepted form of modern Christianity"?[27] BeDuhn's own theological and philosophical biases have been sufficiently documented here. BeDuhn's estimate of the accuracy and bias in translations is the function of his own prior commitments, conclusions that were "decided beforehand," as he puts. His conclusions are prejudiced by his own world view, an aspect of his bias that he has completely "overlooked."

---

[26] Ibid., 168.
[27] Ibid.

CHAPTER 11

"YHWH" NOT "JEHOVAH"

Introduction

Although the name 'Jehovah' is almost universally believed to be the name of the God of Israel, the fact is that the Hebrew Bible rarely uses this form of this name for God, and it is nowhere used in the New Testament. Because of this fact, the Jehovah's Witnesses have often attempted to justify their use of this name, and they have tried to argue that this is indeed God's name. In spite of his aspirations to objectivity, in the minds of his readers BeDuhn confirms his bias toward this cult in his effort to justify the use of this name. In this final chapter we will deal not only with how this name likely arose, but with BeDuhn's efforts to justify the use of the name Jehovah in certain passages of the New Testament by the translators of the New World Translation (NW).

From "Lord" to "Jehovah"

In the Appendix titled "The Use of 'Jehovah' in the NW,"[1] BeDuhn does a brief study of the name 'Jehovah.' His account of how the word 'Jehovah' came into existence seems fairly accurate and informative. He explains, "In ancient Judaism, the Biblical commandment not to profane God's name developed into a taboo against pronouncing it aloud except in very special circumstances. In ordinary reading from the Bible, therefore, it became customary to substitute the euphemistic title *adonai*, 'lord,' whenever one came to YHWH in the biblical text."[2] Eventually the vowels of Adonai became superimposed upon the divine name YHWH (see **Figure 14**) to produce the illegitimate name "Yehowah." The form "Jehovah" is the Latinized form of the Hebrew letters and vowel points. The name "Yehowah" or "Jehovah" is not a biblical name for

---

[1] BeDuhn, *Translation*, 169–81.
[2] Ibid., 170.

God. It is, in effect, the confusion of the vowels of אֲדֹנָי ("Adonai," "Lord" or "my Lord") with the consonants of יהוה YHWH. BeDuhn says, "Of course, 'Jehovah' also appears throughout the NW Old Testament. In this case, the NW is the only accurate translation of the nine we are comparing, since all of the other translations replace the personal name of God, in over six thousand passages, with the euphemistic title 'Lord' (given by many of these translations in all capitals, as 'LORD,' which my students invariably misunderstand as some sort of emphasis)."[3]

Here BeDuhn's personal preference for the NW is evident. Rather than give modern translators the benefit of the doubt that perhaps they are attempting to respect the Jewish tradition of not pronouncing the divine name, or that perhaps they recognize that "Jehovah" is not a legitimate name, and, rather than inventing a name, or rather than using the letters YHWH which would be obscure and unintelligible to most English readers, they opt for the word 'Lord' for ease of reading, BeDuhn immediately charges modern translations with inaccuracy. But the use of the name 'Jehovah' is equally as inaccurate since this was not and is not an actual biblical name. It is just as legitimate and accurate to use 'LORD' as to use 'Jehovah,' and perhaps more accurate since it does not perpetuate the notion that 'Jehovah' is a biblical name. BeDuhn's bias is particularly evident in the fact that he does not charge ancient Jews with inaccuracy because they used what he calls "the euphemistic title *adonai*" rather than pronounce the divine name, but he is ready to charge modern translations with inaccuracy when they use the "euphemistic" title 'Lord.'

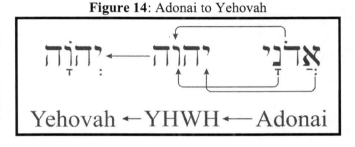

Figure 14: Adonai to Yehovah

BeDuhn goes on to say, "YHWH does appear in the original Hebrew of these passages [six thousand passages], and the only accurate translation is one that renders that name into some pronouncible [*sic*] form."[4] So, modern translations use of 'Lord' is "inaccurate" even though it renders the name YHWH into a pronounceable form and is in fact a real title that is actually used of God in the OT, but the NW is "the only accurate translation" when it uses an illegitimate name, according to BeDuhn, that was never God's name or title.

---

[3] Ibid., 169–70.
[4] Ibid., 170.

New Testament Quotations and NW Translation Principles

BeDuhn's theological bias is evident throughout his book, but perhaps no more so than in his treatment of the NW's placement of the name 'Jehovah' in various NT verses. BeDuhn reports, "In an appendix to the NW, they state that their restoration of 'Jehovah' in the New Testament is based upon (1) a supposition concerning how Jesus and his disciples would have handled the divine name, (2) the evidence of the 'J texts,' and (3) the necessity of consistency between Old and New Testaments."[5] In his analysis of the application of these principles in NW, BeDuhn points to five passages in which the NW translators have become inconsistent: Rom. 11:2; 11:8; Gal. 1:15; Heb. 9:20; 1 Pet. 4:14. Concerning this inconsistency, BeDuhn asserts, "But in five of the verses in the list above, the NW has 'God' rather than either 'Jehovah' or 'Lord' ... I cannot say why the NW editors abandoned their principle of conjectural emendation in these five cases; it makes no difference in the meaning of the text."[6] BeDuhn goes on to say, "Then there are three more verses where, by the principles applied by the NW editors, 'Jehovah' should be used, and yet is not: 2 Thessalonians 1:9; 1 Peter 2:3; and 1 Peter 3:15."[7] Let us look at these passages to see if we can discover why the NW editors did not use the word "Jehovah" in these instances.

2 Thess. 1:9

Table #108: 2 Thess. 1:9

NASBU	"These will pay the penalty of eternal destruction, away from the presence of the Lord and from the glory of His power,"
UBS4	οἵτινες δίκην τίσουσιν ὄλεθρον αἰώνιον ἀπὸ προσώπου τοῦ κυρίου καὶ ἀπὸ τῆς δόξης τῆς ἰσχύος αὐτοῦ,
NW	"These very ones will undergo the judicial punishment of everlasting destruction from before the Lord and from the glory of his strength,"

According to BeDuhn, the principles of the NW editors required them to use "Jehovah" in these verses. The OT passages that are back of this verse are Isa. 2:10, 19, and 21.

---

[5] Ibid., 172.
[6] Ibid., 174.
[7] Ibid., 174–75.

Table #109: Isa. 2:10, 19, 21

Isa. 2:10	NASBU	"Enter the rock and hide in the dust From the terror of the Lord and from the splendor of His majesty."
	BHS	בּוֹא בַצּוּר וְהִטָּמֵן בֶּעָפָר מִפְּנֵי פַּחַד יְהוָה וּמֵהֲדַר גְּאֹנוֹ׃
	GSEPT	καὶ νῦν εἰσέλθετε εἰς τὰς πέτρας καὶ κρύπτεσθε εἰς τὴν γῆν ἀπὸ προσώπου τοῦ φόβου κυρίου καὶ ἀπὸ τῆς δόξης τῆς ἰσχύος αὐτοῦ ὅταν ἀναστῇ θραῦσαι τὴν γῆν
	NW	"Enter into the rock and hide yourself in the dust because of the dreadfulness of Jehovah, and from his splendid superiority."
Isa. 2:19	NASBU	"*Men* will go into caves of the rocks and into holes of the ground before the terror of the Lord and the splendor of His majesty, when He arises to make the earth tremble."
	BHS	וּבָאוּ בִּמְעָרוֹת צֻרִים וּבִמְחִלּוֹת עָפָר מִפְּנֵי פַּחַד יְהוָה וּמֵהֲדַר גְּאֹנוֹ בְּקוּמוֹ לַעֲרֹץ הָאָרֶץ׃
	GSEPT	εἰσενέγκαντες εἰς τὰ σπήλαια καὶ εἰς τὰς σχισμὰς τῶν πετρῶν καὶ εἰς τὰς τρώγλας τῆς γῆς ἀπὸ προσώπου τοῦ φόβου κυρίου καὶ ἀπὸ τῆς δόξης τῆς ἰσχύος αὐτοῦ ὅταν ἀναστῇ θραῦσαι τὴν γῆν
	NW	"And people will enter into the caves of the rocks and into the holes of the dust because of the dreadfulness of Jehovah and from his splendid superiority, when he rises up for the earth to suffer shocks."
Isa. 2:21	NASBU	"In order to go into the caverns of the rocks and the clefts of the cliffs before the terror of the Lord and the splendor of His majesty, when He arises to make the earth tremble."
	BHS	לָבוֹא בְּנִקְרוֹת הַצֻּרִים וּבִסְעִפֵי הַסְּלָעִים מִפְּנֵי פַּחַד יְהוָה וּמֵהֲדַר גְּאֹנוֹ בְּקוּמוֹ לַעֲרֹץ הָאָרֶץ׃
	GSEPT	τοῦ εἰσελθεῖν εἰς τὰς τρώγλας τῆς στερεᾶς πέτρας καὶ εἰς τὰς σχισμὰς τῶν πετρῶν ἀπὸ προσώπου τοῦ φόβου κυρίου καὶ ἀπὸ τῆς δόξης τῆς ἰσχύος αὐτοῦ ὅταν ἀναστῇ θραῦσαι τὴν γῆν
	NW	"in order to enter into the holes in the rocks and into the clefts of the crags, because of the dreadfulness of Jehovah and from his splendid superiority, when he rises up for the earth to suffer shocks."

Verse 9 states that those who will be judged will be taken "away from the presence of the Lord and from the glory of His power." These are undoubtedly references to the Isaiah passages. Yet in each one of the three verses from Isaiah, the divine name יהוה is used and the NW translates these as "Jehovah." Yet when it comes to 2 Thess. 1:9

they use the word "Lord." Why do they do this? Notice that verse 10 of 2 Thessalonians 1 states, "when He comes to be glorified in His saints on that day . . ." (ὅταν ἔλθῃ ἐνδοξασθῆναι ἐν τοῖς ἁγίοις αὐτοῦ . . . ἐν τῇ ἡμέρᾳ ἐκείνῃ.). There can be no question that this is a reference to Jesus Christ. The JW's would certainly not claim that Jehovah is going to come back and be glorified with His saints. But, the association of the verse in 2 Thessalonians indicates that Jesus Christ is Jehovah. The antecedent of "He" in verse 10 is "the Lord" in verse 9.

So, it is the Lord who is coming with His saints from whose presence they will be judged. But since the verse in Isaiah clearly states that it is from the presence of Jehovah/YHWH that they will be judged, this clearly indicates that Jesus Christ is Jehovah. But, this is something that the JW's cannot allow, so they abandon their principle of translation to avoid the obvious meaning of the text. This is clearly a case of theological bias, and yet BeDuhn never calls it that.

1 Pet. 2:3

Table #110: 1 Pet. 2:3

NASBU	"if you have tasted the kindness of the Lord."
UBS4	εἰ ἐγεύσασθε ὅτι χρηστὸς ὁ κύριος.
NW	"provided YOU have tasted that the Lord is kind."

The OT verse that is the basis of the statement in 1 Pet. 2:3 is Ps. 34:8, verse 9 in the BHS and the GSEPT.

Table #111: Ps. 34:8 (H9; GSEPT9)

NASBU	O taste and see that the Lord is good; How blessed is the man who takes refuge in Him!
BHS (v. 9)	טַעֲמוּ וּרְאוּ כִּי־טוֹב יְהוָה אַשְׁרֵי הַגֶּבֶר יֶחֱסֶה־בּוֹ׃
GSEPT (v. 9)	γεύσασθε καὶ ἴδετε ὅτι χρηστὸς ὁ κύριος μακάριος ἀνήρ ὃς ἐλπίζει ἐπ' αὐτόν
NW	Taste and see that Jehovah is good, O YOU people; Happy is the able-bodied man that takes refuge in him.

Once again the NT portrays Jesus Christ as Jehovah God. In 1 Pet. 2:4 the text states, "And coming to Him as to a living stone which has been rejected by men, but is choice and precious in the sight of God." Now the antecedent of "Him" in verse 4 is the Lord in verse 3.

Figure 15: 1 Pet. 2:3–4 Antecedent of 'Him'

1 Pet. 2:3	if you have tasted the kindness of the Lord.
1 Pet. 2:4	And coming to Him as to a living stone which has been rejected by men,

But verse 4 describes the Lord as the stone that was rejected and was seen as the choice and precious stone in the sight of God. Of course this indicates that Jesus Christ is Jehovah God, something the NW editors cannot not abide. So, once again they depart from their translation principles to avoid the theological implications. Another clear example of theological bias, but another time BeDuhn does not identify the practice for what it is.

1 Pet. 3:15

Table #112: 1 Pet. 3:15

NASBU	"but sanctify Christ as Lord in your hearts, always *being* ready to make a defense to everyone who asks you to give an account for the hope that is in you, yet with gentleness and reverence"
UBS4	κύριον δὲ τὸν Χριστὸν ἁγιάσατε ἐν ταῖς καρδίαις ὑμῶν, ἕτοιμοι ἀεὶ πρὸς ἀπολογίαν παντὶ τῷ αἰτοῦντι ὑμᾶς λόγον περὶ τῆς ἐν ὑμῖν ἐλπίδος,
NW	"But sanctify the Christ as Lord in YOUR hearts, always ready to make a defense before everyone that demands of YOU a reason for the hope in YOU, but doing so together with a mild temper and deep respect."

The OT passage behind this statement is Isa. 8:13.

Table #113: Isa. 8:13

NASBU	"It is the Lord of hosts whom you should regard as holy. And He shall be your fear, and He shall be your dread."
BHS	אֶת־יְהוָה צְבָאוֹת אֹתוֹ תַקְדִּישׁוּ וְהוּא מוֹרַאֲכֶם וְהוּא מַעֲרִצְכֶם:
GSEPT	κύριον αὐτὸν ἁγιάσατε καὶ αὐτὸς ἔσται σου φόβος
NW	"Jehovah of armies—he is the One whom YOU should treat as holy, and he should be the object of YOUR fear, and he should be the One causing YOU to tremble."

The problem for the NW editors in 1 Pet. 3:15 is quite obvious. The text explicitly commands that we sanctify Christ as Lord. The Isaiah passage uses the divine name

יהוה, which the NW translates as Jehovah. So here is an explicit statement that Jesus Christ is Jehovah God. But again, the theological bias of the NW editors prevented them from following their own principle of translation, and once again BeDuhn fails to identify this as theological bias.

BeDuhn says, "These three passages present serious problems for the NW translators and their principle of using 'Jehovah' based on Old Testament passages that use YHWH. The fact that they do not, and apparently *cannot*, have 'Jehovah' in these three passages underscores the problem with the whole idea of using 'Jehovah' in the New Testament."[8] Of course the Jehovah's Witnesses cannot use "Jehovah" in these verses because they present Jesus Christ as Jehovah. Yet, with such an obvious instance of theological bias, whether right or wrong, BeDuhn never once makes such a charge against the translators/editors of the NW. However, based on the slimmest and sometimes fabricated evidence, BeDuhn is eager to charge modern translations with theological bias. Whereas, according to BeDuhn, modern translators deliberately add or change or delete words, the NW editors are "inconsistent," or they "shy away from," or they are "interpreting," or they use "conjectural emendations"—apparently BeDuhn never suspects them of "theological bias."

Conclusions

BeDuhn explains the practice of the editors of the NW in their use of the name "Jehovah" in the NT as "Carefully distinguishing God from Jesus by using the name of Jehovah for the former." He claims they have sought to resolve the "ambiguity in a way that keeps these two personages distinct and aids in the formulation of theology and christology by showing which entity is responsible for which activities in the thinking of the biblical authors."[9] An unguarded remark is often an excellent means of getting a peek at one's biases, and this is certainly the case here with BeDuhn's comment. He says the practice of the NW editors shows "which entity is responsible for which activities . . ." The fact that he unguardedly uses the term "entity" exposes his prior theological and philosophical bias. According to the dictionary, an entity is, "A thing that has real and individual existence in reality or in the mind; anything real in itself: essence, essential nature."[10] Now there is a long and orthodox history of belief that Jesus and God are the same Being or Essence and different Persons. Whether right or wrong, this tradition believes that this is the teaching of the Bible. Now, whether this tradition is right or wrong is not the point. The point is, BeDuhn has unguardedly exposed his own theological and philosophical bias by referring to God and Jesus as distinct entities. And there is not a single undisputed verse or passage to which BeDuhn can appeal that unquestionably teaches this view. BeDuhn has pointed to verses that he thinks support

---

[8] Ibid., 174–75.
[9] Ibid., 176.
[10] *Webster's New Twentieth Century Dictionary* (1977), s.v. "entity."

this view, but none of these is beyond dispute. In fact, BeDuhn's conclusions about these verses are clear examples of conclusions prejudiced by his own desired outcome—the outcome of his own world view.

In critiquing the NW effort at clarification, BeDuhn says, "These are reasonable points, but fundamentally matters of *interpretation* rather than translation. The clarification that the NW editors seek to bring to the Bible can only be a matter of translation if it is based upon something in the original Greek text."[11] But what would constitute "something in the original Greek text"? Don't the editors of the NW think and claim that there is in fact "something" in the original Greek text that justifies their efforts? And who is the one to determine what is and what is not a qualifying "something" in the Greek text? It cannot be the actual words of the text since BeDuhn himself advocates changing the words when he thinks this is appropriate. In the question of gender neutrality BeDuhn advocates making the English translation more gender neutral and therefore changing the gender of the actual words in the Greek text. If the "something" in the Greek text were the actual words of the text, then BeDuhn's own proposal about changing the gender would be unjustifiable. Apparently, then, the actual words of the Greek text are not the "something" that justifies what BeDuhn would classify as an "accurate" translation. Unfortunately for his readers, BeDuhn does not specify what that "something" might be other than the actual words of the existing manuscripts, a proposal that contradicts BeDuhn's own practice in other parts of his book.

In fact, what that "something" seems to be is the person's own theological and philosophical world view with which he or she approaches the text and evaluates meaning. Although BeDuhn claims that the NW editors' use of "Jehovah" in NT passages where κύριος (*kurios*) is illegitimate, he places this on the level with using the word "LORD" to translate YHWH and treats them both as illegitimate. The problem is, as we have pointed out, the use of "Jehovah" in either the Old or New Testaments is illegitimate since that is nowhere used of God, whereas the word "LORD" is indeed and in fact used of God. How can an actual word that is used of God be as illegitimate as using a word that nowhere is ever used of God? If BeDuhn wants to claim that in fact the name "Jehovah" is found in certain instances, this flies in the face of his own explanation of the source of the vowels on the divine name. In fact, KBH indicates that the form יְהֹוָה came into existence after the 1st century: "pronounced as אֲדֹנָי in MT, → אָדוֹן since first century AD (Baudissin 2:305f; even earlier; Rudolph 231f, on Lam 331); editions consequently יְהוָֹה, from which BH3 and BHS; usu. understood as שְׁמָא, Arm. for הַשֵּׁם."[12]

BeDuhn claims that the use of "LORD" for YHWH has "no justification whatsoever in the Old Testament translations of the KJV, NASB, NIV, NRSV, NAB, AB, TEV and LB."[13] In fact there is justification for using the word "LORD" in the OT, and this

---

[11] BeDuhn, *Translation*, 176.
[12] KBH, s.v, "יהוה."
[13] BeDuhn, *Translation*, 176–77.

justification comes from the Jewish practice of substituting אֲדֹנָי or אָדוֹן in pronunciation for YHWH. This is precisely what these modern translations are doing, i.e., using "LORD" for YHWH so that when the text is read, the reader will say "Lord," not pronounce the divine name. There is in fact "no justification whatsoever" for BeDuhn to claim that there is "no justification whatsoever" for this translation practice. The only reason for making such a claim is BeDuhn's own theological and philosophical bias and his preference for the NW translation. And there is absolutely no justification whatsoever for claiming that modern translations are "expunging" the divine name.[14]

BeDuhn's "Final Word" wasn't his final word after all, so our concluding remarks and observations about his book can be found at the end of the previous chapter. BeDuhn has utterly failed to demonstrate that the New World Translation is "the most accurate of the translations compared."[15] What BeDuhn has done is successfully to demonstrate that the NW is the closest representative of his own theological and philosophical bias.

Apologetic Points

From our study of the use of 'Jehovah' by the JWs, we can cull the following four apologetic points:

1. The name 'Jehovah' is not a biblical name. It came about because of the confusion of the consonants of the divine name YHWH and the vowels of the word 'Adonai' ("Lord" or "my Lord").

2. The OT passages that are back of 2 Thess. 1:9 are Isa. 2:10, 19, and 21. In each one of the verses in Isaiah, the divine name YHWH is used. This indicates that 2 Thess. 1:9 identifies Jesus as YHWH, the true and living God.

3. The OT verse that is the basis of the statement in 1 Pet. 2:3 is Ps. 34:8, verse 9 in the BHS and the GSEPT. In Ps. 34:8 (H9), the divine name YHWH is used. This indicates that 1 Pet. 2:3 identifies Jesus as YHWH, the true and living God.

4. The OT verse that is the basis of 1 Pet. 3:15 is Isa. 8:19. 1 Pet. 3:15 explicitly commands that we sanctify Christ as Lord. The Isaiah passage uses the divine

---

[14] Ibid., 177.
[15] Ibid., 163.

name יהוה, which the NW translates as Jehovah. So here is an explicit statement that Jesus Christ is Jehovah God.

BIBLIOGRAPHY

Aland, Barbara, et al., ed. *The Greek New Testament*. Stuttgart: Deutsche Bibelgesellschaft, 1993.

Aristotelis, *Opera Omnia*. Parisiis: Ambrosio Firmin-Didot, 1927.

Baker, Mona, ed. *Routledge Encyclopedia of Translation Studies*. London: Routledge, 2000.

Barber, Cyril J. *Introduction to Theological Research*. Chicago: Moody Press, 1982.

Bassnett, Susan. *Translation Studies*. 3d ed. London: Routledge, 2004.

Bavinck, Herman. *Reformed Dogmatics*. Translated by John Vriend. Grand Rapids: Baker Academic, 2003.

Beale, G. K., and D. A. Carson, ed. *Commentary on the New Testament Use of the Old Testament*. Grand Rapids: Baker Academic, 2007.

Beekman, John, and John Callow. *Translating the Word of God*. Dallas, Texas: Summer Institute of Linguistics, 1986.

Biblia Sacra Juxta Vulgatam Clementinam. Romae: Societatis S. Joannis Evang, 1927.

Blass, F., and A. DeBrunner, *A Greek Grammar of the New Testament and Other Early Christian Literature*. Chicago: The University of Chicago Press, 1961.

Blomberg, Craig L. *Interpreting the Parables*. Downers Grove, Illinois: InterVarsity Press, 1990.

Botterweck, G. Johannes, and Helmer Ringgren, ed. *Theological Dictionary of the Old Testament*. Translated by John T. Willis. Grand Rapids: William B. Eerdmans Publishing Company, 1975.

Brenton, Sir Lancelot Charles Lee. *The Septuagint Version of the Old Testament According to the Vatican Text*. London: Samuel Bagster and Sons, 1844.

Brown, Colin. *The New International Dictionary of New Testament Theology*. Grand Rapids: Zondervan Publishing House, 1971.

Elliger, K., and W. Rudolph, ed. *Biblia Hebraica Stuttgartensia*. Stuttgart: Deutsche Bibelstiftung, 1977.

Ellingworth, Paul. *The Epistle to the Hebrews: A Commentary on the Greek Text*. Grand Rapids: William B. Eerdmans Publishing Company, 1993.

Elwell, Walter A., and Barry J. Beitzel, ed. *Baker Encyclopedia of the Bible*. Grand Rapids: Baker Book House, 1988.

Frawley, William J. ed. *International Encyclopedia of Linguistics*, 2d ed. Oxford: Oxford University Press, 2003.

Geisler, Norman L., and Ronald M. Brooks. *Come Let Us Reason: An Introduction to Logical Thinking*. Grand Rapids: Baker Academic, 1990.

Gentzler, Edwin. *Contemporary Translation Theories*, 2d ed. Clevedon, England: Multilingual Matters, 2001.

Glare, P. G. W., ed. *Oxford Latin Dictionary*. Oxford: At The Clarendon Press, 2005.

Hannah, John. *Our Legacy: The History of Christian Doctrine*. Colorado Springs, Colorado: NavPress, 2001.

Harris, R. Laird, Gleason L. Archer, Jr., and Bruce K. Waltke. *Theological Wordbook of the Old Testament*. Chicago: Moody Press, 1999.

Hurtado, Larry W. *The Earliest Christian Artifacts: Manuscripts and Christian Origins*. Grand Rapids: William B. Eerdmans Publishing Company, 2006.

_____. *Lord Jesus Christ: Devotion to Jesus in Earliest Christianity*. Grand Rapids: William B. Eerdmans Publishing Company, 2003.

Jacobsen, Thorkild. *The Treasures of Darkness: A History of Mesopotamian Religion*. New Haven, Connecticut: Yale University Press, 1976.

Kahane, Howard. *Logic and Philosophy*, 2d ed. Belmont, California: Wadsworth Publishing Company, 1973.

Keener, Craig S. *The Gospel of John: A Commentary*. Peabody, Massachusetts: Hendrickson Publishers, 2003.

Kittel, Gerhard, ed. *Theological Dictionary of the New Testament*. Translated by Geoffrey W. Bromiley. Grand Rapids: Wm. B. Eerdmans Publishing Company, 1978.

Koehler, Ludwig, and Walter Baumgartner. *The Hebrew and Aramaic Lexicon of the Old Testament*. Translated by M. E. J. Richardson. Leiden: Brill, 2001.

Kreeft, Peter. *Socratic Logic*. South Bend, Indiana: St Augustine's Press, 2004.

Lamsa, George M. *Holy Bible: From the Ancient Eastern Text*. San Francisco: Harper & Row, Publishers, 1968.

Lebreton, Jules. *The Origins*. Vol. 1, *History of the Dogma of the Trinity from its Origins to the Council of Nicaea*. Translated by Algar Thorold. New York: Benziger Brothers, 1939.

Leiden Peshitta. Leiden: Peshitta Institute Leiden, 2008.

Lewis, Charlton T., and Charles Short. *A Latin Dictionary*. Oxford: At The Clarendon Press, 1966.

Liddell, Henry George, and Robert Scott. *A Greek-English Lexicon*. Oxford: Clarendon Press, 1996.

Louw, Johannes P., and Eugene A. Nida, ed. *Greek-English Lexicon of the New Testament Based on Semantic Domains*, 2d ed. New York: United Bible Societies, 1989.

Morwood, James. *Oxford Grammar of Classical Greek*. Oxford: Oxford University Press, 2001.

Munday, Jeremy. *Introducing Translation Studies: Theories and Applications*. London: Routledge, 2001.

Nash, Ronald H. *Christianity and the Hellenistic World*. Grand Rapids: Zondervan Publishing House, 1984.

Nida, Eugene A., and Charles A. Taber. *The Theory and Practice of Translating*. Leiden: E. J. Brill, 1969.

Nöldeke, Theodor. *Compendious Syriac Grammar*. Eugene, Oregon: Wipf and Stock Publishers, 1904.

Oppenheim, A. Leo. *Ancient Mesopotamia: Portrait of a Dead Civilization*. Chicago: The University of Chicago Press, 1964.

Parker, Francis H., and Henry B. Veatch. *Logic as a Human Instrument*. New York: Harper & Brothers, Publishers, 1959.

Quine, Willard Van Orman. *Word and Object*. Cambridge, Massachusetts: The Technology Press of The Massachusetts Institute of Technology, 1960.

Salzmann, Zdenek. *Language, Culture, & Society: An Introduction to Linguistic Anthropology*. Boulder, Colorado: Westview Press, 1993.

Schmidt, Robert W. *The Domain of Logic According to Saint Thomas Aquinas*. The Hague: Martinus Nijhoff, 1966.

Scorgie, Glen G., Mark L. Strauss, and Steven M. Voth, ed. *The Challenge of Bible Translation*. Grand Rapids: Zondervan Publishing House, 2003.

Seligmann, Kurt. *The History of Magic and the Occult*. New York: Gramercy Books, 1997.

Silzer, Peter James, and Thomas John Finley. *How Biblical Languages Work: A Student's Guide to Learning Hebrew and Greek*. Grand Rapids: Kregel Academic & Professional, 2004.

Smith, J. Payne, ed. *A Compendious Syriac Dictionary*. Oxford: At The Clarendon Press, 1990.

Smyth, Herbert Weir. *Greek Grammar*. Cambridge, Massachusetts: Harvard University Press, 1984.

Sokoloff, Michael. *A Syriac Lexicon*. Winona Lake, Indiana: Eisenbrauns, 2009.

Strauss, Mark L. *Distorting Scripture? The Challenge of Bible Translation and Gender Accuracy*. Downers Grove, Illinois: InterVarsity Press, 1998.

Swanson, Reuben, ed. *New Testament Greek Manuscripts: John*. Sheffield, England: Sheffield Academic Press, 1995.

Turner, Nigel. *Syntax*. Vol. 3, *A Grammar of New Testament Greek*, by James Hope Moulton and Nigel Turner. Edinburgh: T. & T. Clark, 1963.

VanGemeren, Willem A., ed. *New International Dictionary of Old Testament Theology & Exegesis*. Grand Rapids: Zondervan Publishing House, 1997.

Vetus Testamentum Graecum. Auctoritate Academiae Scientiarum Gottingensis Editum. Göttingen: Vandenhoeck & Ruprecht, 1931–2006.

Waard, Jan de, and Eugene A. Nida. *From One Language to Another: Functional Equivalence in Bible Translating.* Nashville: Thomas Nelson Publishers, 1986.

Wallace, Daniel B. *Greek Grammar Beyond the Basics.* Grand Rapids: Zondervan Publishing House, 1996.

Waltke, Bruce K., and M. O'Connor. *An Introduction to Biblical Hebrew Syntax.* Winona Lake, Indiana: Eisenbrauns, 1990.

Westcott, Brooke Foss, and Fenton John Anthony Hort. *The New Testament in the Original Greek.* New York: Harper & Brothers, 1891.

Wilson, Colin. *The Occult.* New York: Vintage Books, 1973.

Made in the USA
San Bernardino, CA
16 April 2018